PICTURESQUE AMERICA

CENTENNIAL EDITION

VOLUME TWO

EDITED BY WILLIAM CULLEN BRYANT

LYLE STUART, INC.   SECAUCUS, NEW JERSEY

CENTENNIAL EDITION 1974
ALL RIGHTS RESERVED
PUBLISHED BY LYLE STUART, INC.
120 ENTERPRISE AVENUE
SECAUCUS, NEW JERSEY 07094
PRINTED BY NOBLE OFFSET PRINTERS, NEW YORK
MANUFACTURED IN THE UNITED STATES OF AMERICA
ISBN 0 8184 0212 1

PICTURESQUE AMERICA;

OR,

THE LAND WE LIVE IN.

A DELINEATION BY PEN AND PENCIL

OF

THE MOUNTAINS, RIVERS, LAKES, FORESTS, WATER-FALLS, SHORES,
CAÑONS, VALLEYS, CITIES, AND OTHER PICTURESQUE
FEATURES OF OUR COUNTRY.

With Illustrations on Steel and Wood, by Eminent American Artists.

EDITED BY WILLIAM CULLEN BRYANT.

VOL. II.

NEW YORK:

D. APPLETON AND COMPANY,

1, 3, AND 5 BOND STREET.

PICTURESQUE AMERICA

VOL. II.

CONTENTS, VOLUME SECOND.

LIST OF ENGRAVINGS ON STEEL.

The steel engravings, reproduced on special
coated paper, following page 32.

VOLUME SECOND.

PICTURESQUE AMERICA.

Poughkeepsie, and its Founderies at Night.

HIGHLANDS AND PALISADES OF THE HUDSON.

WITH ILLUSTRATIONS BY HARRY FENN.

TO those who are willing to accept such unobtrusive companionship as we have to offer, in this artist's voyage among the noblest scenes of our most beautiful and perfect American river, we must say at the beginning that we shall not follow the tra-

ditions of the ordinary guide. To him it matters little by what path he leads a traveller to the most glorious outlook, nor does he care for his observer's frame of mind;
he will suddenly show you the Rhine-fall from the back-door of a dingy beer-house, and
point out your first view of Niagara through the dusty window of a hackney-coach.
To us, the way of approach seems of no little moment; and here especially, among the
scenes we know so well, we have our fixed ideas of the traveller's most satisfying course.

The true way, then, to learn the noblest beauties of the Hudson's grandest region,
is to enter the Highlands with the river's course; beginning the voyage from some
point above, watching the growing picturesqueness of the stream, and noting the gradual
rise of the hills, the increasing grandeur of their outline, and the deepening majesty of
their presence, until, with his heart full of this slowly-gaining beauty, one finds himself
among the perfect pictures which lie in the very midst of the mountain-group.   Let us
enter on our journey in search of the picturesque, then, from some point at a little distance up the river.   Newburg is too near the Highlands; it lies in the shadow of their

The Hudson, south from Newburg.

On the Old Newburg Toll-Road.

very gates; let us begin our voyage at that point of practical as well as theoretical convenience — at Poughkeepsie.

Indeed, our place of departure is itself, in the matter of picturesque outlook, not to be despised. The "rural city," as one of our writers has called it, lies very pleasantly upon its group of gentle hills, and overlooks a bright and sunny portion of the river-view. By day, one may quarrel a little with the smoke of its busy founderies, but by night these become the most strangely beautiful and striking feature in many miles of the Hudson's scenery. They light the river like weird beacons, and the sound of their great furnaces comes across the water in the stillness, as the panting of giants that toil when the weaker forces of the world are all asleep.

Our departure from Poughkeepsie allows us to approach the Highlands by the "Long Reach"—that quiet and sunny portion of the river's course that here lies like a broad, straight avenue between the beautiful banks, for more than twenty miles. Its upper extremity is at Crom Elbow—the *Krom Elleboge* of the old Dutch settlers; its

The Storm-King and Cro'-Nest.

lower is at Newburg. Sailing down it, we pass many points which their history, as well as their beauty, makes noteworthy. Here, on the eastern bank, two miles below the town, is Locust Grove, entitled to remembrance as the summer home of Morse, whose name the wires of his telegraph have told to all the world. A mile or two farther on, where Spring Brook comes into the Hudson, lived stout Theophilus Anthony, the blacksmith, a century ago, who helped to forge the great chain that once guarded the river at Fort Montgomery, below. Farther still in the Long Reach lie the bright little villages of Milton and Marlborough, almost hidden from the river by the high banks; we pass New Hamburg, too, called into sad prominence a year or two ago by one of the terrible disasters that are all too common now; and so, noting picturesque little Fishkill on our left, we come upon the beautiful Newburg Bay — the most perfect of the Hudson's harbors.

Close by the gate of the Highlands, opposite the

WEST POINT, AND SCENES IN VICINITY.

St. Mary's Church at
Cold Spring.

range of the Fishkill hills, and overlooking a stretch of river and shore such as you may hardly find anywhere else in the world, Newburg lies, with its bright group of picturesquely-clustered houses, with memories of old Revolutionary days surrounding it, and every association connected with it that should make it a marked town among our historic places. Here were Washington's headquarters during a part of the stormiest of the war - time; and here, in combating with the strongest and simpliest eloquence, the work of the famous "Newburg Addresses," he perhaps, more than anywhere else, showed how great agents were his strength of will and earnest purpose in the salvation of the country.

It is with the beauty of the old town, however, and not with its history, that we have to do. From the shore below it we have gained one of the most perfect views of this noble part of the Hudson's course. We see the entrance of the Highlands, and the broad expanse of water lying between this and the town. This is the very perfection of an approach to the glorious scenery below. The broad bay forms a kind of enchanted border-region, which the true guide will let his visitor study well; and it and its shores—along which one should pass to fully learn the beauty of the great stretch of sunny river—put one in the truest mood for the first sight of the grander aspects of mountain and stream upon which he is to look with the next stage of his journey. One should pass, we say, along the shore as well as make the voyage upon the river, to catch the full beauty of this scene in Newburg Bay. The old toll-road runs along the western bank of the Hudson here, and gives from time to time such glimpses of the hills below as are worth a day's travel to seek. From one of these Mr. Fenn has shown the very spirit of the whole scene. This is a portion of the journey that no one should miss. And now we are within the gates of the Highlands themselves, in the presence of the great Storm-King and the dark pile of the Cro'-Nest.

To us these two noble mountains are the grandest of the Highland range. They have a charm that might induce a man to live in their shadow for no other purpose than to have them always before him, day and night, to study their ever-changing beauty. For they are never twice alike; the clouds make varying pictures all day long on their wooded sides, and nowhere have we seen more wonderful effects of shadow and sun-

Glimpse of the Hudson from Fort Putnam.

shine. Under the frown of a low thunder-cloud they take on a grim majesty that makes their black masses strangely threatening and weird; one forgets to measure their height, and their massive, strongly-marked features, by any common standard of every-day measurement, and they seem to tower and overshadow all the scene around them, like the very rulers and controllers of the coming storm. And when the sunlight comes back again, they seem to have brought it, and to look down with a bright benignity, like giant protectors of the valley that lies below.

Beyond them, on a remarkable and beautiful promontory, extending into the river at what seems to us the most perfect point of the whole course of the Hudson, lies West Point. It has always been to us an ideal place. In its shores, every view of

View south from the Academy Grounds.

which is full of picturesque charm ; in the dark background of its hills ; in the aspect — somewhat unusual in our America — of its earthworks and defences, and all the surroundings that have been given it by the long years of its occupancy as a military school ; in its broad plain, forming the central ground of human action, on which the great natural amphitheatre of the Highlands looks silently down ; even ·in the grouping of its cluster of buildings, and in the picturesque monuments about it, that call up so many memories, there seems to us a harmony of beauty that makes the site of our important military post one of the most attractive spots in the whole country.

It is from West Point, too, that the most satisfying views of the Hudson itself are to be gained. Whoever has looked out from the broad veranda of the hotel near the parade—the familiar "Roe's"—and seen the broad reach of the river stretching north-ward between the picturesque dark hills, never forgets the perfect vista that lies before him here.

Equally beautiful in sunshine and shadow, and fairly glorious in a storm, this is such a scene as no other river can show. Sit and watch it lying under the sky of a cloudless autumn morning, when its outlines all seem mellowed with a touch of golden haze, and it is framed by the many-colored splendors of the foliage of late October; or see it when the perfect beauty of the new green of spring is over its hills, and the river is just rippled by a touch of air; or, best, perhaps, and certainly grandest of all, when the overhanging thunder-cloud of a summer afternoon comes slowly nearer, and first the sharply-outlined black shadow, and then the distinct, clearly-marked edge of the pelting storm, approach across hills and river, until, with the growing thunder and whirl of rain, you find yourself overtaken by the tempest; see this picture of the Hudson in one of these aspects or in all, and you will grant that no Old World vaunted Rhine can show you more and truer beauty than is thus given in our own home.

But this perfect river-view, which lies always before the visitor, to be enjoyed with-out an effort, and to satisfy even without any thing else, is really only the beginning of what West Point has to offer to a lover of the picturesque. Turn in whatever direction one may from the parade-ground of the academy—the recognized central point of all things at the post—he finds new points of outlook, and new beauty waiting for him everywhere. On the summit of Mount Independence, an irregular hill, some distance back from the river, are the ruins of old Fort Putnam—such ruins as are left of the once stout work; and, climbing to these, one gains a new glimpse of the Highlands and the water. It is useless to try to show in words the different and always fresh charm that each new point of observation gives; nor could the pencil show it with entire suc-cess unless it could fill a volume with sketches, in which even then one would miss the glorious coloring that forms a crowning beauty of these hills. The ruins of the fort are themselves picturesque, with that beauty of ruins that is so rare with us in America— the nameless charm that, even for the least sentimental, always surrounds an old, decay-ing structure that has played its part in the world, and seems resting and looking on dreamily, only an observer now, and not an actor.

Close by the central grounds of the academy there are other relics of old days, monuments that have an interest besides their picturesque aspect, as they lie among the green of the turf and trees. Along the steep shore of the river, that rises so suddenly as to form a series of sharp precipices and rough terraces between them, there are many of these memorials, and many historic nooks. Here, half-way down the slope of the shore, is "Kosciuszko's Garden," where the brave Pole used to make his favorite haunt, and where he would lie and read in his leisure, regardless, according to the story, of the

THE HUDSON AT "COZZENS'S."

fact that shot from the vessels in the river now and then struck the rocks not far away. Along the paths that lead from one to another of these natural terraces are smooth cliffs, on which the names of famous victories have been cut in large, bold letters; the vines and ferns give to these natural frames of green, and the plain records are the most perfect that could have been devised—better than any tablets of less noble simplicity. There is no lack of memorial-stones erected by men's hands, however; here and there a column or an obelisk looks out from the foliage—a monument to some army hero, who once went out into earnest battle from the quiet existence and petty events of "the corps."

Down by the most beautiful part of the shore runs the path—memorable in the lives of countless fledgling soldiers—that has been named by profane souls "Flirtation Walk"—a designation at which the heart of any man over two-and-twenty must sink, in despair of his race. For the path is a perfect ideal of beauty; at every point of its course there are glimpses of hills and river that it makes a man's whole life better to have seen; and yet it must exist for whole generations more of gray-clad youngsters under the title of "Flirtation Walk!" Not that we quarrel with the fact of the flirtation—under sun, moon, or stars, there is no such place for tender passages and summer love-making—but why did not some young hero, with his memory full of these things, christen it by any name, though ever so ultra-sentimental, that would commemorate them better than the chosen title that now rules?

From the shady nooks of the West Point shores one may look out upon parts of the opposite bank that are, in their quieter fashion, also beautiful. Opposite the promontory of the Point lies the little village of Cold Spring—a bright group of houses by the water. Above and below it the shore rises into high, steep banks, and on one of these stands the little church of St. Mary's, which Mr. Fenn has chosen for a picture that might almost persuade one he was looking upon some view of a little chapel crowning the rocks by an old river of Europe, so quaint is it, and so foreign in its features to the ordinary aspect of our American scenes. Near by it the railway runs along the bank and through a rough tunnel in the ragged point; but the little church looks like a mediæval building, as far removed as possible from the practical progress of to-day.

But we must not long digress from the detail—even though it be so meagre—of the beauties that more closely surround the West Point plain. We should be unfaithful to our duties as guide if we did not lead the looker-on at these favorite scenes of ours to some few more of the points from which he will carry away pleasant memories. One of these is the landing-place itself at which he finds himself upon arrival by the ordinary route from the city; for one is carried by the train to Garrison's, on the Hudson's eastern side, and thence in a little steamer across the river, and is landed at the foot of the cliffs of the promontory. Here is a road leading to the plain above, and built by the engineers in a single long slope from the water, along the steep face of the shore, to the point where it again reaches level ground. It is to this road and the views seen from it that we would, in guide-book manner, call the reader's notice. Whoever is sound in wind and limb should walk up the long, regularly-graded ascent, and now and then look down at the river. It lies below him, seen through the branches of the trees, as he will see it nowhere else. Such a sense of overhanging the water is hardly felt even on the Palisades themselves. The rocks above and below the road are grouped in

Anthony's Nose, from the Western Shore.

rough, massive forms; the sense of height is far greater than actual measurement would warrant; and the outlook, wherever one turns, is striking, and such as will be gained from perhaps no other point but this, midway in the slope along the cliff.

On the opposite side of the promontory from this, and some distance beyond the academy grounds, is the cemetery of the post. Overlooking the river to the north and east, and lying in a little level plain above the cliffs, where the sunlight falls all day long, and where every thing in scene and surrounding seems to join in giving quiet and peaceful beauty to it, it is such a resting-place as any man might choose after a soldier's stormy life. Here Scott is buried, and here are many heroes of fame more or less widely spread—all honored by the younger men growing up to take their places, with an honor partly made up of generous ambition to go and do like them, partly of an admiration for bravery in the abstract, and partly of the nameless and indescribable sentiment of veneration that hangs about the memory of "a graduate." To us, the cemetery—overlooked by dark old Cro'-Nest; looking down on the river far below; quiet and peaceful in the sunlight; silent, yet never gloomy, under the stars; scarcely touched, it would seem, even by the winds of the Highland storms—is among the West Point scenes that seems most beautiful.

We must not leave the Point without saying something of the associations, which, besides its beauty, make it a place full of interest to every traveller through the Hudson's scenery. For here are the scenes of not a few events to which every one's memory turns back familiarly, and the whole neighborhood is

Near Anthony's Nose at Night.

among the most famous regions of our history. During the War of the Revolution, West Point was, if not the principal, at least one of the most important military posts in the country. Singular as such a statement must appear to us now, it was looked upon—as an American historian has phrased it—as the key to the passage between the New-England and the Middle States—the colonies of Revolutionary days. It commanded the entrance to the Upper Hudson; it was the centre of the scene of many principal movements of the war; it was invaluable as a deposit for munitions, and troops were mustered within its fortifications, to be sent to every part of the theatre of action. Upon its defences was concentrated much of the attention and effort of the Congress and the leaders of the army. Here, from Gee's Point to Constitution Island (no longer surrounded by the stream), was stretched across the Hudson the huge chain, to which reference has been made already. "It was laid," says the best description that we have at hand, "across a boom of heavy logs, that floated near together. These were sixteen feet long, and pointed at each end, so as to offer little resistance to the tidal currents. The chain was fastened to these logs by staples, and at each shore by huge blocks of wood and stone." Several of the great links of the chain are preserved at the Point; and the work of the stout old blacksmith looks as though it might have borne the wear and rust of centuries; but by the vessels of an enemy its strength was never tested. Here, too, on a conspicuous part of the promontory, Kosciuszko constructed Fort Clinton, in 1778. Of Fort Putnam we have already spoken; and, indeed, the whole vicinity of the post was provided with no mean works for fortification and defence. It is not hard to see, then, apart from other reasons, why Washington and his generals looked upon it as, perhaps, their chief fortress. The fighting colonies had no other military stronghold of such extent and permanent character as this.

All these features of the place contributed to increase the magnitude of the crime which will always be associated with the history of West Point—the treason of Benedict Arnold. It is impossible to forget it as we look at the scene of the plan—impossible even for us, who have come to seek rather the beauty of the present than the stirring recollections of the past. Inevitably we picture again in mind, as we did when school-boys, the September morning when the traitor heard of the miscarriage of his plans, and wonder what feeling came to him as he sat at the table of Beverly House (where Colonel Beverly Robinson had made his home, on the eastern side of the river, nearly opposite the post), and the note was brought to him from his subordinate at the military station below, that said "Major André, of the British army, is a prisoner in my custody." The scene with his wife, the hurried flight, his treacherous surrender of his boatmen—all these things that were wont to stir our blood when we read them in the school-histories, come back to us perforce when we linger at the Highland fortress. It must have been, indeed, a sorry time for more men than Arnold; and one can have a feeling of thorough sympathy for the disheartened commander-in-chief, when

he turned to
Lafayette and
Knox with his
saddened,
"Whom can
we trust now?"
But we are
playing false to our guide's
duty in thus digressing to talk
of the by-gone days, when the
Hudson had added to its
beauties the interest of war.

Anthony's Nose, from Iona Island.

Because we have lingered
so long in the beautiful neighborhood of West Point and its really glorious scenery,
the patient reader must not fancy that the noblest views of the Highlands approach

View from Peekskill.

their end when the picturesque military post is passed.   So far is this
from being the fact, that we fear we have
given to what is, we confess, our favorite of
all the places on the river's shore, more than
its share of time and space.

For we have not yet spoken of Cozzens's, that familiar and
great resort of summer pleasure-seekers, perched high on the
brow of the cliff that is the most prominent on the western
shore for several miles below the Military Academy.   Nothing could be more picturesque than the situation of the great building of the hotel, high up in air, looking
down upon all the noblest of the river-views.   It is several hundred feet above the
water in reality; but it looks twice the real distance from the low shore at the base
of the cliff to the foundations of the house, for the precipice is here so bold and
rugged that the most practised eye is deceived by its appearance of great height.
Along this steep descent runs the road, cut as at the post-landing above, in a well-
graded slope from the river to the summit of the cliffs.   On the shore Mr. Fenn has
found a point of view where 'one may deceive himself into the belief that he looks upon
some legend-haunted ruin near the Rhine or the Neckar, so picturesquely are the outlines of this commonplace old structure by the Cozzens's Landing shaped and scarred by
time and weather.

But we must hasten on, for now, a little distance farther down the river, we come upon another of the most glorious mountain-groups of the Highlands—the most southern of all, forming the lower gate, as the Storm-King and its fellows form the upper. Chief among this new group is the bold height of Anthony's Nose, descending sharply to the water of the river at one of the most perfect bends in all its course. So boldly does the promontory jut out into the stream that it seems actually to close its channel; and the good Hendrick Hudson, as he approached it, thought for a time that his progress was finally brought to a close, and that the arm of the sea, up which he imagined that he was sailing, had ended here among the hills. The steep sides of the headland are dark with rock and forest and thick undergrowth; and the coloring of the whole is so stern and sombre, even in the sunlight, that there is about the mountain an air of majesty that makes it by far the most prominent of the chain in which it stands.

Why this famous height received the name it bears, no one knows; but the veracious Knickerbocker claims to have made discovery of the facts that led to the choosing of the title. "And now I am going to tell," says he, "a fact which I doubt much my readers will hesitate to believe; but, if they do, they are welcome not to believe a word

The Hudson, north from Peekskill.

in this whole history, for nothing which it contains is more true. It must be known, then, that the nose of Anthony the trumpeter was of a very lusty size, strutting boldly from his countenance, like a mountain of Golconda, being sumptuously bedecked with rubies and other precious stones—the true regalia of a king of good fellows, which jolly Bacchus grants to all who bouse it heartily at the flagon. Now, thus it happened that, bright and early in the morning, the good Anthony, having washed his burly visage, was leaning over the quarter-railing of the galley, contemplating it in the glassy wave below. Just at this moment the illustrious Sun, breaking in all his splendor from behind a high bluff of the Highlands, did dart one of his most potent beams full upon the refulgent nose of the sounder of brass, the reflection of which shot straightway down hissing hot into the water, and killed a mighty sturgeon that was sporting beside the vessel. This huge monster, being with infinite labor hoisted on board, furnished a luxurious repast to all the crew, being accounted of excellent flavor, excepting about the wound, where it smacked a little of brimstone; and this, on my veracity, was the first time that ever sturgeon was eaten in these parts by Christian people. When the astonishing miracle became known to Peter Stuyvesant, and that he tasted of the unknown fish, he, as may well be supposed, marvelled exceedingly; and, as a monument thereof, he gave the name of Anthony's Nose to a stout promontory in the neighborhood, and it has continued to be called Anthony's Nose ever since that time."

There are other mountains here that guard, with Anthony's Nose, this southern entrance. Chief among them is the grand Donderberg, jutting sharply into the river from the shore opposite the Nose, and a mile and a half below it in the stream's course. Around this Mountain of Thunder the summer storms collect; and its summit is best known to those who have seen it with the frown of a cloud sweeping over it, and the sound of the coming tempest already heard about its sides.

We are in the very land of Irving now; the whole region is peopled with the creatures of his fancy. Who does not remember the " little bulbous-buttomed Dutch goblin, in trunk-hose and sugar-loaf hat, with a speaking-trumpet in his hand, which, they say, keeps the Donderberg? They declare," Irving says further of the river-captains and their legend, "that they have heard him, in stormy weather, in the midst of the turmoil, giving orders, in Low-Dutch, for the piping up of a fresh gust of wind, or the rattling off of another thunder-clap; that sometimes he has been seen surrounded by a crew of little imps, in broad breeches and short doublets, tumbling head-over-heels in the rack and mist, and playing a thousand gambols in the air, or buzzing like a swarm of flies about Anthony's Nose; and that, at such times, the hurry-scurry of the storm was always greatest."

Of the Sugar-Loaf, Bear Mountain, and the other picturesque hills that form the beautiful southern Highlands, we have not space to speak at length; nor have we looked upon our guide's office as imposing upon us the duty of pointing out to view each several feature of the Highland scenery. Had we done so, we should be open to a thousand charges of neglect. We have rather floated down with the stream, talking with perhaps some garrulity of what first met our eyes; but if we were to yield to temptation, and wander away upon the shore, or penetrate ever so little inland, we should

A Misty Morning on the Hudson.

never end our journey. For there would be then all the picturesque creeks that tumble foaming to the river, and all their long, wild valleys, to follow up; there would be the bright villages, with their legends and their scenes of our old history, to recall; and there would be the hundred thousand points of view to visit and to enjoy, each one more than the last. But we cannot do this; and we must make our farewell to the Highland

The Hudson, at Yonkers.

group, with Mr. Fenn's sketches of the great promontory, and go on into the new scenes of the river below.

As Newburg at the northern entrance of the Highlands, so lies Peekskill near the southern. Very picturesquely the town is placed, with its houses lying on the sloping

The Palisades.

lower shore, and its terraced road on the steep hill - side behind. From this road we again look out on the long reaches of broad and open river; and the wilder and grander aspects to which we have grown accustomed disappear. Yet the quieter scene is very beautiful; and, looking southward from the high terrace, a pleasant country meets the view, where along the river-banks are the little country-places that make homes for crowded-out New-Yorkers.

And now follows a long reach of river of which our title strictly takes no cognizance; it is neither in the Highlands, nor is the greater part of it bordered by the most picturesque portion of the Palisades; yet how can we pass it entirely by without a word—even we who are seeking that which is by nature beautiful, and have nothing, by the stern limitations of our duty, to do with story or reminiscence or manifold attractions of association? We cannot pass by it without at least a word or two; for here, in the part of the river to which we are coming, are scenes that every one knows by heart. We do not mean to speak of Stony Point, where gallant Anthony Wayne led his men so well through the July midnight in 1779; or of Treason Hill, where Arnold's plans were matured, and where André took the papers that betrayed it; or of the hundred other historic localities that lie hereabout; for we will not weary the voyager again with long rehearsal of history, or call him away from his journey. But, when we speak of scenes that every one knows by heart, we mean those that have been touched by Irving's pen, and those among which he himself lived and wrote.

For now we approach the Tappan Zee, and that whole region of the river and its valley which is always connected with the romance and the legendary lore that he created for it. And below is his own home of Sunnyside, standing in classic ground for all Americans. Who can pass, a little above Tarrytown, the shore beyond which lies Sleepy Hollow, or sail past the banks of which every point suggests some memory of the sunny-hearted writer, and not be glad at the thoughts they bring into his mind? Every thing that Irving has touched he has turned into something better than gold.

But, while we have looked only at the eastern shore in this part of the Hudson's course—the eastern shore, to which its associations irresistibly draw the traveller's first glances—the Palisades have already begun, and have grown into an unbroken, massive wall upon the western bank. In strict truth, and geographically, their great escarpments begin in the neighborhood of Haverstraw, and run south along the river-bank for thirty miles or more; but the noblest part of their wall of vertical and columned rock is of much less extent. It is that portion which we call the noblest in which they rise, in rude and rugged but uninterrupted line, to the height of three hundred and even five hundred feet, attaining their greatest magnitude in the enormous and jutting buttress that thrusts itself into the stream nearly opposite Sing Sing.

For miles on either side of this, their giant ridge, like a natural fortress, lies between the river and the bright and fertile region on its west. Here and there the wall is cut by deep and narrow ravines, and through such fissures in the cliffs are gained some of the most perfect views of river and landscape that have greeted us in all our course. It is through such rifts in the rock that one sees the stream lying so far below that it seems almost in another world, and looks across into the blue distance in the east as he might look out from a great and magical window that gave a glimpse into an entirely different life. For nothing could present sharper contrasts than do the two regions separated by this natural wall.   On its west lies the quietest farming country, with its people leading simple, uneventful, pastoral lives—people to whom the busy towns and the noises of the city seem as far away as if they existed only to be read about and wondered over.   But on the eastern side, in the places along the banks of the river, in every kind of dwelling, from great country-seat to smallest suburban cottage, is found a class utterly different.   These are they the chief part of whose days is passed "in town," who have come out, or been driven out, to the beauty of the country for rest and a little freshness and invigoration in their homes, at least. All over the Hudson's banks, from Newburg to New York, these people cluster in villages and little cities, trying hard to bring into the whole region the bustle of their town-life, but gaining good, in spite of themselves, from their surroundings.

At the Foot of the Palisades.

But there is more to be gained from the summit of the Palisades than an outlook at the various aspects of the humanity about their base.   High up upon the crest of the great escarpment one may stand and look far away into the east, or see the most glorious sunsets that ever changed the sky to gold and fire.   To the north lie the Highlands we have passed, stretched out in noblest panorama for his view; and to the south the river flows on in a broader stream, until on its eastern side the city begins, and the stream changes its aspect, and passes between the crowded shores that send out across it the noisy thunder of their busy life; and Palisades, and rocky hills, and long reaches of still stream, and green, pleasant banks, make a sudden end, as the Hudson sweeps grandly and quietly down to the sea.

PHILADELPHIA AND ITS SUBURBS.

WITH ILLUSTRATIONS BY GRANVILLE PERKINS.

Chestnut-Street Bridge, on the Schuylkill.

THE Quaker City! Little did William Penn think, as he stepped out of his boat upon the grassy margin of Dock Creek, that memorable morning of 1682, and walked, with mien sedate and befitting, along the path that led to the pleasant but solitary hostelry of the Blue Anchor, his mind in travail with the scheme of a Philadelphia about to be founded among the "coves and springs and lofty lands" of Coaquannoc—little, beyond peradventure, did he think of the vast possibilities of growth and change that might transform and in one sense alienate, in a future more or less remote, this child of his ambition and his hope! Sagacious and far-seeing as he undoubtedly was, it surely never occurred to him, sitting—as in those days even "friends" did not disdain to sit—in the sanded parlor of the Blue Anchor, and looking, perchance, in a prophetic mood of mind, along the winding shores of the creek, and on what were then the uplands upon the hither bank of the great river in which the creek was lost—surely it could not have happened that his sober fancy pictured so great and

Market Street, looking down from Sixth Street.

Girard College.

Arch Street, looking up.

Philadelphia, from Independence Hall, looking east.

Chestnut Street, looking up from Independence Hall.

Chestnut Street, looking down from Ninth Street.

SCENES IN PHILADELPHIA.

so wonderful a metamorphosis as that which has at this day transfigured the entire landscape into the likeness of the actual Philadelphia! The scope of his forecast may be gauged by the limit of his design. He planned a "town" of thirty streets, crossing each other at right angles, nine east and west, and one-and-twenty north and southward trending—the former serving only as highways from shore to shore of the two streams that held the "lofty lands" in their embrace, with no thought, it would seem, of venturing across these watery barriers, but the latter capable of indefinite extension, subject, of course, to the contingent rights and privileges of neighboring "settlements." Hampered by the memories and traditions of the Old-World towns and cities, he inflicted upon the future metropolis of the Keystone State the same misery that has stayed or stunted the complete and comely development of nearly all the older towns and cities on this continent—the misery of narrow thoroughfares and scanty spaces, blind alleys, dark courts, and a general inadequacy of breathing-room and free circulation, to say nothing—though a great deal should be said—of the lost opportunities for architectural adornment, and the refinement of the popular mind by objects of beauty and grandeur placed constantly before them in their goings up and down the high- and by-ways of daily toil and traffic. Mr. Penn perhaps thought to remedy this to some extent by laying his city out with a fair and, to a mathematical mind, satisfying rectangularity; and, viewed from a thoroughly Gradgrindian stand-point, a city whose streets are intersected by each other at invariable right angles, and consequently traverse the length and breadth of the land in undeviating straight lines, is possibly the most comfortable and convenient of cities. But, looking from a picturesque point of view, such an arrangement is very unfortunate, and a wholesale sacrifice of beauty to utility. Though the sect to which the eminent founder of Philadelphia belonged was not popularly believed to have much sympathy with the allurements of the beautiful, either in Nature or art, yet it will not be denied that there were, and are, many picturesque features in the landscape of the spot chosen by him for the site of his city of fraternal love. Here was a large and pleasantly-undulating plain, rising gently, north and westward, to a country of heavily-timbered hills, and rich uplands pregnant with the promise of future harvests, margined for many a mile by the broad, swift, deep-flowing Delaware, and the shallower, slower, but more beautiful and purer, Schuylkill—twin channels for an apparently illimitable commerce, and an equally exhaustless supply of the vital element that is necessary to the existence of this commerce and of the life that makes it possible—a plain, too, with further accidents of beauty along its borders in the shape of rocky dell and shadowy ravine, hints of mountain and gorge, and all the fascinating marvels of torrent, cascade, and rapid, reproduced in miniature, so to speak, upon the romantic banks and in the sylvan stream of the weird and winding Wissahickon. "It seemed," indeed, as Penn himself said, the very place "appointed for a town;" and surely the phenomena of its growth have gone far to prove the wisdom of his selection.

Tower and Steeple, Independence Hall.

The Philadelphia of William Penn was incorporated in 1701 ; and for a number of years thereafter the tendency of its growth was in a lateral direction, upon or near the shore of the Delaware, north and southward rather than westward toward the Schuylkill. This disposition to cling to the margin of the waters over which the adventurer has sailed from the Old to the New Land is natural, and noticeable in nearly every instance of the early settlements in this country. It was specially so in Philadelphia, where both the business and social life of the city long clustered in the streets bordering or abutting upon the Delaware, leaving most of the upper or western part of the city-plan either in the condition known to real-estate dealers as "unimproved," or occupied as small farms and suburban villas. Even as late as the first quarter of the present century, many of the finest private residences in the city were on Front Street, which was the first street opened by Penn, and ran nearly due north and south along the course of the river. Some of these remain to this day the habitations of wealthy citizens, though jostled by the encroachments of toil and traffic, and their river-side pleasures and privileges usurped by unsightly and unsavory wharves, crowded avenues, and lofty warehouses.

There are, of course, but few historical monuments left standing of the earlier days of Philadelphia. The most venerable, perhaps, and one of the most interesting, is Christ Church, in Second Street, above Market, which dates, in its present construction, as far back as 1727, two years before the laying of the corner-stone of the State-House, since memorable as Independence Hall. Hemmed in, as this stately pile now is on all sides, by the obtrusive and inharmonious aggregations of brick and mortar devoted to the prosaic purposes of trade, it may be difficult, if not impossible, for the artist to find a point of view from which its picturesque features can be brought into full relief; but from its belfry the visitor at least beholds a panorama of land and water which will well repay the fatigue of ascent. The broad expanse of the Delaware, with all its varied aspects of commercial highway and grove-fringed, villa-bordered stream, flows between its level banks for many a mile beneath him. Eastward he looks far across the river to the sandy reaches of New Jersey, with Camden and Gloucester in the foreground, and an indefinite vista of sombre pine-groves beyond.

To the south his roving eye will first be caught by the old Navy-Yard, with its ark-like ship-houses, its tiers of masts and docks, and the green oases of its officers' quarters; while still farther away, where the Schuylkill and Delaware meet on their way to the sea, low and dark on the horizon lies League Island—the Navy-Yard of the future.

If, now, he turn his back on the river, the entire city and its far-reaching suburbs are spread as a map before him from the mouth of the Schuylkill, on the south, to the extremest limit of Germantown, on the north, and westward, far beyond the semi-rural avenues of West Philadelphia, Mantua, and Hestonville, all of which are comprised in the city of to-day. A similar panoramic view will open before him who may gaze from the belfry-gallery of Independence Hall; and a third, and even more picturesque overlook, is obtained from the summit of Girard College, which is itself one of the most magnificent monuments of individual benevolence in this country. The buildings devoted to this noble charity stand upon high ground, in the midst of a park-like plot of forty-five acres, stretching along what was once called the Ridge Road, but now elevated to the more sounding title of Ridge Avenue, in the northwestern part of the city. The principal and central structure, containing the college proper (the other buildings being chiefly dormitories and offices), is a massive Corinthian temple, of white marble, and is justly regarded as the best reproduction of pure Greek architecture in this country. The purpose and history of this institution are too well and widely known to need further recapitulation.

Most of the streets of Philadelphia are, unhappily, narrow, and their rectangularity and straightness offend the artistic eye as well as mar the architectural effect of the

FOUNTAINS IN PHILADELPHIA.

more imposing structures erected upon them. There are, however, on almost all her highways noble and graceful edifices constructed by public or private munificence and taste, massive temples of charity, of religion, of industry, and of art, which go far to redeem the stiffness and monotony of the general plan of the city. Something about the more notable buildings, public and private, may not be wholly inappropriate even in a picturesque article, the less so as some of them are intimately connected with the history and traditions (which are always picturesque) of the place. So, having left the "dim, religious light" that marks the sacred precincts of Christ Church, let us go on to Chestnut Street, and pause at the State-House, with a reverent recognition of its claims, to notice above those of more recent and more ornate constructions.

The edifice is but two stories in height, and built of simple brick, but its associations have given it an interest scarcely less world-wide and thrilling than that attaching to any structure, however magnificent in size or symmetry, throughout Christendom. It is surmounted by a steeple, in which was hung the great and glorious bell, with its prophetic inscription, verified little more than a century after its first echoes woke the good burghers of the royal province of Pennsylvania, when the clangorous pæan was proclaimed of—"Liberty throughout the land, unto *all* the inhabitants thereof." Beneath its roof was pronounced the Declaration of Independence, and in the same chamber, a few years afterward, the system of government which culminated in the establishment of the Great Republic was discussed and adopted.

Market Street is the great central highway of traffic, foreign and domestic, and is chiefly remarkable for its handsome warehouses and mercantile depots, its width, and its turmoil. The traveller in search of the picturesque will not care to linger amid its prosaic bustle. Neither will he find much to arrest his eye on Arch Street, save a graceful spire here and there; but he will be struck by the repose of the street as contrasted with the rattle and hurry of adjacent highways, and with the air of placid respectability that distinguishes the staid denizens of that quiet avenue. It was, and to some extent still is, a favorite street for "Friends'" residences, and partakes, both in its architecture and its human circulation, of the peculiar plainness and primness of the primitive Quakers.

The handsomer private residences are chiefly in the western and northwestern parts of the city. West Philadelphia, across the Schuylkill, is full of elegant villas and tasteful cottages. The western part of Walnut, Chestnut, Arch, Spruce, and Pine Streets, is wholly occupied by what we sometimes hear called palatial mansions; and the spacious and noble boulevard of Broad Street runs for miles between the dwellings of the rich, built of every variety of stone and in every conceivable (or inconceivable) style of architecture, and, in many instances, further adorned by lawns and gardens of most elaborate finish and fruitfulness.

The numerous spots of shade and greenery known as "squares" are pleasant and wholesome features of this city. They were part of the original plan of Penn, and having had the advantage of time, are full of noble and venerable trees, some of which were denizens of the virgin forest that gloomed the soil on which they still stand. In the centre of Franklin Square—the largest and one of the most beautiful of those within the city—there is a fine fountain, with a number of jets falling into a large basin, upon whose clear surface two or more swans were wont to glide, much to the delight

Navy-Yard.

of the children; but these graceful water-fowl have vanished, having, perhaps, been removed to the broader waters of Fairmount Park. The thirsty wayfarer, by-the-by, whether man or beast, will find no lack of fountains whereat to quench his thirst in Philadelphia. There are scores of these grateful drinking-places on the high- and by-ways of the city and suburbs, some of them, as may be seen by the accompanying illustration, not without a picturesque or artistic beauty and fitness in their design, which does

not render the water less refreshing or the pilgrim less appreciative. These street fountains are due to the humane and enlightened labors and taste of a few gentlemen,
who, in 1869, formed themselves into a Fountain Society for this beneficent object, and,
either through their personal and pecuniary efforts and assistance, or by the influence of
their example upon others, these well-springs of wholesome refreshment have been offered
to the parched throats of hundreds of thousands of their fellow-creatures.

In several instances an intelligent advantage has been taken—notably in the Park
and upon some of the pretty roads about the skirts of the city—of the natural accidents of scenery in the selection of the spot and the character of the fountain, and the
result is picturesque, and in harmony with the landscape and associations. It were to be
wished that an equally enlightened taste had been displayed in *every* instance ; but as
some of these—shall we say works of art?—have been the free gift of individual citizens (and, therefore, not to be viewed with the " critic's eye"), there is here and there an
unfortunate specimen of that peculiar taste supposed to belong to the great " Veneering "
and " Podsnap " families. Under the circumstances, however, it would be uncharitable to
seem severely critical, and these blots upon the artistic perspicacity of the Fountain Society shall not, therefore, be more particularly alluded to herein.

Art and science have received careful attention in Philadelphia. For many years
the quiet and modest rooms of the Academy of Fine Arts, in Chestnut Street, were
the resort of art-loving citizens and curious strangers. Here several of the huge canvases
of Benjamin West and Rembrandt Peale were enshrined in state, and received the hom-
age of those who deemed them superlative works of art, the finest of which the country
could boast. Here the annual exhibitions of the works of Philadelphia's artists are held,
and in the basement beneath are casts of the famous statues of antiquity, arranged in
sepulchral rows. All of these treasures, it is believed, will in time be transferred to the
new Academy of Fine Arts, which will be erected on an appropriate site in another
portion of the city.

One of the most remarkable buildings in Philadelphia is the new Masonic Temple,
just erected on the corner of Broad and Filbert Streets. It is constructed of granite,
dressed at the quarry and brought to the site all ready for immediate use. As a piece
of architecture it is a curious imitation of the round and pointed styles of the middle
ages—the outlines, the tower, and certain other features, suggesting the Gothic, while the
windows, the façade, and the minuter details, are thoroughly Saxon in character. Thus,
the deeply-recessed porch, with its dog-tooth ornaments and round arches, might be
copied from one of the old Saxon-built abbeys of England; while the tower, adorned in
a more elaborate style, only needs a spire to be Gothic in general effect if not in detail. Inside the Temple there are various halls, built in the Corinthian, Doric, and
other styles, so as to be in consonance with various phases of masonic practices.

If the Delaware River is the source of commercial prosperity to Philadelphia, the

Coal Depot, Richmond, on the Delaware.

Schuylkill offers to its citizens their most delightful out-of-door pleasures. The Delaware, broad, swift, and majestic, is of utilitarian benefit. The Schuylkill, narrow, winding, and picturesque, gratifies the sense of beauty. It is at Fairmount that the charm of the Schuylkill begins. Below this point there is not much in the stream calculated to interest the visitor, though the graceful iron arches of the Chestnut-Street Bridge will attract attention, as being a work in which engineering skill has effectually availed itself of the curved lines in which it is claimed that beauty dwells. Up to this bridge the largest vessels may approach, their tapering masts and graceful yards presenting a picture which, in a bright, sunny day, might have won the admiration and employed the pencil of Turner. The scene at this point is usually a busy one. Noisy steam-tugs, light sail-boats, scows, canal-boats, and other kinds of craft, crowd the stream, and impart that life and vivacity peculiar to the water-front of a flourishing commercial city. At night, when the bridge is lighted by rows of

A. C. WARREN

G. R. HALL

City of New York

FROM BROOKLYN HEIGHTS

HARRY FENN

S. V. HUNT

West Point and the Highlands

DAVID JOHNSON

G. W. WELLSTOOD

The Mouth of the Moodna on the Hudson

GRANVILLE PERKINS

R. HINSHELWOOD

Philadelphia from Belmont

WEST PARK

J. D. WOODWARD

R. HINSHELWOOD

Connecticut Valley from Mount Tom

City of Baltimore

FROM DRUID HILL PARK

HARRY FENN

S. V. HUNT

The Catskills

SUNRISE FROM SOUTH MOUNTAIN

A. C. WARREN

W. WELLSTOOD

City of Cincinnati

City of Louisville

F. O. C. DARLEY

H. B. HALL

Emigrants Crossing the Plains

F. O. C. DARLEY

F. HOLL

Native Californians Lassoing a Bear

GRANVILLE PERKINS

R. HINSHELWOOD

The Susquehanna

AT HUNTER'S GAP

J. D. WOODWARD

E. P. BRANDARD

City of Boston

FROM SOUTH BOSTON

J. W. CASILEAR

R. HINSHELWOOD

Lake George

A. F. BELLOWS

S. V. HUNT

The Housatonic

A. C. WARREN

R. HINSHELWOOD

City of St. Louis

Quebec

J. F. KENSETT

S. V. HUNT

On the Beverly Coast, Massachusetts

J. M. HART

R. HINSHELWOOD

The Adirondack Woods

C. G. GRISWOLD

S. V. HUNT

East Rock, New Haven

The Rocky Mountains

A. C. WARREN

R. HINSHELWOOD

City of Milwaukee

C. ROSENBERG

G. R. HALL

The Terrace, Central Park

NEW YORK

W. L. SHEPPARD

R. HINSHELWOOD

Washington from Arlington Heights

PHILADELPHIA, FROM BELOW THE NEW SOUTH-STREET-BRIDGE.

Wire Bridge at Fairmount.

gas-lamps, and the masts and cordage loom up in the dim moonlight, the scene assumes a picturesque element which it does not possess by daylight. Below the bridge, on either shore, may be seen the outlines of huge derricks, used in loading coal-barges. Beyond can be discerned various spires and towers, and the cross-surmounted dome of the Roman Catholic Cathedral on Logan Square. Another bridge—known as the South-Street Bridge — is building in this vicinity, and will afford another much-needed means of communication between these populous and busy shores.

Fairmount Water-Works have been for many years one of the recognized "sights" of Philadelphia; but the great improvements recently made in their vicinity have transformed this resort into one of the most charming pleasure-gardens in the world. Twenty years ago "Fairmount" meant only the buildings in which the machinery used in supplying Philadelphia with pure water was enclosed, and the little pleasure-ground and reservoir lying near it.

FAIRMOUNT WATER-WORKS.

Now, the vast expanse of Fairmount Park is included in the generic term, and days might be pleasantly spent in investigating the attractions of this charming spot.

As early as 1800 the necessity of providing for Philadelphia a supply of water greater than that offered by the wells and cisterns was recognized; but it was not until 1818 that the scheme of elevating and turning into it the river Schuylkill, by means of an immense dam, was determined upon. The principal features of this plan are the construction of a dam, over fourteen hundred feet long, which backs the water up the river about six miles, creating a power sufficient to raise into the reservoir ten million gallons a day; the immense forcing-pumps, placed in a horizontal position, and worked by cranks on the water-wheels; and the vast net-work of mains and pipes which convey the water to all parts of the city. The buildings containing this ponderous machinery are open to the public, and the majestic, regular motion of the massive forcing-wheels offers a constant source of attraction to the curious visitor. The peculiar and by no means disagreeable odor produced by fresh water when in broken motion pervades these buildings, and can be detected at some distance as you approach them.

The grounds in the immediate vicinity of the Water-Works, though limited in size, are pleasantly laid out; and wooded paths wind up the Reservoir hill, summer-houses and rustic seats being placed on the various coignes of 'vantage. Projecting from the Reservoir, there is a massive stone belvedere, from which may be obtained an extensive view of the Schuylkill and its picturesque shores on the one hand, and the roofs and spires of the great city on the other. The view of the Water-Works from the opposite side of the Schuylkill is quite unique, a pleasant architectural effect being produced by two little Grecian temples which overhang the water, and by the symmetrical colonnade of the larger of the half-dozen buildings which appertain to the Water-Works.

Embowered in the trees near these buildings is the monument erected to the memory of Frederick Graeff, the designer and first engineer of the works. It is but a few minutes' walk from this spot to the large bronze statue of Lincoln, erected in 1871— probably the most elaborate monument yet erected to the memory of the martyr President.

Fairmount Park, in its entire extent, comprises some four thousand acres, is three times larger than the famous Central Park of New York, and is by far the most extensive pleasure-ground in this country. It lies on both sides of the Schuylkill, and communication between its different sections is maintained by the bridges at Girard Avenue and Schuylkill Falls. There is also, below Fairmount, a wire bridge, which, when it was new, was thought to be a remarkable triumph of engineering skill, and attracted the attention of all visitors to the Quaker City. It is to-day as useful and as sightly as ever, but its celebrity has been long since eclipsed. Fairmount Park was gradually formed through the purchase by the municipal authorities of several of the elegant, well-cultivated estates which lay on either side of the Schuylkill in the vicinity

VIEW FROM WEST PARK.

of the city.   The property includes Belmont, once the country-home of Judge Peters, a noted jurist in the early part of the century, and a personal friend of General Washington; the Landsdowne estate, belonging to a Marquis of Landsdowne, who married Miss Bingham, an American lady; and the Sedgely estate.   These lands are all on the west side of the river.   On the east side the city has acquired Lemon Hill, Eaglesfield, and

Rockland Landing, on the Schuylkill.

all the estates, on that side of the stream, up to the Wissahickon River.   Not only do these acquisitions offer "ample room and verge enough" for one of the most magnificent parks in the world, but the admirable natural advantages—gentle declivities, and a picturesque river among them—were enhanced by the fact that the private country-seats, of which this property is mostly composed, were all richly improved.   The ancestral trees were in excellent preservation and in the fullest splendor of their foliage.   The roads were all laid out, and the grounds showed that for years they had received the careful attention of skilled landscape-gardeners. In fact, the Park authorities had only to combine into one a number of pleasure-grounds already constructed, and to invite the citizens of Philadelphia to the immediate enjoyment of one of the loveliest out-door resorts in the country.

The Schuylkill—View from Landsdowne.

Of course, the points of view, the quiet retreats, and the charming nooks in Fairmount Park are almost innumerable. The windings of the river offer a constant variety of sylvan scenery. At Rockland Landing, for instance, there is an extensive view in both directions until the bend of the stream cuts it off, while directly behind the spectator towers a rocky, perpendicular cliff, on the face of which the various strata of rock are exposed to view in a manner which would delight equally a scientific geologist or the mere casual lover of the picturesque. Above Belmont the stream assumes a wilder character. The shores slope gradually down to the water's edge; and the overhanging trees curve gently forward over the road-way, as if, like the fond Narcissus, they were enamoured of their own reflection in the fair bosom of the limpid stream. From the heights of Landsdowne there is a wider scope of vision. Seated on the rustic benches, overshadowed by stately trees of almost a primeval growth, the lounger may enjoy one of the most delightful bits of river-scenery of the milder order which our country affords. Perhaps among the noblest views which are afforded by the rich variety of the Fairmount country is one to be gained from the West Park. In this view the river is not visible. The eye, wandering over an expanse of billowy foliage, descries in the distance the roofs and spires of the fair city, and the smoke of industry arising from a hundred tall chimneys. Near the centre of this scene arises a graceful and varied architectural grouping, formed by the tower of the Masonic Temple, the sharp spire of the adjacent church, and the swelling dome of the Roman Catholic Cathedral. These buildings are not really near together; but, by the effect of parallax, they seem to form one group, and in their proud majesty dominate the entire city.

The Delaware and the Schuylkill! "The wedded rivers," Whittier calls them in his recent lovely pastoral, "The Pennsylvania Pilgrim." Perhaps the sympathetic visitor,

Schuylkill, above Belmont.

Old Bridge on the Wissahickon.

wandering in Fairmount Park at that sweet hour when day is melting into night, may keenly realize the Quaker poet's description of the city and its vicinage in the colonial days, nearly a century before the colonists were troubled with dreams of independence:

" . . . One long bar
Of purple cloud, on which the evening star
Shone like a jewel on a scimitar,

" Held the sky's golden gate-way. Through the deep
Hush of the woods a murmur seemed to creep,
The Schuylkill whispering in a voice of sleep.

" All else was still. The oxen from their ploughs
Rested at last, and from their long day's browse
Came the dun files of Krisheim's home-bound cows.

" And the young city, round whose virgin zone
The rivers like two mighty arms were thrown,
Marked by the smoke of evening fires alone—

" Lay in the distance, lovely even then,
With its fair women and its stately men
Gracing the forest-court of William Penn—

" Urban yet sylvan; in its rough-hewn frames
Of oak and pine the dryads held their claims,
And lent its streets their pleasant woodland names."

And to this day many of the streets of Philadelphia retain "their pleasant rural names," as Pine, Chestnut, Vine, and others. The great majority, however, are designated by numerals—a prosaic, mechanical system, which seems to be generally adopted in our larger American cities, though it was never found necessary for Paris, London, or Vienna.

In the West Park will be erected, in 1876, the superb buildings intended for the International Exhibition connected with the Centennial Celebration. The central structure will be permanent, and will remain most probably, for ages to come, an ornament to

Drive along the Wissahickon.

the Park, a source of attraction to strangers, and an object of pride to citizens. The crowds of visitors from all parts of the world, who will flock to Philadelphia on the occasion of the official celebration of our hundredth national birthday, will ever recall with pleasure the sylvan beauties of Fairmount Park, and will spread far and wide the fame of this most delightful pleasure-resort. In twenty years, Fairmount will be as famous in its way as the Bois de Boulogne of Paris, Hyde Park of London, the Pincian Hill of Rome, the Cascine of Florence, or the Prater of Vienna. It possesses a greater variety of natural beauty than any of them.

No notice of Philadelphia would be complete without some description of the Wissahickon. This very picturesque little river winds through a narrow valley, between steep and richly-wooded banks, and possesses all the wildness of a stream far from the haunts

Wissahickon, near Paper-Mill Bridge.

of men, though it is but a few miles from one of the largest cities on the continent. Its beauties begin from the moment it pours its crystal current into the waters of the Schuylkill. As it approaches the latter river, it is quiet and peaceful; but it soon becomes almost a mountain-torrent, as it is confined between narrow banks and overshadowed by towering hills. Its water-power has been made available for manufacturing purposes; but, as it has lately been included within the limits of Fairmount Park, it is understood that the unromantic mill-buildings will be soon removed, and nothing allowed to remain which can in any way interfere with its wild and picturesque beauty. Even at present, these objectionable structures are not wholly unsightly; and the factories at the mouth of the Wissahickon are so shaded by foliage that, in conjunction with the arches of the bridges near by, they offer tempting bits of form and color for the artist's pencil. The old log-cabin bridge, which crosses the stream at one point, has attracted the attention of both amateur and professional sketchers nearly as much as the falls which give variety to one of its widest stretches.

A wide carriage-road runs along the bank of the Wissahickon, and is a favorite drive of the Philadelphians, the river dancing along on one side, and high, rocky projections, crowned with wild, overhanging trees and shrubbery, bordering the other. Nothing can surpass the variety of this river-scenery. Even the covered bridge, so often an unsightly object in the rural scenery of America, when compared with the open, arched bridges of Europe, seems to be in keeping here. We can hardly say as much for the so-called "Pipe Bridge," which, to the unprofessional eye, looks as if it were thrown upside-down across the valley.

Various restaurants and houses of resort for pleasure-seekers are to be found on the Wissahickon road. Other spots are noted as the localities of various traditions, generally of a rather apocryphal nature. Near the "log-cabin" is a lane which leads to a well, dug, some two centuries ago, by one John Kelpius, who is generally known as "the hermit of the Wissahickon. This man, a graduate of the University of Helmstadt, in Germany, came to Philadelphia in 1694, with a party of two hundred followers, who had adopted his peculiar religious views. Whittier says that the "Magister Johann Kelpius" was a believer in the near approach of the millennium, and was thoroughly imbued with the mystic views of the German philosophers. He called his settlement by the odd name of "The Woman in the Wilderness." He died in 1704, when only thirty-four years of age, while in the act of preaching to his disciples in his garden. He was the possessor of a "stone of wisdom," which he threw into the river shortly before his death, and which has never been found. He seems to have been a believer in the theories of the alchemists of the middle ages, and during his lifetime was viewed with distrust by the Pennsylvania Quakers. Whittier speaks of him as "the painful Kelpius," who—

> "in his hermit den
> By Wissahickon, maddest of good men,
> Dreamed o'er the Chiliast dreams of Petersen."

There, where "the small river slid snake-like in the shade," he is described as crooning wizard-like over forbidden books, and, by the aid of his magical stone, seeing visions as strange and terrible as those beheld by the inspired eye of the Seer of Patmos.

MOUTH OF THE WISSAHICKON.

OLD LOG CABIN-BRIDGE ON THE WISSAHICKON.

WISSAHICKON FALLS.

SCENES ON THE WISSAHICKON.

Laurel Hill, the famous cemetery of Philadelphia, which for many years has been the subject of artistic illustration, is now, like the Wissahickon, included within the limits of Fairmount Park, though a suitable wall of partition secures to it the privacy becoming a metropolis of the dead. Here rest many of the most noted citizens of Philadelphia, including persons who have won an abiding fame in the worlds of literature and of art. On the opposite side of the Schuylkill is another cemetery, known by the rather cumbrous name of West Laurel Hill. The other cemeteries of the Pennsylvanian metropolis are known as Monument Cemetery (from a monument erected to the joint memories of Washington and Lafayette), Mount Peace, Mount Vernon, Glenwood, Mount Moriah, Woodland, and the Cathedral Cemetery, the latter being the favorite place of interment of the Roman Catholic community. There are, besides these, various smaller cemeteries, belonging to different organized societies.

On the Wissahickon at Sunset.

SCENES IN NORTHERN NEW JERSEY.

WITH ILLUSTRATIONS BY JULES TAVERNIER.

Scene on the Passaic.

ALTHOUGH New Jersey, ever since her admission into the Union, has been the butt for the sarcasm and wit of those who live outside her borders, the gallant little State has much to be proud of. Her history is rich in instances of heroism, especially during the Revolutionary period. Her prosperity is far greater than that of many noisier and more excitable communities. Her judiciary has made the name of "Jersey justice" a terror to the evil-doer. Her territory includes every variety of scenery, from the picturesque hills and lakes of her northern to the broad sand-wastes of her southern counties. Those interested in the statistics of industry will find much that is worthy of notice in her iron-works and other great manufacturing establishments, while those who seek the indolent delights of summer enjoyment cannot fail to be charmed with her famous and fashionable sea-side resorts.

The picturesque features of New Jersey lie almost entirely in the northern section of the State, and are within easy reach of the great metropolis. Indeed, thousands of

EAGLE ROCK, ORANGE.

WASHINGTON ROCK.

the business-men of New York live in the midst of these picturesque scenes, an hour's ride serving to convey them from the turmoil of city occupations to the serene quiet and sylvan charms of rural life.   Jersey City and Newark are flourishing cities, with populations of their own ; but the multitudinous smaller towns and villages, within a radius of fifty miles, owe their existence entirely to the surplus population of New York.

A ride of seven or eight miles brings the traveller from the valley of the Hudson to the valley of the Passaic, the latter being bounded, at some distance inland, by the abrupt, precipitous range of hills known generally as Orange Mountain.   A dozen years ago, this mountain was a wild, uninhabited region.   The Dutch farmers who originally settled in this vicinity were content to nestle in the grassy valleys, preferring for their homes the quiet plains rather than seeking for picturesque nooks on the frowning hill-side.   They built solid one-story houses of gray-stone, covering them with overhanging roofs, and caring in their domestic arrangements rather for comfort than for elegance. Many of these simple yet substantial structures are standing at this day, giving shelter to the descendants of those who built them.   Others have passed into the hands of city-folk, and have been decked out with verandas, furnished with larger windows, and even provided with Mansard roofs, so that it is difficult to recognize in these reconstructed edifices the solid old farm-houses of a hundred years ago.   In no part of the country has speculation in real estate been carried on more vigorously or more successfully than in Northern New Jersey, and many a hard-working farmer has found himself unexpectedly rich through the marvellous rise in the value of the land which his fathers considered as only adapted to the raising of cabbages or potatoes.   In the last few years, railroad communication has increased to such an extent that almost every farm in Northern New Jersey enjoys the advantage of being " near the station "— a privilege which only those who live in the country can fully appreciate.

One of the first and most successful attempts at landscape-gardening on a large scale, in this country, was made by the late Llewellyn S. Haskell, a gentleman who was especially enamoured of rural life, and who to ample means and unflagging energy added a finished and cultivated taste.   He purchased a large tract of land on Orange Mountain, and laid it out as a park, in which he and his friends built a variety of elegant private residences.   No attempt was made to deprive this region of its wild primeval beauty.   Roads were laid out, winding in gentle curves amid the rugged rocks and through the rich and picturesque forests.   Near Eagle Rock, the proprietor of this superb domain erected his own home, at a point which commands a view more extensive than any other in the vicinity of New York.   Beneath the spectator lies the cultivated valley, covered with villages, and partially bounded by the Bergen Hills.   To the south can be seen the gleam of the waters of the bay of New York and of the Atlantic Ocean, and, under favorable atmospheric circumstances, the spires of the great city.   The whole eastern slope of the mountain, for several miles in length, is dotted with resi-

RAMAPO RIVER.

dences, most of which command this delightful view, which increases in diversity and beauty, though not in extent, as you go northward into the prosperous town of Montclair.

At the foot of the mountain there is a well-kept road, which is a favorite drive for the residents of the vicinity, affording as it does, in the warm summer afternoons, that

Terrace House and Thorn Mountain.

"shadow of a great rock in a weary land" of which the Scriptural poet spoke so many thousand years ago; and, at the same time, offering a goodly view of the level plain. From this road—though it is at a much lower elevation than the point of view suggested in our engraving—Eagle Rock is seen towering up in majestic grandeur, as bold and rugged as when only the red-men inhabited this charming region. The eagles, which

BREAKWATER. RAMAPO.

gave it its name, are now but seldom seen; yet the hoary, scarred projection seems to the eye as distant and as desolate as when it was indeed the home of the king of birds.

Still more striking in appearance, and more picturesque in formation, is Washington Rock, on the same range of hills. This rock is divided by a deep chasm into two parts, one of which has evidently been cleft from its fellow by some great convulsion of Nature, and has fallen several rods down the slope of the hill, where it stands firm and upright. From this rock it is said that George Washington viewed the land below, eager

Little Falls.

to trace the course of the British army. At that time the plain was cultivated, it is true; but the pretty little village of Dunellen, which to-day forms so pleasing a feature of the scene, was then unthought of, and the mountain itself was as wild and uninhabited as the far-distant Sierras. Washington Rock is now a favorite resort for picnic-parties, and for the tourist who seeks to gratify his taste for the picturesque.

Farther to the north of the State is the Ramapo River, a stream which finds its way between high hills, and is frequently made use of for manufacturing purposes. Over one of the dams which obstruct its course, the water flows in a graceful cascade, which, but for its prim regularity, would equal in its beauty of motion the natural falls which

THE PASSAIC, BELOW LITTLE FALLS.

are ever such a source of delight to the lover of the beautiful. To such, indeed, the Ramapo offers many attractions. The stream, in its numerous curves, constantly presents fresh points of view. The hills—sometimes abrupt, sometimes rolling—here and there recede from the river's edge, leaving grassy fields or rocky plateaus, on either of which it is a pleasure to stroll, listening, as did Sir Bedivere, to—

> " . . . hear the ripple washing in the reeds,
> And the wild water lapping on the crag."

The sails on the river add to the variety of the scene ; the fisherman's row-boat imparts to it notable life and vivacity ; and the wreathed smoke of the locomotive does not seem wholly inharmonious. In fact, the railroad-train has become quite a prominent incident in our river-scenery. Railroads naturally follow the river-courses, and they give to the wildest and most unfrequented valleys a touch of human life and interest which greatly adds to the effect of mountain solitudes. Heard in the far distance, the whistle of the locomotive sounds really musical. The rumbling of the approaching train—now enhanced by a sudden echo, now deadened by a plunge into a tunnel—grows nearer and stronger, till, as the long line of cars passes by, it becomes less and less distinct, and, dying away in the distance, renders the solitude of the hills, by contrast, still more lonely. There is in all this a certain picturesque effect of sound—if the expression may be allowed—which harmonizes well with the rural scenery. When a railroad was first projected along the shore of the Hudson River, the occupants of the elegant country-seats which adorn the green banks of that noble stream, were highly indignant at what they deemed an invasion of their rights, and an outrage upon the quietude and beauty of their homes. Audubon, the celebrated naturalist, who lived on the Hudson, was so affected by this innovation that his anxiety on the subject is said to have shortened his life. To-day, however, no one complains of the passing trains, which, in fact, add a peculiar element of human interest to the wildest and grandest scenery.

There are many other points of picturesque beauty in Northern New Jersey, to which we can only briefly allude. Greenwood Lake, on the boundary-line between New Jersey and New York, is sometimes called the Windermere of America, and, in its quiet, graceful beauty, will remind the traveller of the famed English lake. It has of late years become a recognized place of resort—perhaps the most noted in the State, with the exception of Cape May, Atlantic City, and Long Branch.

Among the hills and streams of the section of country to which these few pages are devoted may be found many attractive nooks—many quietly-beautiful homes, like Terrace House, which is overlooked by a towering mountain-peak, worthy of companionship with the mountains of New Hampshire. But, as a general thing, the scenery of Northern New Jersey is on a less extensive scale. The hills, rugged and wild as they may be, after all, cannot fairly be called mountains. The lakes are small, and the nar-

PASSAIC FALLS.

row rivers find devious paths among their rocky barriers. Principal among these streams is that on which the largest city of New Jersey is situated. Indeed, the Passaic, to which allusion is made, is, not only in its historic interest, but its great length, breadth and commercial importance, a notable exception among the rivers of New Jersey. For, though rising in and flowing for much of its course through a hilly and rock-bound region, the Passaic River is the most tortuous and the most sluggish, as well as the longest, stream in the State. From its extreme source, in the upper part of Morris County, it flows, as gently as "sweet Avon," between the hills of that county and Essex, taking toll of Dead River as it passes the base of Long Hill, and thence stealing its way, with scarcely a ripple, through narrow vale and broad valley, for twenty miles among the defiles of the Horseshoe Mountain, till it receives the tribute of the vivacious Rockaway. Stimulated apparently by the instillation of this lively little rock-stream, or perhaps awakened to the sense of an impending crisis in its fate, it emerges from the last defile with a sudden start, and almost rushes for a few miles toward its first leap over the rapids of Little Falls, nearly opposite the somewhat uninteresting manufacturing village of that name. This first saltatory experiment of the Passaic, though comparatively of a gentle character, is still not devoid of picturesque beauty, or even of a certain grandeur. The fall is more than three hundred feet broad, and is formed with an obtuse angle opening down-stream, over which the river, just pausing to smoothe its ruffled surface on the brink, leaps in two broad sheets of foam-capped, spray-clouded water, and then glides away serenely to perform a similar feat a short distance lower down, at the Second Fall—the two being possibly in the nature of rehearsals for the final acrobatic struggle at the Great Passaic Falls, some six miles below. The scenery along the river, during its leisurely loiterings through the mountains, and its scarcely more hurried voyage athwart the valleys of its upper course, is of that peculiar character which belongs to such regions. Tall masses of rock rise abruptly, at intervals, on its banks, like great buttresses, or still more like the massive and forest-grown ruins of mighty rock-structures, such as are found here and there along the water-courses of the wondrous Southwest. The river-bed is rocky; yet the flow is hardly fretted into ripples by these up-cropping barriers, but seems to hold the even tenor of its way with a quiet disregard of obstacles that is eminently suggestive of a serene philosophy. At Little Falls the Morris Canal crosses the river by a handsome stone aqueduct; and from the summit of this the artistic loungers may obtain a charming view of the stream, winding down between overhanging hills of greenery, and jutting escarpments of cedar-crowned trap-rock and sandstone, toward Great Falls, and the more level reaches of the Paterson plains and the salt-marshes of Newark. Before reaching this point, however, the river undergoes a second tribulation in the shape of another fall and rapid, which rouse its sluggishness into momentary and picturesque fury, and over and down which it roars in foamy wrath, scarcely subdued in time to collect itself for the struggle five miles beyond. But it does

THE PASSAIC BELOW THE FALLS.

subside, and, assuming once more a tranquil air of unconsciousness, rolls smoothly to the verge, and then plunges boldly, in one unbroken column, over the precipice of the Great Falls, dropping, like a liquid thunder-bolt, sheer ninety feet into a deep and narrow chasm of less than sixty feet in width, through which it dashes and foams in short-lived madness, to rest and glass itself upon a broad, still basin, hollowed by its own labors from the solid rock.   After leaving this basin, the river is vexed no more, but flows pleasantly past many thriving towns and hamlets, giving of its tide to turn the wheels of industry here and there, spanned by bridges of many forms and purposes, from the elaborate iron arch of the railway to the rude rusticity of the wooden foot-bridge.   Its path now lies amid rich uplands and orchards, teeming fields, and the dwellings of a prosperous agricultural community.   But there are still many picturesque glimpses of a wilder nature along its course, and many a spot known to the disciples of the "gentle Izaak" as giving and fulfilling the promise of excellent sport and the added charm of attractive scenery.   From Paterson to Newark the shores spread like an amphitheatre covered with verdure, dotted thickly with dwellings and the monuments of successful enterprise and industry, giving it the appearance of a watery highway through a picturesque succession of close-lying villages and centres of busy life.

Near Greenwood Lake.

THE VALLEY OF THE CONNECTICUT.

WITH ILLUSTRATIONS BY J. DOUGLAS WOODWARD.

THE charms of the beautiful valley of the Connecticut have so often been described that all persons of intelligence in this country must have some knowledge of them. Among the hills of New Hampshire and Vermont the queen of our New-England rivers takes its rise. Flowing in a nearly southerly direction for four hundred miles, it forms the

Saybrook.

dividing line between the two States in which it had its birth. Crossing the States of Massachusetts and Connecticut, it empties into the Long-Island Sound. Through this charming valley we now propose to pass, from the mouth of the river to its northern head, near Canada, our artist meanwhile giving us sketches of some of the leading points of interest, and making us acquainted with the rare beauty of its exceedingly varied and picturesque scenery.

Leaving the cars at the junction of the Shore Line Railway with that of the Connecticut River, if we are good pedestrians we shall not fail to walk the entire length of the broad street on which have been built most of the houses of the ancient town of Saybrook. Although the distance to Saybrook Point—the terminus of the railroad at the mouth of the Connecticut—is not far from two miles, we shall not find our walk a wearisome one. The venerable elms beneath which we pass will remind us of the olden times, and there will be enough of the antique meeting our eye to carry us back to the times when Lord Say and Seal and Lord Brook, in the unsettled period of the reign of Charles I., procured from Robert, Earl of Warwick, a patent of a large tract of land, within which was included the territory on which the town of Saybrook was laid out in 1635. Our walk has brought us to a gentle rise of land, from which we get a distinct view of Long-Island Sound. On our right is a cemetery, through the iron gate of which we pass, and come almost immediately to a very ancient and somewhat rude monument. We read the simple inscription—"Lady Fenwick, 1648;" and we are informed that she was Lady Anne Botler, or Butler, the daughter of an English nobleman, and the wife of General Fenwick, the commandant of the fort erected not far from this spot. Another item of historic interest also comes to our notice. The place where we are now standing was laid out in those early days with great care, as it was expected to

Mouth of Park River.

become the residence of eminent men, and the centre of great business and wealth. Oliver Cromwell, with a company of men who, subsequently, during the period of the English Commonwealth, became so distinguished, actually embarked in the Thames, intending to settle in Saybrook. A square was laid out a little west from the fort, in which the plan was to erect houses for Cromwell, Pym, Hampden, and other well-known commoners of England. What different fortunes might have befallen the mother-country had the project been carried out! Saybrook Point had the honor of being selected as the site for the collegiate school which afterward became Yale College. The building first erected must have borne some resemblance to a rope-walk, being one story in height and eighty feet in length.

THE CONNECTICUT, ABOVE MIDDLETOWN.

Hartford, from East Side of the River.

Leaving Saybrook—a place around which cluster so many venerable associations—we begin our ascent of the river. We soon pass through scenes which remind us, on a diminished scale, of the Highlands of the Hudson River. A sail of thirty miles brings us to one of the most beautiful places on the river—Middletown—a partial view of which our artist has given us, the sketch having been taken above the city. As the writer was walking up from the river to the McDonough House, he had for his companion Professor S——, of the Wesleyan University. On remarking to him that it was his practice while travelling in Europe to seek some elevated spot from which to get a bird's-eye view of the places he visited, allusion having been especially made to the view of Athens obtained from Lycabettus, the professor replied that nowhere abroad had he seen any thing more beautiful than Middletown and its surroundings from some high spot in the western section of the city. As we stood on the top of Judd Hall, one of the buildings of the

Wesleyan University, and let the eye range over the widely-extended scene, we could heartily respond in the affirmative to this remark. The city itself presents a most attractive appearance, with its streets of generous width, adorned with shade-trees and many elegant mansions and public buildings. The Methodists have here one of their earliest and most flourishing seats of learning in the country, founded in 1831. Its oldest buildings were originally built for the American Literary, Scientific, and Military Academy, under the care of Captain Partridge. This institution not meeting with the success which its projectors had anticipated, it was purchased by the Methodists, and, under the care of that denomination, is taking high rank among the best colleges of the land. Some of its buildings, especially the Memorial Hall and Judd Hall, are among the finest of their kind in the country.

Opposite Middletown are the famous freestone quarries, from which some of the most stately and costly buildings in New York and other cities have been erected. According to tradition, the rocks at the northern and principal opening originally hung shelving over the river. They were used for building-material not long after the settlement of Middletown. A meeting was held in that town in 1665, at which a resolution was passed that no one should dig or raise stones at the rocks on the east side of the river but an inhabitant of Middletown, and that twelve pence should be paid to the town for every ton of stones taken. Now the Connecticut freestone is as famous as the ancient Pentelic marble from the quarries near Athens.

The level tracts north of Middletown will not be overlooked by the tourist. These meadow-lands, which are found all along the Connecticut, are exceedingly fertile; and some of the finest farms in the New-England States have been formed out of this soil of exceeding richness. It was these meadow-lands that attracted the attention of the early settlers of the State, and brought to Connecticut some of the best blood of the Plymouth and Massachusetts colonies. Above Middletown, a few miles, is Wethersfield, claimed by some to be the oldest settlement in the Commonwealth. Among those early comers to the lowlands of Connecticut there was one woman, who had a good share of spirit, and, we judge, no small amount of humor, in her composition. It is related that, when the settlers arrived at the place where they were to land, some controversy arose who should first set foot on the shore. While the men were contending with each other for this privilege, good Mrs. Barber, taking advantage of the contention, dexterously sprang forward, and, reaching the shore, had the honor of first treading on the soil. Wethersfield is a venerable, staid old place, long celebrated for a specialty to which its inhabitants have directed their attention—the cultivation of the onion. It is also the seat of the State-prison, which, if we mistake not, the authorities of Connecticut, with their traditional skill in turning an honest penny from all enterprises in which they embark, have made a source of no little income to the State.

We are now approaching one of the most charming cities in our country—the city

HARTFORD, FROM COLT'S FACTORY.

of Hartford. The scenery all about it is of a very picturesque character. Its banks are among the most beautiful levels on the river, and indicate at a single glance that they

Stone Bridge, Hartford.

must be a mine of agricultural wealth to the cultivators of the soil. The original name of the place did not carry with it the euphony which usually characterizes the old In-

Terrace Hill, City Park, Hartford.

dian names, it being called Suckiaug. The story of the hardships of its early settlers is a familiar one. Dr. Trumbull tells us that, "about the beginning of June, 1635, Mr

Hooker, Mr. Stone, and about one hundred men, women, and children, took their departure from Cambridge, and travelled more than a hundred miles through a hideous and trackless wilderness to Hartford. They had no guide but their compass, and made their way over mountains, through swamps, thickets, and rivers, which were not passable but with great difficulty. They had no cover but the heavens, nor any lodgings but those

Main-Street Bridge, Hartford

that simple nature afforded them. They drove with them a hundred and sixty head of cattle, and by the way subsisted on the milk of their cows. Mrs. Hooker was borne through the wilderness upon a litter. The people carried their packs, arms, and some utensils. They were nearly a fortnight on their journey. This adventure was the more remarkable, as many of this company were persons of figure, who had lived in England in honor, affluence, and delicacy, and were entire strangers to fatigue and danger." It does not fall within our design to follow the fortunes of these adventurers. It is out of our power to comprehend the difficulties which they encountered. Among their severest trials was the constant dread in which for years they lived of the attacks of the savages, by whom they were surrounded, who, with ill-concealed chagrin, saw the rich possessions over which, without let or hinderance they had been wont to roam, slipping out of their hands, and the white men becoming the lords of the soil.

The city of Hartford, in our judgment, contrasts favorably with the many places in our country which, if looked down upon by an observer a few hundred feet in the air, look like a checker-board. The very irregularity of its laying-out adds to its charms. It is divided at the south part by Mill or Little River, two bridges across which are seen in the accompanying sketches. We present also a sketch of Terrace Hill, in the City Park, one of the most beautiful spots in the city. Just back of the fine old trees which occupy the centre of the picture are the buildings of Trinity College, an Episcopal institution, which has done good service in the cause of sound learning. On the grounds is a noble statue of Bishop Brownell, in which he is represented in full sacerdotal robes, looking benignantly over the scene on which his eye is supposed to rest. The buildings of Trinity College are soon to be removed to make way for the erection of the Capitol of the State of Connecticut, which bids fair to be one of the most costly and elegant structures of its kind in the country.

Hartford is celebrated as being the seat of some of the best charitable institutions in the United States. Prominent among these are the Asylum for the Deaf and Dumb, and the Retreat for the Insane. The first of these institutions was founded by an association of gentlemen in 1815. It owes its origin to a distinguished clergyman, the Rev. Dr. Cogswell, the father of a beautiful child who lost her hearing at the age of two years, and not long after her speech. Wishing to educate this daughter, and in his deep sympathy including other young persons alike unfortunate, it was arranged that the late Rev. T. H. Gallaudet, LL. D., should visit Europe, and in the institutions for the deaf and dumb in the old country gain all the information he might need for successfully establishing a similar institution in the United States. On his return he was accompanied by Mr. Laurent Clerc, himself a deaf-mute, who, under the celebrated Abbé Sicard, had been a successful teacher for several years in Paris. Under the joint supervision of Messrs. Gallaudet and Le Clerc, the institution soon won its way to popular favor. The number of its pupils increased rapidly, all parts of the country being represented among them. So successfully did the cause of its unfortunate inmates appeal to the public benevolence that Congress granted to the asylum a township of land in Alabama, the proceeds of the sale of which were invested in a permanent fund.

Half a mile, in a southwesterly direction from the centre of the city, on a most sightly spot, is the Retreat for the Insane. Its founders showed their good taste in selecting this place for an institution which, of all others, should be so situated as to secure for its inmates every thing that can charm and soothe a disordered mind. From the top of the building the eye ranges over a scene of rare beauty. In the immediate vicinity is the city of Hartford, with its public buildings, its elegant mansions, and its numerous manufactories, representing the industry and thrift of a busy town. The view of the Connecticut Valley in both directions, north and south, is very extensive, and embraces some of the choicest scenery on the river. Looking west, we see numerous villages, in which are found forest-trees and orchards, beneath whose grateful shade nestle cottages and farm-houses, the very sight of which awakens in the mind most gentle and soothing emotions, making us fancy, for the moment, that

Windsor Locks, Connecticut River.

into such a paradise sin and sorrow have not found their way. The grounds of the Retreat have been laid out in excellent taste. Some twenty acres furnish the most ample facilities for delightful walks and rides; while the old trees, standing either singly or in clusters, invite to quiet repose those whose diseased intellects and wayward imaginations may find rest amid such peaceful scenes. How many morbid fancies. how many strange hallucinations have been put to flight amid these scenes; how changed have been views of life and duty, which have made the world both dreary and desolate, and robbed many a soul of its peace! Let any one with nerves shattered by excessive brain-work, and weary with the daily and constant toils of life, walk through the neat, airy halls of the Retreat, or wander over its beautiful grounds, and breathe the invigorating airs which come from the neighboring hills, and he will at once feel a kindly influence pervading his whole being, and filling him with profound gratitude that Christian benevolence has here put forth her best efforts to alleviate the sorrows of humanity. "The general system of moral treatment at this institution is to allow the patients all the liberty and indulgences consistent with their own safety and that of others; to cherish in them the sentiment of self-respect; to excite an ambition for the good-will and respect of others; to draw out the latent sparks of natural and social affection; and to occupy their attention with such employments and amusements as shall exercise their judgment, and withdraw their minds as much as possible from every former scene and every former companion, and give an entire change to the current of their recollections and ideas. By pursuing this course, together with a judicious system of medication, many of these once miserable beings, cut off from all the 'linked sweetness' of conjugal, parental, filial, and fraternal enjoyment, are now restored to the blessings of health, to the felicities of affection, and to the capacity of performing the relative duties of domestic and social life."

Any allusion to Hartford without reference to the famous "Charter Oak" would be like the play of "Hamlet" with the character of *Hamlet* left out. Although the story is a familiar one to the people of Connecticut, we do not lose sight of the circumstance that we are writing these sketches for hundreds and thousands in our own country, and in other lands, who have not so much as heard that there was a "Charter Oak." This famous tree, now no longer standing, occupied an eminence rising above the south meadows, not far from the ancient mansion of the Wyllys family. Like the great elm on Boston Common, its age is unknown, the first settlers of Hartford finding it standing in the maturity of its growth. Some idea of its great size may be formed when we are told that it was nearly seven feet in diameter. The cavity in which the charter was hid was near the roots, and large enough, if necessary, to conceal a child. The story of the "Charter Oak" is soon told. In December, 1686, Sir Edmund Andros, who had been appointed the first governor-general over New England, reached Boston, from which place he wrote to the authorities of Connecticut to resign their charter. The demand was not complied with. "The Assembly met as usual in October, and the government continued according to charter until the last of the month. About this time Sir Edmund, with his suite and more than sixty regular troops, came to Hartford, where the Assembly were sitting, and demanded the charter, and declared the government under it to be dissolved. The Assembly were extremely reluctant and slow with respect to any resolve to bring it forth. The tradition is that Governor Treat strongly represented the great expense and hardships of the colonists in planting the country; the blood and treasure which they had expended in defending it, both against the savages and foreigners; to what hardships he himself had been exposed for that

SCENES AT SPRINGFIELD.

purpose; and that it was like giving up his life now to surrender the patent and privileges so dearly bought and so long enjoyed. The important affair was debated and kept in suspense until the evening, when the charter was brought and laid upon the table where the Assembly were sitting. By this time great numbers of people were assembled, and men sufficiently bold to enterprise whatever might be necessary or expedient. The lights were instantly extinguished, and one Captain Wadsworth, of Hartford, in the most silent and secret manner carried off the charter, and secreted it in a large hollow tree fronting the house of Hon. Samuel Wyllys, then one of the magistrates of the colony. The people all appeared peaceable and orderly. The candles were officiously relighted, but the patent was gone, and no discovery could be made of it, or of the person who carried it away." The "Charter Oak" was cherished as an object of veneration and affection by the inhabitants of Hartford for several generations. A few years since, in 1856, weakened by age and decay, it fell before the blasts of a severe storm. It lives now only in the memory of a generation which in a few years will, like their fathers, have passed off the stage. It would be easy to extend this sketch of Hartford indefinitely; but we are warned that we must pass on to other scenes.

As we journey on up the valley of the Connecticut, we do not lose our impression of the wonderful beauty of the extensive meadows, and the indescribable charms of the neighboring and overshadowing hills. Had we time we would be glad to linger for a few hours in the ancient town of Windsor, settled as early as thirteen years after the landing of the Pilgrims at Plymouth, and the birthplace of those distinguished men so much honored in the times in which they lived—Governor Roger Wolcott and Oliver Ellsworth, LL. D., Chief-Justice of the United States. We must pause for a few moments at Springfield, one of the busiest, most thriving of all the interior cities of the old Commonwealth of Massachusetts. Let us ascend the cupola which crowns one of the United States buildings, on Arsenal Hill, and survey the scene, and acknowledge that the panorama on which the eye rests deserves all the commendation that has been given it. Rich alluvial meadows stretch far away in the distance along the river, rising gradually to quite an elevation, and terminating in a plain reaching several miles east. Lofty hills rear their heads in all directions, clothed in the summer with the richest verdure. Villages and farm-houses everywhere meet the eye, while the busy city is spread out like a map at our feet. An incessant noise from the rolling wheels of long trains of cars, converging toward or radiating from the spacious railroad station, falls upon our ear, while the smoke that ascends from the factories without number tells us of an activity which tasks the brain and the physical energies of many a skilful mechanic. And this is the Agawam of the olden times, when the wild Indian roamed over this splendid country, whose name—Springfield—was given to it as far back as 1640. It has, like other places to which we have referred, its history and its traditions of fearful sufferings and shocking outrages, when the savages made their attacks on its defenceless inhabitants. The days of barbarous warfare have long since passed away; but the citizens are not allowed to sever themselves from all warlike associations, inasmuch as the United States has here erected one of the most extensive armories in the country. Indeed, if we are not mistaken, it is the largest arsenal of construction in the country, and has always employed a large force of men in the manufacture and repair of tens of

Mount Holyoke.

thousands of muskets, keeping stored hundreds of thousands of weapons of warfare, if any emergency should arise calling for their use. These arsenal-buildings have once been assaulted. In 1786, during the insurrection in Massachusetts, known as the "Shays Rebellion," a vigorous effort was put forth to get possession of the United States Arsenal. At the head of eleven hundred men, Shays marched toward it, intending to carry it by assault. The officer in command of the defensive force— General Shepard—warned the assailants of the danger to which they exposed themselves, but, his warnings not being heeded, he fired upon the attacking party, killing three of their number and wounding one, when the assailants fled in all haste from the scene of

action.   Springfield is emphatically a government city, its prosperity depending largely on the patronage derived from the special department of mechanical labor in which for so many years it has been engaged. In many respects it is by far the most thriving city on the Connecticut River.

Leaving Springfield, we pass

The Connecticut Valley from Mount Holyoke.

rapidly over the level lands on the river, catching glimpses at every turn of scenes of singular natural beauty, and observing the improvements everywhere made by man, pressing into service the immense water-power which he finds so useful as the propeller of the vast machinery here set in motion. Chicopee, and especially Holyoke, will not fail to attract the attention of the tourist, if, with his love of Nature, he combines an interest in works which give scope to human industry, and minister to the comfort and add to the luxuries of life. The scenery along the river, if possible, grows more charming as we advance. The hills are nearer to the river, and begin to assume the name of mountains. We have reached Northampton, in all respects one of the most

The Oxbow—View from Mount Holyoke.

beautiful villages in this or in any other land, situated on the west side of the Connecticut, on rising ground, about a mile from the river, between which and the town lie some of the fairest meadow-lands in the world, covering an area of between three thousand and four thousand acres. Like Hartford, the town is somewhat irregularly laid out, deriving from this circumstance what to many eyes is a great charm—the charm of diversity. It abounds in shade-trees,

Mount Tom from Oxbow.

the venerable appearance of which gives evidence of their great age. Few places of its size can boast of a larger number of elegant mansions and villas. Many persons of intellectual culture and taste have made their homes here, amid the charming scenery of the place, that they may enjoy the many social and intellectual privileges which the village affords.

We will cross the river and take our stand by the side of the doubtless enthusiastic gentleman whom our artist has described as standing near the edge of a precipitous cliff on Mount Holyoke. The imagination can easily picture the exceeding beauty of the scene. The sketch shows to us the river winding through the meadow-lands, which, it needs no words to tell us, are of surpassing fertility. Changing our position, we are at the Mountain House, so distinctly seen in the next picture. Here we are, nearly a thousand feet above the plain below, spreading far away both north and south. From this elevated point let us look about us. We quote from one who writes enthusiastically of this lovely scenery: "On the west, and a little elevated above the general level, the eye turns with delight to the populous village of Northampton, exhibiting in its public edifices and private dwellings an unusual degree of neatness and elegance. A little more to the right, the quiet and substantial villages of Hadley and Hatfield; and still farther east, and more distant, Amherst, with its college, observatory, cabinet, and academy, on a commanding eminence, form pleasant resting-places for the eye. Facing the southwest, the observer has before him, on the opposite side of the river, the ridge called Mount Tom, rising one or two hundred feet higher than Holyoke, and dividing the valley of the Connecticut longitudinally. The western branch of this valley is bounded on the west by the Hoosic range of mountains, which, as seen from Holyoke, rises ridge above ridge for more than twenty miles, checkered with cultivated fields and forests, and not unfrequently enlivened by villages and church-spires. In the northwest, Graylock may be seen peering above the Hoosic; and, still farther north, several of the Green Mountains, in Vermont, shoot up beyond the region of the clouds in imposing grandeur. A little to the south of west, the beautiful outline of Mount Everett is often visible. Nearer at hand, and in the valley of the Connecticut, the insulated Sugar-Loaf and Mount Toby present their fantastic outlines, while, far in the northeast, ascends in dim and misty grandeur the cloud-capped Monadnoc."

The artist has given us another view of the valley from Mount Holyoke, showing a bend of the river which, from its peculiar shape, is known as the Oxbow. We have the same charming scene of meadow and winding river which we had in the other picture. From Oxbow, also, we have a view of Mount Tom, the twin-brother, if we may be permitted to call it, of Mount Holyoke—not as much visited as the latter, but well worth climbing, and not disappointing the highly-raised anticipations of the tourist. The

Mount Holyoke from Tom's Station.

village of South Hadley lies on the east side of Mount Tom. This place has almost a national reputation as being the seat of the famous Mount Holyoke Female Seminary.

Titan's Pier, Mount Holyoke.

There are not a few spots in its neighborhood from which a spectator will get most picturesque views of the surrounding country. The other views which we have intro-

Northampton Meadows.

duced will prove that an artist will find in all this region abundant opportunities for the exercise of his skill, and that the man of taste may wander wherever his inclinations may direct, and be sure of finding enough to gratify his most ardent love of Nature.

South Hadley bears off the palm of being, in many respects, the most beautiful village on the Connecticut. Let the tourist take his stand on the bank of the river, and look toward the northwest. Holyoke and Tom rise with boldness from the valley, standing on either side of the river like watch-towers, from whose lofty summits the observer may look out upon some of the most charming scenery in the world. Through the opening made between these twin-mountains one can see two or three miles up the river, in which will be noticed one or two islands, looking peaceful enough to make another paradise on earth. Scattered over the meadows are the fine old trees whose

summer shadows are so inviting, through whose foliage may be seen the more prominent buildings of Northampton.   Directly above the town the Connecticut, changing
somewhat its usual course, turns northwest.   Making a bend to the south again, it moves
on for a little distance, and then turns toward the east.   In these winding movements,
of nearly five miles in extent, it has enclosed, except on the eastern side, an interval of
singular beauty, containing some three or four thousand acres.   On the isthmus of this
peninsula is the principal street of the village, not surpassed in loveliness by any street
in the whole country.   It is nearly level, is sixteen rods in breadth, and lined with trees,
whose verdure in summer is rich be-
yond conception.   South Hadley is famous as having been the residence of

Table-Rock, Sugar-Loaf Mountain.

Whalley and Goffe, two of the regicides of Charles I., they having sat in
the court which tried the monarch,
and signed the warrant for his execution.   They succeeded in escaping from England
when their lives were in great peril, and, in 1664, they came to South Hadley.   It is
said that "when the house which they occupied was pulled down the bones of Whalley
were found buried just without the cellar-wall, in a kind of tomb formed of mason-
work, and covered with flags of hewn stone."   Not long after the death of Whalley, his
companion, Goffe, left Hadley, and spent the closing days of his life with a son of his
companion in exile in Rhode Island.

We should be glad to linger about these delightful regions of the Connecticut Valley. In no direction would it be possible for us to move without finding something most attractive to the eye, and pleasing to a cultivated taste. Thus, a ride of not far from seven miles east of the river, would bring us to Amherst, the seat of Amherst College, founded in 1821, and one of the most flourishing literary institutions in Massachusetts, many of whose officers have stood in the front rank of the educators of the United States. It may be questioned, indeed, if, in extent and variety of knowledge in the sciences of geology and mineralogy, any man in this country could be compared

Sugar-Loaf Mountain from Sunderland.

with Professor Hitchcock when he was at the height of his professional career. But we must resist the temptation which binds us to spots so full of attraction and interest, and move on our "winding way" up the river. We pass Hatfield and Whately, without special examination, for want of time. In the distance rises a conical peak of red sandstone, reaching an elevation of five hundred feet from the plain. This is Sugar-Loaf Mountain, in South Deerfield, of which we have two views from the pencil of our artist, and both of them will repay examination. Although seemingly inaccessible, Sugar-Loaf Mountain may be ascended without serious difficulty on foot; and the tourist will be

Connecticut Valley, from Rocky Mountain, Greenfield.

amply rewarded for the fatigue of the ascent when he reaches the summit. At the foot of the mountain the attention of the observer will be arrested by a monument erected there to commemorate an event which took place in 1675. It was in the time of King Philip's War, when Captain Lathrop was enticed into an ambush by the Indians with a company of "eighty young men, the very flower of Essex County," and nearly all of them killed. This whole region was once the scene of frightful disaster, when the savages with relentless fury attacked the feeble settlements, and many fell victims to their arrows and tomahawks. Rising some seven hundred feet above the plain on which the village of Deerfield stands, is Deerfield Mountain. Standing on the western verge of this mountain, one gets charming views of the surrounding country. Deerfield River, after passing over a country fifty miles in extent, discharges its waters into the Connecticut, not far from the spot in which the observer stands. The meadows in this neighborhood are especially worthy of note, as

MOUNT CHESTERFIELD.

being among the most picturesque on the river. Other elevations, such as Mount Toby and Mount Warner, are worth ascending, and from their summits may be obtained views, each one of which will have some peculiar charm distinguishing it from all other views.

We have reached Greenfield, which combines the activity of a manufacturing with the quiet of a rural village of New England. The two rivers which pass through the place—Fall River and Green River—furnish an excellent water-power, which has not been suffered to lie unimproved. The beautiful elm-shaded streets, and the neat, and, in many cases, elegant and tasteful dwellings, give us an illustration of one of the better class of New-England villages. The artist has given us a sketch of the valley of the Connecti-

Brattleboro.

cut as seen from Rocky Mountain in Greenfield. What images of summer repose are awakened in the mind as we gaze upon the scene on which the eye rests! We cannot help thinking of the changes through which all this region has passed since the white man first set his foot here. We cease to wonder at the fierce struggles of the red-man, who saw himself driven out of a heritage so fair and beautiful, to exterminate a race of beings who had come hither from far across the waters to set up their new homes, and make this charming valley the scene of their industry, and gather here the reward of their toil. We see before us a region, the capabilities of which are far from having been fully developed, where future generations are to live from the products of its fertile soil and its busy manufactures. A single glance at the " iron horse," dashing across the bridge which spans the Connecticut, sets in motion a train of thought as swift as the locomotive which drags behind itself the cars belonging to its train. How much has the railroad done—how much is it still to do in developing the resources of all this valley, opening a mart for its agricultural products, and the manufactories, whose wheels are run by the waters which flow down these descents! Looking back to an age lying far beyond that of the settlement of the white man, we come to a geological period when this whole country presented a scene far different from the one on which the eye now rests; where—as the researches of such men as Professor Hitch-

Whetstone Brook, Brattleboro.

cock bring to our knowledge—a race of animals, now extinct, left the imprint of its footsteps in soil which, becoming pet- rified, has borne down to our vision the marks of the huge creatures once roaming over these lands. Casting our thoughts forward, we see this valley dotted everywhere with villages and hamlets, in which are gathered a population far outnumbering that which now dwells here, whose homes will be abodes of virtue and intelligence. And if natural scenery has aught to do in develop- ing the love of the beautiful, in refining the taste, and in cultivating the imagination, we may justly expect to find here a cultured people, with large brains and warm hearts, who will be among the best citizens of that vast domain which we delight to call our own, our dear country.

But we can stay no longer on this Greenfield eminence to indulge in these reveries. We descend, therefore, and keep on, in our northerly course, passing through Bernardston, and coming to South Vernon, from which we will take the few miles' ride required to bring us to that beautiful New-Hampshire village—Keene. We shall be particularly struck with the length and width of its streets. The principal street, which is a mile long, is an almost perfect level, and is throughout its entire length ornamented with what adds so much to the charm of our New-England villages—the fine old trees. Blessed be the memory of the fathers, in that they had the good taste to plant these trees, under whose grateful shades their posterity might linger, and whose green foliage might add so much to the beauty of the homes which they were rearing, not for themselves only, but for their children who should come after them. Returning from our short circuit, it does not take us long to reach Brattleboro. We are now getting into a more rugged portion of the country. We crossed the boundary-line of Massachusetts at Vernon, and are now in Vermont. Brattleboro has the well-deserved reputation of being among the most beautiful sites on the Connecticut. As a sanitarium, it is in some respects preëminent, and for many years has been resorted to by persons in search of health. The Asylum for the Insane, long regarded as one of the best institutions of its kind in the country, is located in this place. Brattleboro has also several large and well-conducted water-cure establishments. The water here is said to be of remarkable purity, issuing cool and most refreshing from the hill-sides. The fine, invigorating air, and the romantic scenery which in all directions meets the eye, make this village one to which invalids love to resort. We give a representation of Mount Chesterfield, which presents a singularly regular and unbroken appearance. One is almost tempted to think that good old Izaak Walton has come back from the other world to enjoy in this enchanting region the piscatorial pleasures in which he took so much delight when he was an inhabitant of our earth. Something more than "glorious nibbles" we will fain hope that he gets, and that a basket of fat, toothsome trout, weighing at least a pound each, will reward him for the tramp he has taken from his home to catch them.

Our next stage is twenty-four miles, bringing us to the well-known Bellows Falls. In passing over this stage in our journey we have stopped for a few moments at Dummerston, one of the oldest towns in the State, watered by West River and several small streams, useful as water-power. Near the centre of the town is what is called Black Mountain, an immense body of granite, through which passes a range of argillaceous slate. Our artist has given us a sketch of an old mill in Putney, a few miles north of Dummerston. This village is beautifully situated on the west bank of the Connecticut River, and embraces within its limits an extensive tract of river-level, known as the Great Meadows. Sackett's Brook is a considerable stream, which within a distance of one hundred rods falls one hundred and fifty feet. On the breaking out of the French War, in 1744, a settlement was begun and a fort erected on Great

Meadows. Our route has taken us through West-
minster, whose soil has made it a particularly fine
agricultural region. A semicircle of hills encloses
the place, touching the river two miles above and

Old Mill, Putney.

below the town. While this
has the effect to add to the
natural beauty of the place,
it has been the occasion of
its being deprived of the
water-power which comes from the
hills in so many places along the
Connecticut, the streams being diverted away from the village instead
of flowing through it.

Bellows Falls, of which we have
three picturesque views, is well known
as the stopping-place of the railways,
and, to some extent, a place of summer resort. The falls, which give the chief charm
to the place, are a succession of rapids in the Connecticut. These rapids extend not far
from a mile along the base of a high and precipitous hill, a partial view of which we

Bellows Falls from Distance.

have in one of the sketches which bears the name of Fall Mountain. Standing on the bridge which crosses the river, one looks down into the foaming flood below. The gorge at this point is so narrow that it seems as if one could almost leap over it. Through this chasm the water dashes wildly, striking with prodigious force on the rocks below, and by the reaction is driven back for quite a space upon itself. In a distance of half a mile the water descends about fifty feet. Apart from the falls there will not be much to detain the tourist in this spot. There are several pleasant villages in the vicinity to which agreeable excursions may be made.

Keeping on in our northerly course, we come to Charlestown. At this point there are in the Connecticut River three beautiful islands, the largest—Sartwell's Island—having an area of ten acres, and well cultivated. The other two have not far from six acres each in them. Among the first settlers of this place was Captain Phinehas Stevens. When the fort, of which he was the commandant, was attacked by the French and Indians in 1747, he made so gallant a defence that he was presented by Sir Charles Knowles with a costly sword, in token of his appreciation of the bravery of the heroic captain. In memory of this act of Sir Charles, when, a few years after, the township was incorporated, the inhabitants gave it the name of Charlestown.

No lover of the picturesque will fail to see Claremont, a place watered by the Connecticut and Sugar Rivers, and having a fine, undulating surface, and surrounded by hills with gentle acclivities, from the summits of which are obtained charming views of the surrounding country. Beds of iron-ore and limestone are here found, which have added much to the wealth of the inhabitants. Claremont took its name from Claremont in England, the country-seat of Lord Clare, one of the most distinguished of the governors-general of the East Indies. From this spot we get fine views of Mount Ascutney, of which the accompanying sketch gives us an excellent idea. This mountain is situated in the towns of Wethersfield and Windsor, and is an immense mass of granite. It is well spoken of as "a brave outpost of the coming Green Mountains, on the one hand, and of the White Mountains on the other." It is sometimes called the Three Brothers, from its three peaks, which are so distinctly outlined as we look at the mountain from the point of view which the artist has selected. How extended and how magnificent the view is from its highest summit, which is nearly eighteen hundred feet from the bed of the river, it is not easy to describe.

Windsor is our next point of interest, situated on the elevated bank of the river, somewhat irregularly built, but in all respects one of the most charming villages of Vermont. The number of its elegant mansions and public buildings compares favorably with that of almost any village of its size in the country. Its wide, shaded streets give it a peculiarly attractive appearance, and if one ascends the highlands in the neighboring town of Cornish, or climbs to the top of Ascutney, he will look out upon a scene which he will not soon forget. The location of Windsor is such that it has become the centre of trade, both for the towns on the river and for the fertile interior country. Its men of business have been enterprising and far-sighted, and they have built up a town which has enjoyed, and bids fair still to enjoy, a high degree of prosperity.

We have reached White-River Junction, where the White River empties into the Connecticut, of which the artist has given us a view. It needs but a glance to indicate to us that we are in the midst of the mountains. We can almost feel the invigorating breezes as they blow pure and fresh from the "everlasting hills;" and, as we write this sketch in this hot July day, we fancy that we feel all the cooler and brighter as we look upon the scene before us. It is evident that the artist has intended that his sketch shall represent the evening hour. The new moon hangs over the valley which divides the two mountains in the left of the picture. The wind blows very gently down

Bellows Falls.

the mountain-gorge, bending a little to the right the smoke which ascends from the chimney of the cottage in the rear of the bridge. The whole scene is one of quiet beauty. Sitting there where our friend is—on the river's bank—we think we could

The West Branch of Bellows Falls.

easily throw down the burden of life's cares and worriments, and give up ourselves to the romance of the place and the delicious musings of the hour.

From White-River Junction we go to Hanover, New Hampshire, the great attraction of which is Dartmouth College, situated about half a mile from the Connecticut. The buildings are grouped around a square, whose area is twelve acres, in the centre of the broad terrace upon which the village has been built. This institution, whose career has been so honorable and prosperous, was chartered by a royal grant in 1769, and received its name from William, Earl of Dartmouth. Its graduates have distinguished themselves in all the walks of professional life. Any college from which such men as Daniel Webster and Rufus Choate have gone forth, may well pride itself on account of its sons.

The villages of Thetford, Orford, Bradford, and Haverhill, may detain us for a few

Mount Ascutney.

hours. We shall find, in all this neighborhood, excellent farms, and a busy, industrious population. In Orford, limestone is found at the foot of a mountain some four hundred feet above the Connecticut. Soapstone and granite abound, and some lead has been discovered. Bradford and Haverhill were so called because their earlier settlers came from towns of that name on the Merrimac, in Massachusetts. The town of Newbury is delightfully situated on the west side of the Connecticut River, and comprises the tract to which the name of "The Great Oxbow" has been given. This tract, on a bend of the Connecticut River, is of great extent, and is well known on account of its rare beauty and the fertility of its soil. Here we have one of the most charming of the many pictu-

White-River Junction.

Moose Hillock, from Newbury Meadows.

resque scenes which our artist has given us of the Connecticut. From the meadows of Newbury is seen the elevation called Moose Hillock. A few miles north of Newbury we reach Wells-River Junction, whence the traveller, by one line of railroad, goes to the White Mountains, or, by another, proceeds to Montreal. Not far from this point the waters of the Ammonoosuck empty into the Connecticut.

Our last sketch represents a scene in Barnet, Vermont, one of the best farming towns in the State, and abounding in slate and iron-ore. The water-power on the Passumpsic and Stevens Rivers is one of the finest in all this region. The fall in Stevens River, of which we have a view, is one hundred feet in the short distance of ten rods. Not far from this point the river Passumpsic discharges its waters into the Connecticut. From this point onward it bears the character of a mountain-stream. There are several pleasant villages on either side of the river, as we follow it up to its very source in the northern part of New Hampshire. The lover of Nature may be sure of finding abundant material to gratify his taste for the sublime and the beautiful all through this most picturesque region.

Stevens Brook, Barnet.

BALTIMORE AND ENVIRONS.

ILLUSTRATED BY GRANVILLE PERKINS.

WHEN Captain John Smith adventured upon the wide waters of the Chesapeake Bay in two frail, open boats, we do not find that he explored the broad estuary now known as the Patapsco River. Beaten by storms and driven astray by adverse winds, praying and singing psalms in the old, sturdy Puritan fashion, punishing rigorously all oaths by pouring a can of cold water down the sleeve, he put back hurriedly to Jamestown. On a second expedition he entered the Potomac and the Patuxent, but went no farther. Even when, in 1634, the Ark and the Dove, after a stormy

Washington Monument.

Fort McHenry, at Entrance of Baltimore Harbor.

voyage, landed the Pilgrims of Maryland at St. Clement's Isle, the Potomac was regarded as the future seat of government. The first of the colonists who, either overland through the wilderness, or, as is more probable, entering the river from the bay, stood upon the future site of Baltimore town, is unknown. No romantic legends attend the city's birth. It is certain, however, that it was not until some time after 1634 that the colonists ventured to leave the older towns on the Potomac and brave the dangers supposed to coexist with proximity to the warlike Susquehannas. Even these first settlers had no forecasting of the advantages a city at the head of such an immense stretch of inland water would offer. Their only desire was to be on a navigable stream, where ships could anchor with safety.

The immediate sur-
roundings of this shel-
tered cove on the Pa-
tapsco were nevertheless
such as to render its
borders remarkably at-
tractive. The fresh nat-
ural beauties of the land
which greeted and de-
lighted those who built
here upon the edge of
the wilderness are lost
to their later descend-
ants. Jones's Falls,
which is now a great
and ever-recurring nui-
sance, was then a pure
and limpid forest-stream,
the basin and the harbor
as quiet and peaceful as
any far island-shore in
the depths of ocean.
The woods came down
to the water's edge and
clothed the broken hills
that rise, interlaced by
small but rapid streams
far into the interior.
So even without that
extraordinary foresight
of future growth with
which some historians
would endow the found-
ers of the city, they had
good and sufficient rea-
sons for their choice.
Here, then, in the lat-
ter part of the seven-
teenth century, the va-

Baltimore from Federal Hill.

rious "points" and "necks" which run out sharply into the river were successively patented. Prosaic Jonestown arose, the chief production of which, judging from the old maps, appears to have been almost preternaturally symmetrical rows of flourishing cabbages. Huge hogsheads of tobacco, stoutly hooped, and with an axle driven through the middle so as to form a huge roller, and drawn by horses driven by negroes, were trundled over what are still known as "rolling roads" to town; flourishing mills, tanneries, and other manufacturing industries, soon became established; trade with the neighboring States and with the West Indies increased; and with this prosperity came the demand that the name of Jonestown be discarded, and the cities east and west of the Falls be consolidated under a new title, that of the first proprietary— Lord Baltimore. A picture of this worthy gentleman exists in Washington, painted by Vandyck. It was bartered off by a Legislature of Maryland for a series of portraits of the early governors by Peale. This sponsor of the city could not but have been a conspicuous figure at a brilliant court. His portrait is that of a man tall and finely formed; his smallclothes are of blue velvet, the coat embroidered elaborately, having open sleeves lined with blue silk, and brocaded in the same color; his doublet is worked in gold and colors; his sash is of orange silk; his breastplate of blue steel, inlaid; and the broad sash around his waist shows above it the hilt of a sword studded with jewels. He wears the heavy powdered wig of his times, and black shoes with box-toes and gold buckles. Such, in rich array, as bodied forth by the hand of a master, is the stately figure of Lord Baltimore, the city's patron. There were fitness and propriety in the choice other than that of historic gratitude. Baltimore was long an English provincial town in many of its characteristics. In its society the founder of Maryland would have been at his ease. Gentlemen of the old school, its citizens danced their solemn minuets and cotillons; talked much, but read little; and were eminently sociable, kind-hearted, hospitable, and happy in the repose of unhurried lives. It was a picturesque day for the city when gallants wore the three-cornered cocked-hat, powdered hair and cue; coats many-pocketed, narrow, light-colored, and curiously embroidered; smallclothes, striped stockings, and shoes with wide silver buckles. And then the ladies, witty, sprightly, gay —the Carrolls, the Catons, the Pattersons, the Ridgeleys, and their fair companions. From that time to this Baltimore has never lost its reputation for the beauty and attractiveness of its women, nor for the hospitality and cordial, frank courtesy of the homes they grace.

We find in a scarce pamphlet by a pleasant writer, who visited Baltimore just before the War of 1812: "It is computed that the city under the general name of Baltimore contains forty thousand inhabitants. The people of opulence seem to enjoy the good things, and even the luxuries of life, with greater *gout* than their neighbors to the eastward; the *savoir vivre* is well understood; and their markets, of course, are yearly improving in almost every article that adds to the comfort and splendor of the table."

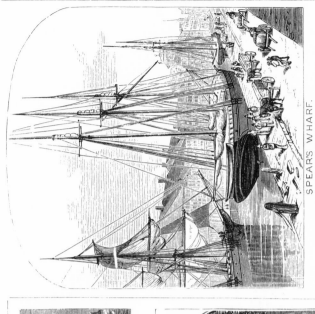

SPEAR'S WHARF.

EXCHANGE PLACE.

PUNGIES COMING UP THE CHESAPEAKE.

NIGHT SCENE IN PATTERSON PARK.

FORT McHENRY.

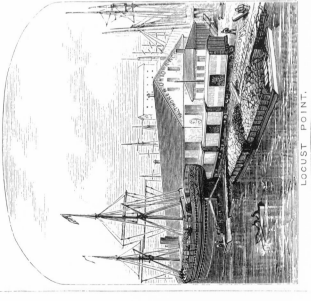

LOCUST POINT.

CALVERT STREET.

SCENES IN BALTIMORE.

Baltimore from the East.

Market — now Balti-more—Street was, in the time of which we are speaking, the favorite prom-enade. Then the avenue was resplendent with " dames and damsels — some with hooped-skirts; some in brocade, luxuri-ously displayed over hoops, with comely bodices sup-ported by stays, disclosing perilous waists, and with sleeves that clung to the arm as far as the elbow, where they were lost in ruffles that stood off like feathers on a bantam. And, then, such faces—so rosy, spirited, and sharp — with the hair drawn over a cush-ion, tight enough to lift the eyebrows with a slight curve, giving a somewhat scornful expression to the countenance ; and curls that fell in cataracts over the shoulders. Then they stepped along with a mincing gait, in shoes of many colors, with formida-ble points at the toes, and high, tottering heels, deli-cately cut in wood, and in towering peaked hats, garnished with feathers that swayed aristocratically back-ward and forward at each step, as if they took pride in the stately pace of the wearer." In the muddy ruts of the unpaved streets, great, clumsy, capacious Conestoga wagons rumbled past, drawn by teams of the finest draught-horses in the country. They were bound for the old inns, with spacious enclosed yards and swinging signs, a few of which, peculiarly English, and comically out of place, still refuse to be improved off the city streets. At night the oil-lamps threw yellow gleams over the galloping gallants who came in from the family seats on the neighboring hills to attend the balls at the old Assembly Rooms, still standing at the corner of Holliday and Fayette Streets.

The town grew slowly. For a long time large swamps existed on the low grounds, and but few of the streets ran down fairly to the harbor. Where is now Centre-Market Space, near the centre of the city, one vast quagmire spread its uninviting extent. As the limits of the town touched the bold hills of Charles Street, the prospect for health and comfort was better. When the city had once firmly planted itself on this plateau, it began slowly to thrust out its streets into the neighboring country. Old wooden build-ings, dozing in shady seclusion by the side of some narrow lane, would find themselves suddenly in the embrace of pretentious brick-and-mortar, and there many of them still are embalmed, with steep, gabled hip-roofs, moss-grown and bleached.

While the business-life of the city still centred around the wharves, the fashionable quarter was constantly changing. Starting along the Falls, it came by the way of Lom-bard Street to Harrison—now redolent of Jews' shops, old clothes, and rusty iron—to Gay. There it remained stationary until it spread into Lexington, North, and Calvert Streets, with outlying suburbs in Barré, Conway, and Sharp Streets, to the west and east, and Franklin Street to the north.

When, however, in 1812, the pure white shaft of the Washington Monument rose in Howard Park, it drew, like a magnet of supernatural proportions, the finest private dwellings around it in four parallelograms facing the four grass plots that radiate from it. The city surmounted at one leap the steep depression of Centre Street, and occupied at once the second plateau.

As was usual with our forefathers, when they had any scheme of public interest and more than usual magnitude to manage, a lottery was the primary means of raising funds for the erection of the monument. A lottery, it must be borne in mind, was then a perfectly legitimate transaction as well as a pecuniarily profitable one. Heavy wagons brought the now well-known Maryland marble sixteen miles over a rough road from Black Rock, on the Gunpowder River.

The design of the monument is simple and effective. The pedestal is fifty feet square by thirty-five in height. Around this are briefly recorded the most notable events in the life of Washington. From it rises majestically, brilliantly clear, polished, and white, the round shaft, for one hundred and sixty feet, and crowning its capped dome is the figure of Washington, of heroic size, holding in his hand the scroll of his " Farewell

SCENES IN DRUID HILL PARK.

Address," delivered in the Senate-Chamber of the State-House at Annapolis. A winding, dark, stone stairway leads to the top, and the visitor is provided with a lantern when about to make the long and tedious ascent. The view of the city and Patapsco is peculiar and far-reaching, but is almost a bird's-eye down-look, and loses in effectiveness. Below is an innumerable multitude, a sea, of roofs, from which, like masts, rise the spires of the churches, the pointed pinnacles of public buildings, and, like huge iron-clads, the glittering rounded metal roofs of the machine-shops and market-halls. To the north and west the hills are dotted with villages and isolated dwellings, or are heavy with forest-growth. To the south the Patapsco stretches far away to the bay, and on a clear day the glittering spire of the State-House at Annapolis, forty miles distant, can be seen. The configuration of the land-locked harbor is especially well defined, the Spring Gardens to the right, the inner and outer harbor in the middle ground, the various points and necks, and the wharves and manufactures of Canton to the extreme left.

Any idea of Baltimore would be nevertheless incomplete without a better water-view. Two prominent points afford this. Patterson Park is in East Baltimore. Here still remain the earthworks thrown up in the War of 1812, when the British landed at North Point, twelve miles below. Patterson Park was formerly known by the less alliterative and euphonious name of Loudenslager's Hill. It was a sop to Cerberus, the many-headed being, represented by the people of East Baltimore, or Old Town, or the city east of the Falls, who were dissatisfied with the appropriation for Druid-Hill Park beyond the western limits of the city, and some six miles distant. The park is a great resort of the beaux and belles of East Baltimore, and many an offer of a row on its lake of a soft summer's evening carries off the lady, by no means reluctant, from the side of her more timid but watchful mother.

Federal Hill, on the opposite side of the harbor, is better known outside of the city than Patterson Park. To many the name will suggest interesting reminiscences of the war. The fortifications then constructed still remain, although guns from their embrasures no longer threaten the city, and from the flag-staff and station shown in the engraving the flag of war has been superseded by the peaceful emblems of commercial prosperity. As the signals go up with their familiar letters, it is known to the pilots that a ship is in the offing. A puff of smoke rises in the harbor, and, with quick, short snorts from her powerful engine, a pert, saucy little tug goes out on the chance of a tow.

Below Federal Hill lies Fort McHenry, and eight miles down the river the round, white, and unfinished walls of Fort Carroll rise above the water from Soller's Flats. A prisoner on board a British man-of-war, Francis Scott Key here wrote the national song of the "Star-Spangled Banner." The flag that then waved over the fort is still in the possession of a descendant of Colonel Armistead. The original flag was thirty-six feet long, with fifteen stripes and fifteen stars. One of the stars has been cut out and given away. On one of the white stripes is written the name of Colonel George Armi-

Druid-Hill Park.

stead, who commanded the American forces during the bombardment. The printer-boy who put the famous song in type still—July, 1873—survives, and the paper in which it was published yet exists. It has only been, indeed, within a few years that the British ship Minden, on board of which it was composed, was broken up as beyond service. Her timbers were eagerly bought by Americans as relics.

From the fort the most agreeable method of getting back to the city is by engaging one of the half-amphibious young watermen that ply between the city and the opposite shore. By this means the wide, sweeping front of the harbor is seen. The water-line is exceedingly irregular, and the wharves are thrust out side by side like the projecting cogs of some vast wheel. Many of these wharves are very old—as old as the city itself, in fact. They are known by the name of the person who built them—as Bowly's Wharf, Spear's Wharf, or Smith's Wharf. The present trade of the port is becoming too great for their capacity. Larger facilities are slowly coming into use. At Locust Point the enterprising Baltimore and Ohio Railroad has built an immense pier and grain-elevator—one of the finest in the United States—for its vast business. Here the Bremen steamers land their freight and passengers, while the immigrants for the West are taken at once on board the cars and shipped to their destination. Coming farther up the river, all the peculiarities of the harbor can be seen. Behind us is Fort McHenry; to the left is Federal Hill, with its signals flying; to the right is the wide expanse of the river, the numerous manufacturing industries that crowd the shore of the Canton Company. In front is a confused and blended mass of buildings—first, the factories and warehouses; then, more inland, the spires of churches; and the outlines, the mere suggestions, of private dwellings. Covering the water, the bay and its tributaries have sent up a peculiar class of sailing-craft; oyster-pungies and the swift-sailing market-boats—there are no better sailers anywhere than these low, rakish vessels—bay-steamers, and the crowd of sail-boats that ply on the Patapsco and the inland waters of Maryland and Virginia; the ocean-steamships and the South-American traders, whose battered sides and dingy sails bear witness to a long voyage; and ships that come from ports along the Atlantic coast from Maine to Florida.

So deep is the indentation of the harbor, from Light Street to the Maryland Institute, six squares distant, that the boats run up within a few hundred yards of the centre of the city. The regular landing-place is near the Institute, and a walk up Lombard Street opens the vista of Exchange Place and the Custom-House. This may be called the commercial centre of Baltimore. To be on Exchange Place is to be, in the majority of cases, a merchant of standing and credit. The Custom-House cost a large amount of money, is imposing, and worth a glance.

Passing out of Exchange Place and through South Street—devoted to brokers, bankers, and insurance agents—into Baltimore Street, and in one short square the restless stream of greatest travel is met. More persons pass the corner of Baltimore and Calvert Streets in the course of the day than over any other spot in the city. Near here are the largest hotels, and seen in the perspective of the sketch is the Battle Monument, erected to those who fell in the War of 1812. To the left is Barnum's, of gastronomic fame, where guests are supposed, from the city's special celebrity, to dine day in and day out on turtle and terrapin, Chesapeake oysters, and soft-crabs.

Here, also, the hackman hovers. It is a curious custom, dating from the first ordinances of the city, that certain hack-stands are established. It has become so much a right, by use from time immemorial, that, although the hacks standing around Battle Monument mar the appearance of the square, the privilege has never been interfered with by the authorities. If accosted, as will inevitably be the case, if the quick-trained eye of the hackman discovers a stranger, with the offer of a conveyance, which the world over invariably follows such recognition, let it be remembered that Druid-Hill Park is too distant for the most vigorous pedestrian, but is a pleasure-ground of which the citizens are justly proud, and one by no means to be neglected by the visitor.

In the year 1858 old Lloyd Rogers was in secure possession of an ancestral estate on the northern suburbs of the city. It had been in the family since the Revolution, and the first owner, an officer in the Revolutionary Army, was a man of taste. Some recollection of the parks and lawns, the stately trees and wide avenues of English country-seats led him to lay out his grounds with admirable judgment. So year after year the rugged, gnarled oaks, the symmetrical chestnuts, the straight and well-massed hickories, and the tall, dome-like poplars, grew in shape and form to please the artistic eye. Down in the valleys and on the hill-slopes the untended forest-growth covered the rich soil in tangled luxuriance. Mr. Lloyd Rogers was an old man when he died, and resided almost alone on the place. Latterly he had given little thought to its improvement.

Hampden Falls.

The family mansion was sadly in need of repair, and the barns and out-buildings were leaky and dilapidated. The whole place had the appearance of having been given over to neglect and decay. When the commissioners appointed to select a tract of land to form a park for the rapidly-growing city offered what was then a high price for this place, the offer was accepted. Public opinion, hitherto divided as to the proper location, crystallized at once in favor of the purchase. So manifold were the advantages, so great the natural beauties of the estate, that dissent from its fitness was impossible.

Druid-Hill Park lies immediately on the northern suburbs of the city, and embraces nearly seven hundred acres of well-diversified surface. Steep, wooded hills rise to two hundred feet above tide, giving glimpses of the surrounding country, and views of the city and the river. Quiet, sequestered dells, and cool, shaded valleys, watered by streams and rejoicing in springs of the purest water; drives that wind through meadows and woods; bridle-paths and foot-ways that seldom leave the welcome shadow of the trees, render the park one of great rural beauty and sylvan seclusion. It is indeed not a made show-ground, but a park with all a park's natural attractiveness of wood and water, grassy lawns, with branching shade-trees and avenues that are lost in forest-depths. All the architectural ornamentation is brought together around the central point—the old family mansion, now restored and enlarged. This is the favorite place of meeting of those who

Jones's Falls.

ride or drive from the city. About twilight of the evenings of early summer or autumn the scene is at its brightest, and horses and carriages, carrying much of the beauty and wealth of Baltimore, shift and change with incessant motion. The favorite drive is around by Woodberry, a sturdy little town of recent growth, and Prospect Hill, and back by the storage-reservoir of Druid Lake. On the approach to the white tower at the head of this lake, the upper part of the city gradually comes into view. To the right is Druid Lake, lying too low to be much affected by the prevailing winds, but stirring and simmering in its restless motion, glassy and reflective, shedding the light as a mirror set in rock. To the left runs the Northern Central Railroad around an abrupt curve. The foreground is cut up by deep, gravelly ravines; the eminence on which stands the Mount-Royal Reservoir; and, immediately in front of the distant suburbs, the depression of North Boundary Avenue. The town beyond is fringed by the outlying spires of the churches upon the northern suburbs; for this northwest section is a perfect nest of churches. They emigrate here by twos and threes from Old Town, or East Baltimore, drawn by the constant

Mill on Jones's Falls.

migration of the members of their congregations to the north and westward. It is only a small segment of Baltimore that is here seen, although the distant view of the river is very extended. In this direction the town is increasing most rapidly, and, like some huge dragon, eating away the green fields of the country. Before these words are many years old the streets, the dwellings, all the unpicturesqueness of lamp and telegraph pole, of

Lake Roland.

curb-stone and gutter, will be up to the limits of the embankment upon which we are standing.

From here one of the peculiar beauties of the vicinity of Baltimore will be remarked—the rolling, elevated, rounded hills that nearly environ it. The chain of lakes and reservoirs, in which Druid Lake is but a link, and which supplies the city with pure water, extends through one of the most beautiful portions of this broken country. Druid Lake itself is but a storage-lake, with the capacity to afford the city, if needful, sixty days' consumption. Nearer the city lies Mount-Royal Reservoir, and, above, Hampden Reservoir. We now follow Jones's Falls, which presents us with some water-views—Hampden Falls, and the Cotton Mills of Mount Vernon—little sketches that are but suggestive types; and then we come to Lake Roland, clasped in the embrace of bold hills, and winding, river-like, around jutting peninsulas. It is a charming scene. In the fresh, dewy sparkle of early morning, or in the soft closing-in of the evening shadows, it is beautiful in varying moods as the ever-changing, ever-new face of the waters answers to the drifting clouds; the heavy hill shadows, the trees that sentinel its margin, or come down a disorderly, irregular troop to mirror themselves in its bosom; or to the fitful caprices of Nature around, now bright with glint and gleam of sun or stars; now sombre and murky under driving winds and masses of low, drifting clouds, pelting with the rain, as with falling shot, the gray surface.

The lake is very deceptive as to size, as only bits of it can be seen from any one point. The official measurement gives it seven miles in circumference and a mile and a half in length. Even this, the fifth in the series, is not the last of the complicated system by which the Baltimore Water-works, costing over five million dollars, are rendered efficient. Seven miles farther up, where the Gunpowder River cuts its way between two narrow hills, is derived, by means of expensive works, a supplementary supply,

Scene on Lake Roland.

yet to become one of the principal sources upon which the city will depend, by an aqueduct ten miles long Pardon us for being statistical for a moment, as thereby we can best show the extent of the present works. Druid Lake has a capacity of four

Lake Roland Dam.

hundred and twenty million gallons; Lake Roland, three hundred and twenty-five millions; Hampden Reservoir, fifty-two millions; Mount-Royal Reservoir, thirty-two millions; and a new high-service reservoir, twenty-seven millions. The Gunpowder works, when completed, will be capable of supplying the city with more than three times the quantity now given by Jones's Falls and Roland's Run.

Lake Roland above the Dam.

All the streams around Baltimore afford scenes of much quiet beauty. Herring Run to the east has been honored by the brush of more than one artist; and Gwynn's Falls, a rapid stream to the west, presents many quaint old mills on its banks, which seem to have fallen asleep listening to the ceaseless monotone of the waters flowing past. Reminiscences these, gabled, steep-roofed, weather-worn, of the time not long after the Revolution, when Baltimore was the largest flour-market in the United States. The Patapsco, in what is known as the North Branch, is also a favorite sketching-ground. With all their beauty these streams are at times terrible agencies of destruction. Down they come, bearing every thing before their resistless force, those freshets and floods of which the history of the city records many. At the Maryland Institute is a mark of

The Patapsco at Ilchester.

the height of the flood of·1868, six feet from the street, and the water backed up to within one square of the centre of the city. An impassable barrier was suddenly thrust between East and West Baltimore—all the bridges over the Falls were swept off—heavy stone mills went down with a crash—wooden buildings were undermined, whirled round, and carried away, and many lives were lost.

The charge that Baltimore, while an elevated, beautiful, remarkably clean, and unexceptionally healthy city, possesses but few places of striking interest, has been often

made. It is unjust now, as the pencil of Mr. Perkins has proved, and in a few years it
will be but fair to presume that it will cease to be uttered. In addition to the objects
of æsthetic or historic interest thought suitable in the preceding pages for the purposes
of the artist, the Potomac Tunnel, of the Baltimore and Potomac Railway, and the
Union Tunnel, of the Canton Company, are surpassed only by the more famous Hoosic,
and girdle the city underground to the north and east. By the generosity of Johns
Hopkins, a university, complete in all its departments, endowed with more than five million dollars, and attached to which will be a park of six hundred acres, has been already
secured. The harbor channel has been deepened, so that the largest class of vessels now
come up to the wharves; and, before long, a ship-canal will be cut across Maryland and
Delaware to the ocean, and the voyage to Europe be shortened two days. From four
to five million dollars are to be spent on Jones's Falls; the stream will be straightened,
floods rendered harmless, and what is now an unsightly ditch will then, it is hoped, be
an ornament to the city. Within a year the City Hall will be completed, and be one
of the finest municipal structures in the United States, occupying an entire square and
facing four streets, with walls of white Maryland marble, and in height, from the ground
to the top of the dome, one hundred and seventy-two feet.

Scene on the Patapsco.

THE CATSKILLS.

WITH ILLUSTRATIONS BY HARRY FENN.

The Mountain House.

ABOUT one hundred and forty miles from the sea, on the western bank of the Hudson, the chain of mountains which, under various names, stretches from the banks of the St. Lawrence to Georgia and Tennessee, throws out a broken link toward the east. Clustering closely together, these isolated mountains, to which the early Dutch settlers gave the name of "Catskills," approach within eight miles of the river, and, like an advanced bastion of the great rocky wall, command the valley for a considerable distance, and form one of the most striking features in the landscape. On the western side, they slope gradually toward the central part of the State of New York, running off into spurs and ridges in every direction. On the eastern, however, they rise abruptly from the valley to a height of more than four thousand feet, resembling, when looked at from the river, a gigantic fist with the palm downward, the peaks representing the knuckles, and the glens and cloves the spaces between them. Thus separated from their kindred, and pushed forward many miles in advance of them, they overlook a great extent of country, affording a wider and more varied view than many a point of far greater elevation. Indeed, from few places, even among the Alps of Switzerland, does the traveller see beneath him a greater range of hill and valley; and yet many an American stands on the summit of the Righi, rapt in admiration of the wonderful prospect, ignorant that a view nearly as extensive, and in many respects as remarkable, may be found in one of the earliest-settled parts of his own country! Nor are the Catskill Mountains famous only for this celebrated bird's-eye view. They contain some of the

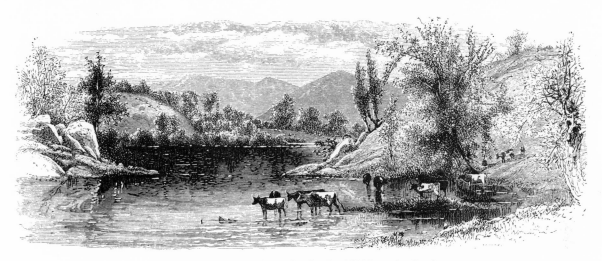

View of Mountains from Creek, Catskill-Mountain Road.

most picturesque bits of mountain-scenery in the world. The beauties of the Clove and the Falls of the Kauterskill have been immortalized by Irving and Cooper and Bryant, passing into the classics of American literature, and awakening in the genius of Cole its loftiest inspiration. After such illustrators, the task of describing the charms of this beautiful group of mountains would seem to be as difficult as the attempt were presumptuous; but a few notes may, perhaps, be useful in explanation of some of the sketches made by Mr. Fenn in this shrine of summer pilgrimage.

It was mid-August when we started for the Catskills. Though it was early when we left New-York City, no air was stirring, and the hot morning gave promise of a hotter day. The train steamed out of the huge depot into the glare of the early sunlight, and the dust began to whirl up beneath the wheels in a white, dry cloud. We have rushed with lightning-speed along the eastern bank of the Hudson—now plunging into a dark, damp tunnel cut through the overhanging rock; now whirling around some promontory, jutting out into the placid river; and, again, seeming to skim over its silvery bosom, as we glided across an elbow of the stream. We have passed beneath Yonkers and Tarrytown, and watched the shadows play on the high wall of the Palisades; skirted the shores of Haverstraw Bay and Tappan Zee; and, entering the giant gates of the Highlands at Stony Point, caught a glimpse of West Point, as we swung around the mountain opposite Cro'-Nest. Newburg and Poughkeepsie have flashed by in the rapidly-changing panorama. The Hudson, bearing many a white-sailed craft upon its bosom, flows tranquilly along between high banks covered with trees, with here and there a pretty cottage nestling among them. Now and then, as we strain our eyes forward, we can catch for a moment a faint outline, toward the north, of high mountains, dark blue in the lessening distance. Suddenly we rush through a dark cleft in the rock, and then out again on the other side. On the western bank of the river you can see a series of ridges covered with trees, rolling away, one after another, eight or ten miles; and beyond the farthest, lifting their wooded sides up into the clouds that have begun to settle on their peaks, are the famous mountains. Yonder round one to the right is Black Head; then, in succession, North Mountain, South Mountain, and Round Top, with High Peak towering over all. Between this last and the South Mountain you see

Rip Van Winkle's House, Catskill Road.

a sharp notch, or depression, terminating in a deep shadow. There lies the Clove, through which the Kauterskill comes tumbling to the plain. High on the face of the South Mountain, or rather between it and its northern neighbor, your eye detects a small speck, hanging like a swallow's-nest upon a wall, white and glistening in the sun. It is the Mountain House, from the broad piazza of which three or four hundred human beings are perhaps, at this moment, looking out over the landscape which lies beneath them like a map, and noting the faint line of white smoke that marks the passage of our train. A scream escapes from the locomotive, and the speed is slackened. Presently we come to a dead stop. Bundles are quickly made; a crowd of travellers hurries from the cars; baggage is thrown about in wild confusion; the locomotive gives a warning whistle; and, amid a cloud of dust, the train whirls up the river, and out of sight on its way to Albany. A ferry-boat lies waiting at the little wharf. A few gasps from the asthmatic engine, and we are off. A few turns of the lumbering wheel, and we have reached the western bank. Old-fashioned stages stand by the landing, awaiting our arrival. In a little while our trunks are strapped on behind; and, seated each in his place, we swing about, and are jolted up and down, as the huge vehicles roll through the little village of Catskill.

South Lake.

We have presently crossed the bridge which spans the mouth of the Kauterskill, and have fairly begun our ride toward the mountains. The day is intensely hot. The road stretches before us white and dusty in the sunshine. On either side the trees stand drooping, unstirred by a breath of air; and often, as our horses slowly pull their heavy burden up a rise in the road, and stop a moment to rest, a locust, perched on a tree by the road-side, begins his grating cry. In the meadows the cows stand under the trees, switching away the buzzing flies; and the recently-cut grass breathes out its life in the soft perfume of new-mown hay. In the distance, the clouds have begun to gather on the tops of the mountains; and, now and then, a long rumble of thunder reverberates through them, and comes rolling down into the valley. Here Mr. Fenn pauses to make his first sketch. Beside us, the little Kauterskill, wearied with its rough journey down from the heights yonder, winds among the trees that line its banks, placidly smiling in the sun. Half a dozen cows are standing in the stream to cool themselves. In front, the valley rolls gradually (about a thousand feet in

First Leap of the Falls.

seven or eight miles) up to the base of the mountains, which rise in the distance like a wall. Round Top and High Peak are buried in a dark cloud, but the scarred head of the North Mountain is in full view, and the Mountain House is clearly defined against a background of pines.

A ride of several hours across the fertile valley, climbing the ridges that lead like steps from the level of the river to the foot of the mountains, brings us at length to a toll-gate, from which we see the road straight before us, ascending steadily. We have now begun to climb in earnest. This excellent road takes advantage of a deep glen, or ravine, through which in the winter the melting snow finds its way into the valley. By clinging closely to the mountain—now creeping around a projecting rock; now crossing the beds of little streams, which, in the midsummer heat, trickle down the mossy rocks beneath the overshadowing trees—it brings us, at last, nearly to the highest point of the ravine. On every side huge trees overhang the road. On the right, the mountain towers straight up above our heads; on the left, the precipice plunges headlong down among the scattered rocks. As you climb up this steep road, and see, here and there, great bowlders lying on the slope of the mountain, covered with moss and fern, and in the perpetual shade of the forest-trees that interlace their leafy arms above you—catching a glimpse, every now and then, through some

CATSKILL FALLS.

opening in the tree-tops, of the valley, a thousand feet below, and the river glistening in the distance—you can hardly blame him who, seeking a scene for Irving's immortal story, wandered into the romantic beauties of this wild ravine, and called it "Rip Van Winkle's Glen." And, indeed, I am reminded of the legend; for, as we stop to rest the horses at a point where the road crosses the bed of a stream, from which we can look at the gorge and see a triangular piece of the valley, set in the dark foliage on both hands like a picture in its frame, a sudden clap of thunder breaks on the peaks, and echoes among the cliffs above our heads, rolling off slowly, fainter and fainter, till it dies away. Here, by the side of a little stream, which trickles down the broad, flat surface of a large rock, is the shanty called "Rip Van Winkle's House," which is represented in Mr. Fenn's sketch. The artist is looking up the glen from a point on the left of the road. On the right, one may notice the corner of a house, built for a tavern some time ago, which serves for a resting-place and half-way house between the foot of the mountain and the hotel on the summit. From this point the glen grows narrower and steeper, until it is finally lost among the crevices on the cliffs of the mountain.

The road now winds around the side of the North Mountain, creeping at times on the edge of the precipice, and steadily ascending. Mr. Fenn has sketched one of its most striking points of view. At a certain place it turns abruptly, and commences to climb in zigzags. At the first turn you suddenly see the Mountain House directly before you, apparently at the distance of half a mile. Perched upon a piece of rock which juts out far over the side of the mountain, in the bright sunshine glistening and white against the pine-clad shoulders of the South Mountain, the pile of buildings forms a singular feature of the view. On the left of the picture you may notice the opening of the Kauterskill Clove, between the sloping side of the South Mountain and that of the more distant High Peak, and, above the clouds, which are floating, like bits of gauzy drapery, about the sides of the mountains, see the valley of the Hudson fading off toward the south. One feature of these views is strikingly shown in this sketch. The face of the cliffs is broken into ledges of rock, sharp and jagged, and often overhanging the precipice for more than a thousand feet.

From this point there is a steady climb of three miles, the last part through a narrow gorge shaded by drooping hemlocks, when you have at last reached the plateau on which the hotel stands. The Mountain House is built on a flat rock, on the very edge of the precipice. Beneath it the cliff falls almost perpendicularly about eighteen hundred feet. The view from the piazza is wonderful. Two or three trees, growing on the broken stones twenty or thirty feet below the level of the house, peep up above the rock in front; and between their waving tops the landscape for miles lies spread out before you. The Indian Ridge, and the smaller ridges beneath you, though in some places as much as seven hundred feet in height, are dwarfed into nothingness; and the hill-country, through which you have ridden from the river, looks like a flat and level

UNDER THE CATSKILL FALLS.

plain. Through the centre of this, at a distance of eight miles, the Hudson winds along like a silver ribbon on a carpet of emerald, from the hills below Albany on the north to where, toward the south, its glittering stream disappears behind the Highlands at West Point. Directly beneath you, the fertile valley, dotted with farms, and broken here and there by patches of rich woodland, is smiling in the sunlight, constantly changing, as the waves of shadow chase each other across the varied mass of green. And, beyond, an amphitheatre of mountains rises on the horizon, stretching, in jagged lines, from the southern boundaries of Vermont to Litchfield, in Connecticut — rolling off, peak after peak, wave after wave of deepening blue, until they are lost in the purple of the Berkshire Hills.

Pudding-Stone Hall.

On the wide face of this extended landscape the atmosphere is constantly producing strange effects. In the morning, when the sun peeps above the distant hills, and the valley is filled with clouds that lie massed a thousand feet beneath you, the effect is that of an arctic sea of ice. At times, Righi himself affords no more wonderful sight than when the rosy light of sunset falls from behind the Catskills upon huge masses of *cumulus* clouds, heaped up upon one another like peaks of snow. Day by day, the scene is changing with the hours, and ever revealing some new beauty. Mr. Fenn's sketch of the view at sunrise (see steel engraving) was taken from a point on the face of the South Mountain, near the entrance to the Clove. The morning had just broken when we scrambled over the edge of the cliff down, a hundred feet or more, to a point where the rocks, broken off from the mountain, stood up like huge monuments, towering out over the abyss below.

As we sat upon a ledge, from which a pebble would have fallen perpendicularly more than five hundred feet, the sun rose up above the hills in Massachusetts, pouring a flood of light upon the western side of the valley. The eastern, from the river to the foot of the distant mountains, was still in shadow, filled with a mass of clouds, out of which the smaller hills peeped up like rocky islets in a frozen sea. Directly beneath us light, fleecy clouds, white as snow, came creeping out of the valley, throwing into bold relief the gnarled and twisted pines that clung to the rocks in front of us. Steadily the sun mounted into the heavens, and the clouds, gathering into a snowy curtain, and for a few moments obscuring all beneath, presently broke into pieces and melted away, and there lay the exquisite landscape smiling in the sun-

Druid Rocks.

shine. The most famous beauty of the region is the Fall of the Kauterskill. On the high table-land of the South and North Mountains lie two lakes, buried in a dense forest. Of one of these, the South Lake, Mr. Fenn has given us a sketch. It was taken from a high ledge on the North Mountain, looking southward. The shores are dark with pines, and the surface of the lake is dotted here and there with the broad leaves of the water-lily, but the most striking feature of the view is the summit of Round Top reflected as in a mirror. A little brook, making its way from these lakes, westward along the shoulder of the mountain, soon reaches the edge of a very steep declivity, over which it leaps into a deep pool in the centre of a great amphitheatre of rock.

Gathering its strength again, the torrent makes a second leap over huge bowlders, which have fallen from the ledges above and lie scattered down the glen, dashing itself into foam in its headlong fury. Tumbling from one ledge to another, it reaches, at length, the bottom of the glen, when, meeting the stream that flows from Haines's Fall, the mingled waters hurry down the stony pathway through the Clove, and out into the valley, until, swollen to a wide stream, they glide placidly into the Hudson at the village of Catskill. There is nothing more beautiful in American scenery than this water-fall as it leaps from the lofty height and dashes into spray in the hollow basin below. The strata of which the mountain is formed lie piled upon one another horizontally, and through them the water has cut its way smoothly like a knife. Some distance above the margin of the pool, in which the fallen waters boil as in a caldron, there is a stratum of soft stone, which has broken up and crumbled in the dampness. Wearing away several yards deep into the cliffs, it has left a pathway all around the Fall, from which you have a fine view, and often, when the stream above is swollen, through a veil of glittering drops dripping from the rocks above. Exquisite as is the effect of the whole Fall, when seen from the rocks at the foot of its second leap, this last point of view is even more striking. Standing on the narrow pathway, you look through the great white veil of falling waters, leaping out over your head and sending up clouds of spray that float off down the gorge. Sometimes, when the sun is shining brightly, a dancing rainbow will keep pace with you as you creep around the semicircle beneath the rock. Here, too, you get an enchanting glimpse of the edges of the Clove, down which the stream goes headlong, and can mark the wild figures of the pines that cling to the verge of the cliffs, and seem, with their black spears, to pierce the sky.

Upon the very edge of the precipice, close to the narrow channel through which the Fall makes his plunge, there is a tree which has grown out from a crevice, and then upward until it juts out over the abyss. To this solitary tree the lad who acts as your guide points with his finger, and tells you of the adventurous young woman who crept out to the rock, and, clasping the slender trunk of the tree with her hands, swung her body far out over the Fall, and then, with a cry of triumph, back again in safety.

Beneath the second fall the gorge is wild in the extreme. On both sides the mountains rise almost perpendicularly, clad with a dense forest, and, through the shade beneath, the torrent roars, ceaselessly, among the rocks.

One of the most beautiful walks is over the South Mountain. Immediately after leaving the House you plunge into a dense thicket of pines, and commence to climb a steep pathway among the rocks. The roots of trees, interlacing across the path, form a series of steps, and, here and there, a huge rock serves for a resting-place in the con-

stant ascent. In a few minutes you have reached the level of a stratum of conglomerate of many feet in thickness, which lies across the top of this and the North Mountain. Some convulsion of Nature has riven off a piece of it, which now lies on the
hill-side, many feet in thickness, and eighteen or twenty high. Between this and the
solid rock is a passage several feet in length and two or three in width, to which some

Looking South from South Mountain.

one has given the name of " Pudding-Stone Hall." Ferns are growing in the dark recesses of the rock, and water drips constantly into the cavity. Your path leads through
this chasm, and, by means of a pile of stones at the farther end, as shown in the
sketch, you climb up to the top of the ledge of conglomerate. Here the trees are
white and dead, having been killed by repeated fires, and the path winds among the
rocks, half buried in long mountain-grass or blueberry-bushes, until it comes out to the

Glimpse of Catskill Clove from Indian Head.

eastern face of the mountain. You are, of course, high above the level of the Mountain House, which lies beneath you to the left, and the view over the surrounding country and the valley of the Hudson is even more extended than that from the piazza of the hotel. With a good glass you can distinguish a round object glittering on the summit of a hill on the northern horizon. It is the Capitol at Albany, forty miles off as the crow flies. Farther along, still keeping southward, and occasionally climbing up steep steps, you find the cliffs exceedingly fine. Some of them are sharply cut, and overhang the tops of the tallest trees that grow from the *débris* at their base. On a promontory of high rock, near the entrance to the Kauterskill Clove, lies " the Bowlder," which is often the goal of walking-parties. It is a huge block of the pudding-stone brought here, doubtless, by the ice in the glacial period, and left by some strange chance on the very verge of the precipice. A few feet farther and it would have toppled over the edge and crashed downward two thousand feet into the bottom of the Clove. Mr. Fenn has sketched the Bowlder and the cliffs on top of which it lies. From his point of view you look southward, across the mouth of the Clove, the great shoulder of High Peak and Round Top rising up abruptly beyond. Here, as in the sketch of the sunrise, the precipitous walls of rock hardly afford foothold for the weather - beaten pines that grow out of the crevices and wave their twisted arms from the dizzy heights. Sometimes, after passing through Pudding-Stone Hall, you keep straight along the path through the woods instead of turning eastward toward the face of the mountain. After a time you come to a point where the bits of rock have fallen from the ledge above and lie scattered along the hill-side, like the bowlders hurled about in the giant warfare of the Titans. The wood is dense and dark : the pines interlacing their arms above your head throw a perpetual twilight on the hill-side, and, as you sit on the soft carpet of their fallen leaves, and see these huge fantastic rocks scattered around you, one cannot but feel that the name of " Druid Rocks," which has been given to the place, is at once suggestive and appropriate. At times the path keeps close along the sloping hill-side, finding a doubtful way beneath the base of tall cliffs

Bridge in Catskill Clove.

covered with moss; at others it climbs through some crevice, and, ascending to the top of the ledge, winds among the gray rocks in the full glare of a summer's sun.

A delightful walk brings you at last to Indian Head. This name is given to a bold promontory which juts out over the Clove until it overhangs the bed of the tumbling, tossing Kauterskill. From this rock the mountain falls eighteen hundred or two thousand feet. Half a dozen tall pines, growing out of the cliff, divided into two groups on either hand, form a sort of dark, rustic frame for the exquisite picture. The Clove at this place is very narrow, and, along the bottom, the Kauterskill goes tumbling and foaming over the stones. Along the base of the cliff, on the left or southern side of the glen, winds the little road that leads from the village at its mouth up to the table-land beyond the famous falls. On both sides, the mountains tower high above your heads, heavily wooded to the summits with chestnut and pine, through the rich green of which, here and there, you can see the rugged face of a huge precipice, scarred and broken by the frosts, and spotted with dark lichen and moss. As we gazed down into the Clove a heavily-laden stage came lumbering into view, looking, as it does in Mr. Fenn's sketch, like a mere speck upon the winding road. We watched it creeping along, often half hidden by the trees, until it passed over the little rustic bridge that spans a brawling cataract, and vanished behind the dark shoulder of the mountain. It was a perfect day. About the great head of High Peak the clouds had thrown a scarf of white, the shadow of which darkened his mighty shoulders and the gorge beneath. The colors were constantly changing with the moving clouds, and the sunlight played and danced upon the walls of rock and the masses of deepest green, while the sound of the Kauterskill came floating up to us from its stony bed, where it dashed along, now sparkling in the sunlight and then plunging over mossy rocks into the shade. The wonderful effect of this play of light and shade is perfectly shown by the accompanying picture. The little rustic bridge which is seen in the view from Indian Head spans the stream at one of the most striking points in the Clove. Of it Mr. Fenn has made a sketch from a rock just below it in the stream. The light structure, hardly strong enough, apparently, to bear the heavy stage that is about to cross it, hangs over the Kauterskill where it comes tumbling over some huge rocks that have fallen in its path. The water boils and tosses into foam, and then dashes headlong down a succession of ledges beneath. On one side, the cliff towers high into the air, sharp and smooth as masonry, looking like the walls of a great mediæval castle. On the other, the spurs of the South Mountain, densely covered with trees, rise rapidly more than fifteen hundred feet. It is a most romantic spot. As you stand upon Sunset Rock and look westward up the Clove, you have one of the most picturesque views in the range of mountain scenery. The rock is broad and flat, projecting far out over the precipice. An old pine-tree stands, like a sentinel, upon its very verge. In front of and behind you, as you sit by the old tree on the dizzy edge, the mountain pushes two great, gray cliffs, bald

Sunset Rock.

and ragged, far out over the glen, and then falls in broken lines a scarred and frowning precipice.

The lines of the South Mountain and of the spurs of High Peak and Round Top blend so gently together, as they meet beneath, that it is difficult to trace the bed of the Kauterskill or its tributary even by the shadows in the dense forest of green.

The Five Cascades, Kauterskill Clove.

Directly in front of you the table-land, which is formed by the shoulders of these mountains, rolls off toward the westward, where the sharp lines of Hunter Mountain are clearly defined against the sky among its sister peaks. Over the edge of this table-land leaps Haines's Fall. As in the accompanying engraving, it looks, from Sunset Rock, like a white spot in the dark forest—glittering for an instant in the sunlight, and then plunging down behind the waving tree-tops.

One of the most beautiful of all the sketches made by Mr. Fenn is that of the Five Cascades, as they are improperly called. A stiff climb from the bottom of the Kauterskill Clove —commencing at the point where the carriage-road leaves it and following the bed of the stream that comes down from Haines's, now clambering over bowlders and fallen trees, and again scrambling up the wet rocks or clinging to the vine-clad banks—brought us at last to the Five Cascades. It was an enchanting spot. The stream, after plunging over the cliff—as shown in the view from Sunset Rock— like a far-off feathery vapor into a large shallow pool, jumps rapidly over a series of ledges from ten to forty feet in height, that lead like steps down into the Clove. Through the succession of the ages it has worn its way among the rocks until, for most of the distance, its path is hidden from the sunshine. In many places the branches of the trees on the high banks above are intertwined across the ravine, down which the little stream dashes in hundreds of beautiful cataracts in a perpetual twilight. There are, in truth, hundreds of these falls, but five of them are peculiarly striking—and three of these are represented in the engraving. As we sat upon a fallen tree and gazed upon the stream, dashing its cold, gray waters over the black rocks, a shaft of sunlight broke through the tree-tops above our heads and fell upon the middle fall. The change was instantaneous. Above it and below, the cataracts were still in shadow, but the central one, in the bright sunshine, threw over the glistening rock a myriad of diamonds. For five minutes the water seemed to rejoice in the glorious light, when suddenly it faded—the spell was broken, and the little cataract went tumbling over the dark rocks in the gloom again.

Stony Clove.

The last engraving is a distant view of Stony Clove—a pass in the mountains famous for the wildness of its scenery. It is always dark and cool, and even in mid-August you may find ice among the crevices of the rocks that have fallen in great numbers from the cliffs above. The sketch was made as we drove toward the northern entrance. A thunder-storm was gathering about the southern gate of the pass, and a rainbow seemed to rest upon the mountains hovering above the Clove.

Such are a few of the attractions of this charming region. Of course there are drives over fine roads among the hill-tops, and countless walks through the forests and over the ledges, with the usual results of torn clothes, sunburnt faces, and hearty appetites. To the dweller in a city of the plain, weary of work and worn with the tumult of its life, there are few places in the whole range of American scenery so attractive and refreshing as the Catskill Mountains.

THE JUNIATA.

WITH ILLUSTRATIONS BY GRANVILLE PERKINS.

Duncannon, Mouth of the Juniata.

AMERICANS are but too apt to rank their rivers by their size, and almost refuse to believe that a stream can be exceedingly lovely that does not flow, at the least, a thousand miles or so. Such a work as the present will go far to remove this way of thinking, since the scenes depicted of many rivers will enable the world to compare and contrast them more accurately; and the comparison will assuredly award the palm of loveliness to the smaller streams.

The Juniata is a tributary—a mountain-tributary—of the far-famed Susquehanna;
and though its short life begins at a point beyond Clearfield, and ends at Duncannon—
a distance of one hundred and fifty miles—yet does it present many scenes of entrancing
beauty. It falls into the Susquehanna, about a mile from the last-named place, in a site
that deserves certainly to have been the theme of poets' song, and the inspiration of
the artist's brush. The village of Duncannon is built at the base of numerous foot-hills,
which lie crouching beneath the colossal mountain-forms that rise to a height of several
thousand feet into the blue air. It is a curious fact that these foot-hills are not from

Night-Scene on the Juniata, near Perryville.

the detritus and washing away of the mountains above; for the former have a limestone
substance, and the latter are of sandstone. Hence the foot-hills are not only fertile, but
singularly adapted for raising wheat, and for the cultivation of the vine. The mountains
are covered from base to summit with a luxuriant growth of forest-trees, mostly oaks,
chestnuts, hickories, pecans, and other hard woods. As one ascends higher and higher
into the mountain-region where the Juniata takes its birth, pines and spruces appear; but
at Duncannon one may look long at the masses of superb foliage without discovering
the dark-green leafage and the upright form of a pine.

Ascending one of the foot-hills, covered with high, waving corn, the spectator obtains

a noble view of the Sus-
quehanna and its lovely
tributary. The first river is
quite broad here, and pours
a brown, whelming flood,
nearly a mile wide, in the
direction of Harrisburg,
though the manner in
which the mountains put
their heads together, as one
looks backward, renders its
course entirely problemati-
cal. Looking opposite from
the Duncannon foot-hill,
there lies in full outline a
superb mountain, at whose
base runs the Northern
Central Railway of Penn-
sylvania, and the canal,
which formerly belonged to
the State, but has since become the property of the
Pennsylvania road. This
mountain, like the others,
is densely wooded; but
there are places where its
sides are bare, and show a
mass of small, broken rocks
approaching shale, which
would entirely destroy any
beauty in these mountain-
forms. The kindly mantle
of green foliage which Nature has given them is an
absolute necessity as regards
the picturesque, though, as
a consequence, the eye in
vain looks for the sheer
descent and the bold, rug-

Windings of the Juniata, near Perryville.

ged outlines which make mountain scenery sublime. Here, on the contrary, every thing has a gentle slope, and one often sees a succession of wooded terraces mounting upward into the air. The manner in which these enormous masses of tree-coverings arrest and detain the blue particles of air has won for them the appellation of Blue Mountains, though geographically they are known as the Kittatinny. Beyond this mountain rises up another of still grander majesty; and just between them is the bridge over which the teams of the canal-boats cross from the Susquehanna to accompany the Juniata. At this point, therefore, the waters meet. The mouth of the Juniata is not very broad, and seems quite narrow when compared with the flood of her big sister; but her stream is much deeper, and her waters of a deep blue. The poets of the locality love to write about the blue Juniata, and speak of it as the gently-gliding stream. In summer-time, no doubt, this name is appropriate; but from the hill of observation above Duncannon one can see the remains of four stone piers—all that is left of the bridge that spanned the Juniata at this point. Regularly every spring, when the snows melt and the ice piles up in masses, the Juniata sweeps away her bridges as if they were feathers, and comes rushing into the Susquehanna with a wealth of blue water that materially changes the color of the big, brown stream. At Harrisburg they know, by the color of the stream that rushes past, when the waters come from the Juniata; and they mutter about lively times down Huntingdon way. There is a broad, bold curve of land on the left bank of the Juniata, which hides all but its mouth from observation; but the Susquehanna can be seen wandering among the foot-hills, and swelling out like a lake in various places.

Following the bank of the blue Juniata, side by side with the canal, one is for a few miles, at first, in a level country. The stream is not broad, but tolerably deep, and abounding in fish, which rise every moment at the flies that hover over the placid surface. Between here and Perryville the river is full of beautiful islands, covered with trees whose branches sweep down to the ground and often hide the bank. With the branches are interlaced wild-vines, with huge leaves; and between them the golden-rod, and the big yellow daisy, and the large-leaved fern, make their appearance. In the low parts of these islands there are beautiful mosses, and a species of water-grass which becomes a deep orange in circular patches. Some of these islands are quite large, comparatively speaking; and one can spy, through the crossed and entangled branches, the glimmer of white dresses, and the glancing of fair faces, belonging to a picnicking party, or perhaps to folks going a-berrying, who, having filled their baskets, have been romantic enough to eat their lunch on the Moss Islands.

Approaching Perryville, the foot-hills disappear, and the bright glimpse of champaign country vanishes. The mountains are once more upon us, looming up into the clear sky like giants. They are on both sides, and in front likewise. On the right there is one huge, solid wall, with hardly an irregularity or a break along the crest, which is

Moss Islands, in the Juniata.

straight as a piece of masonry. On the left the mountains are strung along like a chain of gigantic agates. Each seems to be triangular, and between each is a ravine, where there are not only tall trees, but also fine slopes of high grass. There are deer in there, and there are black bears on the summit; but, to see them, one must live on a farm on the mountain-side, and be one of the sons of the mountain. The *feræ naturæ* do not love the scream of the steam-whistle, and abide far away on the long slopes of the sides, which we do not see, for we are now skirting the bases of their triangular fronts. Nine-tenths of those who pass them never dream how far back these mountains extend; and, indeed, it is somewhat difficult for any one to keep in his head the multiform appearances of the same mountain as viewed from various sides. At night-time, when there is a full moon, the river near Perryville is exceedingly grand — the solemn stillness of the hour; the lapping sound of the gentle water; the whisper of the wind among the trees, that seems more like the falling of a distant cascade than the rustling of leaf on leaf, and the chafing of bough against bough. When the wind rises, then the voices of the mountain speak; and a storm of groans, shrieks, and mutterings, is loosened. Voices of command, of entreaty, threats, muffled or rising high, are borne upon the air; and it seems as if the murky night were being peopled with an invisible creation, with voices that were formless, but had souls that spoke through the endless modulations of sound.

But if the approach to Perryville be most beautiful by night, it is not so beyond. For the great wall sinks behind a line of detached mountains here which come sloping down to the river in long capes and promontories, covered by a profusion of many-hued foliage. On the left bank, the mountains still show their bold fronts, and the stream, forced around the capes on the one side, has worn similar indentations on the other, presenting a most beautiful appearance. The most picturesque part of this lovely region is after we pass the little village of Mexico; and it may be noted here that the nomenclature of the whole place is ridiculous beyond comparison, the pretty names being all cribbed from Ireland, and the others having no meaning or relationship whatever. It is difficult to say whether the river is finer looking forward or looking back. Perhaps looking forward is the best, if one can leave out of the perspective a wretched mountain called Slip Hill, which, having been deprived by the wood-cutters of its forest-mantle, has ever since taken to rolling stones down its great slope, and presents a hideously forlorn appearance. It is covered from apex to base with a mass of small, flat stones, like scales, and about every half-hour there is a movement, and a miniature land-slip goes gliding into the river. As the stones are quite small, the river sends them along, but they have materially changed the bed in places, and made the stream quite shallow. If this unfortunate bit can be hidden, the view is the perfection of the picturesque. It does not amount to sublimity, for the hills are not bold enough for that. But the curves of the stream are so graceful, and the slopes of the mountains covered with green so grand, that the imagination is charmed and the feelings softened.

The next point along the line of the Juniata is one where the river sinks into a very subordinate position, indeed. The hills on both sides, that have hitherto been so amiable, suddenly break off, and the great wall comes into view on the right hand, while

Narrows near Lewistown.

on the left we get the side of a mountain instead of its front. On both banks the hills
are remarkably steep, and they approach so closely together as to confine the little river
within extremely narrow bounds. For seven miles and a half this imprisonment lasts;
and here, perhaps, the mountains show their grandest forms. The bases are often crag-

like, showing huge masses of stone that seem to hang on to the side without any definite support, and threaten momentarily to come down upon one's head. The summits in
a few instances have castellated forms, and beguile the eye with momentary impressions
of battlements, from which the wild-cherry or the vine flings itself to the breeze like a
banner. Unfortunately, these spots are rare, but the general character of the scenery is
much bolder than in other places. It is astonishing how the mist clings here, and how
resolutely the sun is combated. The bright luminary has to be quite high in the

The Forks of the Juniata, near Huntingdon.

heavens before his rays can surmount the barriers which Nature has planted against the
sunlight. Slowly the masses of white mist rise like smoke, clinging to the sides of the
hills in great strata. When the sun reaches down to the surface of the river, the mists
have disappeared, but there are tiny spirals, like wreaths of smoke, which dance upon
the water, and remain for many minutes. At length all is clear, and the blue firmament
smiles down upon us, the golden clouds sail over us, and the sun beams beneficently
down. In the twinkling of an eye the mists have marshalled their hosts, and the whole

TYRONE GAP, VIEW FROM THE BRIDGE.

scene—sky, mountains, and river—is blotted out. Then the battle has to be fought again. Once more the sunbeams triumph, and the beaten vapor clings for protection to the sides of the hills, and the maids of the mist dance upon the waters. But all is not yet over, and the contest often is waged until far in the day, when the sun's triumph becomes lasting. As the entrance into the Narrows was sudden, so the exit is abrupt. One wanders along the tow-path of the canal looking up at the mountains, and wondering how much nearer they intend to come, and whether they are going to act like the iron shroud, and close in and crush us utterly, when, *presto!* the Juniata makes a bold fling to the right, and we find ourselves in Lewistown, with the mountains behind us and a pleasant valley smiling welcome in our front.

Between Lewistown and Huntingdon the scenery is extremely beautiful; but to describe it would be simply a repetition of the phrases applied to Perryville, where the curves of the river are so lovely. But the mountains are decidedly bolder, and the river becomes wilder, and curves in such a multitudinous fashion as to make frequent bridging absolutely necessary. One of the chief charms of this route may perhaps be in the fact that, on the right-hand side, there are two ranges—one always like a Titanic wall, the other a broken line of skirmishers. As one advances higher and higher into the mountain-region, the pines begin to show on the sides of the great cones of sandstone like a shaggy fringe, and the masses of rock are larger and more picturesque. At Huntingdon the hills retire, and leave a pleasant level. Here the Juniata forks, the larger but less picturesque fork striking southward toward Hollidaysburg, and the smaller branch, known as the Little Juniata, going west in the direction of Tyrone. The canal and the Pennsylvania Railroad, which hitherto have faithfully run side by side along the Juniata, now separate also, the canal going with the big branch and the railway with the little one. In consequence of this separation there are many bridges at Huntingdon, and the place looks quite picturesque with its background of mountains and its wandering streams. But henceforth the Juniata ceases to be a river, both branches being just trout-streams, and nothing more. And, what is still more cruel, the Little Juniata loses its beautiful blue color, because it flows through a mining-region, and the miners will persist in washing their ore in its clear wave.

After we leave Huntingdon we are in the mountains altogether. Various creeks join the Little Juniata, which winds so that it has to be bridged every three or four miles. At the junction of Spruce Creek, the mountains on the left, which have been shouldering us for some time back, suddenly hurl a huge barrier over our path in the shape of Tussey's Mountain—a great turtle-backed monster, several thousand feet high. The wall on the right hand closes in at the same time, so that there is no resource left but a tunnel, which, however, is not a very long one. We are now seven miles from Tyrone, the centre of the mountains, and the pines are quite thick. The hills that lie at the base of the mountains show pleasant farm-houses and deep-green-leaved corn. The

SINKING RUN, ABOVE TYRONE.

mountains show us now their fronts and now their bases, but are never out of sight, and at intervals come right up to us. At Tyrone they look as if they had been cleft asunder, for there is a great gap cut between two mountains. This in times past was doubtless the work of the Juniata, and was not so difficult as it looks; for the shaly mountains are very different from the firm limestone, through which the Kanata cuts its way at Trenton Falls. On the right hand, however, the hard sandstone shows for a considerable space, and affords all the stone of which the bridges in the neighborhood are built. Tyrone is built in quite a considerable valley. The mountains open out for some distance to the eastward and to the westward. But north and south they hang on with the persistence of bull-dogs. The river in the olden times must have swelled to a lake here, and cut the gap through the line of mountains that stretch north and south, being aided by countless creeks and nameless streams. Bald-Eagle Creek joins the river here, and, in spring-time, the plain in front of the gap is one stretch of water. The town is built away from the Juniata, and rises in terraces along the Bald-Eagle Creek, the foot-hills being highly cultivated. There is quite a wealth of pine on these mountains, though it is all second growth, every hard-wood tree having been cut down to supply charcoal for the Tyrone forges, which originated the city, though now it is a centre for the mountain railroads. The scenery around is decidedly Alpine in character; and some of the roads made for the lumber business traverse regions of savage beauty. Thunder-storms are of daily occurrence up in these heights, and luckless is the stranger wight who trusts to his umbrella; for the winds will turn it inside out, and will propel it forward, dragging its reluctant owner to the brink of precipices, and, after giving him chills of terror, will at length drag it from his grasp, and leave him umbrellaless, exposed to the pelting storm. The curious thing about these storms is, that one does not last five minutes, and the sun is out and drying one's habiliments long before such a thing could be hoped for. But the clouds whirl about the mountains so furiously that one is sure to be caught several times, and the writer was wetted to the skin three distinct times when descending Sinking-Run Hill, a mountain about six miles from Tyrone. The view presented by the artist is taken from an old road now discontinued for lumber travel, which starts from the side of the mountain, about half-way up, and descends circuitously to the base of the opposite mountain. Wild-cherries and whortleberries grow in abundance, and the route is shaded by pines and hickories, while an occasional spruce-tree adds variety to the foliage. The waters of the run are agreeable to drink, though impregnated by sand. In the spring of the year the mountains are one blaze of rhododendron blossoms. Then is the time to visit them if one is not afraid of wet feet; for the waters are then out in every direction, and tiny runs of water trickle across the road everywhere.

ON THE OHIO.

WITH ILLUSTRATIONS BY ALFRED R. WAUD.

The Ohio, below Pittsburg.

O–HE–YO is a Wyandot word, signifying "Fair to look upon." The early French explorers, floating down the river's gentle tide, adopted the name, translating it into their own tongue as *la Belle Rivière,* and the English, who here as elsewhere throughout the West, stepped into the possessions of the French, took the word and its spelling, but gave it their own pronunciation, so that, instead of O-he-yo, we now have the Ohio. It is a lovely, gentle stream, flowing on between the North and South. It does not bustle and rush along over rocks and down rapids, turning mills and factories on its way, and hurrying its boats up and down, after the manner of busy, anxious Northern rivers; neither does it go to sleep all along shore and allow the forest flotsam to clog up its channel, like the Southern streams. But none the less has it a character of its own, which makes its gentle impression, day by day, like a quiet, sweet-voiced woman, who moves through life with more power at her gentle command than the more beautiful and more brilliant around her.

No river in the world has such a length of uniform smooth current. In and out it

meanders for one thousand
and seven miles; it is never
in a hurry; it never seems
to be going anywhere in particular, but has time to loiter
about among the coal and
iron mines of Pennsylvania;
to ripple around the mountains of West Virginia; to
make deep bends in order
to take in the Southern rivers, knowing well that thrifty
Ohio, with her cornfields and
villages, will fill up all the
angles; then it curves up
northward toward Cincinnati,
as if to leave a broad land-
sweep for the beautiful blue-
grass meadows of Kentucky;
and at North Bend away it
glides again on a long southwestern stretch, down, down,
along the southern borders of
Indiana and Illinois, and after
making a last curve to re-
ceive the twin-rivers — the
Cumberland and the long,
mountain-born Tennessee—it
mixes its waters with the
Mississippi, one thousand
miles above the ocean.

The Ohio is formed
from the junction of two
rivers as unlike as two rivers can be: the northern parent, named Alleghany, which
signifies "clear water," is
a quick, transparent stream,
coming down directly from

Pittsburg, from Soldiers' Monument.

Pittsburg, from Reservoir

the north; while the southern parent, named Monongahela, which signifies "Falling-in banks," comes even more directly from the south—its slow, yellow tide augmented by the waters of the Youghiogheny—a name whose pronunciation is mysterious to all but the initiated, a shibboleth of Western Pennsylvania. These two rivers, so unlike in their sources, their natures, and the people along their banks, unite at Pittsburg, forming the Ohio, which from that point to its mouth receives into itself seventy-five tributaries, crosses seven States, and holds in its embrace one hundred islands. The hills along the Ohio are high, round-topped, and covered with verdure; in some places they rise abruptly from the water five hundred feet in height, and, in others, they lie back from the river, leaving a strip of bottom-land between, whose even, green expanse is a picture of plenty — the ideal fat fields which a New-England farmer can see only in his dreams. On the southern side, when the hills are abrupt and there is no bottom-land, the original forest remains in all its denseness, and we see the river and its shore as the first explorers saw them, when, gliding down in canoes almost two centuries ago, they gave, in their enthusiasm, the name of *Belle Rivière*, which the Indians had given long before. The verdure is vivid and luxuriant; the round tops of the swelling hills are like green velvet, so full and even is the foliage;

and when, here and there, a rocky ledge shows itself on the steep river-side, it is veiled
with vines and tufts of bright flowers, the red-bud and blue blossoms growing in patches
so close to the rock that it looks as if it were *lapis-lazuli.* The river constantly curves
and bends, knotted like a tangled silver thread over the green country. Every turn
shows a new view: now a vista of interval on the north; now a wooded gorge on the
south; now a wall of hills in front, with scarcely a rift between; and now, as the stream
doubles upon its track, the same hills astern, with sloping valley-meadows separating their
wooded sides. There is no long look ahead, as on the Hudson—no clear understanding
of the points of the compass, as on the broad St. Lawrence; the flag-staff at the bow
veers constantly; the boat's course is north, south, east, or west, as it happens, and the
perplexity is increased by a way they have of heading up-stream when stopping, so that,
although you may begin the day with a clear idea which side is Virginia and which
Ohio, by the time the boat has finished the *chassés,* and turns necessarily to its first stop
and reached the bank, you have lost your bearings entirely, and must either join the be-
wildered but persistent inquirers who besiege the captain all the way from Pittsburg to
Louisville with the question, "Which side *is* Ohio, captain, and which side Kentucky?"
or else, abandoning knowledge altogether, and, admiring the scenery as it changes, float
on without a geographical care, knowing that you will reach Louisville some time, *et
præterea nihil.* For exercise there is always the carrying of chairs from one side of the
boat to the other, as the frequent turns bring the afternoon sunbeams under the awning;
you may walk several miles in this way each day. It is a charming way of travelling
in the early spring, when the shores are bright with blossoms and fresh with verdure.
The river-steamers, with their wheels astern and their slight, open hulls, like summer-
houses afloat, go slowly up and down, and whistle to each other for the channel, according to their load. The crews are motley, black and white, and, as the boats pass each
other, you can see them lying on the lower deck, idle and contented, while the jolly
laugh of the negro echoes out almost constantly, for he laughs, as the birds sings, by instinct. On the northern shore of the Upper Ohio, the railroad to Pittsburg is seen;
the long trains of yellow cars rush by, their shrill whistles coming from the steep hill-
side over the water, as if remonstrating with the boats for their lazy progress. In truth,
the boats do their work in a leisurely way. A man appears on the bank and signals,
but even he is not in a hurry, finding a comfortable seat before he begins his waving;
then the captain confers with the mate, the deck-hands gather on the side to inspect the
man, and all so slowly that you feel sure the boat will not stop, and look forward toward
the next bend. But the engine pauses, the steamer veers slowly round, runs its head into
the bank; out comes the plank, and out come the motley crew, who proceed to bring
on board earthenware, lumber, or whatever the waving man has ready for them, while
he, still seated, watches the work, and fans himself with his straw hat. To eyes accustomed to the ocean, or the deep lakes and rivers of the North, with their long piers,

solid docks, and steamers drawing many feet of water, this landing with the ease of a row-boat is new and strange. The large towns have what they call a levee—pronounced *levy*—which is nothing more than a rough stone pavement over the sloping bank; but the villages off the railroads, where the steamers generally stop for freight, have nothing but an old flat-boat moored on the shore; and many of them have not even this. The large, handsome, well-filled steamboats run right up into the bank, so that even a plank is hardly necessary for landing, and all you have to do is to take your bag and step ashore. The steamers, large as they are, draw but a few feet of water; their bulk is above, not below, the tide; they float along like a plank; and there are no waves to dash over their low, open decks. If they run aground, as they often do in the varying channel, down comes a great beam, fastened with tackle like a derrick, on the bow, and, this having been pushed into the river-bottom, the engine is started, and the boat pried off. If there is a fog at night—as there often is—the captain ties up his boat to the bank, and all hands go to sleep, which is a safe if not brilliant course to pursue. In this way the voyage from Pittsburg to Cincinnati becomes uncertain in duration; but wherefore hurry when the Ohio farms, the Virginia mountains, and the Kentucky meadows, are radiant with the beauty of spring?

The mouth of the Ohio River was first discovered in 1680, but its course was not explored until seventy years afterward, its long valley having remained an unknown land when the Mississippi and the Red River of the South, as well as Lake Superior and the Red River of the North, had been explored and delineated in maps. In 1750 the French penetrated into the Ohio wilderness, the first white navigators of the Beautiful River. They claimed the basins of the lakes and the Mississippi and its tributaries as New France, and began a line of forts stretching from their settlements in Canada to their settlements in Louisiana. The head-waters of the Ohio, at the junction of the Alleghany and Monongahela, was a commanding point in this great chain of internal navigation, and, at an early date, became a bone of contention, for the British were jealously watching every advance of their rivals as they pushed their dominion on toward the south. In 1750 Captain Celeron, a French officer, was sent from Canada to take possession of the Ohio-River Valley; this ceremony he performed by depositing leaden plates along the shore, and then returned, satisfied that all was well. Three of these talismans have been discovered in modern times. The following is a translation of one of the inscriptions: " In the year 1750, we, Celeron, commandant of a detachment by Monsieur the Marquis of Gallisonière, commander-in-chief of New France, to establish tranquillity in certain Indian villages of these cantons, have buried this plate on the Beautiful River as a monument of renewal of possession which we have taken of said river and its tributaries, and of all the land on both sides; inasmuch as the preceding kings of France have engaged it and maintained it by their arms and by treaties, especially by those of Ryswick, Utrecht, and Aix-la-Chapelle."

SOUTH PITTSBURGH.

ALLEGANY CITY.

SOUTH PITTSBURG AND ALLEGHANY CITY.

These plates, buried with so much ceremony by the officers of Louis XV., could not have exercised much moral influence through the ground, for, from that time on, there was fighting along the Beautiful River and its tributaries for more than sixty years, and no " tranquillity " in those " cantons," from Braddock's defeat to Aaron Burr's conspiracy, from George Washington's first military expedition to the brilliant campaigns of young Harrison, whose tomb can be seen from the steamer a few miles below Cincinnati.

In pursuance of their plan, the French, in 1755, built a fort near the present site of Pittsburg, naming it Duquesne, after the Governor of Canada, having taken possession of the unfinished work which the Virginians, on the recommendation of the young surveyor, George Washington, had commenced there. The war at that time going on between England and France had been so unfortunate for the former nation that Horace Walpole had said, " It is time for England to slip her cable and float away into some unknown ocean."

Braddock had been defeated on the Monongahela, owing to his ignorance of Indian warfare ; he died during the retreat, and was buried under the road in the line of march. But when Pitt, the great statesman, took the English helm, he changed the current of events, and, toward the close of 1758, General Forbes took Fort Duquesne from the French, rebuilt the burned walls, and named it after the Earl of Chatham, a name the present city has retained.

After several years, during which the little post maintained a precarious existence in

The Ohio, from Marietta.

At Muskingum.

the wilderness, Pontiac's conspiracy burst upon the country, and Fort Pitt, with its handful of men, was closely invested by the Indians, who had succeeded in capturing nine of the British forts in the west, Detroit and Niagara alone escaping. Colonel Bouquet, a Swiss officer, whose flowery name brightens the sombre pages of Ohio-River history, as his deeds brightened the sombre reality, came to the rescue of Fort Pitt, supplied the garrison with provisions, and dispersed the Indians. Soon after this the French gave up their claim to the territory, and then began the contest between the Americans and the British. But the river-country was far away in a wilderness beyond the mountains; and in 1772 General Gage, the commander-in-chief of the British forces, sent orders to abandon Fort Pitt, and accordingly the post, which had cost the English Government sixty thousand pounds, and which was designed to secure forever British empire on the Beautiful River, passed into the hands of the Americans.

The present city of Pittsburg has the picturesque aspect of a volcano, owing to its numerous manufactories; a cloud of smoke rests over it, and at night it is illuminated by the glow and flash of the iron-mills filling its valley and stretching up its hill-sides, resting not day or night, but ever ceaselessly gleaming, smoking, and roaring. Looking down on Pittsburg at night from the summit of its surrounding hills, the city, with its red fires and smoke, seems satanic. Quiet streets there are, and pleasant residences; the

Baltimore and Ohio Railroad-Bridge, Parkersburg, Va.

two rivers winding down on either side, and uniting at the point of the peninsula, the graceful bridges, the water-craft of all kinds lying at the levee, some coming from far New Orleans, and others bound up the slack-water into the interior, are all picturesque. But it is the smoke and the fires of Pittsburg that give it its character. Imaginative people, beholding it by night, are moved to sulphurous quotations, and bethink themselves of Dante's "Inferno;" and, as Mr. Brooke, of Middlemarch, would say, "that sort of thing."

Anthony Trollope wrote, "It is the blackest place I ever saw, but its very blackness is picturesque." Parton said, "It is all hell with the lid taken off." In the face of the facts to the contrary, you fancy that Pittsburg must be a wicked city; and, as the boat glides away, verses come to your memory about "the smoke of her torment ascending forever and ever." What a grand, lurid picture Turner, Ruskin's art-god, would have made of Pittsburg by night!

The river starts away in a northwestern direction. On its banks, nineteen miles from Pittsburg, is the quaint German town of Economy, founded by Father Rapp, a German pietist, who emigrated with a colony from Würtemberg in 1804. The little band of believers, in what seems to us a dreary creed, made one or two changes of location; but, after selling their possessions. in Indiana to the well-known Robert Owen, a man of kindred enthusiasm but opposite belief, they came to the Ohio River, where their village, with its Old-World houses, tiled roofs, grass-grown streets, and quiet air, seems hardly to belong to this practical, busy, American world. Economy is a still abode of the old; there are no homes, no children there, only gray-haired brothers and sisters, who are waiting for a literal realization of the promises of the millennium. The society is rich in land, oil-wells, and other possessions, all held in common; and the thought arises, Who is to inherit this wealth when the last aged brother has been buried in the moundless, stoneless cemetery, where the pilgrims lie unmarked under the even sod?

The course of the river here is dotted with old derricks—tombstones of high hopes; in the little ravines, where the creeks come down to the Ohio, these gaunt frameworks stand thick, like masts in a harbor, as far as you can see. They are pathetic spectres in their way, for they tell a story of disappointment. One would suppose that the great beams were worth taking down; but, generally, the buildings and engine-house are all complete, abandoned just as they stood.

The State of Ohio reaches the river at Columbiana County. This was a fancy name, formed from Columbus and Anna. One asks, "Why Anna, more than Maria or Jane?" and this, no doubt, was the feeling of that member of the Ohio Legislature, who, pending its adoption, rose and proposed the addition of Maria as more euphonious, thus making a grand total of Columbianamaria! Opposite, as the river turns abruptly down toward the south, is the queer little strip of land which Virginia thrusts up toward the north, the ownership of which is probably due to some of the fierce quarrels and compromises over land-titles which came after the Revolution, and made almost as much trouble as the great struggle itself. This northern arm is called the Pan-Handle, Virginia, undivided, being the pan. A railroad going west from Pittsburg has taken the name, much to the bewilderment of uninitiated travellers, who frequently called it Pen-Handle, with a vague idea that it has something to do with stocks and accounts.

Three miles below Steubenville was an old Mingo town, the residence of Logan, the Mingo chief. This celebrated Indian was the son of a Cayuga chieftain of Pennsylvania, who was converted to Christianity by the Moravian missionaries, the only rivals of the Jesuit fathers in the West. The Cayuga chief, greatly admiring James Logan, the secretary of the province, named his son after him. Logan took no part in the old French War, and remained a firm friend of the whites until the causeless murder of all his family on the Ohio River, above Steubenville. From that time his hand was against the white man, although, from the curt records of the day, we learn that he was sin-

SCENES ON THE OHIO.

gularly magnanimous to all white prisoners. The last years of Logan were lonely. He wandered from tribe to tribe, and was finally murdered by one of his own race on the banks of the Detroit River, as he sat before a camp-fire, with his blanket over his head, buried in thought. But his words live after him. Logan's speech still holds its place in the school reading-books by the side of the best efforts of English orators.

The river, as it stretches southward, is here fair enough to justify its name. The Virginia shore is wild and romantic, full of associations of the late war, when its mountain-roads were a raiding-ground, and its campaigns a series of cavalry-chases, without those bloody combats that darkened the States farther south. There was not much glory for either side in Western Virginia, if glory means death; but there were many bold rides and many long dashes over the border and back again, as the dwellers in the rambling old river farm-houses, with their odd little enclosed upper piazzas, know. At Wheeling the national road, a relic of stage-coach days, crosses the river on its westward way. This turnpike was constructed by the national government, beginning at Cumberland, in Maryland, crossing the mountains, and intended to run indefinitely on westward as the country became settled. But railroads took away its glory, and the occasional traveller now finds it difficult to get an explanation of this neglected work, its laborious construction and solid stone bridges striking him as he passes through Central Ohio, although the careless inhabitants neither know nor care about its origin. In the Old World it would pass as a Roman road.

Marietta, in Washington County, Ohio, is the oldest town in the State. It is situated in the domains of the New-England "Ohio Company," which was originally organized to check the advance of the French down the river. Marietta has a picturesque position, lying in a deep bend where the Muskingum flows into the Ohio, with a slender, curved island opposite, like a green crescent, and, beyond, the high, rolling hills of Virginia on the southern shore. The Ohio Company owned one million five hundred thousand acres along the river; and, in November, 1787, they sent out their first colony, forty-seven men, who, taking Braddock's road, originally an Indian trail over the mountains, and trudging on patiently all winter, arrived at the Youghiogheny, or "Yoh," as they called it, in April, and, launching a flat-boat, sailed down to the mouth of the Muskingum, where they made a settlement, naming it Marietta, in honor of Marie Antoinette. These pioneers were New-Englanders; their flat-boat was called the Mayflower; and their first act on landing was, to write a set of laws and nail them to a tree. Washington said of them, " No colony in America was settled under such favorable auspices as that on the Muskingum." A little stockade-post, called Fort Harmar, had been built here two years before. It was occupied by a detachment of United States troops, who did good service in protecting the infant colony from the Indians, and then moved on toward Cincinnati. Emigrants, soldiers, and Indians, are always, like poor Jo, "moving on." The little village on the bank of the Muskingum bears the name of the old post, Harmar. At Marietta were found the remains of an ancient fortification—a square, enclosed by a wall of earth ten feet high, with twelve entrances, containing a covert way, bulwarks to defend the gate-ways, and various works of elaborate construction, including a moat fifteen feet wide, defended by a parapet. These are supposed to belong to the era of the mound-builders. At this little inland settlement ship-building was at one period the principal occupation, and the town was made a port of clearance. There is a curious incident connected with this. In 1806 a ship, built at Marietta, sailed to New Orleans with a cargo of pork; and, as at that time the American vessels were the carriers for the world, it went on to England with cotton, and thence to St. Petersburg, where the officer of the port seized the little ship, declaring that its papers were fraudulent, since there was no such seaport as Marietta. But the captain, with some difficulty procuring a map, pointed out the mouth of the Mississippi, and traced its course up to the Ohio, and thence on to Marietta. The astonished officer, when this seaport in the heart of a continent was shown to him, allowed the adventurous little vessel to go free. Thirteen miles below Marietta is Parkersburg, in West Virginia; the old Belpré, or Beautiful Meadow, in Ohio, opposite; and near by, in the river, Blennerhassett's Island, which has gone into history with Aaron Burr.

At Parkersburg the Little Kanawha flows into the Ohio, which is here crossed by the massive iron bridge of the Baltimore and Ohio Railroad. Farther on is Gallipolis, where, in 1790, a French colony laid out a village of eighty cabins, protected by a stockade, and, even in the face of starvation, took time to build a ballroom, and danced there twice a week. Anxious to get away from the horrors of the Revolution, ignorant of the country, deceived by land-speculators, these poor Frenchmen—carvers, gilders, coach- and peruke-makers, five hundred persons in all, with only ten laborers among them—sold all they had, and embarked for the New World, believing that a paradise was ready for them on the banks of the beautiful river. They named their village the City of the French; and, unfitted as they were for frontier-life, they worked with a will, if not with skill. Early accounts give a ludicrous picture of their attempts to clear the land. A number of them would assemble around some giant sycamore; part would pull at the branches with ropes; and part would hack at the trunk all around until the ground was covered with chips, and the tree gashed from top to bottom; a whole day would be spent in the task, and, when at last the tree fell, it generally carried with it some of its awkward executioners. To get rid of a fallen tree they would make a deep trench alongside, and, with many a shout, push it in and bury it out of sight— certainly a novel method of clearing land. Little is now left to show the French origin of Gallipolis save a few French names.

At the mouth of the Great Kanawha, on the Virginia side, is Point Pleasant. This stream is the principal river of West Virginia, rising in the mountains and winding through a picturesque country northward to the Ohio. Point Pleasant was the site of

CINCINNATI, VIEW FROM THE CARLISLE HOTEL.

Fourth Street, Cincinnati.

the bloodiest Indian battle of the river-valley, when, in 1774, one thousand Americans were attacked by the flower of the Western tribes under the chieftain Cornstalk. The battle raged all day, but the Indians were finally overpowered, and retreated to their towns on the Chillicothe plains.

Kentucky, which comes up to the Ohio at the mouth of the big Sandy River, is one of the most beautiful States in the country. It is wild without being rugged, luxuriant but not closely cultivated; once seen, its rolling meadows are never forgotten. It is like some beautiful wild creature which you cannot entirely tame, in spite of its gentleness.

Stretching back from the river are vast parks; there is no underbrush, few fences, and few grain-fields; the trees are majestic, each one by itself, and here and there stands a bold hill, or a river comes sweeping over a limestone-bed. It is the grazing-country of America; the wealth of its people is in their flocks and herds; and there is a tradition that they love their horses better than their sweethearts (let us rescue that last sweet old word from misuse). Some miles back from the river lies the famous Blue-Grass Country, so called from the blue tinge of the grass when in blossom. This district embraces five counties, the loveliest in Kentucky, where you may ride for miles through a park dotted with herds, single trees, and here and there a grove shadowing the rolling, green turf. Until 1747 no Anglo-Saxon foot had touched Kentucky, whose

"The Rhine."

forests were the Indians' favorite hunting-ground; the immigration, when it did commence, came from Virginia and Maryland. Daniel Boone is the type of the Kentucky hunter. Leaving North Carolina in 1769, he came westward to examine the new hunting-fields, and, after three years of wandering, he returned to bring his family to the wild home he had chosen. The country is full of legends of Boone, and his name lingers on rocks and streams. The old man became restless under the growing civilization, and went to Missouri, where he could hunt undisturbed. He died, almost with gun in hand, in 1820, at the age of eighty-nine. A prophet is not always without honor in his own country: the people of Kentucky brought back the body of the old hunter, and interred it on the banks of the river he loved in life—in Kain-tuck-ee, the "Land of the Cane."

Cincinnati, the Queen of the West, was first settled in 1778. It lies in Symmes's Purchase—land stretching between the Great and Little Miami, called in early descriptions the Miami Country. Judge Symmes's nephew and namesake was the author of the theory of "Concentric Spheres," a theory popularly rendered as "Symmes's Hole." He was buried on the Purchase, and his monument is surmounted by a globe, open, according to his theory, at the poles. Cincinnati—too generally pronounced *Cincinnater*—received its high-sounding name from General St. Clair, in honor of a military society to

View on the Rhine.

which he belonged. The general rescued the infant town from a worse fate, since it was then laboring under the title of Losantiville—*L*, the first letter of the river Licking, which flows into the Ohio, on the Kentucky side; *os*, the mouth; *anti*, opposite to; and *ville*, a city. The author of this conglomerate did not long survive.

Cincinnati was founded in romance. There were two other rival settlements on the river, and all three were striving for the possession of the United States fort. North Bend was selected, the work begun, when one of the settlers, observing that the bright eyes of his wife had attracted the attention of the commanding officer, moved to Cincinnati. But immediately Cincinnati was discovered to be the better site, and materials and men were moved up the river without delay. North Bend was left to its fate, and Cincinnati, owing to the bright eyes, obtained an advantage over her rivals from that time, steadily progressing toward her present population, which, including her suburbs, is nearly four hundred thousand. The city proper is closely built in solid blocks, rising in several plateaus back from the river; it is surrounded by a circle of hills, through which

The Tyler-Davidson Fountain.

flow the Little Miami and Mill Creek. There are many fine buildings in Cincinnati; but the beauty of the city is in its suburbs, where, upon the Clifton Hills, are the most picturesque residences of the entire West—beautiful, castle-like mansions, with sweeping parks and a wide outlook over the valley. The people of Cincinnati do not live in their city; they attend to their business affairs there and retire out to the hills when work is over. They have an air of calm contentment and indifference to the rest of the

LOUISVILLE, FROM THE BLIND ASYLUM

world; they know they are masters of the river. Pittsburg is lurid and busy; Louisville is fair and indolent; but Cincinnati is the queen. She has no specialty like Buffalo with her elevators, Louisville with her bourbon-warehouses, Cleveland with her oil-refineries, and Pittsburg with her iron-mills; or, rather, she has them all, and therefore any one is not noticeable. Within the city is one picturesque locality—the German quarter—known as "Over the Rhine," the Miami Canal representing the Rhine. Here the German signs, the flaxen-haired children, the old women in 'kerchiefs knitting at the doors, the lager-beer, the window-gardens and climbing vines, the dense population, and, at evening, the street-music of all kinds, are at once foreign and southern. In the centre of the city is the Tyler-Davidson Fountain—one of the most beautiful fountains in the world. The figures are bronze, cast at Munich, Bavaria, at a cost of one hundred thousand dollars. The fountain is a memorial, presented to the city by one of its millionnaires, in memory of a relative. It bears the inscription, "To the People of Cincinnati;" and the people are constantly drinking from the four drinking-fountains at the corners, or looking up to the grand goddess above, who, from her beneficent, outstretched hands, seems to be sending rain down upon a thirsty land.

Below Cincinnati are the vineyards, stretching up the hills along the northern shore. Floating down the river in the spring and seeing the green ranks of the vines, one is moved to exclaim, "*This* is the most beautiful of all," forgetting that the mountains of Virginia and the parks of Kentucky have already called forth the same words. The native Catawba wine of the West was first made in Cincinnati, and the juices of the vineyards of the Beautiful River have gained an honorable name among wines.

Bellevue, in Kentucky, and Patriot, in Indiana, are charming specimens of river-scenery, the latter showing the hill-side vineyards.

The navigation of the Ohio is obstructed by tow-heads and sand-bars, and by the remarkable changes in its depth, there being a variation of fifty feet between high and low water-mark. In the early days a broad river was the safest highway, as the forests on shore concealed a treacherous foe who coveted the goods of the immigrant; hence once over the mountains, families purchased a flat-boat and floated down-stream, hugging the Kentucky shore. These Kentucky flats were made of green oak-plank, fastened by wooden pins to a frame of timber, and calked with tow, and, upon reaching their destination, the immigrants used the material in building their cabins. As villages grew up larger craft were introduced, keel-boats and barges, the former employing ten hands, the latter fifty; both had a mast, a square-sail, and coils of cordage, known as *cordilles*, and when the wind was adverse they were propelled by long poles, the crew walking to and fro, bending over their toilsome track.

The boatmen of the Ohio were a hardy, merry race, poling their unwieldy craft slowly along, or gliding on under sail, sounding a bugle as they approached a village, and shouting out their compliments to the girls, who, attracted by the music, came down to the shore to see them pass. They wore red handkerchiefs on their heads, turban-fashion, and talked in a jargon of their own, half French, half Indian; a violin formed part of their equipment; and at night, drawn up at some village, they danced on the

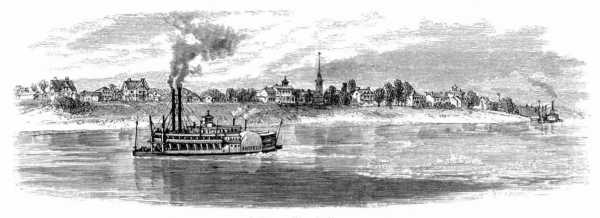

Jeffersonville, Indiana.

flat tops of their boats—the original minstrels. In this way, as the old song has it, "They glided down the river, the O-hi-o." At the present day these flats, or arks, are still seen, propelled with great sweeps instead of poles. They keep out of the steamboat channel, and lead a vagabond life, trading at the settlements where the steamers do not stop. They are seen drawn up in the shallows, all hands smoking or lying half asleep, as if there was no such thing as work in the world. A canal-boat is a high-toned, industrious boat compared with one of these arks; for a canal-boat is bound somewhere, and goes on time, although it may be slow time, while the ark is bound nowhere in

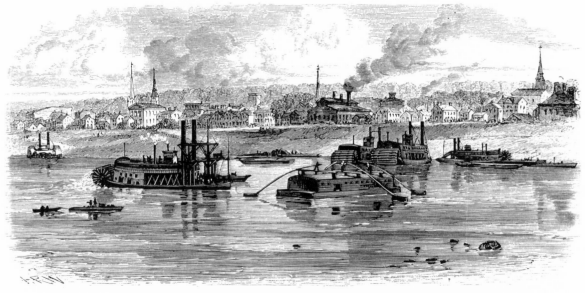

New Albany, Indiana.

particular, and is as likely as not to take a whole summer for one trip down the river. The majority of the Ohio-River craft are tow-boats, black, puffing monsters, mere grimy shells to cover a powerful engine. If tow means to pull, then the name of tow-boat is a misnomer; for these boats never pull, but always push. Their tows go in front, two or three abreast, heavy, open flat-boats, filled with coal or rafts of timber, and behind comes the steamer pushing them slowly along, her great stern-wheel churning up the water behind, and her smoke-stacks belching forth black streams. Negroes do most of the work on the river, and enliven toil with their antics. A night-landing is picturesque; an iron basket, filled with flaming pine-knots, is hung out on the end of a pole, and then, down over the plank stream the negro hands, jerking themselves along with song and joke, carrying heavy freight with a kind of uncouth, dancing step, and stopping to laugh with a freedom that would astonish the crew of a lake-propeller accustomed to do the same work in half the time under the sharp eye of a laconic mate.

Jeffersonville, Indiana, is a thriving town nearly opposite Louisville. Here is the only fall in the Ohio River—a descent of twenty-three feet in two miles, a very mild cataract, hardly more than a rapid. Such as it is, however, it obstructs navigation at low stages of water, and a canal has been cut around it through the solid rock. New Albany, Indiana, a few miles below, is an important and handsomely-situated town.

Louisville—pronounced *Louyville* at the North, but *Louisville*, with the *s* carefully sounded, by the citizens themselves—is a large, bright city, the pride of Kentucky. It was first settled by Virginians in 1773, and remained for some time under the protection of the mother-State; even now, to have been born in Virginia is a Louisville patent of nobility. The city is built on a sloping plane seventy feet above low-water mark, with broad streets lined with stately stone warehouses on and near the river, and beautiful residences farther back. Louisville has a more Southern aspect than Pittsburg and Cincinnati. Here you meet great wains piled with cotton-bales; the windows are shaded with awnings; and the residences swarm with servants—turbaned negro cooks, who are artists in their line; waiting-maids with the stately manners of their old mistresses; and innumerable children—eight or ten pairs of hands to do the work for one family.

In the Court-House is a life-like statue of Henry Clay, a man whose memory Kentucky delights to honor. His grave is at Lexington—the most stately tomb in the West, if not in all America. At Louisville, also, begin the double graves of the late war. The beautiful cemetery contains two plats where the dead armies lie—Confederate soldiers on one side, Union soldiers on the other. The little wooden head-boards tell sad stories: "Aged twenty-two;" "aged twenty-three." Often there are whole rows who died on the same day, the wounded of some Southwestern battle, who came as far as Louisville in the crowded freight-cars, and died there in the hospital. While the fathers and mothers, while the widows of the dead soldiers live, there will continue to be two Decoration Days. But the next generation will lay its wreaths upon all the graves alike, and gradually the day will grow into a holy memory of all the dead, citizen and soldier, as Time sends the story of the war back into the annals of the past.

THE PLAINS AND THE SIERRAS.

WITH ILLUSTRATIONS BY THOMAS MORAN.

Witches' Rocks, Weber Cañon.

THE present banishes the past so quickly in this busy continent that to the
younger generation of to-day it already seems a very dreamy and distant heroic
age when men went out upon the great prairies of the West as upon a dreaded kind

of unknown sea. Even now, perhaps, there is a little spice of adventure for the quieter New-England citizen, as he gathers around him the prospective contents of a comfortable travelling-trunk, and glances at his long slip of printed railway-tickets, preparatory to thundering westward to look out at the great stretch of the Plains from the ample window of a perfectly-upholstered sleeping-car; but how remote the day seems when men tightened their pistol-belts and looked to their horses, and throbbed (if they were young) with something of the proud consciousness of explorers; and so set out, from the frontier settlement of civilization, upon that great ocean of far-reaching, level grass-land and desert, to cross which was a deed to be talked of like the voyage of the old Minyæ! A single title of Mr. Harte's has preserved for us the whole spirit of those seemingly old-time journeys; he has called the travellers "the Argonauts of '49," and in this one phrase lies the complete picture of that already dim and distant venture—the dreaded crossing of "the Plains."

But, although the "prairie schooner"—the great white-tented wagon of the gold-seekers and the pioneers—and its adjuncts, and the men that rode beside it, have disappeared, we cannot change the Plains themselves in a decade. We encroach a little upon their borders, it may be, and learn of a narrow strip of their surface, but they themselves remain practically untouched by the civilization that brushes over them; they close behind the scudding train like the scarce broader ocean behind the stoutest steamer of the moderns—a vast expanse as silent and unbroken and undisturbed as it lay centuries before ever rail or keel was dreamed of. It is our point of view that has changed, not they; and for all of us there remain the same wonders to be looked upon in this great half-known region as were there for the earliest Indian fighter—the first of the adventurous souls that went mine-hunting toward the Golden Gate.

Our time, it is true, attaches a different signification to the title, "the Plains," from that which it bore little more than a quarter of a century ago. In reality, there extends from the very central portion of the now well-peopled Western States to the very foot of the Rocky Mountains one vast reach of prairie—the most remarkable, in all its features, on the globe. On the eastern portion of this are now the thoroughly settled, grain-bearing States—full of fertile farms and great cities, and no longer connected in our minds, as they were in those of men a generation before us, with the untried lands of exploration and adventure. For us, the boundary of the region of the comparatively unknown has been driven back beyond the Mississippi, beyond the Missouri, even; and the Eastern citizen, be he ever so thoroughly the town-bred man, is at home until he crosses the muddy, sluggish water that flows under Council Bluffs, and hardly passes out of the land of most familiar objects until the whistle of the "Pacific express," that carries him, is no longer heard in Omaha, and he is fairly under way on the great level of Nebraska.

The route of the Pacific Railway is not only that which for many years will be the most familiar path across the Plains, and not only that which passes nearest to the well-known emigrant-road of former days, but it is also the road which, though it misses the nobler beauties of the Rocky Mountains, shows the traveller the prairie itself

Red Buttes, Laramie Plains.

in perhaps as true and characteristic an aspect as could be found on any less-tried course. It passes through almost every change of prairie scenery —the fertile land of the east and the alkali region farther on; past the historic outposts of the old pioneers; among low *buttes* and infrequent "islands;" and over a country abounding in points of view from which one may take in all the features that mark this portion of the continent. To the south, the great level expanse is hardly interrupted before the shore of the Gulf of Mexico is reached, and the Mexican boundary; to the north, the hills and high table-land of the Upper Missouri are the only breaks this side of the Canadian border. Through almost the middle of this vast and clear expanse the Union Pacific Railway runs east and west—a line of life flowing like a river through the great plain—the Kansas Pacific joining it at the middle of its course, a tributary of no small importance.

Omaha—most truly typical of those border towns that, all the world over, spring up on the verge of the civilized where the unexplored begins—stands looking out upon the muddy water of the Missouri, and watching with interested eyes that transient traveller whom it generally entices in vain to linger long within its precincts—a town that has been all its life a starting-place; to which hardly anybody has ever come with the thought of staying, so far as one can learn from hearsay; and yet, in spite of the fact

DIAL ROCK, RED BUTTES, LARAMIE PLAINS.

that every man seems to arrive only with the thought of departing, a prosperous, thrifty town, not without a look of permanence, though not of any age beyond the memory of the youngest inhabitant. In its directory, which the writer once chanced to read with some care, in a waiting hour, you may find facts that will startle you about the rapidity of its growth and the splendor of its resources. At its station, one feels a little of the old-time pioneer feeling, as he seems to cut the chain that binds him to Eastern life, and is whirled out upon the great grassy sea he has looked at wonderingly from the Omaha hills.

The word "valley," in this apparently unbroken plain, seems a misnomer; but it is everywhere used—as in regions where its significance is truer—for the slight depression that accompanies the course of every stream; and an old traveller of the Plains will tell you that you are "entering the valley of the Platte," or "coming out of the Papillon Valley," with as much calmness as though you were entering or leaving the rockiest and wildest cañon of the Sierras. And the valley of the Platte, whereof he speaks, lies before one almost immediately after he has left the Missouri behind him. There is only a short reach of railway to the northwest, a sharp turn to the westward, and the clear stream of the river is beside the track—a clear, full channel if the water is high, a collection of brooks threading their way through sandy banks if it is low. For more than a whole day the railway runs beside the stream, and neither to the north nor south is there noteworthy change in the general features of the scenery. A vast, fertile plain, at first interrupted here and there by bluffs, and for some distance not seldom dotted by a settler's house, or by herds of cattle; then a more monotonous region, still green and bright in aspect; farther on—beyond Fort Kearney, and Plum Creek, and McPherson, all memorable stations with many associations from earlier times—a somewhat sudden dying away of the verdure, and a barren country, broken by a few ravines. This, again, gives place, however, to a better region as the Wyoming boundary is approached.

Along this reach of the railway, in its earlier days, stood ambitious "cities," two or three whose ruins are the only reminders now of their existence. They are odd features of this part of the great prairie, these desolate remains of places not a little famous in their time, and now almost forgotten. The walls of deserted *adobe* houses, wherein men sat and planned great futures for these towns in embryo, look at you drearily, not seldom watching over the graves of their owners, whose schemings were nipped in the very bud by the decisive revolver-bullet or the incisive bowie, as the unquiet denizens of the mushroom metropolis extirpated their fellow-citizens like true pioneers, and "moved on" to the next "terminus of the road."

The Wyoming border crossed, a new region is entered. The Plains do not end, but they are already closely bordered, within sight, by the far-outlying spurs of the Rocky Mountains. Beyond the civilized oasis of Cheyenne, the scenery takes on a darker look, and, if one chances to come to the little station of Medicine Bow when

Buttes, Green River.

the sunset begins to cast long shadows from the black mountains on the southern side of the North Fork of the Platte, there is something almost sombre in the aspect of the shaded plain. The Laramie plains have just been passed; indeed, they still lie to the northward. Hills break the monotony of their horizon, and here and there the regular forms of castellated *buttes* stand out sharply against the sky. The far-off Red Buttes are most noteworthy and most picturesque of these;

grouped together like giant fortresses, with fantastic towers and walls, they lift ragged edges above the prairie, looking lonely, weird, and strong. Among the singular shapes their masses of stone assume, the strangely-formed and pillar-like Dial Rocks tower up— four columns of worn and scarred sandstone, like the supports of some ruined cromlech built by giants. About them, and, indeed, through the whole region about the little settlements and army-posts, from the place called Wyoming, on to Bitter Creek—ominously named—the country is a barren, unproductive waste. The curse of the sage-brush, and even of alkali, is upon it, and it is dreary and gloomy everywhere save on the hills.

Only with the approach to Green River does the verdure come again—and then only here and there, generally close by the river-bank. Here the picturesque forms of the buttes reappear—a welcome relief to the monotony that has marked the outlook during the miles of level desert that are past. The distance, too, is changed, and no longer is like the great surface of a sea. To the north, forming the horizon, stretches the Wind-River Range—named with a breezy poetry that we miss in the later nomenclature of the race that has followed after the pioneers. To the south lie the Uintah Mountains.

At some little distance from the railway the great Black Buttes rise up for hundreds of feet, terminating in round and rough-ribbed towers. And other detached columns of stone stand near them—the Pilot, seen far off in the view that Mr. Moran has drawn of the river and its cliffs. And through all this region fantastic forms abound everywhere, the architecture of Nature exhibited in sport. An Eastern journalist—a traveller here in the first days of the Pacific Railway—has best enumerated the varied shapes. All about one, he says, lie "long, wide troughs, as of departed rivers; long, level embankments, as of railroad-tracks or endless fortifications; huge, quaint hills, suddenly rising from the plain, bearing fantastic shapes; great square mounds of rock and earth, half-formed, half-broken pyramids—it would seem as if a generation of giants had built and buried here, and left their work to awe and humble a puny succession."

The Church Butte is the grandest of the groups that rise in this singular and striking series of tower-like piles of stone. It lies somewhat further on, beyond the little station of Bryan, and forms a compact and imposing mass of rock, with an outlying spur that has even more than the main body the air of human, though gigantic architecture. It "imposes on the imagination," says Mr. Bowles, in one of his passages of clear description, "like a grand old cathedral going into decay—quaint in its crumbling ornaments, majestic in its height and breadth." And of the towering forms of the whole group, he says: "They seem, like the more numerous and fantastic illustrations of Nature's frolicksome art in Southern Colorado, to be the remains of granite hills that wind and water, and especially the sand whirlpools that march with lordly force through the air—literally moving mountains—have left to tell the story of their own achievements. Not unfitly, there as here, they have won the title of 'Monuments to the Gods.'"

CLIFFS OF GREEN RIVER.

This point on the Plains, where the mountains—the main chains running northwest and southeast—seem to send out transverse ranges and outlying spurs to intersect the prairie in all directions—if, indeed, we may speak of prairie any longer where the level reaches are so small as here among the Rocks—has interests beyond those of its merely picturesque scenery. While we have spoken of the cliffs and *buttes*, the route we are pursuing has crossed the "backbone of the continent"—that great water-shed where the waters that flow through the whole east of the country separate from those that descend toward the west. It is at Sherman—which its proud neighbors and few residents will haughtily but truly describe to you as "the highest railway-station in the world"—

Church Butte, Utah.

that the greatest elevation is reached; for the little group of buildings there lies eight thousand two hundred and thirty-five feet above sea-level. It is impossible to realize that this height has been attained, the ascent has been so gradual, the scenery so un-marked by those sharp and steep forms which we are accustomed always to associate with great mountains.

It is a characteristic of this whole portion of the Rocky-Mountain chain, and one that disappoints many a traveller, that there are here no imposing and ragged peaks, no sharp summits, no snow-covered passes, and little that is wild and rugged. All that those who remember Switzerland have been accustomed to connect in their minds with great

Castle Rock, Echo Cañon.

groups of mountain-masses must be sought elsewhere. The Plains themselves rise; one does not leave them in order to climb. Over a vast, grass-covered, almost unbroken, gradual slope, extending over hundreds of miles of country, the wayfarer has come imperceptibly to the great water-shed. It is scenery of prairie, not of hills and peaks, that has surrounded his journey.

For the last fifty miles, indeed, before the arrival at Sherman, the rise has been barely appreciable; but that is all. A new circumstance makes the descent from the great height much more perceptible and enjoyable through a new sensation. It is then that the traveller over duller Eastern roads, who has flattered himself that the "lightning express" of his own region was the highest possible form of railway speed, first learns the real meaning of a "down grade." The descent from Sherman to the Laramie Plains is a new experience to such people as have not slid down a Russian ice-hill, or fallen from a fourth-story window. Let the hardy individual who would enjoy it to the full betake himself to the last platform of the last car, or the foremost platform of the front one, and there hold hard to brake or railing, to watch the bewitched world spin and whirl.

But we have returned a long distance on our course. We have reached the Church Butte, beyond Bryan, and had crossed Green River, near the place where, on the old overland stage-route and the emigrant-road, travellers used years ago to ford the stream—no unwelcome task, with that great Bitter-Creek waste of alkali still fresh in the memories and hardly out of their view. At Bryan Station, too, there is an offshoot from the regular path, in the form of a long stage-road, leading away into the northeast to the picturesque mining-region of Sweetwater, a hundred miles distant, where man has spent endless toil in searching for deceptive "leads."

The main line of the great railway goes on beyond Green River through the valley of a stream that flows down from the Uintah Mountains; and, leaving at the south Fort Bridger and crossing the old Mormon road, enters Utah. A little farther, and we are among the noblest scenes of the journey this side the far-away Sierras.

As on the Rhine, the long stretch of the river from Mainz to Cologne has been for years, by acknowledgment, "*the* river," so that portion of the Pacific Railway that lies between Wasatch and Ogden, in this northernmost corner of Utah, will some day be that part of the journey across the centre of the continent that will be especially regarded by the tourist as necessary to be seen beyond all others. It does not in grandeur approach the mountain-scenery near the western coast, but it is unique; it is something, the counterpart of which you can see nowhere in the world; and, long after the whole Pacific journey is as hackneyed in the eyes of Europeans and Americans as is the Rhine tour now, this part of it will keep its freshness among the most marked scenes of the journey. It is a place which cities and settlements cannot destroy.

A short distance west from Wasatch Station the road passes through a tunnel nearly eight hundred feet in length. The preparation for what is to come could not be better; and, indeed, the whole bleak and dreary region that has been passed over adds so much to the freshness and picturesqueness of these Utah scenes that it may very possibly have contributed not a little to the enthusiasm they have called forth. From the darkness the train emerges suddenly, and, tunnel and cutting being passed, there lies before the traveller a view of the green valley before the entrance to Echo Cañon. Through it flows the Weber River, bordered with trees, and making a scene that is suddenly deprived of all the weirdness and look of dreary devastation that has marked the country through so many miles of this long journey. The valley is not so broad, so pastoral in aspect, as that which comes after the wild scenery of the first cañon is passed; but it is like a woodland valley of home lying here in the wilderness.

WEBER RIVER–ENTRANCE TO ECHO CAÑON.

Near the head of Echo Cañon stands Castle Rock, one of the noblest of the great natural landmarks that are passed in all the route—a vast and ragged pile of massive stone, fantastically cut, by all those mighty forces that toil through the centuries, into the very semblance of a mountain-fortress. A cavernous opening simulates a giant door of entrance between its rounded and overhanging towers; the jagged points above are like the ruins of battlements left bristling and torn after combats of Titans; the huge layers of its worn sides seem to have been builded by skilful hands; and the great rounded foundations, from which the sandy soil has been swept away, would appear rooted in the very central earth. It surmounts a lofty, steep-sided eminence, and frowns down with an awesome strength and quiet on the lonely valley below it.

It is a great ruin of Nature, not of human structure; and its grandeur is different in kind and in degree from those other relics in an older world, wherewith human history is associated in every mind, which hold for us everywhere the memories of human toil and action. It is a strangely different feeling that this grand pile, made with no man's hands, gives us as we look up at it. It has stood alone longer than whole races have been in the world. Its lines were shaped with no thought, it seems, of those that were to see them; the purposeless wind and sand and rain have been busy at it for vast cycles of time, and at the end it is a thing of art—a great lesson of rude architecture.

Beyond it the road enters the Echo Cañon itself. It is a narrow gorge between rocky walls that tower hundreds of feet above its uneven floor, along which the river runs with a stream as bright and clear as at its very source. Not simply a straight cut between its precipices of red-and-dark-stained stone, but a winding valley, with every turn presenting some new variation of its wonderful scenery. On the mountains that form its sides there is little verdure—only a dwarfed growth of pine scattered here and there, leaving the steeper portions of the rock bare and ragged in outline. Now and then there are little openings, where the great walls spread apart and little glades are formed; but these are no less picturesque than the wilder passages.

There are memorable places here. Half-way down the gorge is Hanging Rock, where Brigham Young spoke to his deluded hundreds after their long pilgrimage, and pointed out to them that they approached their Canaan—preached the Mormons' first sermon in the " Promised Land." Full of all that is wild and strange, as is this rocky valley, seen even from the prosaic window of a whirling railway-car, what must it have been with the multitude of fanatics, stranger than all its strangeness, standing on its varied floor and looking up at the speaking prophet, whom they half believed, half feared? The weary multitude of half-excited, half-stolid faces turned toward the preacher; the coarse, strong, wild words of the leader echoing from the long-silent rocks—why has no one ever pictured for us all of the scene that could be pictured?

A relic of the early Mormon days, but not a proud one, is some miles away from

MONUMENT ROCK, ECHO CAÑON.

this, high on the rocks; an unnoticeable ruin of the little fortifications once for a very short time occupied by the United States troops, in the presidency of Buchanan, when a trifling detachment of soldiers made a perfectly vain and indecisive show of interfering with the rule of the rebellious saints. The ruin is hardly more important than the attempt; yet it deserves mention, if only as commemorative of an episode that the future historian, if he notes it at all, will connect with this rocky region of hard marches and ill-fated emigrants.

The cañon is not long; the train dashes through it at sharp pace; and suddenly, without passing any point of view that gives the traveller a warning glance ahead, it turns and dashes out into the beautiful and broad valley beyond, halting at Echo City— most picturesque and bright of little villages, destined, perhaps, to realize its ambitious name some time in the remotest future.

The scene here is—as has been said in advance—a really pastoral one. The broad plain, left by the encircling mountains, is green and fresh; the river winds through its grassy expanse in pleasant quiet, without brawl or rush; the trees are like those in a familiar Eastern country-side. Only the great outlines of the surrounding hills, and here and there the appearance on the horizon of some sharper, higher, more distant peaks, show the traveller his whereabouts, and take his mind from the quieter aspect of what lies about him. Near by, in valleys leading into this, are various Mormon settlements; for we are already in the country of the saints.

But the grandest gorge is still to come; and the road enters it almost at once after crossing the little plain. It is Weber Cañon—the greatest of these Utah ravines. Its immense walls are grander by far than those of Echo; the forms of their ragged edges and the carvings of their surfaces are more fantastic; and the deep, dark aspect of the whole narrow valley gives in every way a nobler scene. It should be viewed on a cloudy, gloomy day, to realize its whole look of wild grandeur. The little river brawls at the left of the track; the thunder of the locomotive echoes from the high precipices at its sides; the rush of the train's onward motion adds a certain additional wildness to the shadowy place.

The old emigrant-road passes through the cañon, like the railway. It crosses and recrosses the river, and winds among the trees along the banks, sometimes lost to view from the train. Little frequented as it is in these days, the writer has seen, within a very few years, a "prairie schooner" of the old historic form passing along it; a rough, strong emigrant riding beside it; children's faces looking out between the folds of the cloth covering; and household goods dimly discernible within. And at one of the river-crossings is a mark that must often have given renewed hope or pain to many a one among this family's predecessors—the famous old "Thousand-Mile Tree," that stands at just that weary distance from Omaha, even farther from the great city by the Golden Gate.

DEVIL'S GATE, WEBER CAÑON.

Whoever follows the nomenclature of Weber Cañon would be led to think the enemy of mankind held there at least undisputed sway. All the great glories of the view are marked as his. The Devil's Gate—a black, ragged opening in one part of the great gorge, through which the foaming waters of the river rush white and noisy—is one, but it is well named. A very spirit of darkness seems to brood over the place. On each side, the broken cliffs lie in shadow; the thundering water roars below; there is no verdure but a blasted tree here and there; great bowlders lie in the bed of the stream and along the shore. In the distance, seen through the gap, there are black hills and mountain-summits overlooking them. And there is a cool wind here, that is like a breeze blown across the Styx, and that is never still, even in the hottest summer day.

It is worth the while to think, in this wonderful valley, of the engineering skill that was needed to carry the iron road through its depths. All through the cañon are evidences of the difficulties of the task. Here a truss-bridge and web-like trestle-work carry the rails from one point of the rocky wall to another beyond the stream; here, for a great space, the road-bed is cut from the very sides of the great cliffs, where the gorge narrows and leaves no room for more than sand and river. And, as if to mock at it all, Nature has tried her hand, too, at construction, with a success at once weird, sublime, and grotesque. On the left hand of the route,

Devil's Slide, Weber Cañon.

TERRES MAUVAISES, UTAH.

Salt Lake.

on the steep front of the rocky cliff, appears at one point the very mockery of human work—the singular formation called "The Devil's Slide"—by that same rule of nomenclature that we have mentioned once before. Two parallel walls of stone, extending from summit to base of the precipice, and enclosing between them a road-way, regular and unobstructed. An editor, whom your guide-books will be sure to quote, has written a good, though somewhat too statistical, description of this singular place; we have found it in a well-used route-book, and quote it, in default of words that could say more:

"Imagine," the writer says, "a mountain eight hundred feet high, composed of solid, dark-red sandstone, with a smooth and gradually ascending surface to its very pinnacle, and only eight or ten degrees from being perpendicular. At the foot of this mountain the Weber River winds its devious course. From the base of the immense red mountain, up its entire height of eight hundred feet, is what is called 'The Devil's Slide,' composed of white limestone. It consists of a smooth, white stone floor from base to summit, about fifteen feet wide, as straight and regular as if laid by a stone-mason with line and plummet. On either side of this smooth, white line is what appears to the eye to be a well-laid white stone-wall, varying in height from ten to twenty feet. This white spectacle on the red mountain-side has all the appearance of being made by man or devil as a slide from the top of the mountain to the bed of Weber River."

This odd freak of Nature has nothing sublime about it; the whole idea that it conveys is that of singularity; but it is strangely picturesque and striking.

And now we are nearing the very centre of Mormondom; for only a little beyond the Devil's Gate, which, though first named, is farther toward the western extremity of the cañon than the "Slide," we come to Uintah Station, glance at the Salt-Lake Valley, and are hurried on to Ogden, whence the trains go out to the City of the Saints itself. Ogden lies in the great plain of the valley, but from the low railway-station you see

Plains of the Humboldt.

in the distance long ranges of mountains, more picturesque than almost any distant view you have had thus far; and all about the town are green fields—yes, positively fenced-off fields—and beyond them the prairie; but here no longer without trees.

Whoever will may leave this station—a great central point of the line, for here the Union and the Central roads meet and cause the dreary business of changing cars —and, adding a day or two to his journey, may take the sonorously-named Utah Central Railway—as if, indeed, the Territory boasted a net-work of iron roads—and journey down to Salt-Lake City to see the curious civilization he will find there. "It lies in a great valley," says the statistical and accurate description of this city of the Mormons— a description which we prefer to partly set down here rather than to run risks of error by trusting our own memory for any thing more than picturesque aspects—"it lies in a great valley, extending close up to the base of the Wasatch Mountains on the north, with an expansive view to the south of more than one hundred miles of plains, beyond which, in the distance, rise, clear cut and grand in the extreme, the gray, jagged, and rugged mountains, whose peaks are covered with perpetual snow." (Oh, unhappy writer in statistical guide-books! How much more "grand in the extreme" is that view in its bright reality than any words of yours or mine can show to those who have not seen it! Let us keep to our statistics.) "Adjoining the city is a fine agricultural and mining region, which has a large and growing trade. The climate of the valley is healthful, and the soil, where it can be irrigated, is extremely fertile. . . . The city covers an area of about nine miles, or three miles each way, and is handsomely laid out. The streets are very wide, with irrigating ditches passing through all of them, keeping the shade-trees and orchards looking beautiful. Every block is surrounded with shade-trees, and nearly every house has its neat little orchard of apple, peach, apricot, plum, and cherry trees. Fruit is very abundant, and the almond, the catalpa, and the cotton-wood-tree, grow side by side with the maple, the willow, and the locust. In fact, the whole nine square miles is almost one continuous garden."

So it will be seen that even a city on the Plains has elements that entitle it to a place in this record of the picturesque, and that it is not as other cities are. But Mr. Charles Nordhoff tells us, in his "California," that "Salt Lake need not hold any mere pleasure-traveller more than a day. You can drive all over it in two hours; and when you have seen the Tabernacle—an admirably-arranged and very ugly building—which contains an organ, built in Salt Lake by an English workman, a Mormon, named Ridges, which organ is second in size only to the Boston organ, and far sweeter in tone than the one of Plymouth Church; the menagerie of Brigham Young's enclosure, which contains several bears, some lynxes and wild-cats—natives of these mountains—and a small but interesting collection of minerals and Indian remains, and of the manufactures of the Mormons; the Temple Block; and enjoyed the magnificent view from the back of the city of the valley and the snow-capped peaks which lie on the other side—a view which you carry with you all over the place—you have done Salt-Lake City, and have time, if you have risen early, to bathe at the sulphur spring. The lake lies too far away to be visited in one day."

But, in spite of its distance, the great inland sea should certainly be seen. It is a remarkable sight from any point of view, and as you come suddenly upon it, after the long days of travel, in which you have seen only rivers and scanty brooks, it seems almost marvellous. A great expanse of sparkling water in the sunshine, or a dark waste that looks like the ocean itself when you see it under a cloudy sky, it is an outlook not to be forgotten in many a day.

Here, before we leave the Salt-Lake region, we must say a word to correct one very false idea concerning it—that which obtains concerning its great fertility and natural

PALISADE CAÑON.

wealth of soil. This point is referred to in Mr. Nordhoff's book, and, so far as we know, almost for the first time correctly; but we have never passed through Utah by the railway, or passed a day in this portion of the country, without greatly wondering why the common, unfounded theory had kept its place so long. It is popularly supposed that the Mormons have settled in a very garden of the earth, and that their Canaan was by no means all visionary; and there are not a few good people who have agitated themselves because these heathen had possession of one of the noblest parts of the American territory.

This is all entirely wrong. The region is really, by Nature, an arid desert, made up of veritable "Terres Mauvaises," though not such picturesque ones as lie, dotted with monumental rocks, but a little distance from the lake. The Mormons can truly boast that they have made their land "blossom like the rose;" but only by the greatest toil and care, and by an expenditure of wealth utterly disproportionate to its results. "Considering what an immense quantity of good land there is in these United States," says Mr. Nordhoff, "I should say that Brigham Young made what they call in the West 'a mighty poor land speculation' for his people. 'If we should stop irrigation for ninety days, not a tree, shrub, or vine, would remain alive in our country,' said a Mormon to me, as I walked through his garden. 'Not a tree grew in our plains when we came here, and we had, and have, to haul our wood and timber fourteen to twenty miles out of the mountains,' said another. The soil, though good, is full of stones; and I saw a terraced garden of about three acres, built up against the hill-side, which must have cost ten or twelve thousand dollars to prepare. That is to say, Young marched his people a thousand miles through a desert to settle them in a valley where almost every acre must have cost them, in labor and money to get it ready for agricultural use, I should say not less than one hundred dollars. An Illinois, or Iowa, or Missouri, or Minnesota farmer, who paid a dollar and a quarter an acre for his land in those days, got a better farm, ready-made to his hand, than these people got from Brigham, their leader, only after the experience of untold hardships (which we will not now count in), and of at least one hundred dollars' worth of labor per acre when they reached their destination." It will some time be more widely appreciated how completely the whole pleasant pastoral scenery here is the work of men's hands; for the present, the passage just quoted is so true that it shall serve as the only reference here to the subject.

West from Ogden lies the second great reach of the long overland journey. Salt-Lake City, an oasis of humanity, if not of a very high order of civilization, serves to mark the half-way point in the modern crossing of the Plains. The railways meet at Ogden Station, and the continued journey toward the western coast is made on "the Central," as the affectionate abbreviation of the railway-men calls the latter half of the great iron road. It passes westward through Corinne, a station which derives its life and prosperity chiefly from its communication with the Utah silver-mines, and reaches Prom-

Pleasant Valley, Truckee River.

ontory — properly, it seems, called "Promontory Point," which appears a strange bit of tautology. Here is a noteworthy place, and one which all historians of the future ought to celebrate, each after his manner. Close by the station, which the road reaches after skirting the shore of the great Salt Lake for a little time, and then suddenly curving away, the great iron line, pushed westward from the east, met and joined that which for many months had grown slowly toward it from the west—the last links of the iron chain were riveted. There were jubilant ceremonies when the great day of ending the road came at last, on the 10th of May, 1869. A rose-wood "tie" joined the last rails; and solemnly, in the presence of a silent assembly, a golden spike was driven with silver hammer—the last of the thousands on thousands of fastenings that held together the mightiest work made for the sake of human communication and intercourse in all the world. The engines met from the east and west, as Bret Harte told us—

> "Pilots touching—head to head
> Facing on the single track,
> Half a world behind each back"—

and there was a girdle round the earth such as the men of a century before had not dared even to dream of.

Beyond the memorable Promontory comes a dreary waste—the dreariest that has yet been passed, and perhaps the most utterly desolate of all the journey. Nothing lives here but the hopelessly wretched sage-brush, and a tribe of little basking lizards; yes, one thing more—the kind of gaunt, lank animals called "jackass-rabbits," that eat no one knows what on this arid plain. The horizon is bordered by bare, burned mountains; the ground is a waste of sand and salt; the air is a whirl of alkali-dust. Kelton, and Matlin, and Toano, dreariest of Nevada stations! Could any man wish his direst enemy a more bitter fate than to be kept here in the midst of this scene for a decade?

There is some mineral wealth, farther on, hidden near the route of the railway; but, apart from this, there would seem to be nothing useful to man obtainable from all this region. We dash across the sterile space in a few hours, but imagine for a moment the dreary time for the old emigrant-trains, which came on to these gusty, dusty levels in old days, and found neither grass, nor water, nor foliage, until they came to Humboldt Wells, blessed of many travellers, lying close together within a few hundred yards of the present road, and surrounded with tall, deep-green herbage. There are nearly a score of these grateful springs scattered about in a small area; and they are of very great depth, with cool, fresh, limpid water.

They herald the approach of another and a different district, for now we soon come to the Humboldt River itself, and for a time have all the benefit of the growth of trees along its sides, and the fertility that its waters revive along its course. The soil here is really arable; but go a little distance away from the river, and the few water-pools are alkaline, and the land resumes the features of the desert-soil. The scenery here, in the upper part of the Humboldt Valley, is for a time varied, and in many places even wild and grand. The road winds through picturesque cañons, and under the shadow of the northernmost mountains of the Humboldt Range, until the important station of Elko is reached. This is a noteworthy supply-station for all the country around it, in which are numerous mining settlements. The town is a place of great import to all the guide-books of this region. It has a population of more than five thousand, as we learn from one account of it; and there are a hundred and fifty shops of various kinds, great freight-houses, an hotel, two banks, two newspapers, a school, and a court-house. Truly a most promising prairie-town is this, to have grown up in three hurried years, and to flourish on the borders of a desert!

For now we have a little more of sage-brush and alkali, ant-hills, and sand. Let him who passes over the Humboldt Plains on a hot August day, and feels the flying white dust burning and parching eyes and mouth and throat, making gritty unpleasantness in the water wherewith he tries to wash it away, and finding lodgment in every fold of his clothing, be sufficiently thankful that he is not plodding on with jaded

Truckee River, Nevada.

horse by the side of a crowded emigrant-wagon, with days of similar journeying behind him, and some of it still to come.

Emigrant or passenger by luxurious Pullman car, he will be glad to come near to the refreshing grandeur of scenery of the Palisades—though the finest of this is not seen without leaving the established route, and penetrating a little into the mountains at one side. It is here that you come upon such glimpses and vistas as the one Mr. Moran has drawn—breaks in the rocky wall, through which one looks out on really perfect mountain-pictures. There are hot springs here; and in one valley a host of them sends up perpetual steam, of sulphurous odor, and the ground is tinged with mineral colors, as at the geysers of

California. All around us, too, are mining districts, some of them old and exhausted, some still flourishing. To the pioneers they all have association with "lively times;" the veterans talk of "the Austin excitement," and the famous "Washoe time"—periods which seem like a distant age to us.

The railway and the emigrant-road have long followed the course of the Humboldt River, but this is not always in sight after Battle Mountain—named from an old Indian combat—is passed; and finally it is lost to view altogether, and the road runs by the fresh, bright-looking little station of Humboldt itself; past Golconda, and Winnemucca, and Lovelock's, and Brown's—names that have histories; and finally Wadsworth is reached, cheerfully hailed as the beginning of the "Sacramento division," a title that reads already like the California names. And here the Plains are done—the Sierras fairly begin.

The monotony of the view begins to change; the mountains slope about us, as we enter the well-named Pleasant Valley, through which Truckee River flows, and at last, passing through well-wooded land again, reach Truckee itself, a little city in the wilderness, standing among the very main ridges of the Sierra chain. The town—the first of the stations within the actual limits of California—is a picturesque, bright place of six thousand inhabitants—a place that has had its "great fire," its revival, its riots, and adventures, not a whit behind those of the larger mining towns farther toward the interior of the State.

Along the rocky shores of its river lie the noblest scenes; the tall cliffs are ragged and bare, but pine-tree-crowned; the rock-broken water ripples and thunders through gorges and little stretches of fertile plain; and the buzzing saw-mills of an incipient civilization hum with a homelike, New-England sound on its banks. From the town itself, stages—the stages of luxury and civilization, too—carry the traveller to the beautiful and now well-known Donner Lake, only two or three miles away. The great sheet of clear and beautiful water lies high up in the mountains, between steep sides, and in the midst of the wildest and most picturesque of the scenery of the Sierra summits. The depth of the lake is very great, but its waters are so transparent that one can look down many fathoms into them; they are unsullied by any disturbance of soil or sand, for they lie in a bed formed almost entirely of the solid rock.

Few things could have more perfect beauty than this mountain-lake, and its even more famous neighbor, Lake Tahoe, some fifteen miles farther to the south. The scene is never twice the same. Though it lies under the unbroken sunlight through a great part of the summer weather, there is perpetual variation in the great mountain-shadows, and in breeze and calm on the surface. There is a climate here that makes almost the ideal atmosphere. It is neither cold to chilliness nor warm to discomfort, but always bracing, invigorating, inspiring with a kind of pleasant and energetic intoxication. Already invalids come to these saving lakes from east and west, and find new life up among the

DONNER LAKE, NEVADA.

pines and summits. There are trout in the waters around, and fishing here is more than sport—it is a lounge in dream-land, a rest in a region hardly surpassed anywhere on the globe.

Here, as elsewhere in the Sierras, the rock-forms are picturesque and grand at all points of the view. Castellated, pinnacled, with sides like perpendicular walls, and summits like chiselled platforms, they give a strangely beautiful aspect to every shore and gorge and valley. The road, twelve miles in length, by which Lake Tahoe is reached from Truckee, affords some of the most remarkable and memorable views of these formations, with all their singularities of outline, that can be obtained in any accessible region in this part of the range; and it would be impossible to find a more glorious drive than is this along the edge of the river-bed, over a well-graded path, through the very heart of one of the noblest groups of the Sierra chain. It is a ride to be remembered with the great passes of the world—with the Swiss mountain-roads, and the ravines of Greece—in its own way as beautiful and grand as these. The great cañons, and such noble breaks in the rock-wall as can give us glimpses like that of the Giant's Gap, and a hundred others, are certainly among the vistas through which one looks upon the chosen scenes of the whole world.

It has been said that the traveller is here in the very centre of the mountain-range. The general features of structure in this most noble region of the continent have been better described elsewhere than we can show them in our own words.

"For four hundred miles," says Mr. Clarence King, who knows these mountains, better, perhaps, than any other American, "the Sierras are a definite ridge, broad and high, and having the form of a sea-wave. Buttresses of sombre-hued rock, jutting at intervals from a steep wall, form the abrupt eastern slopes; irregular forests, in scattered growth, huddle together near the snow. The lower declivities are barren spurs, sinking into the sterile flats of the Great Basin.

"Long ridges of comparatively gentle outline characterize the western side; but this sloping table is scored, from summit to base, by a system of parallel, transverse cañons, distant from one another often less than twenty-five miles. They are ordinarily two or three thousand feet deep—falling, at times, in sheer, smooth-fronted cliffs; again, in sweeping curves, like the hull of a ship; again, in rugged, V-shaped gorges, or with irregular, hilly flanks—opening, at last, through gate-ways of low, rounded foot-hills, out upon the horizontal plain of the San Joaquin and Sacramento. . . .

"Dull and monotonous in color, there are, however, certain elements of picturesqueness in this lower zone. Its oak-clad hills wander out into the great plain like coast promontories, enclosing yellow, or, in spring-time, green, bays of prairie. The hill-forms are rounded, or stretch in long, longitudinal ridges, broken across by the river-cañons. Above this zone of red earth, softly-modelled undulations, and dull, grayish groves, with a chain of mining-towns, dotted ranches, and vineyards, rise the swelling middle heights

LAKE TAHOE.

of the Sierras—a broad, billowy plateau, cut by sharp, sudden cañons, and sweeping up, with its dark, superb growth of coniferous forest, to the feet of the summit-peaks. . . .

"Along its upper limit, the forest-zone grows thin and irregular—black shafts of Alpine pines and firs clustering on sheltered slopes, or climbing, in disordered processions, up broken and rocky faces. Higher, the last gnarled forms are passed, and beyond stretches the rank of silent, white peaks—a region of rock and ice lifted above the limit of life.

"In the north, domes and cones of volcanic formation are the summit, but, for about three hundred miles in the south, it is a succession of sharp granite *aiguilles* and crags. Prevalent among the granitic forms are singularly perfect conoidal domes, whose symmetrical figures, were it not for their immense size, would impress one as having an artificial finish.

"The Alpine gorges are usually wide and open, leading into amphitheatres, whose walls are either rock or drifts of never-melting snow. The sculpture of the summit is very evidently glacial. Beside the ordinary phenomena of polished rocks and moraines, the larger general forms are clearly the work of frost and ice ; and, although this ice-period is only feebly represented to-day, yet the frequent avalanches of winter, and freshly-scored mountain-flanks, are constant suggestions of the past."

There could not well be a more satisfactory, faithful, and vivid general characterization of the Sierra chain than this that we have quoted from the account of one of our greatest American mountaineers. Its faithfulness will be confirmed by every view, gained from whatever point, of the series of giant peaks that lie in long line to the north and south of our own special route through the range.

Far off from the railway-route, in those parts of the Sierras known as yet only to a few mountaineers, there is Alpine scenery, not only as grand as the great, world-known views in the heart of Switzerland, but even of almost the same character. Whoever reads Mr. King's "Ascent of Mount Tyndall" will find no more inspiriting record of mountain-climbing in all the records of the Alpine Club. Indeed, this range will be the future working-ground of many an enthusiastic successor of the Tyndalls and Whympers of our time, and the scene of triumphs like that of the great ascent of the before unconquered Matterhorn ; perhaps—though Heaven forbid !—the witness of disasters as unspeakably terrible as the awful fall of Douglas and his fellows.

In reading what Mr. King and his companions have written of the wonderful hidden regions of the great chain, which, for a time at least, we must know only through these interpreters, we, and every reader, must be particularly struck by one characteristic, which they all note in the scenes that they describe. This is the majesty of their desolation— the spell of the unknown and the unvisited. Mighty gorges, with giant sides, bearing the traces of great glacial movements, and watched over by truly Alpine pinnacles of ice and snow, are the weird passes into the silent region that surrounds the highest peaks

SUMMIT OF THE SIERRAS.

Giant's Gap.

within the limits of the United States. In the bottom of these deep cañons are lakes, frozen during the greater part of the year, and at other times lying with motionless water, never touched by canoe or keel.

Against the great precipices of the ravines are piles of *débris* such as are familiar to every traveller through the passes of the Alps. Snow, encrusted with an icy, brittle crust, lies heaped against other portions of the rocky walls, and crowns their tops.

High up, there are vast glacial formations; moraines, that lie in long ridges, with steeply-sloping summits, so narrow and sharp that it is almost impossible to walk along them. Here, too, are structures of ice, pinnacles and needles and towers, and sometimes piles which have formed against walls of rock, but have melted away until they are like great sheets of glass standing on edge, while through them a blue, cold light is cast into the chasm that now intervenes between them and their former precipitous supports. Almost every phase in the phenomena of Alpine scenery is repeated here—often with greater beauty than in that of Switzerland even, with which the very word "Alpine" has become so entirely associated by usage.

In this region of hidden grandeur lies the ground of hope for those cosmopolitan tourists who complain that the world is a small place, full of hackneyed scenes, after all. So long as there is locked up here in our great mountain-chain such a glory as the few who have penetrated into its fortresses have described, even the mountaineer who fancies he has exhausted two continents, need never despair.

One noble feature of the whole Sierra—of all of it save that which lies above the level of any vegetable life—is its magnificent forest-covering. It may well be doubted if the growth of forests of pine is ever seen in greater perfection than is found here. These tall, straight, noble shafts are the very kings of trees. Covering the great slopes with a dense mantle of sombre green, they lend a wonderful dignity to the peaks, as one looks upon them from a distance; and, to one already in the forest, they seem the worthy guardians of the mountain-sides. They are magnificent in size, as they are admirable in proportion. No mast or spar ever shaped by men's hands exceeds the already perfect grace of their straight, unbroken trunks. They are things to study for their mere beauty as individual trees, apart from their effect upon the general landscape, which even without them would be wild and picturesque enough.

Of all these features of the noble Sierra scenery, of which we have said so much, and spoken with such positive enthusiasm, the traveller by the railway sees little or nothing. For through the very finest regions of the mountains the track is of necessity

The San Joaquin River.

OAKS OF OAKLAND.

covered in by strong snow-sheds, extending, with only trifling breaks, for many miles. Indispensable as they are, no one has passed through their long, dark tunnels without feeling a sense of personal wrong that so much that is beautiful should be so shut out from view. Through breaks and openings he looks down into dark cañons, with pine-covered sides, and catches a glimpse of a foaming river hundreds of feet below, when suddenly the black wall of boards and posts closes in again upon the train, and the picture is left incomplete. That happiest of men, the lover of the picturesque who has the leisure to indulge his love, must not fail to leave the travelled route here for days, and to satisfy himself with all the grander aspects of what he will find about him.

The railway passes on from Truckee, climbing a gradual slope to Summit, fifteen miles farther, the highest station on the Central Pacific, though still lower than Sherman, of which we spoke long ago. Summit, standing at the highest point of this pass through the range, is at an altitude of seven thousand and forty-two feet above the level of the sea; and, to reach it, the track has ascended twenty-five hundred feet, say the guides, in fifty miles; and in the hundred and four miles between this and Sacramento, on the plain beyond, the descent must again be made to a point only fifty-six feet above sea-level.

This part of the journey—the western descent from Summit—is one that the writer has several times reached just at the most glorious period of sunrise. There can be no more perfect scene. The road winds along the edges of great precipices, and in the deep cañons below the shadows are still lying. Those peaks above that are snow-covered catch the first rays of the sun, and glow with wonderful color. Light wreaths of mist rise up to the end of the zone of pines, and then drift away into the air, and are lost. All about one the aspect of the mountains is of the wildest, most intense kind; for by that word "intense" something seems to be expressed of the positive force there is in it that differs utterly from the effect of such a scene as lies passive for our admiration. This is grand; it is magnetic; there is no escaping the wonder-working influence of the great grouping of mountains and ravines, of dense forests, and ragged pinnacles of rock.

But soon the mountains seem to fade away, and before we realize it we are among the foot-hills—those oak-clad or bare brown hills, that, as Mr. King told us in the passage we quoted, "wander out into the great plain like coast promontories, enclosing yellow, or, in the spring-time, green bays of prairie." And so out upon the plain of the San Joaquin. We might fancy ourselves back again upon the Plains were it not for the still farther range of heights before us. These are brown, bare, unpicturesque, outlying hills, and we dash through them by Livermore's Pass, having passed Sacramento, and go on our way toward the coast.

Civilization appears again; houses and towns begin to line the track; the stations are like similar places in the East; the prosaic railway-pedlers come back again with their hated wares; for us, the picturesque is over; and already the hum of the still distant city seems almost to reach our ears, as we dash in under the great green oaks of Oakland.

THE SUSQUEHANNA.

WITH ILLUSTRATIONS BY GRANVILLE PERKINS.

THE Susquehanna is considered with justice one of the most picturesque streams of America. It is true that the scenery along its banks seldom reaches to sublime effects; but these do not touch the artist's inmost heart so deeply as the softer beauties which are displayed from its sources almost to its entrance into the Chesapeake Bay. There are no yawning precipices, no bare, tremendous cliffs, no savage rocks, no "antres vast." But, in their stead, there is a constant succession of bold mountain-forms, wooded from the base to the summit; of deep ravines, where the pines stand in serried shadow, like spearmen of Titanic mould in ambush; of winding banks, whose curves are of the most exquisite beauty; of broad sheets of brown water, swift and untamable, whose rapid flow has never been subjected to the curbing of navigation; of a superb vegetation, that clothes with equal splendor the valley and the hill-tops, the banks, the islands of the river, and the undulating plains here and there breaking through the leaguer of the mountain-ranges. All these attractions—these gifts of a tender, loving mother Nature—have been bestowed upon the Susquehanna; and the tourist who has drunk them in

Above Columbia.

with rapture would be loath to exchange them for mountains that invade the skies, and whose sullen peaks are covered with a snow-mantle fringed with glittering glaciers. For the Susquehanna is not only beautiful in itself, but its attractions are greatly enhanced by the soft, silvery haze through which they are presented. This gives to its scenery an indescribable charm, which defies alike the pencil and the pen, but which never fails to make itself felt by the heart.

It must be admitted that all of the Susquehanna scenery is not beautiful. The ending is dull and prosaic; and the long stretch south of Columbia, in Lancaster County, Pennsylvania, to Havre de Grace, in Maryland, presents nothing worthy of commemoration by the pencil or comment by the pen. All that can be seen is a broad stretch of brown waters, and bare, dull banks, with patches, here and there, of luxuriant vegetation, and intervals of cultivated ground. Above Columbia, commences the beautiful land. Here several railroads make a junction, and the trunk-line then follows the path of the river, which is due northward. Here we meet the hilly country—waves of the main ranges of the Blue Mountains, so called because, being wooded to the very summits, an unusual amount of the cerulean haze is seen by the eye at a distance, and the hills appear intensely blue. The Muse who presides over geographical baptisms has not ratified the nomenclature of the people, and has ignored the name of "Blue Mountains," preferring the Indian denomination of "Kittatinnies," a word which is easier to pronounce than it appears, and

Harrisburg, from Brant's Hill.

has a soft swell about it, very pleasant to the ear, like most of the old Indian names. The railway skirts the base of these mountains, running along the eastern bank of the river, and affords, from the windows of its cars, ample opportunities for inspection and admiration. To the right, the mountains rise up in grand, rounded masses, with an inexhaustible wealth of noble trees down their sides. Nowhere can one see such superb forms of vegetation as on the side of a mountain, for here they are fully developed, whereas in the forests they grow spindling, having excessively tall, thin trunks, and a head of small branches, but nothing in the middle. They are choked for want of air ; and so they aspire toward the sky, having no marked development save that

Glimpse of the Susquehanna, from Kittatinny Mountains.

which is upward. But on the mountain-side every tree has all the airy food it needs ; and so they become perfected, and put forth in every direction, having superb branches on every side, and great roots that clasp with intense embraces masses of solid rock, often split asunder by this twining. On the bowlder-covered ground is a superbly colored carpet of many kinds of undergrowth convolvuli and creepers, wild grape-vines and huckleberries, flowers of a hundred different kinds, and humble strawberries that cling to the ground as if to hide themselves and their delicate points of crimson fruit. On the left hand rushes the river, sweeping onward to the sea, bearing no traces of that lumber-trade which in the upper parts is all in all. Scattered over the surface of the gleaming waters are islands, too small to be habitable, covered with the densest vegetation, that fairly glows with vivid hues of green. Around the edges of these islets—these gems of the stream—are often bands of broad-leaved rushes, that sigh plaintively as the wind passes over, as if there was much excellent music in them, like Hamlet's flute, if one knew how to get it out. Onward rushes the train with its freight of tourists and business people, and soon reaches Harrisburg, the political capital of the State of Pennsylvania, and a thriving manufacturing town, where there are many chimneys vomiting volumes of black smoke. It is built along the right bank of the river, the houses of the principal inhabitants being on Front Street, which faces the stream. The town occu-

Dauphin Rock.

pies the ground between the river and the hills, which here retreat considerably. The foot-hills, or low spurs, are close to the city, and are beginning to be built upon.

Brant's Hill is almost in a direct line with the crest of ground, in the centre of the town, on which the capitol is built; and the city, therefore, can be seen most excellently from this point—lying, indeed, spread out before one like a panorama. But the view from Brant's Hill is open to the serious objection that one cannot from it see the Susquehanna, its bridges, and its islands. To view these, one must be on the cupola of the capitol. From this position, still more elevated than Brant's Hill, not only can one survey all the city, with its climbing spires, its massive manufactories, and their aspiring chimneys, but the

Scene at Lockhaven

Columbia Tunnel

Northumberland

Canal at Lockhaven

Williamsport

Williamsport Lumber-Mills

W.H.MORSE.SC.

Emporium

West-Port

SCENES ON THE SUSQUEHANNA.

bold scenery to the northward comes into view, and one has a distant though beautiful glimpse of Hunter's Gap and the range of mountains through which the Susquehanna has to fight its way. There are no less than three ranges, tier upon tier, standing out in bold relief against the sky, each range having a different tinge of blue. Escaping from these, the river bursts, as it were, into a frenzied joy, and from the cooped-up imprisonment of its sandstone walls widens its bed prodigiously, and makes a tremendous sheer to the west before it strikes due south. Hence, opposite Harrisburg, the river is unusually wide, and therefore extremely shallow, which increases the brown appearance of its waters; for in many places the stream is not a foot deep, and the sandstone bed is plainly visible, the eye even catching all the lines of its cleavage. In the centre of the sheer which the river makes is the pretty village of Fairview, to which the Harrisburgers go as to a summer resort. In the centre of the river, straight in a line from the glittering, whitewashed cottages of the village, are three islands, covered with fine trees, and of such a size that picnics are possible on them. They are very close together, but there is a pass between them, through which shallops can glide, though overhead the trees commingle their branches. It is glorious to be in a boat here at sunset, for the sun goes down in summer-time just behind these islands, or, to be more accurate, behind the ranges of mountains in a line with the islands. Just when the sun is beginning to sink behind the farthest crests, the haze that wraps their forms is turned into a golden haze of supreme glory, and the last rays come shooting through the commingled foliage of the islands like veritable arrows, and fall upon the water in long pencils of reflected fire. These grow more and more dusky and dreamy, until they become only faint blotches of dim light, and at last the brown stream rushes through unglorified. In the mean while there has been a battle between the golden haze and the blue upon the mountains. At first, the golden carries every thing before it, save at the bases, which seem mantled in a brilliant green. This spreads and spreads until it covers all the mountain-forms, and then it slowly, slowly changes to its accustomed blue. As this takes place, so the bold crests of the ranges, hidden at first by the wealth of golden fire, struggle into existence, and, at length, show vividly against the clear pallor of the twilight sky.

This is the appearance of Hunter's Gap at a distance. Close at hand, it has no such gorgeous transformations of color, but it presents its own distinguishing beauties. The river turns and twists, writhing like a fever-burned mortal, or some animal trying to escape from a trap. The mountains compass it about on every side; they hem it in about, around, east, west, north, and south, making what the lumbermen call a kettle, which is more poetic than it seems to be; for, if the gentle reader will imagine himself a cricket at the bottom of a copper kettle, swimming around and looking upward despairingly at the huge walls that prison him, he will appreciate the language of the lumbermen. But, though the general aspect is terrifying, there are quiet sylvan nooks, where the mountains show their gentler sides, and, instead of presenting their fronts, turn to us

North Point.

huge, undulating flanks, covered with glorious pines and noble oaks, spreading hickories and dark hemlocks. These are the places where the trout - streams come singing through the ravines, murmuring their thanks to the pines for their shelter and companionship. The water of the Susquehanna is too warm in summer - time for the speckled favorites of the hunter, and they all fly for refuge into these little mountain - streams, which are their summer resorts. Along the banks of these pleasant, meandering waters there are deer still feeding, and bears occasionally show their black muzzles, so that the name which was given to this gate of the river in old times is still merited, and there is plenty of sport for those that love it. But there is still better sport in ascending the mountains, not for game, but for scenery; and, from the overhanging branches of the trees that crown the slopes of the Kittatinnies, gazing upon the glimpses of the Susquehanna that open out far below. All the rush and roar of the water has then passed out of hearing; all the fury, the vexation, and the struggle of the imprisoned stream has disappeared, and the waters seem to slumber peacefully beneath the kisses of the sun. Still more exquisite is it in the moonlight; and many a hunter, from the solitude of his camp-fire, has watched the white beams stealing over the ripples of the river, and transmuting them to molten silver. The gap proper is the last gate-way cut by the river through the hills; but there is, in fact, a succession of gaps, through which the Susquehanna in times past battled fiercely every spring-time; for three distinct ranges lie right across its path, which runs due south, the hills sweeping from northeast to southwest. Hence the gap-district extends for nearly thirty miles. At Dauphin Point is perhaps the most tremendous of these mute evidences of the past struggle. Here the mountains are considerably higher than at the commencement of this region, and the forms are very much bolder. There is, in parts, an appearance of castellated rock, jutting out from the trees which grow over all the mountains. Here and there are crags which are truly precipitous; and these, contrasting with the softer, milder features of the mountain do not oppress the senses with a feeling of awe, but only heighten and intensify the general effect, acting as high lights do in a picture. Here the railroad that accompanies the Juniata in her wanderings crosses over to the left side of the Susquehanna, leaving this stream altogether at Duncannon, where it unites with the bold, whelming, brown flood of the big river. The meeting of the waters is the termination of the gap-region; for, although there are huge hills, and plenty of them, along the river, it is not crossed in the same manner by any succession of main ranges.

The scenery now takes on a much more composed aspect, for, from this point up to Northumberland, where, according to the language of the country, the river *forks* into North and West Branches, the hills retire, and the banks of the stream are for the most part bordered by foot-hills, which are cultivated with a careful, intelligent husbandry, that makes this part of the country of a most smiling appearance. Cornfields wave their tall stems in the lowlands; wheat whitens in broad patches along the slopes of the hills, up to the summits; and the vicinity of the stream, where the richest soil is, will generally be found occupied by tobacco, which flourishes here surprisingly. As one approaches Northumberland, however, these foot-hills become larger, higher, and less pastoral in character, until, at the actual point of junction of the two rivers, those on the east bank are actually precipitous; and, moreover, they are ruder in appearance than elsewhere, being almost entirely denuded of timber. The scene here is a very interesting one. The West Branch at this point runs due north and south, and receives the North Branch, running nearly due east. The latter is very nearly as large a stream as the former; but the majesty of its union is somewhat marred by a large, heavily-timbered island, which occu-

PINE FOREST ON WEST BRANCH OF THE SUSQUEHANNA.

pies the centre of the current. The whole region is permeated by canals which abound with locks. The canal-boats here have to make several crossings, and there are always a few idlers at the ends of the long wooden bridges to watch them crossing the streams.

Everywhere around Northumberland are strong hints that the tourist is getting into the lumber-region; and the next point of importance, Williamsport, is the very headquarters of the lumber-trade in the eastern part of the United States. The West Branch of the Susquehanna at this place has taken a bold, sweeping curve due west, and has left behind it a spur of the Alleghanies. Here comes in the Lycoming River, down which thousands of logs float. But down the Susquehanna come hundreds of thousands of oak and hemlock, and, above all, of pine. One cannot see much live pine at Williamsport; but down by the river-side, and at the boom, one can see nothing but logs of every size and length. The children of the street play upon them, fearlessly jumping from one to the other, as if there were no cold, black water underneath. But, though there undoubtedly is, it cannot be discerned. Wide as the space is, the eye catches nothing but a low, wide plain covered with timber. Of water not a speck is visible. Close by the opposite bank of the river the hills rise up very grandly, but on the other side of the town they are far away, for the valley of the Susquehanna at this point is quite broad. It begins to narrow a little as we approach Lock Haven, which is also a lumber-place—a minor sort of Williamsport. It is a very charming little place, very bustling, very thriving, and more picturesque than the larger town of Williamsport. The canal at Lock Haven is fed with water from the Bald-Eagle-Valley Creek, which falls here into the big river, after traversing the whole valley from Tyrone, not far from the head-waters of the Juniata, the principal tributary of the Susquehanna. Lock Haven is on the left or south bank of the river; and the railroad here crosses over to the north side, and continues there for a very considerable distance. Very shortly after this crossing, the mountains come down upon the river, and hem it in. These are several thousand feet in height, and present a singular variety of forms—all, however, pleasing by grandeur more than sublimity. At North Point, especially, the mountain-forms fairly arrest the eye of the most phlegmatic. In one direction, one mountain proudly raises itself like a sugar-loaf; in another, the side is presented, and it is not unlike a crouching lion; in a third, the front is shown, and the mountain then turns in so peculiar a fashion as to uncover its great flanks, giving it the appearance of an animal lying down, but turning its head in the direction of the spectator. Close by is another pyramidal-shaped mass, whose body meets the flank of the former, forming a ravine of the most picturesque character, where the tops of the pines, when agitated by the breeze, resemble the tossing waves of an angry lake.

The trees along the Susquehanna are now of various kinds—oaks, pines, maples, hickories, hemlocks, tulip-trees, birches, wild-cherry, etc.—but the lumberers say that the pines were the indigenous children of the soil, and that the others have sprung up since

FERRY AT RENOVO.

they were felled. This, perhaps, is so; for, in places where there is no access to the river, the woods are all of pine. The lumberers only cut the timber where it can be. rolled down or hauled to the river, to be floated with the whelming spring-floods to the timber-yards of Williamsport and Lock Haven, so that those places which offer no favorable opportunities of this kind are altogether spared. Those persons who have never wandered up a mountain covered with pine-trees have no conception of the sublimity of such a place. There is a silence, a solemnity, about a pine-wood, which at once impresses the senses with a sentiment of awe. In other forests the ear and eye are greeted with many sounds of life and glancing forms. But through the dim aisles of the tall pines there is neither sound nor motion. It has its own atmosphere, also, for the air around is loaded with the strong fragrance which these trees breathe forth. To speak with candor, it is overpowering to delicate nostrils; but for strong, robust natures it has a wonderful attraction. The lumberers have a passionate love for the "piny woods," as they call them, which artists fully share with them.

But, superb as is the sight of a pine-wood in all its pristine splendor, the spectacle of one, after the lumberers have been felling right and left, is by no means admirable. The ground that was once carpeted with the delicate white stars of the one-berry flower and the low glories of the wood-azaleas, is now covered with chips and bark and twigs, and trees felled but abandoned, because discovered to be unsound and useless. The place is a slaughter-house, and the few trees that have escaped serve but to intensify the un-pleasant aspects of the scene.

Accommodations in the lumber-region are not of the best; and the adventurous trout-fisher, though he will have plenty of sport, will also have plenty of annoyances. It is em-phatically a land where you can have every thing that you bring along with you. Of late years the railway company have become alive to the natural advantages of their route and the influence that beautiful scenery has upon traffic. They have recently erected a fine hotel at Renovo, which is the only stopping-place of importance between Lock Haven and Emporium. This almost immediately became a favorite summer resort, being located at a most picturesque point on the river, in the immediate vicinity of many beautiful mountain-streams, in which the trout shelter during the hot weather. The valley of the Susquehanna at Renovo is nearly circular in shape, and not very broad. The mountains rise up almost perpendicularly from the south bank, which is most picturesque, the other bank being low and shelving. The hotel, surrounded by beau-tifully-kept lawns adorned with parterres of brilliant flowers, becomes a marked point in the landscape, although in the early summer its blossoms are put to shame by the wild-flowers of the surrounding mountains; for at this time the slopes of the giant hills are everywhere covered with the pale-purple rhododendrons, which, when aggregated into large masses, fairly dazzle the eye with the excess of splendid color. Later, when all the flowerets of the wild-woods are small and insignificant, the buds

SCENES ON THE NORTH BRANCH OF THE SUSQUEHANNA.

North Branch of the Susquehanna, at Hunlocks.

of the cultivated lawns come forth and renew the rivalry with the wild scenes around
them more successfully. Just opposite the hotel a mountain rises to a height of twenty-three hundred feet in one vast slope of living green, ascending without a break
in a grand incline right up from the water's edge, whose brown flood is not here broad
enough to reflect the entire outlines of the stupendous mass. For here the river narrows
considerably, and is very deep under the mountain-side, becoming shallower as the bed

approaches the northern bank.
The little town of Renovo is
stretched along the Susquehanna side, its breadth being in-
considerable, although the valley here must be nearly half a
mile wide. The hills on the
other side are not so high as
the one that bids defiance to
the city folks in the hotel, daring, as it were, their utmost
efforts to climb up it. As
there is no road, and plenty
of rattlesnakes, few people are
bold enough to accept the
mute challenge. But on the
other side of the valley the
mountains are easily accessible,
and, in fact, are the daily resort of tourists who love to
shoot, or to pick blackberries
or huckleberries, which last
grow in immense quantities
around Renovo. There is a
mountain-road here which penetrates through the country to
the southward, and the teams
cross the river in a dreadfully
rickety ferry. This is a species
of flat-boat, which is propelled
across by a man hauling on a
rope suspended from the high
south bank to a huge pole on
the other shore. In the win-
try days, when the river is
turbulent and the winds are
high, the crossing here is not
very pleasant ; but in the
jolly summer-tide it becomes

Canal at Hunlocks.

a kind of pastime, and the visitors from large cities are so amused at this rude method of progression that they cross repeatedly for the fun of it. The view from the centre of the stream is beautiful exceedingly. One gets a better idea of the circular shape of the valley, and the manner in which the hills have retired to let the little town have a foothold. And there are islands in the channel covered with beautiful mosses. and stretches of shallow water where rocks peep up, on which gray cranes perch with solemn air, busily engaged in fishing. The shadows of the mountain's bank, too, are thrown into relief by the sunshine on the water, and the mountains to the westward form a brilliant background, with their tree-laden slopes brightened with golden tints.

At this point, though the eye cannot discern them because they are hid by the mountains, the tourist is in the immediate vicinity of numberless trout-streams. These runs have queer names, such as Kettle Creek, Hammersley's Fork, Young Woman's Creek, Fish-dam Run, Wyckoff's Run, Sinnemahoning Run, etc. The last is a stream of considerable size, and is one of the principal tributaries of the West Branch of the Susquehanna. It runs up beyond Emporium, and much lumber is sent down its current in the spring. The Susquehanna, after receiving the cold waters of Kettle Creek, begins to incline southward, and, from its junction with the Sinnemahoning, makes an abrupt turn due southward toward the town of Clearfield. From this point it ceases to be a river, branching off into numerous creeks that rise from the mountains of this region, where it is all either hill or valley, and where a plain is a rarity. The land here is cultivated with care and success, but the prevailing industry is mining, all the mountains here containing iron-ore. There is some considerable difficulty in floating down logs to the main stream of the Susquehanna below Clearfield, and most of the timber cut is used for the purpose of smelting or for forges, where the charcoal hammered iron is made. The scenery is not so wild as might be imagined, the forms of the mountains seldom varying from somewhat monotonous grandeur, relieved by the beauty of the forest-trees upon their sides. But for the geologist the region is singularly interesting, since everywhere are presented vestiges of the grand battles of old days between the imprisoned waters and their jailers, the huge hills.

To describe the north branch of the Susquehanna, it will be necessary to retrace our steps to Northumberland, the point of junction. The North Branch runs here almost due east, rushing right through a majestic range of mountains, which pass under the generic title of "Alleghanies." The railway is on the northern side, and, for a considerable distance, is built on a sort of shelf at the base of the mountains, close to the river's edge, but separated from it by the Pennsylvania Canal, which fringes this branch of the Susquehanna almost from its sources in New-York State. The mountains here are far bolder, more rocky, and with far less timber, exhibiting huge crags of a picturesque character, very unlike the small fragments that cover the hills of the Western Fork. The many chimneys vomiting black smoke at Danville, the first place of importance

PILLSBURY KNOB.

the tourist reaches, remind him forcibly that he is not out of the iron-region; and the coal-cars, which pass him on the road, tell him that he is approaching the very centre of the famous Pennsylvania coal-mines. Beyond Danville the river makes a bend away from the overhanging mountains of the northern side, and approaches more closely to the southern, which are far more densely wooded, and have consequently many more runs brawling and bubbling down their sides. The scenery here has a peculiar charm of its own, which is hard to describe or to localize. The hills on the northern bank are distant, but there are foot-hills that come down to the river. These are often cultivated, the fields of corn being broken by dark patches of waving pines and hemlocks. At the foot of these hills runs the railroad. In immediate proximity comes the canal— a quiet, peaceable, serviceable servant of commerce, vexed with few locks. Between the canal and the river is only an artificial dike of little breadth; but this has either been planted with trees and bushes, or Nature has sent her winged seeds there to take root, to fructify, and to render beautiful that which of itself was but plain and insignificant. This dike is quite a feature, impressing every eye with an idea of *leafiness*, which seems to be the prevailing charm of the district. Beyond it the river, some feet lower in level, rushes vigorously onward to join its waters with those of the West Branch. Its stream is more rapid, and its waves are of a clearer hue, than that which glides past Renovo, Williamsport, and Lock Haven. Rising up from the southern bank are wood-covered mountains, boasting fewer oaks and hickories than we have seen in our progress hitherto, but having a sombre grandeur of tone from the more numerous evergreens. The extreme background is veiled by a soft haze, through which the river looks silvery and the mountains an ethereal blue. At times the sweet sylvan character of the landscape is broken by a numerous gang of workmen drilling away huge blocks of limestone; for the foot-hills are of that structure, though the mountain-ranges are of sandstone. Again we come to a rough, irregular stone structure, black as ink, and surrounded by rudely-arranged scaffolding of a peculiar form. This is a coal-mine, or rather all that can be seen externally of it. Of iron-furnaces there are many, and of rolling-mills more than a few. These seem at first like blots upon the landscape, but they serve to diversify the monotonous beauty of the scenery. But the finest points to the artist are the places where the rushing, tumbling, foaming creeks from the mountains come raging down to join the river, and to frighten the canal from its staid propriety, necessitating great enlargements of the dike and beautiful bridges. These swellings of the dike gladden an artistic eye; for they are often covered with fine, large trees, and produce all the effects of islands hanging, as it were, over the brink of the river. There are several places where these bits of scenery exist—at Mifflin, Shickshinny, but, above all, at Hunlocks. Hunlocks Creek is not very long, but it has a commendable breadth and so precipitous a course that it is more like a cataract than a creek; and its turbulent, shallow stream carries down bowlders of a most respectable size. There is a coal-mine at Hunlocks, close upon the brink of the creek, and the miners down the shaft can hear the growling of the water-course in the spring, like distant thunder. For then its waters are swollen from the mountain snows; and it carries away, encumbered with its ice-masses, tons upon tons of rocks, which go hurtling down the stream, dashing against each other, and crashing with as much noise and fury as if an avalanche had been precipitated by the melting of a glacier. In our illustration on page 217 is a group of illustrations of this

Below Dam at Nanticoke.

region—the furnace on Hunlocks Creek, Nanticoke ferry, Danville, the hemlock-gatherers, the stone-quarry, etc.

After passing Pillsbury Knob, a remarkably bold promontory on the northern bank, the tourist arrives at Nanticoke, where the river expands considerably, becoming very shallow. Here there is a dam erected for the lumberers, though the business is yearly decreasing in this part. There are on the southern side broad stretches of fertile land below the bank, and these are cultivated with profit—principally for the raising of tobacco. The hills here rise in three several ranges upon the northern side and two upon the

NANTICOKE DAM.

southern, and the effect from the lowlands on a level with the river is very grand. The majority of the hills to the northward are not well wooded, and their prevailing hue is a dull, purplish brown. To the south the mountains are better wooded, but the slope is very considerable and the height not very great. Between these the river winds in a serpentine form, creating a thousand *coups d'œil* of transcendent loveliness. For here we

Wyoming Valley.

are actually entering the famous Wyoming Valley, so renowned for its beauties. The hills are not high, never exceeding two thousand feet, but the banks of the river and the river itself form such combinations of form and color as kindle the admiration of the most apathetic. The railway is on the northern bank, which is the more elevated; and, as the hills on this side are more picturesque than the other, it is impossible to get the best view until the river is crossed. This the railway does not do; and it will be best for the tourist to stop at Kingston and cross over to Wilkesbarre, at once the centre of the anthracite-coal region, the centre of the Wyoming Valley, and one of the most charming and prosperous towns in the country.

There is an island in the river just opposite the town, of which the bridge takes advantage. From the centre of this there is a lovely view. One sees to the left the Wyoming-Valley Hotel, built in Tudor style of gray-stone, and forming quite a picturesque feature; beyond it are all the houses of the local aristocracy stretched along the bank for half a mile. At this point the river makes a superb curve, like the flashing of a silver-sided fish, and disappears, showing, however, through the trees, broad patches of gleaming white. But this is only a slight glimpse. The real place for a striking view is from Prospect Rock, about two miles behind the town, nearly at the top of the first range of hills on the southern side of the river. This post of observation is on the summit of a jutting crag, and from its picturesquely-massed bowlders one can survey the whole of the Wyoming Valley, which, from Nanticoke westward to Pittston eastward, lies stretched before the eye of the visitor like a lovely picture. It is not broad; for, from Prospect Rock to the topmost crest of the first range of opposing hills, the distance, as the crow flies, is not more than four miles, and the farthest peak visible not six. But this is a gain rather than a loss; for the views that are so wide as to be bounded by the horizon are always saddening. Step by step the landscape leads you beyond the winding river, and beyond the swelling plain, to vast distances, which melt by imperceptible gradations into the gracious sky, and impress the heart with a conviction that just beyond your powers of sight is a better, nobler clime—a lovely land, where all is beautiful. Such prospects seem indeed the ladder by which the patriarch saw angels ascending and descending. They fill the soul with longing and despairing expectation. They stir the depths within us, and send tears of a divine anguish unbidden to the eyes. It is not so with Wyoming Valley. Its narrow boundaries of northern hills, tossing their crests irregularly like a billowy sea, steeped in clear, distinct hues of a purplish brown, and having every line and curvature plainly in sight, compel the eyes to rest within the green and smiling valley, dotted with countless houses, ever scattered sparsely or gathered thickly into smiling towns. Through the points of brilliant light with which the sun lights up the white houses, the Susquehanna glides like a gracious lady-mother, making soft sweeps here and noble curves there, but ever bordered by fringes of deep, emerald green. The whole valley is green, save where the towns toss up to heaven their towers and spires from numberless churches, and where behind, as if in hiding, black mounds and grimy structures mark the collieries. The contracted view gives no sadness of spirit, stirs no unquiet heart, like the expanded prospect. Far otherwise: the soul itself expands with love and pride at the sight of so much peaceful beauty, so much prosperity and happiness, so much progress. The beyond is out of sight, out of thought,

WYOMING VALLEY, FROM PROSPECT ROCK, WILKESBARRE.

WYOMING VALLEY, FROM CAMP HILL.

MONUMENT.

VIEW FROM KINGSTON.

out of ken, and the soul enjoys, without any drop of bitterness, the full cup of pure earthly happiness. He must be a sordid wretch, indeed, whose pulses are not stirred at the sight before him. Too far to be vexed with details, too near not to see distinctly, the gazer on Prospect Rock views the landscape under just such circumstances as will delight him. Therefore, all who have stood upon these masses of sandstone, and have watched the cloud-shadows sweeping over the broad plain, and have seen the sun go down in beauty, and the stillness of twilight overstretching the happy valley, have gone away with hearts satisfied and rendered at ease. But this was not always a happy valley, and the time has been when this fair stretch of smiling green was smoking with the fires of burning homes, and the green turf was gory with the blood of men defending their families from the invader and his savages; when the Susquehanna shuddered at the corpses polluting her stream, and the mountains echoed back in horror the shrieks of wretches dying in torture at the Indian's stake. For, where the little village of Wyoming rises beside the softly-flowing river, the telescope discerns a plain stone monument commemorating the awful massacre of the 3d and 4th of July, 1778. The valley was defended by Colonel Zebulon Butler, with such militia as could be gathered, against the attack of a very superior force of British, assisted by a numerous band of Iroquois. After the inevitable defeat, which happened on the 3d, the conquered retreated into the fort with their women and children. They surrendered on the 4th, with promises of fair terms, and the British commander, to his eternal disgrace, gave them up to the fiendish savages, who were his auxiliaries. Then followed that massacre which sent a thrill of horror through the civilized world, and which has formed the subject of the noblest poems and the finest pictures. Out of misery came bliss; out of defeat, bloodshed, burning homes, and captured wives and daughters, came tranquil happiness and a material prosperity almost unequalled. The whole valley is one vast deposit of anthracite coal; and is now only in the dawning of its prosperity. What it will be in the full sunlight of fortune it passeth here to tell.

BOSTON.

WITH ILLUSTRATIONS BY J. DOUGLAS WOODWARD.

THERE was little of the "picturesque," to the eyes of the Puritan colony which took up its abode on the main coast where now stand Charlestown and Bunker Hill, in the bold, bald, bleak, triple-hilled peninsula which confronted them on the southwest. It is true that one effusive Puritan, with peripatetic habits, wandering in the late spring-time in the neighborhood, found it possessed of "fair endowments," the hil-

Brewer Fountain, Boston Common.

locks "dainty," the plains "delicate and fair," and the streams "clear and running," and "jetting most jocundly." His less imaginative brethren esteemed the promontory bare

Fort Independence, from South Boston.

and drear, even in the season of budding and flowering Nature; for one of them describes it to be "a hideous wilderness, possessed by barbarous Indians, very cold, sickly, rocky, barren, unfit for culture, and likely to keep the people miserable."

The Puritans named it, with prosaic sense, "Tri-Mountain;" the Indians called it, with poetic suggestiveness, "Shawmut," or "Sweet Waters;" and the gratitude of its earliest settlers, who came from old Boston of the fens of English Lincolnshire, christened their new abode "Boston." The Charlestown colony, like the children of Israel, suffered from exceeding want of water, and moved to Tri-Mountain, which they purchased of its reverend owner, Blackstone, for the absurd sum of thirty pounds, because of the "sweet waters" which the Indian Shawmut promised. Thus began to exist Boston, with its teeming memories, its dramatic history, its steady growth, and its manifold picturesque and romantic aspects.

To him, however, who approaches Boston by the bay, it is difficult to distinguish the three hills upon which Winthrop and his fellow-colonists perched themselves. The city wears the appearance of a single broad cone, with a wide base lining the water's edge for miles on either side, ascending by a gradual plane to the yellow-bulb apex afforded by the State-House dome. Only now and then is the plane broken by a building looming above the rest, and pierced by the white, pointed steeples or fanciful modern towers of the churches, or an occasional high, murky, smoke-puffing, brick chimney rising amid the jumble of dwellings and warehouses. Boston presents the singular contradiction of symmetry in general outline, and irregularity in detail. One scarcely imagines, as he gazes upon this almost mathematically cone-shaped city, rising, by equal and slow gradations, to its central summit, that it is, of all places, the most jagged and uneven; that its streets and squares are ever at cross-purposes; that its general plan is no plan at all, but seemingly the result of an engineering comedy of errors; that many of its thoroughfares run so crazily that a man travels by them almost around to the point whence he started, and many others run into blank no-thoroughfare; and that, by no process of reasoning from experience otherwhere, can he who sets out for a given destination reach it.

The visitor who reaches Boston, indeed, by water, can hardly fail to be struck with the natural beauties—heightened now by artificial adornment—of the harbor, narrowing, as it does, in even curves on either side, dotted with many turfy and undulating or craggy islands—long stretches of beach being visible almost to the horizon, now and then interspersed by a jutting, cliff-bound promontory, or pushing out seaward a straggling, shapeless peninsula of green. Almost imperceptibly, the coast of the noble bay vanishes into villages—now upon a low, now a lofty, shore—which, in their turn, merge as indistinctly into the thickly-settled, busy suburbs, and the city itself. The islands, which in Winthrop's day were bare and wellnigh verdureless, are now mostly crowned with handsome forts, light-houses, hospitals, almshouses, and "farm-schools"—edifices for the most part striking, and filling an appropriate place in the varied landscape. Fort Warren and Fort Independence—in the former of which the Confederate Vice-President Stephens, and Generals Ewell and Kershaw, were incarcerated—are imposing with their lofty ramparts, their yawning casemates, their sharp, symmetrical outline of granite, and their regular, deep-green embankments. Nearer rise, from a lofty hill in South Boston, the great white sides and cupola of the Perkins Institution for the Blind, which Dickens so graphically described after his first visit to America. To the right of the State-House dome looms, distinct and solitary, the plain granite shaft of Bunker-Hill Monument. Below, on either hand, are the wharfs and docks, crowded with craft of every size, shape, and nationality, from the little fishing-yachts which are wafting, on a summer's morning, in large numbers hither and thither on the water, to the stately Cunarder, whose red funnel rises amid the masts in its East-Boston slip. An eye-glance from the harbor takes in nearly the whole of the Boston shipping. It is modest, compared with the

VIEW FROM STEEPLE OF ARLINGTON-STREET CHURCH.

forests of masts and funnels which cluster along the East and North Rivers ; but its extent and movement give evidence of a busy and prosperous port. The water-view of Boston betrays its industrial as well as its commercial character. Large, many-windowed factories, tall, smoke-stained chimneys, appear at intervals throughout the stretch of thick settlement from City Point, in South Boston, in the south, to the limits of East Boston and Chelsea, in the north, indicating the weaving of many fabrics, the fruits of deft handiwork, and the transformation of the metals to useful purposes.

On its harbor-side, Boston exhibits its trade and industry, its absorption in the businesses of life, the sights and scenes of engrossing occupation. Transferring the point of view from the eastern to the western side of the city, the results, instead of the pro-

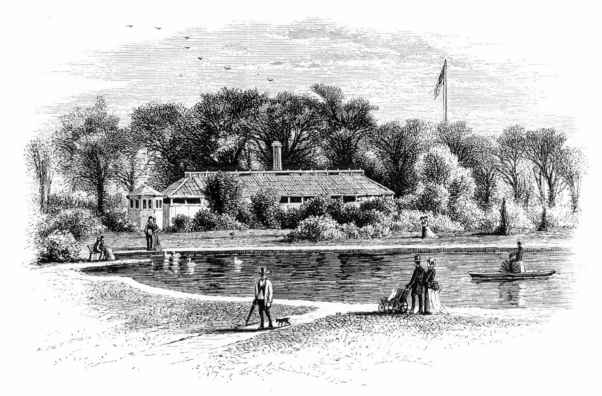

Scene in the Public Garden.

cesses, of wealth appear. From the arch in the steeple of the Arlington-Street Church [picture No. 3], you gaze upon one of the most striking and noble scenes which any American city presents—a scene of brightness, beauty, luxury, adorned by the elegances of horticultural, architectural, and sculptural art, enriched by the best effects of native taste, and gifted by Nature with fine contrasts of elevation, declivity, and outline—a scene which includes all that of which Boston is most proud in external aspect. In the immediate foreground lies the Public Garden, on a space redeemed, within a quarter of a century, from the waters of the Back Bay ; for, up to that period, the waves reached up nearly to the edge of Charles Street, which separates the garden from the Common. Without possessing the pretensions of Central Park or Fairmount, the Public Garden is a gem of a park. It is not certain that now, in its days of young growth, it is not more lovely than it will be when its trees have grown into leafy arches, and its clumps of shrubs into opaque copses. Its edges are even now lined with thriving trees along the iron railings; winding paths lead in among exquisite flower-beds, umbrageous shrub-arbors provided with rustic seats, fountains playing in marble basins, statues of Washington and Everett, and commemorative of the discovery of anæsthetics, and "Venus rising from the Sea," about whose form the light spray shimmers. The borders of the lawns are adorned by beautiful combinations of vari-colored and vari-leafed plants. In the centre is a pretty serpentine, crossed by a heavy granite bridge, and upon whose waters there float swans and ducks, as well as canopied barges and queer little craft, let to the public at moderate prices. Close to the lake is a pretty conservatory, blooming with hot-house plants—the whole park being enclosed in a setting of spacious streets and mansions, park and mansions lending to each other the aspect of enhanced elegance. Beyond, almost hidden in its wealth of mature foliage, is the Common—the old, historic, much-praised, and laughed-at Common—rising, by a graceful plane, to the State-House at its summit, here and there interspersed with hillocks, whose sides peep through openings in the trees, and at whose feet are broad, bare spaces for military manœuvres and popular out-door games. Behind the Common you catch glimpses of the steeples and public halls of Tremont [Tri-Mountain] Street; the historic steeple of the Old South, saved by a miracle from the great fire, which stopped under its very shadow; the steeple of the Park-Street Church, only less memorable in the annals of Boston; the comparatively plain, old Masonic Temple, now used as a United States court-house; and that noble and lavish specimen of Gothic architecture, the pinnacled, granite, new Masonic Temple, rich in decoration, and rising far above the surrounding edifices. On the left, the aristocratic Beacon Street—on the site of the cow-pastures of the last century—rises majestically toward the State-House—its buildings piled irregularly one above another, of brick and brown-stone and marble, of many shapes and colors—the street of the family and moneyed "high society" of the Hub. The view in this direction is most striking. To him who has gazed, at Edinburgh, from Prince's Street along the high, piled-up buildings rising to and capped by the hoary old castle, this scene of Beacon Street, with the State-House at the top, vividly resembles, in general outline and effect, that most picturesque of British cities. The principal difference is that, in place of the hoary keep and ramparts, there is the big, yellow dome, with its gilded cupola, and its American flag floating from the top.

Boston Common! Sacred to the memory of Puritan training-days, and the ruminating of Puritan cows; to the execution of witches, and stern reprimands of women branded with Scarlet Letters; to fierce tussles with Indians, and old-time duels; to the intense exhortations of George Whitefield, and the solemn festivals of the Puritan colonists; to struggles with British troops, and the hanging in effigy of red-coat foes; not less to the memory of thousands of lovers, dead and gone, from the time when it was the favored retreat "where the Gallants, a little before sunset, walk with their Marmalet-Madams, till the bell, at nine o'clock, rings them home!" A "small but pleasant common!" says old Josselyn, who saw it with his critical English eye, fresh from Hyde Park, just about two centuries ago. A small, perhaps, and certainly pleasant common, still, it

Old Elm, Boston Common.

is in these later days. Indeed, for more than two centuries the Common has been the lung of the town and city, the most central and the most agreeable of its open-air resorts, at once the promenade for grown people, and the play-ground and coasting-tryst of the children. Occupying a space of nearly fifty acres, there has been room enough for all; and, while the Common was long the outer western edge of the city, it is fast becoming its centre, as the spacious streets and squares of stately brown-stone and swell-front mansions are gradually stretching out upon the constantly-increasing "made land" of the Back Bay. The beauty of the natural position of the Common, and the richness of its soil, have required but little art to make it a charming park, gifted with all the variety and pleasant prospect worthy of a great and thriving city. It sweeps down the slope of the hill on the edge of which is Beacon Street, and at the summit of which is the State-House—broken, now and then, by undulations crowned by trees and carpeted with softest turf—until it reaches a lowest limit at Boylston Street, on the south. Its foliage no efforts of artistic cultivation can anywhere surpass. Many of the trees are centuries old. The noble rows of elms which, on the Great Mall running just below and parallel with Beacon Street, rise to a stately height, and, bending toward each other on either side, form a grand, natural, arched cathedral-nave, were planted one hundred and fifty years ago; while those of the Little Mall, running at right angles to the first, were set out by Colonel Paddock, rather more than a century ago. These are the two main avenues. The thick, cool shade is gratefully resorted to in summer; seats are ranged along for public use; here *Punch* revels in his quarrelsome squeak; and candy-venders, and lung-testers, and blind organ-grinders, and patent-medicine men, ply their out-door trades; and here the "gallants" still walk, as of yore, with their "madams" in the slowly-deepening twilight and the soft, moonlit nights. The Common is intersected by a maze of irregular, shaded avenues, its foliage being spread thickly over the larger portion of its surface; while its expanses of lawn, kept with assiduous pains, are as velvety and bright green as those of the boasted London parks. On every hand, the Common betrays evidences and memorials of its venerable age and its teeming history, as well as of the tender care with which it is maintained by modern Boston. In one corner is an ancient graveyard, with hoary tombstones, on which the inscriptions are half effaced, and which here and there lean over, as if at last weary of celebrating, to indifferent eyes, the virtues of the forgotten dead; and with embedded vaults, whose padlocks are rusted, and whose roofs are overgrown with grass and moss. Just behind the graveyard is a small, encaged deer-park, where the nimble and graceful denizens of the forest graze, or sleep, or eat, mild and tame, and apparently indifferent to the gaze of the curious passers-by, who linger a moment at the grating to watch their movements. Near the centre of the Common is the "Frog-Pond," a much-abused but pretty bit of water, provided with a fountain and a granite lining, situated just at the foot of one of the umbrageous hillocks, and always a pet resort for the children, who, in summer, sail their miniature yachts and frigates on its clear waters, and, in winter, skate on its glossy surface. Hard by the Frog-Pond is the still proud "Great Elm," a wonder of Nature, and a landmark of history. For more than two centuries its immense trunk and wide-spreading limbs have been the admiration and the shelter of Bostonians. An iron railing preserves it from rude abuse; an inscription tells of its venerable but unknown age, its historic significance, and perils by wind and storm. It is jagged and sear, but still stands vigorous

BOSTON SCENES.

and hale, with its circumference of nearly twenty-two feet, and its more than seventy feet of height; while the spread of its branches extends across eighty-six feet. Near by the Park-Street Mall stands the noble fountain given to the Common by Gardner Brewer, and appropriately called, after him, the "Brewer Fountain." It is an exquisite product of Parisian art, with a lower large and upper small basin, the water jetting from a topmost knob and through spouts in both basins, half veiling the bronze figures of old Neptune and Amphitrite, of Acis and Galatea, which sit in picturesque posture beneath. The fountain stands amid a cluster of noble elms; and above it rises the narrow and pointed spire of the Park-Street Church. At the lower or west side of the Common is a broad, bare space, where reviews are held, and base-ball games are played, the hillocks above converting it into a half amphitheatre, and affording a fine stand-point whence to view the displays and sports.

Leaving the Common, and passing along Beacon Street and by the Public Common, you reach the quarter of elegance and luxury and lavish taste which has sprung up entirely within twenty years, and is known as the "Back Bay" Penetrating this quarter, you have quite lost sight of all that is old, staid, and historic, about the Puritan capital. The aspect bespeaks forgetfulness of the past; it symbolizes Boston in its present and future prosperity; it tells the story of what fruit, in domestic luxury and architectural display, persistent thrift in commerce, and the busy competition in the active walks of life, bring forth in these latter days. The Back Bay is stately, without being cheerless; it is new, and not glaring; it is modern and ornamental, yet the substantial New-England character is impressed upon its firm, solid, yet graceful blocks, and broad, airy streets and squares. It stretches from Beacon Street, on the one side, southward nearly two miles, almost to the limits of what once was Roxbury; and here a vast area of residences—all of the better sort, and ranging from pretty, tempting rows of brick "swell-fronts" of two stories and French roof, for the family of moderate means, to great, square, and richly-adorned palaces of brown-stone—has been built in wide streets, and wider, tree-lined avenues, with now and then a statue, and oftener a church of the modern, showy Gothic or Flemish style. Mansard is the tutelar architectural saint of the whole quarter.

A sudden contrast is it to turn off from the view of this really splendid and brilliant quarter into cosey, umbrageous Charles Street, famous as the residence of Holmes, Andrew, and Fields, to pass up through the sedate repose and dignified presence of the "Beacon-Hill" district. Here, in Mount-Vernon Street, and Chestnut Street, and Louisburg Square, is the older aristocratic quarter, cast into a majestic shade by its plethora of ancient elms, notable for its tall "swell-fronts," with neat, small gardens in front, and carriage-ways up to the sombre doors. Many of the staid old families—the "high respectabilities"—continue here, disdaining the temptations of the brighter and more showy sphere of the Back Bay.

BOSTON, FROM MOUNT BOWDOIN.

Out of this sleepily-tranquil neighborhood, on the eastern slope of the hill, you suddenly come upon the bustle and clatter, the wide-awake world of trade and shopping. The tide of business is caught at Tremont Street, to rise into a rushing, half-pent-up torrent on ancient Newbury, now Washington Street. And now you are in the midst of business, official, and historic Boston. In Boston, above all American cities, the charm of natural situation, and the painstaking of generously-patronized art, are enhanced by historic associations which will surely find a place in the great American epic of the future. In that part of it which lies between Tremont Street and the water are most of the memorable spots and edifices around which clings the aroma of past heroic deeds and noteworthy scenes. Here, too, are the buildings used for public purposes and the assemblages of the citizens—passing down School Street, the high, granite City-Hall, with its half-dome of the Louvre type, its singular complexity of architectural design, its broad esplanade adorned by the bronze statue of Franklin, and its appearance of busy absorption in municipal affairs; near by it is the historic, Saxon-towered King's Chapel, with the graveyard ensconced in the midst of the living bustle; and opposite the lower

Boston Highlands.

Jamaica Plains, from Boyleston.

end of the street stands the yet more historic Old South Church, staid and plain, which Burgoyne turned into a riding-school for the British soldiery, after using the pulpit and pews to light fires, where Whitefield preached and Franklin worshipped, and, since the great fire of 1872, serving the purpose of the post-office; and just around the corner from the Old South is the site of the house wherein Franklin was born.

The historic relics of old Boston—some of which, to be sure, have passed out of existence, swept away by the exigencies of modern convenience—are to be found scattered over the northern and eastern end of the peninsula; but the tortuous region included between the head of State Street and the northern limit is perhaps the most thickly studded with memorable spots and ancient mementos. At the head itself of State Street, in the middle of the thoroughfare, stands the old State-House, a grave old pile, with a belfry, looking down gravely upon the haunts of the money-changers and "solid men," for whom State Street is the centre and nucleus, and now given up to tailors' shops, telegraph and insurance offices, lawyers' chambers, and the Merchants' Reading-room. Passing from State Street through a narrow lane, you come upon the most notable of Boston edifices, standing in a somewhat narrow square, surrounded by a constant and hurried bustle of trade, but preserving still the architectural, and, in a measure, the useful features of a century and more ago. Faneuil Hall, built and presented to Boston by Peter Faneuil as "a town-hall and market-place," is a town-hall and market-place still. It is a large, rather square, thoroughly old-fashioned building, with three stories of arched windows, surmounted by a cupola, which is all too diminutive in comparison with the rest of the structure. On the ground-floor is the market, which overflows on either side upon the pavements; the second floor is devoted to the great public meeting-hall, with galleries on three sides, a large platform opposite the entrance-doors, and, over the platform, the large and imposing picture, by Healy, representing the United States Senate in session, and Webster, on his feet, making the memorable reply to Hayne. The walls are studded here and there with portraits of busts of eminent men, old Governors, and other Massachusetts worthies, among which may be recognized Faneuil himself, the three Adamses, Hancock, Gore, Sumner, Lincoln, and Andrew. Here are held all sorts of political and other meetings, orations, campaign-rallies, and general conferences of the citizens. The reader need scarcely be informed that it was in Faneuil Hall that the citizens of Boston were aroused to resistance against the British, and that many of the most memorable scenes in the earlier stage of the Revolution took place there.

Proceeding from this historic quarter southward by Tremont Street, and along the Common, one reaches, first, the ornate and imposing Masonic Temple, with its arched windows and lofty pinnacles; and, just beyond, is the stately, sombre-colored, substantial Public Library. At this point all the principal public buildings are left behind, and a newer Boston is approached. Those who are not yet beyond the climacteric of age can remember when the space which separated thickly-settled Boston from the suburb of Roxbury was but a narrow neck of land, which in some places almost converted Boston into an island, and whereon were but a few scattered wooden houses. Now, however, this part of the peninsula is as fully occupied as its more ancient quarter, but in a very different style of streets and buildings. The narrow neck of land has been widened by the filling in of new land, and now constitutes a wide, well-built reach between Boston and Roxbury. The whole quarter is called the " South End." The main thoroughfare, Washington Street, is, unlike its aspect in the west, wide, straight, spacious, umbrageous, adorned with many handsome buildings, marble hotels, the great new Catholic cathedral, and long lines of bright and tempting stores. The squares and streets are regularly built, and, but for the long blocks of houses constructed exactly alike, which give a monotonous appearance, the " South End " might well bear comparison for its beauty with the handsomest quarters of other cities. The " South End " has, however, plenty of light, air, and elbow-room.

The suburbs of Boston have been well compared to those of Paris; and Brookline, especially, has been called the Montreuil of America. The amphitheatre of the hills, in which the peninsula is set as in a frame, is almost circular; these eminences are undulating, rising now into cones, now into broad rotundity, broken here and there by jagged cliffs and abrupt descents, dipping deep into leafy valleys, and then sloping off almost imperceptibly to wide, flat, fertile plains. Nature has endowed this surrounding series of hills with all that could beautify and make picturesque ; it is not a single circle, but many circles, of uneven elevations, one without the other ; and, from many of the farther summits, the city, with the yellow dome and glittering cupola of the State-House at its apex, may be seen throughout its extent, enclosed in a magnificent framework of the foliage of the hills which intervene. Especially striking is the view of the city, thus enclosed, from Mount Warren, where the General, Warren, is buried, Mcunt Hope, Mount Dearborn, and Mount Bowdoin, the latter of which eminences stands just south of the old town of Roxbury [picture No. 7]. Upon the groundwork thus provided by Nature, all that in modern art and taste, and in generous expenditure, could conduce to elegance and luxury of aspect, and comfort of residence, has been added to the landscape. Almost all the Boston suburbs are fairly bedded in rich foliage, much

Jamaica Pond.

of it comprising the old forest-trees, and much also due to the careful cultivation of succeeding generations. Perhaps nowhere in America are the English arts of lawn and hedge culture, of garden decoration, more nearly imitated, or more successfully. There is the greatest variety in exterior adornment, as there is in architectural design. In the midst of large areas of lawn and copse, the square, compact, little-ornamented, sloping-roofed mansions of a century ago are followed by imposing, newly-constructed mansions, with fanciful French roofs and towers, an amplitude of verandas, and the protuberance on all sides of jutting bay-windows. In some of the suburbs are estates which would far from shame an English duke who dated from the Conquest; with their roods of hedge lining the roads, their broad avenues, winding through ravishing prospects for half a mile before reaching the mansion, their large conservatories and cottages, their close-cut terraces, and their gardens abloom, in the season, with rare flowers and a wealth of native shrubbery. Any of the suburbs may be reached by rail from the centre of the city within half an hour, and most of them in half that time; and here the heads of old families and the "merchant-princes" delight to vie with each other in the beauty and refinement of their home-surroundings. The suburbs of Dorchester, which overlooks the harbor, and of Roxbury, next west from Dorchester, both of which are now included within the city boundary, occupy the higher elevations in the immediate vicinity of Boston, and, although so near, afford many retreats where one may easily imagine himself in the depths of the country. Both are built on the sides and summits of rather jagged and irregular hills; and, if we once more compare Boston with Edinburgh, and the State-House to Auld Reekie Castle, it may be said that Roxbury well represents Calton Hill. It is the most thickly settled of the southern suburbs, and has a pretty and busy business square; advancing beyond this, you walk along shady streets, taking sudden turns up-hill, or plunging downward with an easy or sharp descent.

Next beyond the eminences of Roxbury, the almost flat expanse of Jamaica Plains is reached. But the beauty of the plain, lying coseyly and shadily among a circle of hills, with pretty streams flowing through it, with a grateful variety of home-like residences, wide, airy, and tree-lined streets, and a snug appearance which is even more perceptible here than upon the heights, is not less attractive than the more lofty suburbs. Many a quiet, rural nook, where the idler may sprawl upon the yielding turf, and angle, meditate, or read, forgetful of the nearness of the big, bustling metropolis, or even of the more contiguous suburban settlement, may be found just aside from the village of Jamaica Plains.

The most attractive spot in this suburb is a placid lake, lying between the plain on one side and sloping hills on the other, fringed with overhanging foliage, broken here and there by well-trimmed lawns, which stretch down from picturesque cottages or old-fashioned mansions to the water's edge, with now and then a bit of sandy beach. Here take place, in summer, suburban regattas and much boat-rowing, while, in winter, "Jamaica

BOSTON SUBURBS.

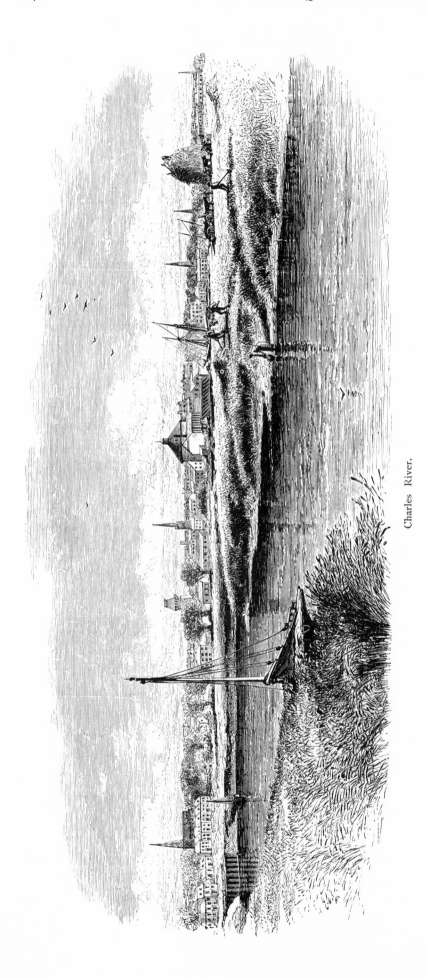

Charles River.

Pond" is a pet resort for Boston skaters. Just beyond the Pond, the loveliest of Boston suburbs, Brookline, is reached. Brookline, on its southern side, comprises a series of beautiful highlands, occupied almost exclusively by large, handsome mansions, in the midst of spacious and picturesquely - wooded parks. It is a snug, highly-cultivated, home-like environ, the favored retreat of the Winthrops, the Lawrences, the Sargeants, and other of the older and wealthier Boston families. Its streets are broad, and wind in and out under elms, maples, and chestnuts, presenting changing aspects of elegance and luxury at every turn, charming bits of landscape suddenly appearing between the trees, and lordly residences of brownstone, brick, granite, and wood, disclosing themselves at the end of arched avenues, and on the summit of graceful eminences. Sometimes broad lawns sweep down the hill-sides to dead walls facing the streets; sometimes only the cupolas and turrets of the mansions peep above the thick copses. It is hard to conceive any style of picturesque architecture in which Brookline is wanting, from the Elizabethan to the Mansard. Nor is it without historic edifices: one house, the ancestral residence of the Aspinwalls, which still stands in a wide, open field, near the centre of the town, sturdily supports its two centuries' existence. Brookline is as noteworthy for the beauty of its churches as for the air of luxurious comfort which its residences betray. The avenues leading from Boston "Back Bay" through Brookline are the favorite drives of the city people, and, on pleasant afternoons, are crowded with showy turnouts, horseback-riders, and family carriages. The old reservoir occupies the crest of a noble hill, and the drive around it is full of pleasant prospects; while the new reservoir, "Chestnut Hill," lying on the northern edge of the town, is surrounded by broad roads along the granite embankments, and affords an agreeable limit to the

College Buildings.

drives from the city. The public buildings of Brookline, mainly consisting of the new Town-Hall and the Public Library, are striking for the tastefulness of their design, and their combination of beauty and convenience. Both are in the French style, the Town-Hall being lofty, of granite, and capped with a high Mansard façade. The Public Library is a snug little edifice of red brick, with Mansard roof, and having a pretty,

Washington Elm, Cambridge.

close-cut lawn in front. The village square, lined with tall brick and wooden stores, is one of the brightest and pleasantest of the many village squares around Boston. At one end of it is the railway-station, whence trains start every hour for Boston, reaching it in fifteen minutes, and returning quite as frequently; and from the square, in all directions, the streets branch off irregularly, invariably lined with shade-trees, and betraying the evidences of domestic taste and comfort.

Fresh Pond, Cambridge.

Beyond Brookline the river Charles
flows through flat, marshy tracts, westward
from the Back Bay, to the hilly districts of Wal-
tham and Auburndale, some miles beyond; and,
on its northern bank, lies the University of Cambridge, situated on a broad plain, extending from
the Charles to the eminences of Somerville. Cambridge wears the same aspect of
umbrageous adornment, spacious streets, and elegant mansions, characteristic of all the
Boston suburbs; and, nearly in its centre, is Harvard University, with its various
edifices standing, without apparent order, in a spacious and shady park. Here are
plain, old, brick dormitories, built more than a century ago; bright new dormitories,
with much ornament; a Gothic, granite library, Gore Hall, with pinnacles, buttresses,
and painted windows; the picturesque Appleton Chapel; the cosey Dane Hall, where
the law-lectures are given, with its heavy pillars and severely plain front; the square,
marble recitation-hall; the solid granite anatomical museum; and other large edifices of
various styles, for the different uses of the university. The high elms, forming majestic
natural archways, the quiet that reigns throughout the scholastic purlieu, the singular
contrasts between the new buildings and the old, the rare collections which have

been gradually formed for generations, the venerable age of the university, its illustrious catalogue of alumni, its noteworthy share in the history of the nation—all render a visit to "Old Harvard" one of peculiar interest. Beyond the colleges a broad, winding thoroughfare, Brattle Street, leads past comfortable and sometimes very handsome dwellings, in somewhat more than a mile, to the beautiful, hilly cemetery of Mount

Lake and Fountain, Mount Auburn Cemetery.

Auburn ; but, on the way, several places of note are to be observed. One is the grand old mansion now occupied by the poet Longfellow, memorable as having been the headquarters of Washington during the siege of Boston, a large, square, wooden mansion, painted yellow, with a veranda under wide-spreading elms at one side, a garden behind, and a pretty lawn extending to the street in front. The next house beyond was occupied by Dr. Worcester, the compiler of the dictionary, till his death ; while, farther on,

Mount Auburn Tower.

toward Mount Auburn, down
a cool, shady lane, is the house,
not very unlike Longfellow's,
which is the ancestral home of the poet
Lowell. Branching off from Brattle Street,
Fresh Pond, a lovely expanse of water,
much resembling Jamaica Pond, is reached;
and thence it is but a brief jaunt to the
most beautiful of New-England "cities of the dead," Mount Auburn. This cemetery
is built on the sides and summits of graceful hills, and in the shaded valleys between
them; and, while Nature has been lavish with foliage and picturesque prospects, art
has bestowed every various and appropriate adornment. There are lakes and ponds,
elaborate tombs and monuments, nooks and grottos, and an abundance of flowers,
quiet paths beside modest graves, and, on the summit of the highest hill, a large gray
tower rising above the trees, whence a panorama of Boston and its suburbs, for miles
around, opens upon the view. Beyond Cambridge is the new suburban city of Somer-

ville, built on the side of a hill, and then comes the long, flat city of Charlestown, with the granite shaft of Bunker Hill looming conspicuous and solitary among its mass of buildings, steeples, and chimneys. This, with Chelsea, completes the circuit of the Boston suburbs; and, after one has made it, he cannot but confess that the Pilgrim wilderness has been made to blossom like the rose, and that no American city has been more amply blessed in the beauty, comfort, taste, and picturesqueness of its surroundings.

Charlestown, from Brighton.

LAKE GEORGE AND LAKE CHAMPLAIN.

WITH ILLUSTRATIONS BY HARRY FENN.

IT is somewhat remarkable that in the physical conformation of our country the northern part should be studded with innumerable lakes, while below the southern boundary of New-York State this feature should disappear. Apart from those grand inland seas which form the northern limits of the Union, there are gathered within the borders of New York a number of charming expanses of water that may be equalled, but are certainly unexcelled, in natural attractions by any lakes in the world. There are beautiful lakes in Maine, in New Hampshire, and in Vermont; in these States there are, indeed, famous contributions to our far-northern lake-system; but New York may claim the palm, both as regards the number and beauty of its inland waters. It is preëminently a State of lakes. In the great northern woods their name is legion; and not only is the western boundary encircled by lakes, but the interior is fairly crowded with these beautiful miniature seas, of which we have only to mention Cayuga, Seneca, Canandaigua, Otsego, Oneida, to recall to the reader a succession of pleasing pictures. Below New York the lake-system disappears. In Pennsylvania there are none much above the dignity of ponds, and but few of these. In Northern New Jersey there are two handsome sheets, one of which extends across the border into New York. All the vast mountain-region of Virginia, East Tennessee, and North Carolina, is utterly without lakes—a singular circumstance, inasmuch as the

LAKE GEORGE FROM PROSPECT MT.

Lake George, from Glen's-Falls Road.

conditions would appear to exist for the formation of these water-expanses.

Of all the New-York lakes, Champlain and George are the most famous historically, the most beautiful in picturesque features, and the best known to tourists and pleasure - seekers. They are united by a narrow stream, through which the waters of one flow into the other; and, as we glance at them upon the map, the lesser lake would seem to be merely a branch of the larger one. The name of "Horicon," which the Indians applied to the lake, is said to mean "Silver Water;" they also had another designation for it —"Andiartarocte," meaning "the Tail of the Lake." It is to be regretted that the most beautiful of our lakes should be the only one without either a pleasing or a distinctive name. Had the lake been a less busy scene, had it filled a less important place in our early annals, the Indian name of Horicon would gradually have been accepted by the occasional hunters and pioneers that would have reached its shores, and thus attained a recognition before ambitious captains had sought to impress the name of their far - off king upon it. The French, also, sought to rob it of its Indian designation. It was they, of the white races, who first discovered it; and so struck were they with the transparency and clearness of its waters that they called it Lake St.-Sacrement, and actually prized its water so highly as to transmit it to Canada for baptismal purposes.

Lake George is situated in Warren County, New York, about sixty miles, in a direct line, north of Albany. It is thirty-four miles long, from one to four miles wide, and is said to have a depth, at places, of nearly four hundred feet. Its long, narrow form gives it the character of a river rather than of a lake, or, at least, of the popular idea of a lake; but many of our lakes have this elongated form, Cayuga and Seneca being almost identical with Lake George in the general features of their conformation.

Fort George.

The waters of Lake George flow into Champlain by a narrow rivulet at its northern extremity, the distance which separates the two sheets of water being not more than four miles. The surface of Lake George is dotted with many small islands—one for each day in the year, so it is popularly asserted—while its shores lift themselves into bold highlands. The lake is fairly embowered among high hills—a brilliant mirror set in among cliffs and wooded mountains, the rugged sides of which perpetually reflect their wild features in its clear and placid bosom. "Peacefully rest the waters of Lake George," says the historian Bancroft, "between their rampart of highlands. In their pellucid depth the cliffs and the hills and the trees trace their images; and the beautiful region speaks to the heart, teaching affection for Nature."

Approaching Lake George from the south, the tourist takes the Saratoga Railway at Albany for Glen's Falls; thence the lake is reached by stage-coach, a distance of nine miles. If the traveller is fortunate enough to secure an outside seat upon the coach, the ride will prove to him an entertaining one throughout, but specially charming will be the first glimpse of the lake as the coach approaches the terminus of its route at Caldwell. One especial sensation is in reserve for him. The spacious Fort William Henry Hotel, situated upon the site of the old fort of the same name, stands directly at the head of the lake, with a noble expanse of its waters spread out before it. The coach is driven with a sweep and a swirl through the grounds of the hotel, and, suddenly turning a corner, dashes up before the wide and corridored piazza, crowded with groups of people—all superb life and animation on one side of him, and a marvellous stretch of lake and mountain and island and wooded shore on the other—such a picture, in its charm and brightness and completeness, as the New-World traveller rarely encounters. The scene, moreover, never seems to lose its charm. Always there is that glorious stretch of lake and shore bursting upon the sojourner's vision; he cannot put foot upon the piazza, he cannot throw open his hotel-window, he cannot come or depart, without there ever spreading before him, in the soft summer air, that perfect landscape, paralleled for beauty only by a similarly idyllic picture at West Point, amid the Highlands of the Hudson.

At Caldwell one may linger many days, learning by heart the changing beauties of the scene. There is a superb bird's-eye view of the lake that may be obtained from the summit of Prospect Mountain, on the southern border of the lake. A road from Caldwell leads to the top. Formerly the view from this mountain was wholly obstructed by trees, but an observatory has been erected, from the summit of which a glorious picture of the whole region is spread out before the spectator. Some conception of this prospect—it is but a faint one, for art struggles always inadequately with large general views—may be gathered from the first illustration accompanying this paper. A more agreeable idea of the conformation of the southern part of the lake may be obtained by means of the second engraving, this view differing little from the one obtained from the piazza of the hotel. This prospect, it will be observed, stretches down what is called the North Bay (see initial picture), the main course of the lake being shut from view by projecting points of land, which form what is known as the Narrows. At this point is one of the most charming features of the lake—a great cluster of islands, numbering several hundred, varying in size from a few feet to several acres. The nearest island to Caldwell is known as Tea Island, lying about a mile distant from the landing. Its name is derived from a "tea-house" erected there for the accommodation of visitors, but of which only the stone-walls now remain. This island is covered with noble trees, and bordered with picturesque rocks. Here parties come for picnics; here lovers come to saunter among the shaded walks, or to sit upon the rocks and watch the ripples of the

DOME I⁰ & TONGUE M⁺.

SABBATH-DAY POINT.

"AS YOU ARE" I⁰

FITCH M⁺.

SCENES ON LAKE GEORGE.

Lake George, South from Tea Island.

transparent waters. There are many beautiful islands dotting the surface of Lake George, but none more picturesque and charming than this.

There are several ways of enjoying the scenery of Lake George. A steamboat makes a daily trip to its northern terminus, thirty-four miles distant, returning the same day. A small pleasure steam-craft may also be chartered for an independent exploration of the lake; or, if one chooses, he may course the entire circuit of its shores with a row-boat or sail-boat. There are public-houses along the route, at which he may rest.

Sloop Island.

Lake George, North from Tea Island.

The winds from the mountains, however, are fickle, and a sail must be managed with more than ordinary precaution and care. But no more delightful expedition could be devised than a sail around this American Como, as we frequently hear it called. The wild and rugged shores, the charming little bays and indentations, the picturesque islands, the soft beauty of the waters, the towering mountains—all make up a continually changing picture, full of a hundred subtile charms. One may, in such an expedition, go prepared to camp at night, thus adding another relish to the pleasure of the jaunt. Camping-parties are a special feature of Lake George; in the summer months they may be seen on almost all the larger islands, adding a very picturesque feature to the scene.

The Hermitage.

Let us imagine ourselves on the steamer Minnehaha, gliding out from the landing at Fort William Henry Hotel, on a voyage down the lake. Our first point of interest is Tea Island, already described. A mile and a half farther on is Diamond Island, so called on account of the beautiful quartz-crystal found in abundance here. Beyond are the Three Sisters; and along the eastern shore is Long Island, which from the lake appears no island at all, but the main shore. We pass Bolton, ten miles from Caldwell; the Three Brothers; a richly-wooded island called Dome Island, near Tongue Mountain, which forms the east side of Northwest Bay; and then come to the Hermitage, or Recluse Island, where a gentleman from New York has erected a neat villa among the trees, and thrown a graceful bridge to a little dot of an island at hand. A more charming situation for a summer sojourn could scarcely be imagined. Near Recluse Island is Sloop Island, so called for reasons which the reader will readily detect by glancing at our illustration. There is no prettier island in the lake. We now come to Fourteen-Mile Island, at the entrance of the Narrows, where there is a large hotel. At the Narrows the shores of the lake approach each other, the space between being crowded with islands. This is one of the favorite portions of the lake; the tourist can have no greater pleasure, indeed, than a winding sail around and among these wooded and charming islets. Here also, on the eastern shore, is Black Mountain, the highest of the peaks that line the lake-shore. It is well wooded at its base, although frequent fires have swept over its surface, while the summit of the mountain stands out rocky and bare. Its height is a little over two thousand eight hundred feet. The view from the summit is very extensive, but, like all panoramic pictures, not easily represented by the pencil. The ascent is laborious, but is often undertaken by tourists, guides being always ready for the purpose. Here also may be made an agreeable diversion to Shelving-Rock Fall, situated on a small stream which empties into Shelving-Rock Bay about a mile south of Fourteen-Mile Island. It is a very picturesque cascade, and is specially appreciated because there are very few water-falls in this immediate vicinity. It is a beautiful spot, and much resorted to by picnic-parties. Beyond Black Mountain we reach the Sugar-Loaf Mountain; Bosom Bay, with the little village of Dresden; and Buck Mountain on the left. Buck Mountain is so called, according to report, from the tragical fate of a buck, which, being hotly pursued by a hunter and his dogs, leaped over the precipitous side of the mountain facing the lake, and was impaled on a sharp-pointed tree below.

The next place of importance that we reach is Sabbath-Day Point. Why this tongue of land bears this designation, is unknown. It was once supposed to have been so named because General Abercrombie, in his descent of the lake in 1758, in his expedition for the capture of Fort Ticonderoga, landed his troops here on Sunday; but it is now known that the point was reached by him on Wednesday, instead of Sunday. There is also evidence that the place was known as Sabbath-Day Point at an earlier period. This tongue of land juts out from a tall, precipitous hill, just beyond which is another hill of corresponding height. The intervening space is known as Davis's Hollow. Mr Fenn has sketched this scene from the north, showing it just as the declining afternoon sun is sending a flood of radiance through the hollow, forming a rich and glowing contrast of light and shadow. From Sabbath-Day Point, the view up the lake is grand, Black Mountain assuming a commanding place in the picture. The next most noticeable point is Anthony's Nose —a bold, high hill, whose borrowed title is an offence. There can be but one rightful Anthony's Nose, and that we look for on the Hudson. Two miles beyond is Rogers's Slide, another abrupt rocky height, at a point where the lake becomes very narrow. The steamer hugs the precipitous, rocky shore, the narrow passage forming almost a gate-way to the main body of the lake for those who enter its waters from the north. This mountain derives its name from an incident that befell, according to tradition, one Rogers, a ranger conspicuous in the French and Indian War. The story runs that, in " the winter of 1758, he was surprised by some Indians, and put to flight. Shod with snow-shoes, he eluded pursuit, and, coming to this spot, saved his life by an ingenious device. Descending the mountain

Black Mountain, from the Narrows.

Shelving-Rock Falls.

until he came to the edge of the precipice, he threw his haversack down upon the ice, unbuckled his snow-shoes, and, without moving them, turned himself about and put them on his feet again, with the heels in front. He then retreated by the way he came, until he reached the southern brow of the rock, where he found a ravine, down which he escaped, and sped away on the ice toward Fort George. The Indians in the mean while came to the spot, and, seeing the double set of tracks, concluded that they were made by two persons who had thrown themselves down the cliff rather than fall into their hands. But, on looking about, they saw Rogers disappearing in the distance on the ice, and, believing that he slid down the dangerous and apparently impassable cliff, hastily assumed that he was under the special protection of the Great Spirit, and so gave up the chase." This is the story, but, of course, there are numerous skeptics who throw doubt on the narrative, and not without reason, as it appears that Rogers was a notorious braggart, whose deeds and misdeeds fill no little space in the local history of this region.

Beyond Rogers's Slide the lake is narrow, the shores low and uninteresting, the

Davis's Hollow, Sabbath-Day Point.

water shoal, and soon the northern border of the lake is reached. From the steamboat-landing Concord coaches run to Ticonderoga, on Lake Champlain, four miles distant. The waters of Lake George flow through a narrow channel, at Ticonderoga village, about midway between the two lakes, tumbling down a rocky descent in a very picturesque fall. A portion of the water is here diverted, by a wooden viaduct, for the uses of a mill. Mr. Fenn has depicted this scene at the hour when he saw it, with the sun just sinking in the western sky, and a twilight shadow darkening the tumbling waters. The

Black Mountain, from Sabbath-Day Point.

vagueness of the semi-light gives, with a certain charm of mystery, a melancholy tone to the picture. At another hour, of course, the waters dance and sparkle in the light; but there are beauties in the gray shadows of the evening full of a sweetness and poetry of their own.

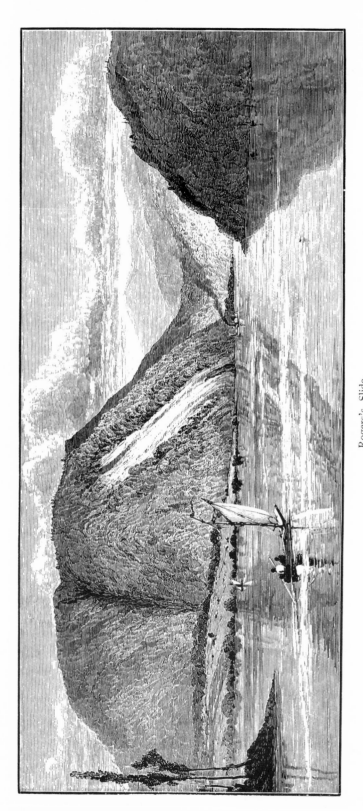

Rogers's Slide.

Lake George has many associations as well as charms. Few places in our country are more associated with historical reminiscences, or so identified with legend and story. Just as Scott has made the Highlands of Scotland teem with the shadows of his imagination, Cooper has peopled the shores of this lake with the creations of his fancy. Who can wander along its shores without thinking of Cora and Alice, and Hawkeye, and, more than all, of that youthful figure in whose melancholy eyes is foreshadowed the fate of the last of the Mohicans? In all American literature there is no figure so enveloped in poetic mystery, so full of statuesque beauty, as Cooper's Uncas; and, on these shores, the too frequent vulgar nomenclature should give place to an heroic name like that of the brave and beautiful Mohican. We have Rogers's Slide, and Flea Island, and Sloop Island, and Hog Island, and Anthony's Nose, and Cook's Island, and Black Mountain—but on what spot have Hawkeye and Uncas, whose shadows ever seem to haunt the lake and its shores, impressed their immortal names?

Lake George fills a large place in the colonial history of New York. The lake was first seen by white men in 1646, the discoverer being Father Jagues, who was on

Falls, Ticonderoga Village.

his way from Canada to the Mohawk country, to perfect a treaty with the Indians. He arrived in a canoe at the outlet of the lake on the eve of the festival of Corpus Christi, and named it "Lac du Sacrement" (Lake of the Blessed Sacrament). But, in 1609, nearly forty years earlier, Champlain had heard of the lake from the Indians, and, in ascending that lake which now bears his name, with a party of friendly Indians, he endeavored to reach it; but a battle occurred at Crown Point with the Algonquins, which, although victorious for the Indian allies of the Frenchman, frustrated his design.

We hear of the lake being visited by various scouting-parties, and forming the channel of communication between the Canadian French and the Indian tribes southward; but it was not until the French War of 1745 that the lake came into conspicuous notice. It then became the great highway between the North and places southward; armies reached

Fort Ticonderoga.

its borders and were transported over its silvery waters, but as yet no contest had stained it with blood. In 1755, General William Johnson, designing to operate against the French at Crown Point, on Lake Champlain, reached its shores with a small army; and this zealous captain, with the view of asserting the supremacy of his sovereign over this region, ordered that it should be known as Lake George, a command which has been only too literally obeyed. While here, the French General Dieskau, with an army partly composed of Indians, appeared on the scene. Colonel Williams, with twelve hundred men, was dispatched to meet him. A battle took place at a brook about four miles east of the lake. Colonel Williams was drawn into an ambush; he was killed at an early part of the conflict, and the command devolved on Colonel Whiting; a retreat was ordered to the main body at the lake; Dieskau followed, and another battle ensued at the place where now stand the ruins of Fort George. Johnson had thrown up a slight breastwork of logs; this defence enabled him to repel the attack of the French, who, after five hours' fighting, were compelled to retreat. After this contest a fort was thrown up near the spot, and named Fort William Henry, in honor of the Duke of Cumberland, brother to the king, the site of which is now occupied by the hotel of the same name. After this event we hear of numerous minor contests on the lake and its shores. The English sent scouting-parties and troops down the lake; the French sent them up the lake; and hence ensued an endless number of collisions, with not a few romantic incidents pertaining thereto. Among these contestants was one Israel Putnam, whose later career in the struggle of the colonies for independence all the world knows. Two years later, in 1757, occurred a momentous contest at the southern boundary of the lake. The Earl of Loudon was in command of the English forces in North America. He was planning a general attack upon the Canadas. Colonel Munro was in command at Fort William Henry. Several unsuccessful attempts had been made by the French upon the fort; but now General Montcalm, the French commander, determined upon a concentrated effort for its capture. He embarked from Montreal with ten thousand French and Indians. Six days were occupied in reaching Ticonderoga; then, after some delay, the main body of the army were transferred to Lake George, and ascended the lake in boats. It is a stirring picture that comes up before the imagination — this placid sheet, these sylvan shores, all astir with the "pomp and circumstance of war." All was in preparation for defence at Fort William Henry and Fort George. Fort William Henry is described as a square, flanked by four bastions. The walls were built of pine-trees, covered with sand. It mounted nineteen cannon and four or five mortars, the garrison consisting of five hundred men. Seventeen hundred men occupied a fortified position on the

Fort Ticonderoga, from Eastern Shore.

Looking south from Fort Ticonderoga, Lake Champlain.

site of the ruins of Fort George. The siege lasted six days, but the courage of the English soldiers was unavailing. They were compelled to surrender, the conditions being that the garrison and the troops of the fortified camp should march out with the honors of war, in possession of their arms and baggage; but the Indian allies were uncontrollable, and a horrible massacre ensued. This bloody incident was soon followed by another brilliant spectacle. In July, 1758, sixteen thousand men assembled, at the head of the lake, under General Abercrombie, and, in a fleet of one thousand boats, descended in stately procession to the northern terminus, with the purpose of attacking Ticonderoga. The expedition was unsuccessful. But, one year later, General Amherst, with about an equal force, traversed the lake on a similar, and, as it proved, more successful expedition. His capture of the forts on Champlain brought peace to the shores of Lake George; but afterward in the Revolution it became the centre of stirring scenes at the time of the Burgoyne invasion.

Ticonderoga Landing.

It is only four miles from the steamboat-landing on Lake George to Ticonderoga, on Lake Champlain, a distance traversed by Concord coaches in connection with steamers on both lakes. Fort Ticonderoga is a picturesque ruin — one of the few historic places in America that is untouched by the hand of improvement and unchanged by the renovations of progress. Its crumbling walls are full of history; few places in America, indeed, have so many romantic associations, or have undergone so many vicissitudes of war. It was built in 1755 by the French, who had already occupied and fortified Crown Point, on the lake-shore, some ten miles northward. The French called it *Caril-lon* (chime of bells), so named in allusion to the music of the water-falls near it. We have already mentioned General Abercrombie's attempt to capture it in 1758, and Lord Amherst's more successful campaign in the following year. The French, being unable to maintain the fort, abandoned and dismantled it on the approach of the English forces. Soon after, Crown Point was also abandoned. The English enlarged and greatly strengthened the two fortifications, expending thereon ten million dollars, at that time an immense sum for such a purpose. The fort and field-works of Ticonderoga

extended over an area of several miles. After the cession of Canada, in 1763, the fort
was allowed to fall into partial decay. At the breaking out of the Revolution, in 1775,
it readily fell into the hands of the Americans, under the eccentric leader Colonel
Ethan Allen. In 1776 there was a struggle, before the walls of the fort, between
British and Americans, in which the latter were compelled to take refuge under

Lake Champlain, near Whitehall.

its guns. In June, 1777, General Burgoyne invested it, and, July 4th, having gained
possession of the summit of Mount Defiance, which commanded the fortifications, compelled the garrison to evacuate. In September of the same year, the Americans endeavored to recapture it. General Lincoln attacked the works, took Mounts Hope and
Defiance, captured many gun-boats and stores, but failed to get possession of the fort

Lake Champlain, near Ticonderoga.

itself. After the surrender of General Burgoyne, it was dismantled, and from that time
was suffered to fall into ruin and decay.

Mr. Fenn has given us several interesting drawings of this relic, showing, at the
same time, the beauty and character of the surrounding shores. There is one picture
that vividly recalls a verse from Browning:

"Where the quiet-colored end of evening smiles
Miles and miles
On the solitary pasture where our sheep
Half-asleep
Tinkle homeward through the twilight, stray or stop
As they crop—
Was the site of a city great and gay,
(So they say)."

But all artists delight in bringing these suggestions of peace in contrast with the associations of strife.

We are now on Lake Champlain. There is a very striking difference in the shores

Crown Point and Port Henry, Lake Champlain.

of the two lakes. On Lake George the mountains come down to the edge of the waters, which lie embowered in an amphitheatre of cliffs and hills; but on Lake Champlain there are mountain-ranges stretching in parallel lines far away to the right and left, leaving, between them and the lake, wide areas of charming champaign country, smiling with fields and orchards and nestling farm-houses. There are on Lake Champlain noble panoramas; one is charmed with the shut-in sylvan beauties of Lake George; but the wide expanses of Lake Champlain are, while different in character, as essentially beautiful.

It is in every way a noble lake. Ontario is too large—a very sea; Lake George is perhaps too petty and confined; but Champlain is not so large as to lose, for the

Split Rock, Lake Champlain.

voyager upon its waters, views of either shore, nor so small as to contract and limit the prospect. The length is one hundred and twenty - six miles, its width never more than thirteen miles. The traveller who reaches it at Ticonderoga from Lake George loses a view of the extreme southern portion ; but this is scarcely a matter for regret. The head of the lake is narrow, and, at Whitehall, the shores are mainly low and swampy. North of Ticonderoga the lake begins to widen, and, at Burlington Bay, expands into a very sea. The first point of interest above Ticonderoga is Crown Point, the history of which is closely identified with that of Fort Ticonderoga. The steamer makes several stopping-places ; but the villages, while attractive-looking, have no claims to the picturesque. Some miles below Burlington, a spur of the Adirondacks stretches down to the shore, forming the only steep cliffs directly on the border of the lake. These cliffs extend for several miles, and terminate in a point of land known as Split Rock, where a portion of the rock is isolated by a remarkable fissure, and converted into an island. From this point opens a broad expanse of water stretching for sixty miles. There is almost always a wind upon this sea of waters, and at times the blasts that come sweeping down from the north are full of vigor. There are occasions when the waves come tumbling upon Split Rock like an ocean-surf; so fiercely, indeed, do the seas assail the spot, that, in many a winter storm, the spray is dashed over the tall light-house, where it enshrouds the round walls in a robe of ice. Even on a calm summer's day the traveller discovers a difference as he enters this spacious area, for the placid sweetness of the lake-surface has given place to a robust energy of motion, and a certain brilliant crispness replaces the mirror-like calm of the lower portion. Here, too, the distant mountain-views are superb. The Green Mountains, on one side, purple in the hazy distance; the Adirondack Hills, on the other, mingle their blue tops with the clouds. One may study the outlines of Mansfield and Camel's Hump, the highest of the famous hills of Vermont, and search for Whiteface amid the towering peaks of the Adirondacks. At Burlington Bay the lake is very wide, numerous islands break its surface, and the distant Adirondack Hills at this point attain their highest. From Burlington to Plattsburg (one hundred miles from Whitehall) the shores are of varying interest, similar in general character to those below. At Plattsburg the lake has its widest reach, but a long island breaks the expanse nearly midway between the two shores. St. Albans is on the eastern shore of the lake, near the northern boundary of Vermont. Between Plattsburg and this place Mr. Fenn has grouped a succession of views which tell their own story with sufficient fulness. Rouse's Point, twenty miles from Plattsburg, is at the extreme boundary of a western fork of the lake, situated in

Burlington Bay.

LAKE CHAMPLAIN, FROM PLATTSBURG TO ST. ALBANS.

Canada, on the border-line between the two countries. From this point the waters of the lake flow into the St. Lawrence by a narrow stream known as Sorel or Richelieu River.

Champlain, like Lake George, has a romantic and stirring history. It was discovered in 1609 by Samuel de Champlain, commander of the infant colony of the French at Quebec. He had left the colony with a small number of Indians, who were proceeding to give battle to a hostile gathering of the Algonquins. He was accompanied by only two French companions. Making a portage at the Chambly Rapids, the party reëmbarked, and soon emerged upon the great lake, which, if our records are correct, then, for the first time in the long ages, knew the presence of the white man. The French officer promptly named it after himself—a vanity we shall not complain of, inasmuch as the designation is simple, euphonious, and dignified. On this expedition Champlain reached a point between the later fortifications of Crown Point and Ticonderoga, where ensued a contest between the Iroquois and Algonquin Indians, which speedily resulted in victory for the former. The discovery of this superb inland sea led the French to ambitiously plan a great state upon its shores. At Crown Point they built a fort called Fort Frédéric, and laid the foundation of an extensive settlement, under the expectation of making this place the capital of the new empire. Twenty years later the fort at Ticonderoga was built. But, in 1759, as we have seen in our brief history of Ticonderoga, the power of the French on the lake was overthrown, and their magnificent projects vanished into air. During the Revolution, the lake saw but little fighting after the fall of Ticonderoga and Crown Point; but, in 1814, it was the scene of a naval battle of no little magnitude, in which the American Commodore Macdonough defeated the English Commodore Downie. The contest took place at Plattsburg, on Sunday morning, September 11th. The American fleet consisted of fourteen vessels, eighty-six guns, and eight hundred and eighty men; while the English force numbered sixteen vessels, ninety-five guns, and one thousand men. It is stated that, before going into the fight, Commodore Macdonough assembled his officers and crew on the deck of the flagship Saratoga, and solemnly implored Divine protection in the approaching conflict. The result of the battle was the surrender of the entire British fleet, with the exception of a few small gun-boats. Commodore Downie was killed. While this struggle was going on upon the lake, a body of fourteen thousand men on land, under General Provost, were attacking an American force, at Plattsburg, of inferior numbers, under General Macomb; and this contest also resulted in victory for the Americans.

From that day to the present hour the lake and its shores have known unbroken serenity. Fleets of vessels have traversed its waters, but they have been on peaceful errands. Vast armies have sailed up and down its channels, invaded its towns, penetrated the forests and assaulted the mountains that surround it, but they have been armies of pleasure-seekers.

MOUNT MANSFIELD.

WITH ILLUSTRATIONS BY HARRY FENN.

Rock of Terror.

VERMONT is, and perhaps ever will be, the most purely rural of all the older States. Though bordered by Lake Champlain, and pretty well supplied with railways, she seems to be aside from any great thoroughfare, and to hold her greenness nearly unsoiled by the dust of travel and traffic. Between the unyielding granite masses of the White-Mountain range on the one side, and the Adirondack Wilderness on the other, lies this happy valley of simple contentment, with its mellower soil and gentler water-courses, its thriftier farmers and more numerous herds, its marble-ledges, its fertile uplands, and its own mountains of gentler slope and softened outline.

Nearly through the middle runs the Green-Mountain range, giving rise to a thousand murmuring rivulets and modest rivers, that lapse down through green-browed hills and crumbling limestone-cliffs and sunny meadow-lands, now turned quickly by a mossy

ledge, and now skirting a bit of native forest, until they lose themselves on the one side in the deep-channelled Connecticut, or on
the other in the historic waters of Lake Champlain.
Quiet industry, pastoral contentment, out-door luxury, and in-door comfort—these are the characteristics that continually suggest themselves to the visitor,
wherever he loiters among the valley-farms or pleasant villages of the Green-Mountain State. It impresses him as a land where wealth will seldom ac-
cumulate, and men should never decay—whose dwell-

The Old Woman of the Mountain.

ers may forever praise God for the
greenness of the hills, the fertility of the
soil, the purity of the streams, the delicious atmosphere,
and the mellow sunshine—where the earth extends such a genial invitation to labor
that all must be allies, striving together for a living out of the ground, and none need
be enemies, scheming to get it out of each other.

When Jacques Cartier, a third of a millennium ago, descried these peaks from

Corduroy-Bridge, Mount-
Mansfield Road.

Mount Royal, by the St. Lawrence, he looked upon a land whose history was yet to be, where we look upon one whose history, in the romantic sense of the term, is probably closed. For nicely-worded statutes and accurate surveyors' lines have taken the place of vague royal patents, bounded by unknown rivers; and the contention between New Hampshire and New York, that kept Vermont out of the Union during the Revolution, can have no repetition or parallel. There was one Bennington—there need be no more; there was one Ethan Allen—there can never be another. But, though the days of colonial jealousies and rebellious warfare are over, and this quiet people are counting their cattle and weighing their butter-firkins where their grandsires shouldered their muskets and lighted beacon-fires, the glory of manhood has not departed with the romance of frontier-life. It was the sons of the men who carried Ticonderoga and Crown Point who annihilated Lee's forlorn hope at Gettysburg, turning the battle that turned the civil war. Vermont, too, may have a history of literature and art, which is but just begun. Here lies the marble-quarry of America, and here sprung America's earliest and best-known sculptor. One of her most famous journalists here spent his boyhood, learning the use of pen and type; and here, also, his aptest pupil was reared. And, for the extremes of literature, one of our earliest humorists, and one of our most celebrated philologists, were born in these same verdurous valleys.

If Professor Rogers's theory of mountain-formation be correct—that elevated ranges have been produced by a sort of tidal wave of the earth's once plastic crust—then the Green Mountains must be the softened undulation that followed the greater billow which crested and broke in Mount Washington and Mount Lafayette, leaving its form forever fixed in the abrupt and rugged declivities of the White Hills and the Franconia group. The Green Mountains form the northern portion of what is known as the Appalachian Chain. Their wooded sides obtained for them from the early French settlers the term *Monts Verts*, and from this phrase is derived the name of the State in which they are situated. The continuation of the range through Massachusetts and Connecticut is also known to geographers as the Green Mountains, but by the inhabitants of those States other names are applied to them —as the Hoosac Mountains, in Massachusetts, for that portion lying near the Connecticut River, and constituting the most elevated portion of the State between this river and the Housatonic; and the Taconic Mountains for the western part of the range, which lies along the New-York line. These ranges extend into Vermont near the southwest corner of the State, and join in a continuous line of hills that pass through the western portion of the State nearly to Montpelier. Without attaining very great elevation, these hills form

View from Mountain-Road.

an unbroken water-shed between the affluents of the Connecticut on the east, and the Hudson and Lake Champlain on the west, and about equidistant between them. South from Montpelier two ranges extend—one toward the northeast, nearly parallel with the Connecticut River, dividing the waters flowing east from those flowing west; and the other, which is the higher and more broken, extending nearly north, and near Lake Champlain. Through this range the Onion, Lamoille, and Winooski Rivers make their way toward the lake. Among the principal peaks are Mount Mansfield, Camel's Hump, both situated near Burlington; Killington's, near Rutland; and Ascutney, in Windsor County, near the Connecticut, and which has been illustrated in our article on the Connecticut River.

Mount Mansfield, the highest of the Green-Mountain range, is situated near the northern extremity, about twenty miles, in a direct line east, or a little north of east, from Burlington, on Lake Champlain. This mountain has been less popular among tourists and pleasure-seekers than the White Mountains and the Catskills, principally because its attractions have been little known. The pencil of Gifford has made it familiar to art-lovers; but literature has so far done little toward making its peaks, cliffs, and ravines, known to the general public. That it possesses points of interest and picturesque features quite as worthy the appreciation of lovers of Nature as the White Mountains or the Catskills do, Mr. Fenn's illustrations fully show. Of recent years, it has been more visited than formerly; and a good hotel at Stowe, five miles from its base, has now every summer its throng of tourists. There is also a Summit House, situated at the base of the highest peak known as the Nose, where travellers may find plain but suitable accommodation if they wish to prolong their stay on the mountain-top overnight. Mansfield is conveniently reached by rail from Burlington to Waterbury Station, on the Vermont Central Railway; and thence by Concord coaches ten miles to Stowe. From Stowe a carriage-road reaches to the summit of the mountain.

As in the case of nearly all mountains, there is some difference in the various estimates of the height of Mansfield, the most generally accepted statement being four thousand three hundred and forty-eight feet—a few hundred feet in excess of the highest of the Catskills. Popularly, the summit of Mansfield is likened to the up-turned face of a giant, showing the Nose, the Chin, and the Lip. It is not difficult, with a little aid of the imagination, to trace this profile as the mountain is viewed from Stowe. The Nose, so called, has a projection of four hundred feet, and the Chin all the decision of character indicated by a forward thrust of eight hundred feet. The distance from Nose to Chin is a mile and a half. The Nostril is discovered in a perpendicular wall of rock. This mountain is, moreover, not without the usual number of faces and resemblances to familiar objects, among the most notable of which is that described as the "Old Woman of the Mountain," represented in one of our engravings. She leans back in her easy-chair, and her work has fallen into her lap, while she gazes out, in dreamy meditation, across the misty valley.

The ascent of the mountain is not difficult, which the hardy pedestrian would be wise to attempt on foot. Carriages from Stowe make the journey at regular periods. The ride up the steep road-way is full of interest, the changing views affording momentarily new and beautiful pictures. The mountain, until near the summit, is very heavily timbered; and the glimpses downward, through entanglements of trees into the deep ravines, are full of superb beauty. Neighboring peaks continually change their positions; lesser ones are no longer obscured by their taller brothers; while successive ravines yawn beneath us. Now the road passes over a terraced solid rock, and now it jolts over the

Glimpse of Lake Champlain, from Summit.

crazy scaffolding of a corduroy-bridge that spans a chasm in the mountain-side; soon the forest-growths begin to thin out perceptibly; and at last we reach the Summit House, amid masses of bare rocks, at the foot of the huge cliff known as the Nose.

Cave under Lower Lip.

The path up the Nose, on its western side, is quite as rugged as the ordinary climber will wish; but, with the help of the cable, its ascent may be accomplished. The view from the top is one of the finest in our country. To the eastward are the White Mountains, dwindled by distance. The isolated and symmetrical form of Ascutney rises on the southeast. Southward are Camel's Hump and Killington Peak, and innumerable smaller elevations of the Green-Mountain range—respectable and respected in their own townships, doubtless, but here losing much of their individual importance, like monstrosities at a fair. Westward lies a considerable expanse of lowland, with many sparkling streams winding about among the farms and forests and villages, the city of Burlington in the distance, and beyond them the beautiful expanse of Lake Champlain, with the blue ridges of the Adirondacks serrating the farthest horizon. On the northwest is the Lamoille Valley, watered by the Lamoille and Winooski Rivers, that tumble through the depressions of the outliers, and dream their way across

Climbing the Nose.

the plain. And far northward are Jay Peak and Owl's Head, the stately St. Lawrence, the spires of Montreal, a score of nameless mountains, and Lake Memphremagog, familiar to many readers by the means of Whittier's pleasing verse. The difficulty, however, with all views from mountain-tops is, to find an occasion when the atmosphere is sufficiently clear to take in the prospect. Mr. Fenn was three days on the summit of Mansfield, during all which time a dense, gray vapor enveloped all the facial features of that grand profile, and veiled the surrounding scene as completely as the curtain at the play shuts from view the splendors behind it. At last, the misty veil lifted a little; and we have as a result, in one of the illustrations, a glimpse, through this parting vapor, of Lake Champlain and the distant Adirondacks. Another view shows us the mountain-cliffs looming

through the mist, affording a glimpse of
what is known as Smuggler's Notch, one
of the most interesting features of this
mountain. In the far West this notch
would be called a cañon. It differs from
the cañons of the Sierras mainly in being
more picturesque and beautiful — not
so ruggedly grand as those rocky

Smuggler's Notch.

walls, it must be understood, but the abundant moisture has filled it with superb forest-growths, has covered all the rocks with ferns and lichens, has painted the stone with delicious tints. The sides of the Notch rise to an altitude of about a thousand feet, the

Rocks in Smuggler's Notch.

upper verge of the cliffs rising above the fringe of mountain-trees that cling to their sides. The floor of the Notch is covered with immense bowlders and fallen masses of rocks, which in this half-lighted vault have partly crumbled, and given foothold for vege-

LOOKING TOWARD SMUGGLER'S NOTCH, FROM THE NOSE.

tation. Mosses and ferns cover them, and in many instances great trees have found nourishment in the crevices, sometimes huge, gnarled roots encircling the rocks like immense anacondas. The painter could find no more delightful studies in color than this scene affords. At the time visited by the artist and the writer, there had been a three days' rain. The stream that flowed through the gorge was swollen into a torrent. Over the top of every cliff came pouring extemporized water-falls and cascades, while the foliage, of fairly tropical abundance, shone with a brilliant intensity of green. Smuggler's Notch has a hundred poetical charms that deserve for it a better name. It is so called because once used as a hiding-place for goods smuggled over the Canada border.

Another very charming picture in this Mansfield gallery is Moss-Glen Cascade, a water-fall that comes tumbling down, in successive leaps, through a narrow gorge. The pipe, or flume, supported by the rude ladders on the right, conveys a portion of the water to the wheel of a saw-mill. It seems like an impertinence to introduce any mechanical contrivance into so exquisitely wild a bit of scenery as this; for the brook is emphatically "a gushing child of Nature," not intended for homely usefulness.

Moss-Glen Cascade.

THE VALLEY OF THE HOUSATONIC.

WITH ILLUSTRATIONS BY J. DOUGLAS WOODWARD.

Mouth of the Housatonic.

THERE are few New-England rivers of any considerable length which do not present, in the range of their flow, not only a great variety, but also a striking contrast, of aspects. Rising ordinarily in the hills as sparkling rivulets, they dance and chatter, or foam and fret, into the valleys, slowly gaining sobriety of motion with the rapid growth of their bulk, which they roll, at length, with imposing amplitude and becoming dignity, into broader waters, or into the arms of the all-embracing sea

The Housatonic River is no exception to this rule. It springs in the beautiful Berkshire region of Massachusetts, where its first ripples reflect the crests of grand hills; and, after flowing for a century of happy miles amid scenes that do not suffer it to quite forget its mountain-cradled laughter, it glides gravely enough through the plains of old Stratford, on the Connecticut shore, and is lost thereafter in the expanse of Long-Island Sound.

The journey along the valley of the Housatonic, and beyond it to that of the Hoosic,

The Housatonic at Derby.

upon which the reader of this sketch should imagine himself to accompany us, may be fitly symbolized to him by the mid-October day with whose faint, early light it was begun. The gray, misty gleams of the young morning harmonized well with the broad, pale shimmering of the river that was merging—consciously, it may be—its individuality into the wide waste of waters beyond it. There was beauty enough, however, in the

Housatonic Valley, near Kent Plains.

pink dappling of the sky, tinge-
ing the clouds, the quiet river
and bay alike, with Aurora's
first glad smile; in the gentle swell of the green land,
dotted over with white homes; in the flush of the
wooded slopes, where the maples were mocking the
eastern horizon with the faintly-kindling splendor of
their ripened leaves—there was charm enough in all
this to give pause to impatient feet, until the Sun had rent the veils of mist and cloud,
and poured from his golden chalice a partial glory upon the scene chosen by our artist
for the frontispiece of this sketch.

The change from quietness to romance in the aspects of the Housatonic Valley,

Old Furnace, at Kent Plains.

from its broad mouth upward toward the hills, if less rapid than that of the cool, gray dawn into the warm and shadowless beauty of the day, was still not less real; and our advance, helped at one point by the swift progress of the railway-train, brought us ere long into a region where such speed, amid the surrounding loveliness, would have been an impertinence, if not, indeed, a penalty.

Housatonic Falls, Falls Village.

That brief passage on the
railway will be quite long
enough for the recital of a few initial facts of
interest to the reader. The beauties of the
Housatonic Valley were little known, and still
less pictured, before the opening of the Housatonic
Railway, which connects the sea-coast of Connecticut with the mountains of Massachusetts. That railway,
beginning at the handsome and thrifty city of Bridgeport, enters the valley of the Housatonic only above
Brookfield. Thence it traverses the valley closely through nearly all its remaining extent; and there are few stations beyond at which the tourist might not tarry, and, with
brief excursions to the right or left, fill his eye with the charms of mountain-outlines,

valley-reaches, crystal lakes, and silvery water-falls. There is, therefore, quite a long interval of the valley of the Housatonic which the tourist cannot, if he would, follow by the railway. He may, however, pursue it, for its first half-score of miles, from Stratford, on the rails of the Naugatuck road; and this will afford him pleasing glimpses of the river where it is joined by the noisy Naugatuck, and where the busy manufacturing interests of such villages as Derby and Birmingham subsidize and utilize the water-power of the streams, with little regard to picturesqueness of appliance or effect.

Of the bridges that span the rivers here, one, at least, is pretty enough to have taken the eye of our artist; and, with the accessories of fine old elms, and the placid, mirror-like face of the stream, it can hardly fail to renew its fascination on the page.

From Derby to New Milford the river is unterrified in its course by the shrill whistle and the crashing roll of the locomotive. There is too little, perhaps, of the romantic in this twenty-mile interval to tempt any one but the determined pedestrian to follow the banks of the stream.

An aside, by way of Stratford again, and of Bridgeport, will speedily overpass all the initial tameness of the merely undulating region near the coast, and bring into view the swelling symptoms of those hills which are soon to overhang—now with gloom, and anon with purple glow—the silvery lapses of the Housatonic.

If this sketch were not shut up to narrow limits, but diffusiveness were allowed, the question of the origin and meaning of the name "Housatonic" might be discussed. There was the usual variety of orthographic variations in it before it reached its present easy and euphonious form, which is a grateful refinement, probably, of the aboriginal title by which the Indians designated it. Its signification is "Flowing (or Winding) Waters;" and it is therefore no misnomer. There is the authority of one antiquarian for a primitive name of the river, of which the present appellation gives not the faintest prevision. The old Stratford records, we are told, make it the "Paugusset;" and we are quite content to have this name as mythical as it is remote.

This brief digression, historical and otherwise, has taken less of our time than the train requires from Bridgeport to New Milford. And now the railway tourist must use his eyes diligently to catch a tithe of the picturesque shapes which will pass before them as he is whirled—all too swiftly—along the west bank of the lovely river. He must be satisfied with glimpses only. The western hills, which will soon be mountains, shift rapidly their wavy outlines; and the autumnal hues of their thick forest-growth, which are fast deepening in tone, flash on his sight with weird effects. All the scene is, to him, simply kaleidoscopic—hill and vale, river and rustic bridges, white farm-houses and red barns, mingling together to surprise rather than really to satisfy the eye, which yet declines to linger on the attractive scene.

At Kent Plains the valley opens with such charming aspects as to well repay the patient tourist for his pause, even if it is brief. He will find it worth while to do a little climbing, if it is only to obtain a clear idea of the shape and scope of the noble valley he is traversing, girt closely on the west by almost abrupt hill-sides, and, on the other hand, spreading out into sweet pastoral reaches and green undulations.

His "*little* climbing" will not avail, however, to lift him to the level of the Spectacle Ponds, which are two very unique, but quite elevated, oval lakelets, fringed by

Old Bridge, Blackberry River, near Canaan.

dense woods, and connected by a slender water-belt, or strait. These lie west of the river, and are on the way to a fine hill-top, which commands distant and beautiful views across the Hudson.

The old furnace which the artist has so faithfully reproduced with his pencil will suggest to the mind one of the industries of the Housatonic Valley—the working of the iron which is found in many localities.

It would be doing less than justice to happy historic memories not to recall, at Kent, the story of the Schaghticoke Indians, among whom, long ago, the Moravians founded a mission, and of whom there are yet to be found descendants of a mongrel order, their aboriginal nature and habits strangely mingled and overlaid with the externals of civilization.

A day or two would be well spent between Kent and Canaan—a northward reach of twenty-five miles, which brings the valley of the Housatonic close upon the dividing line between Connecticut and Massachusetts. This interval is rich in picturesque delights. The lofty ridge has now assumed a true mountain-aspect, and lifts up, here and there, such noble crowns to the sky as tempt the tourist to unfold, with the legendary youth—

> "A banner with the strange device,
>   'Excelsior!'"

Falls Village is the centre of some of the chief attractions of the section under notice. There is a chance here, moreover, for the enjoyment of thoroughly rural entertainment, at a little hostelry nestled in a glen on the side of the river opposite to the village, which, like many of the Housatonic villages, is less picturesque than its accessories. Close at hand are the falls of the Housatonic—the most prominent, perhaps, of the cataracts in Connecticut. They are worthy of attention, but it is difficult to avoid some feeling of vexation on finding that near views of them are blemished by the unsightly encroachments of that barbarism which, under the misnomers of "civilization" and "progress," clutter our water-falls and rapids with the ugly shanties and shops where dwell and toil the gnomes of factories, forges, and furnaces, useful indeed, but which we would fain banish into caverns, or at least into unlovely corners. These falls are commonly known as the Canaan Falls, and fill up the whole breadth of the stream with their tumultuous dash and roar over a steep, terraced ledge of dark rock. Their descent possibly exceeds fifty feet; and, seen at a distance, and especially under the sweet, soft magic of the moonlight, they inspire no small degree of admiration in the sensitive mind.

Mount Prospect rises about two miles from these falls, in a northwestern direction; and its very summit may be reached in a carriage, by the rude track which the woodmen follow with their teams. When gained, it opens to the view of the tourist such a scene as he can obtain from few other mountain-crests in the valley, though some are of more renown than this. The great bosom of the interval between the east and west ranges of hills is heaving with its green billows beneath him. A thousand wavy crests are in his view; and, threading its way near and afar, the silvery line of the river stretches amid picturesque homesteads, which now and then cluster into villages. A deep, dark, and ugly fissure into wild, outlying rocks, at the foot of this mountain, bears the appropriate but not attractive name of the Wolf's Den.

Within an hour's walk of the Great Falls lies the pretty village of Salisbury, which, while it is not a railway-station—to its positive advantage in all picturesque respects— is, nevertheless, the social centre of the beautiful and populous county of Litchfield. Lying close under the deep shadows of the great Taconics, Mount Riga may be said to

Old Mill, Sage's Ravine.

be its especial guardian, whose noble crest, known as Bald Peak, alternately smiles upon it in sunshine and frowns upon it in storm.

It would carry the reader quite out of the Housatonic Valley to press him beyond Bald Peak on to the Dome, and westward still, a dozen miles, until we came to the renowned ravine of Bashbish, and its grand but gloomy water-fall, closely overlooking the little iron-working village of Copake, in New York, and on the line of the Harlem Railway.

Without overpassing the ridges of the Taconic, and quite within the legitimate compass of our theme, it is

Silver Cascade, Sage's Ravine.

proper for us to explore a mountain-gorge less known than Bashbish, with less of the terrible, but with far more of the beautiful, in its aspect. Sage's Ravine is but an easy walk — or a delightful drive, if preferred — of four miles from Salisbury. Whether it is more a Berkshire than a Salisbury "lion," let us leave in the doubt we cannot now resolve. It lies along the dividing line of towns and States alike, and is certainly a grand bisector.

At the mouth of this noble ravine there are a fine old mill, and a picturesque bridge spanning the torrent which comes dashing and foaming down the wild cleft. The suggestion of trout-treasures in the pools and eddies of this noisy brook, which the artist has put in his picture, is by no means gratuitous. That eager-eyed fisherman is sure of his game, unless his looks belie him; and, if he were a mile above the mill, with his rod and line he might still fill his creel with the speckled beauties, and be happy.

Leave the roar of the falls and the clatter of the mill-gear behind, and go up the ravine, with some one to show you the possible paths—if it should be young Gilmore, of the contiguous iron-furnace, you will be fortunate.

There is hard climbing before the Twin Falls of our picture are reached. Your feet will sink in clumps of moss and decayed wood, upsetting you if you are not wary. You must cling to birch-boles, and often to slenderer stems. as you swing round opposing barriers of rock. You may get a foot-bath, or worse, as you cross the foaming torrent to find an easier path on the other side. But here and there, all along the wild way, are pretty cascades, tortuous twists of the stream, gayly-lichened or dark-beetling rocks, mossy nooks or gloomy tarns, and, overhead, maples and birches, mingling their rare autumnal splendors of red and gold with the sombre greens of hemlocks, and cedars, and pines. The glory above, and the dash and foam at your very feet, will stir your soul, if Nature's charms can ever do so. Two hours will suffice for the ravine, and tire you at their close, but no consciousness of fatigue will avail to mar your sense of the rare beauty and picturesqueness of the whole scene.

The thrifty Berkshire farmer, whose hospitable homestead lies just north of the old mill, is the descendant and inheritor of him who gave his honest though unromantic name to the ravine, "a hundred years ago."

A week in Salisbury would be none too much time for the leisurely enjoyment of the many charming views to be found in its neighborhood. There, very near to the iron-smelting hamlet of Chapinville, spread the sweet waters of the Twin Lakes—the Washinee and Washineën—encompassed by winding drives, with ever-shifting visions of the kingly Taconic crests, and these, on the nether slopes, displaying, in the bright autumn days, such splendors of variegated color as would intoxicate with delight the heart of a devotee of illuminated missals.

These pretty lakes lie in enticing proximity to a limestone cave, into which the tourist may be induced to venture by the promise of rare visions

"... of stalactites and stalagmites,
In chambers weird and dim."

And, lest he should yield to the temptation and do as we did once—go into the cave with an inadequate supply of candles, and pay for the improvidence by half a day's incarceration in total darkness and in equally dense impatience—let him be warned to take care with whom he goes, and, above all, to take with him some extra "dips." With these precautions, it is quite possible that the Salisbury Cave may be for him a place of pleasanter memories than it is to us, as we review our adventures in that part of the Housatonic Valley.

Canaan, near the outgoing of the river and valley from the Connecticut border, is an important station on the two railways—the Housatonic and the Connecticut Western—at their common intersection. A pretty village in itself, it has its special picturesqueness along the pleasant little valley of the Blackberry River, on whose banks it lies.

Leaving it, the tourist crosses, almost immediately, the southern boundary-line of the

Mount Washington, from Sheffield.

renowned Berkshire County, a region not surpassed, in picturesque loveliness, throughout its whole longitude of fifty miles and its average latitude of twenty miles, by any equal area in New England, and perhaps not in all this Western world.

The slave to the railway and its "rapid car" will not, probably, discover the truth of this broad generalization. He may, and indeed, unless he sleeps in the transit, or does the next most heathenish thing—reads some narrow-printed page instead of that open volume where God has imprinted his own grand symbols of beauty and power—he *must*, see a surpassingly-varied landscape, with perhaps astonishing atmospheric effects, though

Prospect Rock, East Mountain, Great Barrington

for these he needs to bide through changing skies, and hours, and moods of Nature. Off the railway, in village-nooks, in glens and by-ways, upon near crests and remote hill-tops, the lover of the beautiful will find innumerable views to gaze upon, to sketch, or haply to daguerreotype only on his memory.

Sheffield is a good lingering-point for those who do not wisely shun, amid Nature's charms, the shrill pipe of the engine, and the sharp click of the electric hammer.

From Sheffield the ascent of Mount Washington —one of the Taconic giants—is easily made; and the toil it requires will be a cheap purchase of "far prospects," exchanged for the "level bliss" of the vale at its foot. Mount Washington was once a part of the great Livingston Manor, and its summit commands a view of the rich and lordly domain once included in that now half-forgotten name.

The tourist who is not in hot haste to get through his route, as if it were a task, and not a treat, could hardly do better than to take up his abode for a little while at the Mount-Everett House, in South Egremont, a few miles east of the railway, and just under the lofty crest whose name this quiet summer hotel bears. Thence, at his own sweet will, he may go and climb or ramble. He may scale the mountain, by way of "its vast, uncultivated slope, to a height of two thousand feet." There—to his astonishment, if not before informed—he would find a village, whose ten or twelve score of inhabitants are literally mountaineers, and whose eyes are familiar, by daily outlook, with such a panorama as a sensitive valley or sea-side dweller would go into ecstasies to behold. It is not finer, perhaps, though far broader, than that obtainable from Prospect Mountain; but then it takes in half the whole stretch of the Housatonic River, and below the eye lie lakes and woodlands, lawns and villas, gleaming spires, and little rifts and puffs of smoke from furnaces and creeping engines; and all this so far away, so still, that it is more like a picture on canvas than a real scene. East and west, the eye has broad extent of vision into Connecticut and New York. The Catskills make a blue and wavy western horizon; and the Hudson, in the interval, twins the nearer Housatonic in its

Green River, at Great Barrington.

sparkling flow Here one may fitly repeat Thomson's panegyric on a vision not altogether unlike it, perhaps, but in Old rather than in New England:

> " Heavens! what a goodly prospect spreads around,
>   Of hills and dales, of woods and lawns and spires,
>   And glittering towns and gilded streams, till all
>   The stretching landscape into smoke decays!"

The practical man, who shuns the toilsome clamber to Mount Everett's crest, may go afoot, or in his light wagon, from his inn, to see the famous marble-quarries of Egremont, whence were hewn the white columns and walls of the Girard College, more than a third of a century ago, and where to-day the old proprietor is still busily blasting and

Monument Mountain.

blocking out the brill-
iant stones, with far
easier access to the
market than when he
sent them by ox-teams to the Hudson.

Great Barrington — a name from
which the modesty, perhaps, of its people is gradually eliminating the adjec-
tive—is a most attractive point in the
valley of the Housatonic. The river, losing all the while in volume, is gaining
in picturesqueness. Its narrowing banks wear greener and lovelier fringes, and its tones
ring more musically in the swift, broken and impetuous lapses of its waters. Barrington
has many summer charms, in its splendid elms shading its streets, in its attractive drives
over fine roads, and in its pleasant society. All around the village one may find new and
lovely outlooks on the closely-encompassing hills. The stout-hearted pilgrim may think
it worth while to covet the seat and copy the example of the adventurer whom the artist
has giddily enthroned upon the very verge of Prospect Rock.

A stroll along the road that leads to the two Egremonts—North and South—will bring the visitor to a charming bit of land-and-water view at the rural bridge over Green River, a babbling stream that flows along as if in sweet and delighted consciousness of the beauty it here and there discloses.

It would be a great mistake of the explorer of Berkshire to go from Barrington to Stockbridge by rail, unless, indeed, he had exhausted the interval by slower inspection. The highway is the shorter by nearly two miles, and not a furlong of it all is tame or tedious, for it is thick set with those sweet surprises that characterize ridge-roads in Berkshire.

Its half-way wonder is the renowned Monument Mountain, which Stockbridge numbers, with allowable pride, among her special attractions. This mountain was called by the Muh-hek-a-new Indians—the old Stockbridge tribe—" Maus-was-see-ki," which means " The Fisher's Nest." Its present appellation was given to it, perhaps, on account of a cairn found upon its southern crest, which has connected with it an Indian myth of a dusky maiden who, disappointed in love, jumped from the precipice, and was killed—a love-lorn sacrifice which the braves commemorated by flinging a stone upon the fatal spot whenever they passed by it. With or without legend, it is a weird and romantic spot.

From Monument Mountain to the village of Stockbridge is less than half an hour's drive, when the carriage-road has been regained. This village—the " Housatonnuc" of past generations—is of a romantic beauty. Its houses and churches, its library and academy, its fountain and monuments, are pretty mosaics set in the emerald of wonderful elms. There are few—if, indeed, there are any—villages in our land that can rival it in rare and fascinating aspects of rural beauty, in immediate surroundings of unwonted charms, in worthy and precious historical associations, and in the renown of noble sons and daughters. The beauties of Stockbridge lie in many directions. To the north, the pretty lake Mahkeenac—more familiarly known as the " Stockbridge Bowl "—spreads its translucent waters, shapely, in its outline, as a gigantic basin, on whose margin Hawthorne once lived for a succession of seasons. A mile or more from the village is found that wonder of Nature, the Ice Glen, which pierces the northern spur of Bear Mountain; and in its long and awsome corridors and crypts, formed by massive and gloomy rocks, and huge but prostrate trees, the explorer may find masses of ice in the heart and heat of midsummer. The passage of this glen, though not perilous, requires nerve and patience, and the cheer of glowing torches withal. The heights that overhang the village are " beautiful for situation," and studded with pleasant villas, whose fortunate possessors may gaze at will over the fair interlocking valleys of the Housatonic and the Konkapot.

Among the names that memory loves to recall in connection with old Stockbridge, none will live so long or so prominently in history as that of Jonathan Edwards. This distinguished divine was not a native of the village, and, indeed, lived there only a few years; but he was so closely identified, for that time, with all the interests of the place, and especially with its religious and missionary work, that he grew rapidly into the reve-

Housatonic River, at Stockbridge.

rential regard and love of its people. It was there that he wrote his famous work, "The Freedom of the Will," undoubtedly his master-work. The salary of this great preacher—as the pastor of the Stockbridge Church, and distinct from his remuneration as missionary to the Indians—was, in money, less than seven pounds sterling per annum, and two pounds more in value paid in wood! Stockbridge honored the memory of this remarkable man by erecting to him, on the village green, a monument of polished Scotch granite.

On leaving Stockbridge, the tourist may scarcely venture to promise himself a beauty beyond that he has already enjoyed; and this may be suggested without disparagement to the varied scenery of Northern Berkshire. It may hardly be doubted that the rare and numerous attractions of this whole region—so aptly called "the Palestine of New England"—are crystallized, in excess of loveliness, around Stockbridge as a nucleus. If this verdict had gathered something of weight to the judgment from the acknowledged union in Stockbridge of all the forces—natural, historical, social, intellectual, and religious, alike—which have given to Berkshire its enviable renown, the influence would be, nevertheless, legitimate and just.

There is, however, much beyond this picturesque centre deserving the regard of all the lovers of Nature. And this *much* comprehends novelty, as well as similarity, of landscape and water view. It is, indeed, only that one half of Berkshire has been seen, that the other half will possibly present fewer "delicious surprises" than otherwise to the eye of the explorer. There are new outlines of the mountains to be studied; new groupings of their massive forms, with new details and specialties of glen, and lake, and water-fall, to be noted.

The Hoosac range of lofty hills, on the east, comes now into distinct and close rivalry with the Taconics, on the west; and far away, in the northern end of the county, the lordly Graylock lifts his blue crest with such preëminence of majestic mien that the many peaks already named sink inferior to its grand central prominence.

Lee and Lenox are the two villages that lie in the Housatonic Valley between Stockbridge and Pittsfield, which latter village is rapidly growing into the rank of a city, and is the metropolis of all the Berkshire region.

At Lee, through which the railway passes, the river is quite as useful as it is beautiful, lending its force and purity alike to the paper-mills which have contributed so much to build up and enrich the village. Another and perhaps the chief industry of this thriving and attractive place is the quarrying of its fine, white building-marble, which represents Berkshire, with such solid and permanent effect, in the walls of the Capitol at Washington. Lee has a pretty lake, within a pleasant half-hour's walk on the road to Lenox; but, for heavier charms, its summer guests make excursions to quaint old Monterey and to Tyringham, on the east, and to Lenox and Stockbridge, between which places it is about equidistant.

Lenox lies two miles apart from the line of the railway, having a station only at Lenox Furnace. At few—if at any—points immediately on the iron track we are following is there so much to charm and detain the eye as at this station. The sweet, translucent river, its rustic bridge, the swelling knolls of the interval, and the bold, grand sweep of the near mountains, make up a most exquisite picture, to which no artist's eye could be indifferent, even amid the profusion of charming views springing up on every hand.

At Lenox Furnace the double industry of glass and iron working gives occupation to numerous workmen. The recent production there of excellent plate-glass, from the fine-granulated quartz of the region about it, is a noteworthy incident in the manufacturing annals of Berkshire.

Of Lenox itself—reached by a drive of constantly-increasing picturesqueness—these chronicles can make but inadequate mention. Professor Silliman designated it, in his enthusiastic admiration of its pure, exhilarating air, and its lovely views, "a gem among the mountains." It deserves the praise. Till recently, it was the shire-town of the region, and term-time gave it a measure of importance and influence which it has since lost. But it cannot lose its beauty, and the summer doubles its population with hundreds of happy pilgrims from the cities, some of whom occupy their own villas, while more crowd its hotel and the numerous boarding-houses which challenge this periodical influx.

Ice Glen, Stockbridge.

All around Lenox, the crests and slopes of its constituent and outlying hills are covered by mansions and villas, which one might remember for their architectural individuality, if this were not always eclipsed by the surpassing breadth and beauty of the outlook.

To describe this, would be to repeat—only, perhaps, with new allocations of epithets—what has been said of the more southern part of the valley. Here, however, the dwellings are far more numerous, and a richer social element mingles with and enhances the simply picturesque in the landscape.

That gifted and genial woman, Frederika Bremer, is but one of a score of literary notabilities who, living, or lingering for a while at least, amid the charms of Lenox, have recorded their admiration of it in glowing words. Hers may serve as a type of their kindred utterances. She writes: "The country around Lenox is romantically lovely, inspired with wood-covered hills, and the prettiest little lakes." In describing the Housatonic scenery more generally, she justly uses these emphatic expressions—"wonderfully picturesque, and sometimes splendidly gloomy."

It was at Lenox that Fanny Kemble lived, and expressed the wish to be buried, saying: "I will not rise to trouble any one, if they will let me sleep here. I will only ask to be permitted, once in a while, to raise my head and look out upon this glorious scene."

The English origin of this delightful place is commemorated, after the lapse of more than twelve decades, in its name, which was the patronymic of the Duke of Richmond.

The fine view which the "Ledge" contributes to the embellishment of this paper will be its own best commentary on the breadth and manifold charms of the Lenox landscape. The summer guests of Lenox find great delight in gazing out from its noble "coignes of vantage." For still wider range of vision, they go to Perry's Peak, a bald and lonely summit on the west, easily reached in an hour's ride, and standing like a grim sentinel on the New-York border.

There is a scientific interest, also, about Perry's Peak, in that it is strewed with the fine bowlders which are traced, in seven parallel lines, across the Richmond Valley, intervening between the peak and Lenox Mountain. These stones attracted the careful notice and diligent review of that eminent English geologist, Sir Charles Lyell. On this peak, also, in 1869, some local scientific associations held a "field-day" for the especial commemoration of the centennial anniversary of Humboldt's birthday. A fine photograph of the grand old *savant* was uncovered, and a tribute-poem read, on the pleasant occasion.

Among the attractive points included in the magnificent overlook from the peak are the Shaker villages of both Lebanon, in New York, and Hancock, in Massachusetts, the former being, perhaps, the metropolis of the sect of Shakers. The Boston and Albany Railway passes close by the village of the Hancock Shakers, and has a station there. The town of Hancock is itself one of the outlying characteristics of the Housatonic Valley. It is altogether mountainous, being only a long and narrow tract on the backbone and slopes of the Taconic range, with a single hamlet crouching in a beautiful cove, or interval, near the northern end of it. The roads which cross this attenuated township are very romantic and very rough, except, perhaps, those from Lebanon and Hancock villages direct, which are fine in summer, and much travelled.

Pittsfield is the terminus of the Housatonic Railway, one hundred and ten miles from Bridgeport; and here the Housatonic River dwindles greatly by its division into two arms, one of which flows from Pontoosuc Lake just northward, and the other, with far greater meandering, from distant northeastern hills in Berkshire towns.

Lenox Station.

Pittsfield commemorates in its name the fame of England's noble statesman, William Pitt. It is one of the handsomest villages in New England, and perhaps the "New-England Hand-Book" anticipates events only the least in calling it a "city." It might be so, but it is not now. It is already suburban in its aspects, and exhibits fine architectural ambitions in several recent public buildings.

Its just pride in its history, and in that of the county it represents, had a happy

View from the "Ledge," Lenox.

exposition, nearly twenty years ago, in the Berkshire Jubilee, a festival which gathered the sons and daughters of Berkshire by hundreds "from near and from far," and made a bright and memorable page of history for the place. The historic elm-tree of Pittsfield

Banks of the Housatonic, at Pittsfield.

which stood and bourgeoned for more than three centuries in the very centre of the village, was necessarily cut down in 1864; and the ground it once shaded is now a pretty park, adorned with a fountain and a soldiers' monument designed by Launt Thompson.

The industry of Pittsfield is chiefly directed to manufactures of cotton and wool,

Graylock Mountain, from South Adams.

facilitated by the fine water-power which the Housatonic, though shrunk to narrow streams, still avails to furnish.

The large church to which the late Dr. Todd ministered for twenty years is the foremost of half a dozen of various denominations, which are all in vigorous growth. Several banks represent the wealth of the village. It has good schools, both public and private. Of the latter, Maplewood Female Seminary, situated upon charming grounds, has won a fair renown.

Such is Pittsfield, the capital of the Housatonic Valley, at a slight external glance A closer view would reveal more than ordinary social culture among its inhabitants. Music and the fine arts have their happy influence there; and a generously-endowed institution, known and incorporated as the "Berkshire Athenæum," is destined to be an elevating and refining power in the community.

Pittsfield is situated at an average elevation of nearly eleven hundred feet above the sea. Its position is peculiar, as being the geographical centre of valleys and defiles, affording opportunities for crossing its flanking mountains such as are found at no other single point. Pittsfield is the centre of perhaps as many distinct attractions for the summer tourist as any other Berkshire village; and its growing likeness to a city in the special facilities it affords—railway, postal, hotel, shopping, and social—makes it an excellent place for the headquarters of the visitor in all the length and breadth of its matchless shire.

In every direction from the village, fine, natural roads lead to lovely scenes. The Taconic and the Hoosac ranges of mountains are about four miles distant, on the west and east respectively; and from their slopes, or their summits, Berkshire—both Southern and Northern—opens broad vistas to the eye.

Some of the reaches of the Housatonic River near the village are of great beauty; and there are places on the banks of its eastern confluent where it would be meet to sit, of a summer eve, and read or quote Tennyson's dainty rhymes of the brook that would "go on forever."

One of the fairest views in all the county—the especial pride, perhaps, of the people of Pittsfield, as it well may be—is that which takes in and overpasses the exquisite contour of Onota Lake, two miles to the west. This view, besides its immediate loveliness, in the silvery sheen of its waters, and the sweet variety of the pastoral and wooded banks that environ them, has for its central but remote background the splendid outline of old

> " Graylock, cloud-girdled on his purple throne."

In the near east rises the fine range of the Washington Hills, of the Hoosac Chain, over which the Boston Railway is carried by sharp gradients of eighty feet in a mile. On their crest is a romantic lakelet, called Ashley Pond, the water of which is brought into the village—at present only a barely adequate supply for its demands, but soon to be reënforced from a neighboring pond, a recent purchase of the Pittsfield Gas and Water Company.

Roaring Brook, the outlet of a contiguous pond, is a wild mountain-torrent that dashes down the side of the mountain in a rugged cleft known as Tories' Gorge. This brook is a tributary of the eastern branch of the Housatonic. To the eastward, also, lies the village of Dalton, with its busy paper-mills; and beyond it, on the acclivity of the Boston Railway, the village of Hinsdale, from which point, as also from Dalton, the very pretty Windsor Falls may be reached by a brief carriage-drive. These falls lie at the extreme limit of the review which this article will make of the Housatonic Valley. Beyond them the "winding waters" narrow into shining becks and brawling brooks, and make up the vision pictured by Holmes in his pleasant verses of

> ". . . the stream whose silver-braided rills
> Fling their unclasping bracelets from the hills,
> Till, in one gleam beneath the forest-wings,
> Melts the white glitter of a hundred springs."

West of Pittsfield, beyond Onota already named, a mountain-road leads across Hancock Town to Lebanon Springs, and to the village of the Lebanon Shakers, affording, all the way, lovely prospects, but, from its highest point, a scene never to be forgotten. It takes in the whole expanse of the sweet vale of Lebanon, and, beyond this, stretches away to the Catskills, vague and violet-hued.

Northward of Onota, on the slopes of the Taconics, are found delightful bits of

Hoosac River, North Adams.

Nature—here, the Lulu Cascade, a much-frequented haunt of those who fain would find where the "shy arbutus" hides; there, Rolling Rock, a huge and nicely-poised bowlder; and far above it, on the table of a giant crest, as pretty a mountain-lake as the eye could covet. It is called Berry Pond, but not for the profusion of raspberries to be found there in summer. The name is said to be that of a stout-limbed and brave-hearted

Natural Bridge, North Adams.

man who once lived on its borders, and wrested from the scanty soil about the pond a living for himself and family. The lakelet has crystal waters, a sparkling, sandy beach, is fringed by masses of evergreen and deciduous trees, and to these charms adds that of a clear, fairy-like echo to all sounds upon its margin.

Northward of Pittsfield lie Pontoosuc, a populous mill-suburb, and a lake bearing its name; and, three miles beyond, old Lanesboro' is reached by a delightful drive. Here the visitor should not fail to make a slight circuit, and gain, either afoot or in a carriage, the summit of Constitution Hill, lying just west of the village and the iron-furnace. Of the view to be obtained by this excursion let a resident of Berkshire, and a contributor to APPLETONS' JOURNAL of some popular papers on the glories of that region, afford the reader a few glimpses:

"Though you can drive to the very summit if you are sure of your horse, you will grow dizzy as your eye rests on the grand prospect outspread before you—green, fertile valleys, reminding one of that which shut in the happy Rasselas; blue lakes; Pontoosuc at your feet, Onota farther south, and Silver Lake east of Pittsfield; great stretches of table-land, well tilled, and spanned by shady roads; forests that look as old as creation, and hills mantled with a fresher growth; the line of rich foliage which marks the course of the streams that unite to form the Housatonic; Lanesboro' basking on the hill-side, with its great elms drooping over its old homesteads and quaint road-corners; Stearns-ville and Barkersville, farther off; the whole extent of the chief town in the valley, its spires gleaming in the light; Lenox, Lee, and Stockbridge, through the opening in the hills; sunny farm-houses, grazing cattle, browsing sheep, brown grain-fields, flying cloud-shadows—and all domed by a brighter than an Italian sky."

The route we are now pursuing is aside from the track of the railway which connects Pittsfield with Adams and the north; and the true tourist would greatly prefer to follow its rural windings, along the course of the supposed Upper Housatonic, now scarcely more than a rapid, laughing brook, sliding along under its alder and willow fringes. A few miles still farther north, in the town of New Ashford, it is lost in silvery threads from the hills. The road from the "deserted village" of New Ashford to the Williamstowns is solitary, but beautiful, with its ever-shifting views of grand mountain-outlines, bringing one at length into the deep shadows and sweet repose of the close-encompassing hills that keep solemn watch and ward over the time-honored sanctuaries of wisdom at Williams College.

This hasty generalization has done no justice to the interval of twenty miles over which we have glided with haste that would be impertinent, if these notes were not necessarily telegraphic for brevity. Williamstown is a unique and delightful village, with a green park for its main street, and the sparkling, hurrying Hoosac singing along its borders. It is a fit place for study, and a charming one for summer life and recreation, though hardly for fashionable dissipation, to which, indeed, its vigilant wardens evermore oppose their classic *procul.*

Visitors at Williamstown, who are familiar with Swiss scenery, are wont to say that the splendid views and wonderful atmospheric effects they see there more nearly resemble Alpine pictures than those of any other mountain-recesses in this land.

Our promise, in the opening of this sketch, that it would carry the reader beyond the Housatonic Valley, has been fulfilled. He is now in the valley of the Hoosac, and not far from the termination of these autumn rambles.

Whoever follows the railway from Pittsfield to this region passes twenty miles through a country contrasting strangely with the deep rural isolation of that just glimpsed along the by-road through New Ashford. It is a tract of new activities and industries, of glass - furnaces and sand - quarries, of lumber-mills and cotton - looms, of woollen-mills and populous hamlets—in succession, Berkshire, Cheshire, South Adams, until he comes at last to North Adams, where he will wonder more and more, as more he sees, how so large and flourishing and ambitious a town has contrived to find "room and verge enough" amid the encompassing, encroaching, overhanging hills, for its steady, sturdy growth.

It is a pushing rival

Profile Rock, North Adams.

of Pittsfield; behind it, probably, in general, but making well-founded boast of excelling it in the value of its school-property, as it does equally in the cost and elegance of its chief hotel, which would be a credit to any city. North Adams is a rich manufact-

Hoosac Mountain and Tunnel Works.

uring village, where "Chinese cheap labor" has been a specialty and a success for years in the shoe-shops. It is the upper "metropolis" of Berkshire, and is more thickly studded about with wild and romantic spots than its southern sister. Graylock, the loftiest mountain in Massachusetts, is within easy distance, though not visible from its streets. It is perhaps more easily reached from South Adams, a less bustling village, four miles below, whence the commanding summit may be seen in all its royal pomp, rising majestically just over its pleasant homes.

This is the less picturesque, however, of the two or three routes by which the top of Graylock may be reached. The mountain exercise already taken by the Housatonic explorer, when he comes within the shadows of Graylock, will stand him in stead as he contemplates the conquest of the kingly height. It is no child's play, especially if he chooses the North-Adams and Bald-Mountain route, by that mountain-cluster, the "Hopper." All the roads need great improvement, and there should be one, at least, kept in excellent condition. But there is no reaching the top without toil, without fatigue—no "royal road," though the end of the way is most royal.

When Graylock, and the Hopper, and Money Brook, have been explored—or between these explorations, as separate adventures—there are dainty and most compensating "bits" about North Adams, which should not be left unseen. Some of these lie close about that curious object, the Natural Bridge, a rare freak of the waters of a pretty brook among the rocks—itself a scene for the painter, as it and its accessories so commonly are for the photographer. The Natural Bridge is a vast roof of marble, through and under which a mere brook has yet contrived, with incessant, fretting toil, to excavate a tunnel—a passage five or six yards wide, and ten times as long. This wonderful viaduct is loftily arched over the torrent, and displays its marble sides and ceiling sometimes of a pure white, but oftener with strange discolorations, as of mineral stains or lichen - growths. Through this weird corridor the brook flows with thunderous echoes, booming up to the ear and filling the mind of the beholder with strange, wild fancies.

In the ravine of this brook there are many picturesque points to arrest the tourist's attention, but next in interest to the bridge itself is a strange, columnar group of rocks, which at its overhanging crest assumes, to a facile imagination, the aspect of gigantic features, and bears, therefore, the appellation of Profile Rock. These and other scenes are within a mile or two of the village, where there will be found inducements for more than ordinary lingering, and still more reluctant leave-taking, on the part of the visitor. Those who have enjoyed the magnificence and varied charms of the eight-mile coach or carriage drive from North Adams to the east end of the great Hoosac Tunnel, during its long working, will doubtless almost lament that it is now an accomplished fact, because the splendid road across the great Hoosacs will now be no more needed, and will very likely fall into disrepair, thus spoiling a most unique and almost unparalleled mountain-ride. That road climbs the Hoosacs by easy-returning gradients, affording all the way up, and across, and down on the east slope, marvellously-fine prospects. The west mouth of the tunnel is only two miles from North Adams, and lies amid the picturesque scenery of the Hoosac Valley, and full in front of the monarch of the Berkshire hills.

The Hoosac Tunnel is a bold and fortunate feat of engineering skill. Second in length only to the famous Mont-Cénis Tunnel under the Alps, it pierces the solid micaceous slate of the Hoosac Range with a grand artery nearly five miles in length, and thus opens, after incredible toil and immense outlay, a railway-passage between Boston and the Hudson River, about ten miles shorter than any preëxisting route. Long before these pages have reached their final numbering, this tunnel, already open from end to end, will be the scene of swift and multitudinous transit for passenger and freight trains speeding between the Atlantic and the Pacific Oceans.

Upon that busy and tireless flow and ebb of life and labor, old Graylock, and his compeers of the Taconic and Hoosac Ranges, will look down as peacefully as they did upon the turmoil and trouble and disaster with which the western end of the vast work was wrought to proud completeness, adding something to the physical and moral, if not to the natural, beauty and grandeur of the Berkshire hills.

THE UPPER MISSISSIPPI, FROM ST. LOUIS TO ST. ANTHONY'S FALLS.

WITH ILLUSTRATIONS BY ALFRED R. WAUD.

Grand-Tower Rock, below St. Louis.

IN the description of American scenery the Mississippi River, as of royal right, claims a leading place. It is our Nile, our mythic stream, with which are connected all the golden-hued tales of the early travellers. Monsters like Scylla, whirlpools like Charybdis, were reported to lurk in its waters, eager to seize upon the canoes of adventurous travellers, and drag them below its whelming flood. The voices of spirits—messengers of the awful Man-i-tou—reverberated from bluff to bluff, or issued with grewsome sound from the dismal evergreens of its southern banks. The tribes that hunted on its bordering prairies were cannibals, false in friendship, implacable in war, having the tomahawk ever brandished, and the arrow-point poisoned. But, if there were these dreadful things to encounter, there were also prizes worth the winning. There were regions entirely of flowers, where the foot crushed at every movement the rarest blossoms; there were nooks inhabited by fairy beings of extreme beauty, and prompt to form the tenderest connections with the brave knights who dared all dangers to seek them. These were, like the gardens of the enchantress Armida, of supernatural beauty, tinted by a purple glamour that was akin to the atmosphere of Paradise. The blooms never faded, the turf never withered, the trees never shed their leaves, in these bowers of enchantment—these gracious climes, where all was well. In the midst of this happy land was a golden fountain, in whose waters whosoever bathed issued forth restored to his first radiant youth. The wrinkles upon the brow faded away; the thin cheek became plump and rounded; the shrunken limbs resumed their graceful outlines; the few gray locks that straggled over the worn brow were at once luxuriant and golden, or jetty black, or silky brown. Here was the material paradise, here the rest so dear to the wanderer, here that perfect calm which the unquiet heart seeks and shall find only in heaven. Whatever the spirit longed for unavailingly was said to exist here, in the region of the *Michesepe.* Expedition after expedition, under Spanish auspices, struck out from Florida to find the unknown land, watched over by ampler, bluer skies than had been known to mortals. While De Soto discovered the river in the south, the first white men who reached its northern portion were two Frenchmen from the North—Father Marquette and

Devil's Backbone, below St. Louis.

THE LEVEE AT ST. LOUIS.

M. Joliet, a trader; and the first who descended its course from its region of ice to where its waters swell the tropic wave was the Chevalier de la Salle, a man cast in a most heroic mould. Father Marquette descended the Wisconsin in June, 1673; and, on the 3d day of July, his canoe floated on the rippling waves of the great river. It was then truly virgin. The red-men lived on the prairies that here and there break through the solemn regularity of its limestone walls in the northern part, or in the wide savannas that lie behind the densely-wooded banks of its southern region. They were by no means uniform in character or in degree of civilization. Some not only hunted and fished, but applied themselves to a rude agriculture, and spun a coarse cloth, making no trade of war, but simply repelling the attacks of more ferocious neighbors. There were others who lived only for battle, and whose glory consisted in the number of the scalp-locks which adorned their wigwams. Neither was their speech uniform. Besides the great variety of dialects which follows necessarily from the immense local changes of unwritten tongues, there were two great languages altogether dissimilar. These things were noted by the good French priest as the rapid current bore him down the stream; but, unfortunately, those who followed after cared nothing for philology, and modern science now deplores vainly the absence of data on which to found any general conclusions concerning the peoples of this great region, who have now entirely disappeared. Their place has been taken by the thrifty and energetic pale-faces, who have made the Mississippi's borders a long succession of smiling fields and cheerful habitations, and who have built up great cities, destined to be in the future what Nineveh and Babylon were to Asia.

The scope of this article is confined (with the exception of two illustrations of striking scenes below the city) to the Upper Mississippi, from St. Louis to the Falls of St. Anthony. It is easier to describe the ascent of the river than its descent, both because the traveller generally takes the steamboat from St. Louis up to St. Paul, and because there is a natural climax of beauty in the scenery in this way. Near St. Louis the views, it must be confessed, offer little that is admirable to the gaze. As we ascend toward Keokuk, the landscape becomes bolder and more striking; between Keokuk and Dubuque it still becomes more and more grand; from Dubuque to Trempealeau the advantages of Nature are still more enhanced; the scenery of Lake Pepin still strikes an ascending chord, until a culmination of the beautiful is reached in the Falls of St. Anthony and Minnehaha. It is better, therefore, to lead the reader on from that which interests but slightly to things that fairly enchain and enchant, than to commence with the beautiful and simmer slowly down into the absolutely prosaic. We will, therefore, begin with St. Louis (with a glance or two at the high bluffs that are found below the city), premising that the pilots consider this city the termination of the Upper Mississippi, the region between St. Louis and New Orleans constituting the lower river. The city of St. Louis disputes with Chicago the title of Metropolis of the West. But, unlike

5th St. near the Barracks

New Court House

Lafayette Park

St. Louis

Olive St.

On Chestnut St.

A nook in McDowell's College.

On Chouteau Avenue.

On the Fair Ground

ST. LOUIS.

Hothouses
Shaw's Garden.

Entrance
Shaw's Garden.

Eq'ble Ins. Bldg
Locust St.

Fourth St.

High School
Olive Street

At the Waterworks.

The Elevator.

SCENES IN ST. LOUIS.

its great rival, its history dates back to an early period in American history. It was settled in 1762, by the French; in 1764 its inhabitants numbered one hundred and twenty all told, while its population to-day is believed to be nearly three hundred and fifty thousand. The city is situated on the west bank of the river, on a bluff elevated above the floods of the stream. It is built on two terraces, the first, or lower, rising abruptly about twenty feet from the river, and the second making a more gradual ascent of forty feet from the lower, and spreading out into a wide and beautiful plain. The corporate limits of the city extend over six miles along the river, and from three to four miles back of it. The older streets are narrow, but the new avenues are wide, and those in the resident portions lined with elegant mansions. The public buildings are imposing, the warehouses handsome, the public parks singularly beautiful. Among the famous places are Shaw's Garden, with an extensive botanical garden and conservatory, and the Fair-Grounds. The Fair-Grounds are made the object of special care and cultivation, supplying in a measure the want of a large public park. With an amphitheatre capable of seating twenty thousand persons, an area of over forty acres, filled with choice shrubbery, artificial lakes, fountains, rustic bowers, and numerous handsome structures for the exhibition of goods, it is one of the institutions of which St. Louis is justly proud. Shaw's Gardens are a munificent gift by a wealthy citizen to the public. Here is gathered every variety of tree, shrub, and plant, that can be grown in this country by natural or artificial means. St. Louis is destined for a great future. The magnificent bridge just completed, one of the largest and handsomest in the world, over which all the trains from the East directly enter the city, will have a great effect upon its fortunes. One distinguishing feature of the city is the number of huge steamboats that line its levee; but this feature is scarcely so notable now as it was a generation ago, before railroads had competed with steamboats for freight and passenger traffic. The steamers of the largest class descend the river to New Orleans; smaller ones of light draught ascend the Missouri almost to the mountains, and the Mississippi to the Falls of St. Anthony.

Taking our passage-tickets on one of the handsomely-fitted steamers that ply between St. Louis and St. Paul for at least seven months in the year, the upper river being closed from the middle of November to the middle of April by ice, we turn our backs upon St. Louis, its shot-towers and elevators, its high church-spires, and the magnificent cupola of its capitol. The banks are low on each side—rather higher on the west—and of a sandy brown. The aspects are by no means picturesque, and the junction of the Missouri and the Mississippi is not accompanied by any features of striking beauty. The city of Alton, about three miles above this junction, is perched upon a grand limestone-bluff, nearly two hundred feet high, and of a uniform light-brown color. There is a tradition that there were Indian paintings here, but they have disappeared, if they ever existed. One notices here that the water is much bluer than it was at St. Louis, and that the islands which everywhere dot the broad current have a look of greater age.

Those below seem to have formed themselves within a few months, and the hasty vegetation on them confirms the impression. But here we have the common willow, and occasionally the maple, both growing to a respectable height.

As we proceed upward, the bluffs become more numerous, and at Keokuk begin to gain the appearance of a range of hills with sloping ravines between. One might

Group of Islets.

imagine that the country in the rear was of the level of the river, or nearly so ; but it is not so, for the tops of the bluffs are on a line with the prairie-land beyond. The city of Keokuk is on the western bank, in the State of Iowa ; and the city of Warsaw, in Illinois, is opposite to it. Close to Warsaw the Desmoines River falls into the Mississippi, forming what are known as the Desmoines Rapids. It is only in the fall of the

ROCK ISLAND, ILLINOIS.—DAVENPORT, IOWA.

year that these are perceptible, and at that season they offer some hinderance to freight-boats, but the packet-steamers pass through the troubled waters without the least diffi-culty. The scenery at this point begins to give a promise of what awaits the tourist higher up. The stream is of a deep-blue color, or rather appears so from contrast with the limestone-bluffs on each side. The islands begin to be more and more numerous. Sometimes there are clusters of islets, only a few rods in extent, close to the bank—forming, as it were, a little archipelago. The stream, in these sequestered nooks, loses the steady strength of its current, and seems to linger with fondness amid the pleasing scenes. The edges of the isles are fringed with broad-leaved rushes, and often with the

Old Arsenal, Rock Island.

purple iris. Lilies spread their broad, green pads over the smooth water, presenting every variety of blossom, fully opened, half opened, just opening, and simply in the bud. There are also the bright-yellow flowers of the water-bean. In such spots as this the trees upon the islands attain quite a respectable growth, the cotton-woods especially becoming very tall. Nearest the water's edge one sees generally willows and scrub-oak, the latter grow-ing very thick and bushy. There is generally, at the extremity of the islands, a long spot of clear, white sand, which will grow into other islands if the current does not wash it away, which, however, it is sure to do sooner or later. Few can be consid-ered permanent; some only flourish for a few brief years, and then are washed away;

but there are others, which have been formed near the shore, which become protected by sand-bars, and flourish exceedingly, until some sudden thaw in the spring sends down an avalanche of floating ice, and whelms them utterly.

Forrest-Roads, Rock Island.

Leaving behind Keokuk, the steamer resumes its gliding motion over the gentle Mississippi, and the never-ending panorama of water, islands, and bluffs, recommences. About seventy miles higher up, the Iowa River joins the stream, coming in on the left hand. Fifty miles of the same identical scenery, without a change, brings the traveller to one of the few features of this part of the river. Most of the islands in the Mississippi are temporary formations of sand; in fact, there are but three of rock; and we have now come to the largest and the most important, named Rock Island. It is three miles long, and has an area of nearly a thousand acres, the greater part of which is cleared, the rest being covered with fine forest-trees. The soil is, of course, limestone, and has been utilized for building government fortifications and arsenals of quite a formidable character. The old arsenal, of which a sketch is presented, was at one time the headquarters of the famous General Scott during the Black-Hawk War. This has long been abandoned, and has been replaced by limestone structures of the most enduring character; for here the United States has its armory headquarters, and the whole island

BRIDGES ON THE MISSISSIPPI, AT DUBUQUE.

has been developed, until it resembles, in the beauty of its drives and its military buildings, the station of West Point, on the Hudson, where the great military school of the nation is quartered. On the eastern bank, in Illinois, is the city of Rock Island. Opposite to it, on the other shore, is the city of Davenport, in the State of Iowa. These are both connected with the island by bridges, through which steamers pass by means of draws. These bridges were the first that spanned the Mississippi, and they met intense opposition from the steamboat-men, who hired gangs of desperadoes to burn them down as fast as the workmen erected them. But at last the cause of order triumphed, and the river-men consented to an act which they declared would forever ruin the commerce of the river. A candid and impartial mind will be forced to admit that the steamboat-party were not altogether in the wrong, for Nature here has done so much to obstruct navigation by rapids that the draw-bridges were really like putting the last straw on the camel's back. So powerful are the rapids here that in the fall freight-boats are sometimes prevented altogether from ascending, and it is easy to see that there might be seasons of water when a very little thing, such as the draw-bridges, would be sufficient to turn the scale against the boats. The passenger-packets feel the difficulty, but in a far less degree. It cannot be doubted that, within a few years, the railways will be compelled to pattern after the great St.-Louis Bridge invented by Captain James Eads, in which spans of cast-steel give an uninterrupted opening of over five hundred feet.

From the moment that we strike the rapids, we begin to notice a change in the bluffs. They are less hilly than heretofore, and they begin to become more like Cyclopean walls; their height, also, is greatly increased, and they are much lighter in color. The first effect upon the mind is unquestionably grand. The enormous masses of stone, which in their stratification resemble masonry, cannot but deeply impress the beholder. One marvels at the extraordinary regularity of the lines, and the conclusion comes upon one with irresistible force that there was a time when the water was on a level with these walls, three hundred feet high, and that the regular action of the river has exposed their strata with this seemingly strange uniformity. The Mississippi must be here about two miles wide, and is full of islands, which present every variety of form in their masses of vegetation. The water, on a fine summer's day, is perfectly clear, perfectly smooth, and all the indentations in the rocks, every streak of brown upon the whitish-gray sides, every boss protruding, every tuft of grass that has gained footing, every bush upon the slope at the base, every tree on the summit, are pictured in the cool shadows with undeviating fidelity. There is a mingling of the ideas of grandeur with those of rest and peace and happiness, which is inexpressibly pleasant; and there are few things in life more agreeable than to sit on the upper deck and watch the panorama that the river offers. Everywhere one gets delicious effects, specially where a curve in the river brings the trees of the islands sharply against the light background of the bluffs, or where the limestone-walls, receding, leave the islands in the centre, and

DUBUQUE, FROM KELLY'S BLUFF.

the tops of the cotton-woods are defined upon the blue sky. Nature harmonizes her blues and greens, if artists cannot. Then, it is pleasant to watch the working of her general law in the hills themselves. Sometimes, indeed, we see bluffs unsupported; but almost invariably there is a noble, perpendicular wall for two-thirds of the descent, and a great, sloping buttress of fragments for the remainder. It is on the latter that vegetation thrives, though here and there we come to long stretches of bluffs that are made reddish brown in color by a covering of minute lichen.

A Cross-Street in Dubuque.

As we approach Dubuque, three hundred and sixty miles from St. Louis, the rocks begin to be castellated, and, probably from some softness in the limestone, to be worn into varied shapes. But the full extent of this peculiarity is not seen until one passes Dubuque. Below that point the change is mostly manifested in the appearance of broad ledges at the top, that look like cornices, and in an occasional fragment of perpendicular structure, to both of which forms waving weeds and the long tendrils of wild-vines add a peculiar grace. At Dubuque the bluffs are nearly three hundred feet high, but they do not come sheer down to the water's edge, as at Alton, nor is there a long, sloping buttress; but at the base there is a broad level, about sixteen feet above the Mississippi. On this plateau are all the business-houses, the hotels, and the factories. Above, connected with paths that have been cut through the solid limestone, are the streets of the dwelling-houses.

The approaches to these upper houses are mostly by stairs that might easily be called ladders, without exposing one to a charge of being sarcastic; but it is worth the trouble of mounting these ladders a few times every day, to have such a landscape unrolled before the eye. There is a stretch of bare, sandy island in the centre of the river, across which comes the railway-bridge of the Illinois Central Railroad. There is, at the farther end of the island, a large shot-factory, and close to it the shot-tower, which darts up into the blue sky like a light flame. Beyond rise the bluffs of the eastern shore, which here are very hilly, and present beautiful contrasts of green verdure with glaring white. The tops of many are quite covered with a dense vegetation. Far beyond rolls the dreamy

Eagle Point, near Dubuque.

prairie, melting in the distance into the sky, which, blue above, becomes paler and paler as it nears the horizon, until it is an absolute gray. This is the outward look. The inward has plenty of quaint effects. There is an absolute confusion of lines. Here is a wall, there a stairway. Above that wall is a house, with more stairways. Then comes another wall, and perhaps another house, or a castellated mass of limestone, overlooking the architectural muddle. It is as quaint as any of the scenes in the old cities of Lombardy upon the slopes of the mountains, among the terraces cultivated with the grape, the olive, and the fig.

Just beyond Dubuque we come upon one of the landmarks of the pilots of the upper river—Eagle Point, a splendid bluff, some five hundred feet high. The railroad from Dubuque to St. Paul runs upon the western side here, and continues to do so until it crosses at Hastings, a long way north. It runs at the base of the bluffs, and commands the picturesque points almost as well as the steamer. At this point the bluffs are unusually high and massive, presenting often another variety of mountain-form, in which the summit rolls down, as it were, and the perpendicular walls beneath seem like a short column supporting a monstrous dome. Eagle Point is not of this kind, however; but the sloping portion blends so gradually with the perpendicular that, to the eye, it seems one enormous wall, descending from the forest above to the water beneath. The

Buena Vista.

trees here attain a large size, and dot the champaign country that stretches far away on every side. Sometimes the cliffs have been so changed by the action of water as to produce those colossal sloping banks which are called "downs" in England, where not a particle of the limestone is visible, the whole being covered with a rich mantle of green. The effect of these downs is peculiarly pleasing in sudden turns of the river, when in the distance a portion of the Mississippi seems to be isolated, and fancy cheats us with the belief that the broad, gleaming sheet is the commencement of a romantic lake among the hills. Then these great roofs of green become a most exquisite background, more especially when the landscape is tamed down by a thin, silvery mist. Perhaps one of the causes of this lake-like appearance is the comparative freedom of this part of the Mississippi from islands. There are small dots of green, willowy land here and there, but not in such numbers or proportions as to contract the view of large expanses of water. Right in the centre of this beautiful region is the little village of Buena Vista, which owes its name, and indeed its existence, to the appreciative taste of a Westerner who fixed his household-gods here in the centre of all that was lovely in Nature. The place is well known to pilots, because in the vicinity there is an outcropping of lower silurian, which resembles exactly ruins of some gigantic structure. It is not precisely an outcropping, because it has become visible by the washing away of the soil that concealed it. There is at its base an indescribable mass of fragments, round which creepers and wild-vines have twined themselves in picturesque confusion, and on each side of it the forest-trees grow in the greatest luxuriance. The ravines on each side are broad and

At the Mouth of the Wisconsin.

Steamboat Landing Lacrosse.

Scenery above Lacrosse.

LA CROSSE, AND SCENERY ABOVE.

picturesque, but give no idea or suggestion of what the bluff was before it crumbled away, leaving, as it were, its skeleton visible.

The mouth of the Wisconsin is broad, but the water is shallow, and the channel is obstructed by sand-bars, covered with rank vegetation. The bluffs here, on the opposite side, are covered with trees, and, both in their contour and general appearance, remind one very much of the hills along the western branch of the Susquehanna. On the western side we are still in the State of Iowa but the eastern shore belongs to Wisconsin,

Three Miles above La Crosse.

one of the great wheat-raising regions. All along the line of the river here, the towns have something to do with the traffic in cereals, but most of it is becoming concentrated in Dubuque. Somehow, whether it is imagination or not can scarcely be analyzed, but the air here seems purer and more bracing than it did below, yet the sun's rays are immensely powerful. The bluffs, that are directly exposed to the full force of the summer sun, are bare of vegetation as the palm of one's hand—masses of white rock. But, wherever a curve gives a shelter to vegetation, the trees spring up joyously to the blue air, and the wild-vines hang their festoons around the fantastic spires and jutting cornices of the limestone. This is, in sober truth, an exquisite part of the river, from the greater variety of the scenery, the wooded hills, and the exquisitely pure character of the water, which is clear and limpid as that of Lake Leman. The bluffs alternate from massive, deeply-wooded hills to long walls of limestone, with bases and huge cornices and bartizan towers, deep crypts, and isolated chimneys. Often, from the deep heart of the oaks and maples crowning a majestic bluff, starts up a skeleton splinter of bare lime, white as alabaster, in the pure air, a little reminder that the hill had been much higher. Sometimes it will not be a pinnacle, but a regular series of towers or donjon-keeps, with wild-vine

Queen's Bluff, below Trempealeau.

banners waving from the outer ramparts. In other places, the summits will be entirely denuded of timber, but will be covered with a bright mantle of emerald turf. In the ravines between, the trees are low, thick, and bushy, the very place for the covert of a deer, and one watches instinctively to see some motion in the leafy shade, and to detect the brown antlers of some leader of the herd. In the midst of these wonders there comes a break, where a little river pours its waters into the Father of Streams. A smiling prairie, level as a billiard-table, is spread on each side of the mouth for several miles. Here is the town of La Crosse, built upon the prairie where all the Indian tribes, for hundreds of miles around, used to have their great ball-playing, that game which the French travellers called "la crosse," and which has given its name to this stirring city, bustling with manufactures, and noisy with the screams of locomotives. And still we are on the right bank of the river, and still in the State of Wisconsin; the opposite shore is in Minnesota, also a great grain and lumber mart. Here we begin to see big rafts coming down the stream, with often twelve men tugging away at the clumsy, huge oars, battling against the swift current. Above La Crosse, the valley of the Mississippi widens considerably, and the hills recede, leaving long slopes of upland, covered with noble trees. The river is perfectly studded with islands; in fact, one is never out of sight of them. They are all low, composed of alluvial soil, washings from the banks, and are covered with a dense growth of shrub-oak, from which occasional cotton-woods soar up to considerable height. Sometimes they are in the centre, sometimes they fringe the banks; but, in every position, they add greatly to the beauty of the scene.

Scenery below Trempealeau.

Approach to Trempealeau.

The bluffs here are, in many cases, over six hundred feet high, and of varied shapes, the pyramidal beginning to appear with persistent recurrence.

Queen's Bluff, a fragmentary pyramidal bluff, is one of the landmarks by which the pilots know that they are approaching the fairy region of Trempealeau. Queen's Bluff has not only been cleft in twain by the greater Mississippi of the past, but its face has been scooped out by the winds, and Nature has kindly filled up the gloomy void with fine trees. Its southern side is exposed directly to the noonday sun, and is a bare, precipitous mass of glaring white, without so much as a blade of grass to shade it from the sun's fierce kisses. There are great cracks in it, which are positively blue in shadow, from the intensity of the glare.

The steamboat glides onward over the glassy tide, and nears rapidly one of the three rocky islands of the Mississippi. The first was at Rock Island, the second is here at Trempealeau, about eighteen miles above La Crosse. It is sometimes called Mountain Island, for its rocky height attains in one part an altitude of five hundred and sixty feet. But the name which the French *voyageurs* gave it is so poetical that it would be a sin to change it. It rises sheer out of the water in the centre of the channel, and the French called it "Mont qui trempe à l'eau" (Mountain which dips in the Water). Nothing can be conceived more beautiful than the approach to this most romantic and picturesque spot, which, in the writer's opinion, exceeds in positive beauty the far-famed scenery of Lake Pepin, twenty-five miles up the river. The river lies like a lake in the

Trempealeau Island.

bosom of the hills, which are so varied in beauty that they defy description. They do not present an amphitheatre of peaks, but are rather like an edging or the setting of emeralds around a diamond. Their forms offer every possible combination of picturesque lines, every known conformation of limestone-rocks, blended with ever-changing hues of green, from the deep tints of evergreens to the bright emerald of grassy plains. The river seems to sleep below, its placid surface giving back all the glorious beauty of its environing. The locomotive creeps at the base of the great bluffs, as if conscious of

Chimney Rock, near Fountain City.

intrusion, and emits its whistle in a plaintive, deprecatory manner, that the hills echo and reëcho with increasing pathos. The islets that nestle around the huge form of Trempealeau are mostly covered with sedge-crashes, waving with the slightest puff of air. The mountain is by no means bare. There are parts which are covered by thick forests, growing with the greatest luxuriance on the steep ascent; and there are spaces where nothing but the barren rock is seen, with all its huge stratification exposed to view. Spots of the barren rock are covered with a minute lichen, which gives to the limestone a warm, rich effect, like red sandstone; in other spots it is dazzling white, like marble. There is a winding path up Trempealeau for those who care to make the ascent, and, in autumn, the sides of this road are lined with berry-bushes. Nothing is more sugges-tive in the distance than this same winding foot-way, especially when behind it a golden-edged cloud of cumulus formation is slowly sailing by; then it seems a path to El Dorado, to the cities of elf-land, where, in silence, await the bold adventurer, beauteous maidens, in fountained courts, rich with the perfume of celestial flowers, and where birds sing strains of a sweetness never heard from mortal instrument, but akin to those divine airs that flit through the brain, as pitilessly beyond the grasp as the golden-cornered cloud itself. Trempealeau is a study for the painter, a theme for the poet, a problem for the geologist, a clew for the historian. Whosoever will study it with his soul rather than his wit shall not fail of exceeding great reward.

It is hard to say under what aspect Trempealeau looks the best—whether from the distance below, or from a nestling-place in the islets at its feet, or from the village of Trempealeau, five miles above. This little place ought to be visited by every painter and poet in America, and should become the headquarters of every one who loves the scenery of his country, during the summer months. It is a grief that Americans should wander off to the Rhine and the Danube when, in the Mississippi, they have countless Rhines and many Danubes. What does it matter if every peak along the former has the dismantled walls of some robber-baron's den? Is Drachenfels one whit more castel-lated than any of the nameless bluffs about and around Trempealeau? All that is beau-tiful in lake-scenery, in lower mountain-scenery, in river-scenery, is garnered here. The

LAKE PEPIN.

MAIDEN'S ROCK, LAKE PEPIN.

great trees that line the bases of Trempealeau are worthy of the Titan that has nour-
ished them, and develop such trunks, such branches, as do the eyes good to see. The
little isles crouch at the foot of the mountain-island as if seeking protection from the
rush of the spring waters or the live bolt of the storm. They are of every shape, and
the combinations of their trees and their sedgy banks offer a thousand hints of beauty

Limestone Natural Walls, below St. Paul.

and suggestions of romance to the intelligent glance that takes them in. Sometimes the
cotton-trees clump themselves as in a park ; anon, by a few strokes of the oar, and in
a trice, one gazes at a vista of branches through which, obscurely in the distance, one
sees through the tremulous summer a great broad flank of darkened limestone. And the
clear, limpid water that glides around them, and that laves the rocky sides of the grand

Trempealeau, gleams with such brightness, and glows so under the sunlight, and sleeps in silvery lengths under the moonlight, that one cannot but love it. In the distance, looking back regretfully from the village of Trempealeau, every cape and headland is softened, and the green hues of the forest-clad sides become a warmish gray, verging in blue. The little isles appear like dots of trees, springing up out of the silvery wave that spreads itself out in a dazzling sheet of reflected sunshine. And, if any one, after seeing these things, shall pine for the castled crags of the Rhine, let him come and survey Chimney Rock, near Fountain City, some twenty-five miles higher up. It is true that the hand of man never wrought at these things, but, for all that, it is the precise image of Chepstow

Near St. Paul.

Keep, in "merrie England," and is, to all intents and purposes, as much a castle as any ruin of the German river. The spectator who views this peculiar mass of limestone from above the river will fail to see why it received its name. But, from below, and passing abreast, one observes that the extreme mass on the right hand is altogether detached, and presents a very striking resemblance to the enormous stone chimneys which are built up *outside* the houses in Virginia. The castle rises from a dense growth of trees, mostly of maples, and at the base of the bluff there is a sort of natural terrace, very broad and even, which is free from vegetation of any kind, and looks not unlike the terrace of a proud palatine home. Below this is an accumulation of soil, washed down by the river in spring tides, which has offered a resting-place to wandering seeds. These have grown into a belt of scrub-oak, very low and very compact, forming a pleasant foreground to the scene above.

We now approach Lake Pepin, the first glimpses of which are truly charming. The Mississippi here swells into a large expanse of water, in some parts five miles across, and this widening extends for twenty-five miles. By many this region is considered the finest that the river affords, but most artists will decide for the vicinity of Trempealeau. The water here is very deep, and, in the summer-time, is so calm, so unruffled, so still, that one cannot discern with the eye any appearance of a current. So easily do the side-wheel steamboats pass through the water that they seem to be moving through air, so gentle and equable are the pulsations. And it is really an annoyance to be passed by a stern - wheeler; the great machine in the rear tosses the water about and churns it into foam, destroying the serene impressions that had been left upon the mind. Looking northward, on entering the lake, one observes a high rocky point on the left shore, elevating itself like a sentinel of a fairy host guarding the entrance to the enchanted land. In the mid - distance another promontory of high and menacing aspect juts out into the lake, concealing from view the sweep of the upper end of the lake, which here makes a bold curve to the eastward. A superb amphitheatre of bluffs encloses the lake, many of which have an elevation of five hundred feet. These present every variety of form, some of them being square masses, like the keep of an old castle; others flow out in a series of bosses; others are angular, others conical. Here, in one direction, is a pyramid, with numerous depressions and ravines mottling the white mass with veins of shadow; and here, in another, is a vertical wall, with perfect mouldings of cornices and plinths. Anon, steals into the view a gently-sloping mound, covered with herbage and trees. All of these does the delicate-hued surface of the lake reflect with perfect fidelity, excepting that the light objects are elongated, and their outlines are lost; but the dark, stern capes are given back with scrupulous exactitude, line for line, bush for bush, mass for mass.

This is Lake Pepin in a calm. But this daughter of the hills is not always in a good-humor, and, when her waves are ruffled by the angry winds, she rages with a fury that is by no means innocent. Its vicinity to St. Paul makes it a favorite resort for those who are fond of boating, and the surface in the summer is often dotted with the white sails of miniature yachts. These have a hard time in stormy weather, for the waves are very high and very short, and succeed each other with a rapidity which makes steering almost impossible. Many a sailing-boat has been dashed by the mad waters right into the forests that here, in every direction, come sloping down to the water's edge. In all the little villages nestling in the amphitheatres of the lake, there are stories of such disasters, though they never yet taught prudence to any one. The great tradition of death and sorrow belongs to Maiden's Rock. The tale of Winona's tragical suicide

ST. PAUL, FROM DAYTON'S BLUFF.

has been widely circulated, but it is so much a part of Lake Pepin's attraction that it cannot be passed over in silence. Winona was a young girl of that confederacy, named by itself Dah-co-tah, which the French called Sioux, but whose real name is Tetone. She loved a hunter of the same division of the confederacy, but her parents wished her to marry a warrior of the Wapesha division, and, by threats and actual blows, extorted from her a promise of compliance. The day before the union she ascended a bluff of great height, whose upper part is a sheer precipice, and began chanting her death-song. Soon the base was surrounded by the tribe, and all those who possessed any influence over the girl shouted to her to descend, and that all should be well. She shook her head in disbelief, and, breaking off her song, upbraided them bitterly, not only for wishing to marry her against her will, but for their folly in preferring the claims of a warrior, who did nothing but fight, to those of a hunter, who fed the tribe. Then she continued her interrupted chant, and threw herself, at its conclusion, from the height, being dashed to pieces in the great buttress of rocky *débris* below.

Frontenac is in the centre of the lake-region, and is left behind with veritable regret. When we get once more into the river it seems quite narrow, though this is the effect of contrast. At Hastings, the railroad which has hitherto faithfully accompanied us on the left side makes a change to the other shore, just in the region of the limestone walls. These are not very high, but they produce a forcible impression by their length and regularity. The bluffs rise over them in great green domes, and often large trees crown their ledges; but there are spots where, for miles upon miles, these walls stand alone, unadorned by vegetation—white, glaring, and monotonous. Still, there is a quiet strength and sternness about this formation, which impress some organizations more forcibly than actual beauty, and the spots where these ramparts are partially covered with great trailing wild-vines are indeed highly picturesque. The river-scenery at this point is essentially lovely. There is a multiplicity of islands, showing every possible massing of vegetation, and, in many cases, the bluffs are quite low, and admit a broad view of woodland and prairie. The effect is park-like, and, when a powerful sun pours upon the scene a flood of light, nothing more softly beautiful can be imagined. Looking northward in the distance, we obtain faint glimpses of St. Paul; but it is impossible to get a good view of this picturesque city from the river. This is the getting-off place, the end of navigation on the Mississippi, and therefore every one is sure of being able to go to Ball's Bluff, or, better still, to Dayton's Bluff, on the east side of St. Paul, where, with one sweeping glance, the eye takes in the city, its towers, and its elevators, the railroad-bridges, the opposing rocky shores, and the graceful curve of the river.

The chief attraction, of a picturesque nature, in this vicinity, however, is not upon the Mississippi, but on the little Minnehaha River, an outlet of Lake Minnetonka, whose waters are poured into the Minnesota not far from the junction of that river

FALLS OF MINNEHAHA.

with the Mississippi. The famous falls here are by no means what one would imagine from the poem of Longfellow. There is but little water, yet what there is is more admirable at its lowest than at its highest volume. For the chief beauty of the fall is in the crossing of the delicate spiral threads of water, producing an effect which reminds one of fine lace. About two hundred feet below there is a bridge, and, as this is only thirty feet long, it will assist the reader in forming a correct idea of the proportions of this somewhat too famous cataract. The gorge is elliptic in form from the centre of the falls to the bridge, and quite narrow everywhere. The depth is about sixty feet. On each side of the top of the falls are numerous birch-trees, and the summits of the gorge crowned with various forest-trees. Below the bridge, the bluffs or banks on each side cease to be precipitous, and come sloping down to the water's edge, with all their trees, the branches of many actually dipping into the brink. The veil of the fall-

Minneapolis, St. Anthony, and St. Anthony's Falls.

ing water is so thin that one can see the rock behind it. There is a good path behind, which even ladies can follow, except when the wind blows directly opposite, when the adventurous traveller would get well drenched.

By rail from St. Paul to St. Anthony, on the Mississippi River, the distance is about ten miles, and every pilgrim in search of the picturesque ends his journey here. Minneapolis is on one side of the river, and the city of St. Anthony on the other. The falls can be seen with equal advantage from either side, though, if one wants to try both views, the suspension-bridge enables one to do so with perfect ease. The rapids above the cataract are very fine, in fact much finer than the fall itself, for the river is broad above, nearly seven hundred feet wide, and, within the last mile, makes a descent of fifty feet. As the falls are only eighteen feet, they often disappoint the spectator, more especially as commerce has interfered with them, and converted them into water-power, second only to that of Rocky Island at Moline. The rapids are in reality splendid, even in the summer-time. The jostling waters heave up great surges several feet high, from which the wind strikes sheets of spray. In the centre there is a broad, well-defined mass of water, like a ridge, elevated over the stream on each side. Furious eddies boil and circle in this with a deep, gurgling sound, and, when a pine-tree comes down, it goes under, and comes shooting up into the air hundreds of feet below, but with every particle of bark stripped off, and great splinters wrenched from the hard wood by the battling currents underneath. Just above the fall, on the very verge, the waters steady themselves for the leap, but, before that, the waves cross and recross, and stagger with blind, furious haste. The best view seems to be from the centre of the suspension-bridge, for there you can see the grand rapids, and do not see the dams and factories on either side. Looking up the falls, however, you do gain something, for you have a full view of the extraordinary piles of limestone-slabs forced off by the united action of the currents and the ice. These are heaped in many places along the shore with the greatest regularity. The slabs are like the tops of tables, many of them as smooth as possible, this being the distinguishing characteristic of limestone-cleavage. And, the force of the water being in one direction below the falls, the slabs are not broken in the descent, but are gently left by the receding waves along the shore in regular rotation. Still, from this point of view, the dams and other obstructions are too plainly in sight, and, though they cannot make one forget the immense volume of the river that comes leaping onward, yet they do destroy all the romance and much of the beauty of the water-fall.

THE VALLEY OF THE GENESEE.

WITH ILLUSTRATIONS BY J. DOUGLAS WOODWARD.

THERE is said to be a mountain-peak in Potter County, Pennsylvania, standing upon which the observer may mark the fountain-head of two rivers. Though flowing through adjacent gorges, their courses are soon divided, the one tending southward, while the other marks out a winding way to the harbor at Charlotte, there losing itself in the waters of Lake Ontario. To follow down the pathway of the southward-flowing stream would lead the traveller through every variation of climate and verdure that our land affords—now shadowed by the rugged peaks of the Alleghanies, then over rough rapids and dangerous shallows, till the smoky precincts of Pittsburg are reached, with the blending waters of the Monongahela. Still farther, and bearing west by south, its course leads through fruitful valleys, and along the busy wharves of Cincinnati, Louisville, and Cairo. Here the clear, fresh waters of the mountain-rivulet are finally merged and lost in the expanse of the Mississippi ; and, afloat on the bosom of the Father of Rivers, we are borne on its sluggish current to the delta, and the borders of the Southern gulf.

Railroad-Bridge, Portage.

This tour of fancy ended, the river-voyager retraces his path till he stands again upon the Northern summit, and girds himself for the second and northward journey.

This, though short as compared with his southward course, will yet prove one of exceeding beauty, and rich in all those varied phases which unite to form what we call the picturesque. It is to the "beautiful Genesee" that we now turn; and, as the valley that bears its name, and owes its richness to the river's turbulent moods, lies far to the northward, in the limits of the neighboring Empire State, we hasten toward it, trusting to the paths through which the river first made its way.

In its early course, the Genesee is not marked by any exceptional beauty or peculiar charm of surroundings. Nor is it till the falls at Portage are reached that the river asserts its claim to recognition as one of the most beautiful and picturesque of all our Eastern streams.

The summer tourist, if he leave the car of the Erie Railway at Portage Village, will be first attracted by what is the least picturesque though an important feature in the foreground; and that is the great bridge which spans the ravine and river at this point— a work which will well repay a careful survey, since it is regarded as a triumph of the bridge-builder's skill. This bridge, or, more properly, viaduct, is said to be the largest wooden structure of its kind in the world. It crosses the river at a point hardly a stone's-throw above the brink of the First or Upper Fall; and its lightly-framed piers, with their straight lines reaching from the granite base to the road-way above, contrast strangely with the wild roughness of the natural chasm it spans.

The reason given by the artist for not presenting an extended and architecturally complete view of this great work is not without force. "This is a tour in search of the picturesque," he says; "and the straight lines, sharp angles, and cut-stone buttresses of a railway-bridge do not belong to that order of beauty." Assenting to this just estimate of the artist's mission, we turn away from this hasty survey of the bridge to the contemplation of the rough-hewn, rugged walls of the chasm it spans.

Divided for an instant by the stone buttresses of the bridge, the waters of the river unite again, just in time to present a bold and unbroken front upon the brink of the first fall. As the body of water which passes over these falls is comparatively small—except in seasons of flood—and as the first precipice is but sixty-eight feet in height, the effect would be of little moment, were it not for the striking character of the surroundings.

Entering the gorge a short distance above the brink of this Upper Fall, the river has cut for itself a wild, rugged channel, the walls of which rise in a perpendicular height of from two to six hundred feet, each successive fall resulting in a deepening of the chasm, and a consequent increase in the height of the rocky barriers.

It is this chasm that constitutes the distinctive feature in the upper course of the Genesee. Beginning abruptly at a point not far above the Upper Fall, it increases in depth and wildness until the village of Mount Morris is reached, at which point the stream makes its exit from the rocky confines as abruptly as it entered them, and, as

Middle Falls, Portage.

though to atone for the wildness of its early course, settles at once into a gentle and life-giving current, gliding through rich meadows and fertile lowlands, its way marked by a luxuriant growth of grass and woodland. But there are other features in the region of Portage which deserve more extended notice, and to these we willingly return.

Having recovered from their first bold leap, the waters unite and flow onward in gentle current, with an occasional ripple or miniature rapid, for the distance of half a mile, when the brink of the second and highest fall is reached. Over this the waters pour, in an unbroken sheet, a distance of one hundred and ten feet. At the base of this fall the waters have carved out, on the western side, a dark cave, which may be approached by a wooden stairway, standing at the foot of which we see the sky as from the depths of a crater.

Ascending again to the plateau that reaches out on a line with the brink of this fall, we come in sight of Glen Iris, a rural home, the fortunate owner of which is evidently the possessor of a sympathizing and appreciative taste for the beauties with which he is surrounded.

Lower Falls, Portage.

Upon the lawn that divides Glen-Iris Cottage from the brink of the precipice stands a rude log-cabin, which is in the possession of a history so closely linked with that of the first inhabitants of this wild region that it becomes at once a monument of peculiar interest. The form of this cabin is given by the artist with so careful a regard for truth that a description is not needed. We have called it merely a log-cabin; and yet it is, in truth, an ancient Indian council-house, and stands alone, the only ruin of what was once a village of the Iroquois. This ancient council-house of Caneadea stood originally upon a bluff of land overlooking the Genesee, about twenty-two miles above its present site. It was the last relic of aboriginal sovereignty in the valley, and it is not surprising that it should be so jealously guarded by its present owner, Mr. Letchworth, on whose lawn it stands. During the Indian wars, all the white captives brought in from the South and East were here received, and compelled to run the gantlet before this council-house, its doors being their only goal of safety. Among the famous captives who were thus put to the test was Major Moses van Campen, a name distinguished in the annals of the wars with the Iroquois. This building sheltered Mary Jemison, "the white woman of

Indian Council House.

the Genesee," after her long, fearful march from the Ohio to her home and final resting-place in the valley beyond. It was here that the chiefs of the Seven Nations were wont to hold their councils of war. There is no record of the date of its construction, but upon one of the logs is the sign of a cross, the same as that which the early Jesuit fathers were known to have adopted as the symbol of their faith. Besides this single evidence of the presence of the stranger, the old council-house bears upon its rough sides the marks and signs of the Indians who are now without a home or a country, and yet who once could call all these wild passes, royal forests, and broad acres, their own, by virtue of a long inheritance. When the Indians took their departure to more western

High Banks, Portage.

reservations, the old council-house came into the possession of a white squatter, who guarded it against decay, and made it his home for fifty years.

It is this council-house that now stands on the lawn at Glen Iris, in full view of the distant bluffs, and within but a stone's-throw of the Middle Fall. Prompted by his own worthy interest in this last relic of the old league, Mr. Letchworth caused the council-house to be removed from its original site at Caneadea, and erected where it now stands. In effecting this removal, great care was taken to place the building precisely as it originally stood, each stick occupying the same relative position to the others. At the rededication of the building, in the autumn of 1872, there were present twenty-

two Indians. Among these justly-distinguished guests were the grandsons of Mary
Jemison, Cornplanter, Red-Jacket, Tall Chief, Captain Brant, Governor Blacksnake, and
other chiefs whose names are associated with the early history of this region. Many
of these strange guests wore the costumes of their tribes. The council-fire was again
lighted; the pipe of peace—the identical one presented by Washington to Red-Jacket—
was passed again around the circle of grave and dignified chiefs, many of whom were
natives of the valley, and whose ancestors were once the sole possessors of all this land.
These men were said to be fine representatives of their race; and the speeches that
followed the first silent ceremony were delivered in the Seneca tongue, with all the old
eloquence and fire. It was an occasion worthy of a lasting record, as this was, no doubt,
the last Indian council that will ever be held in the valley of the Genesee.

After the Revolutionary War the league of the Iroquois was broken, the Mohawks,

High Banks, Mount Morris.

with Brant at their head, entering the service of the British, while the Senecas remained true to the new claimants of their soil. Thereafter, Mohawk and Seneca met only as enemies; nor was the feud healed until the day of this their last council, when the grandsons of Brant and Cornplanter shook hands across the council-fire, and there smoked the pipe of peace.

The lonely council-house, the dying embers, and the dull rustle of the falling autumn leaves—all seemed in accord with this the last scene in the history of that wild race whose light has gone out with the rising of the new sun.

Turning again to the river, we follow down a wild mountain-road for the distance of two miles, at which point a narrow, winding foot-path leads down a steep and rugged defile. Descending this, and guided by the rush of waters below, we suddenly come upon the Lower Falls. Here the waters of the river are gradually led into narrower channels, until the stream becomes a deep-cut canal, which, rushing down in swift current between its narrow limits, widens out just upon the brink of the fall, that more nearly resembles a steep rapid than either of the others. Standing upon one of the projecting rocks which are a feature of this fall, we can only catch occasional glimpses of the cavern's bed, so dense and obscuring are the mist-clouds. A second and more hazardous pathway leads from these rocky observatories to the base of this the last of the Portage falls; and the course of the river now lies deep down in its rock-enclosed limits, until the broad valley is reached.

To this rocky defile the general name of High Banks is given—a name rendered more definite by a prefix denoting their immediate locality. Thus we have the High Banks at Portage, the Mount-Morris High Banks, and, at the lower end of the valley, the High Banks below the lower fall at Rochester.

To the tourist who is possessed of a full measure of courage and strength, a journey along the river's shore from the lower falls to the valley will reveal wonders of natural architecture hardly exceeded by the cañons of the far West. Here, hidden beneath the shadows of the overhanging walls of rock, it is hard to imagine that, just beyond that line of Norway pines that forms a fringe against the sky above, lie fertile fields and quiet homes. A just idea of the depth of this continuous ravine can best be secured by an ascent to one of the projecting points above, where, resting on a ledge of rock, the river is seen at one point six hundred feet below, a distance which changes with the varying surface of the land above. At certain points the river seems to have worn out a wider channel than it can now fill, and here are long, narrow levels of rich, alluvial soil; and, if it be the harvest-season, we can catch glimpses of life in these deep-down valleys, pigmy men and horses gathering in a miniature harvest of maize or wheat; while, at noonday, the rich golden yellow of the ripened grain contrasts strangely with the deep, emerald green of the sloping sides or the dull gray of the slaty walls beyond.

Although the point where the river enters the ravine at Portage is but twelve miles in a direct line from that of its exit at Mount Morris, the distance, following its winding course among the hills, is much greater. Having traversed this distance, however, we are brought suddenly into the presence of a scene the direct antithesis of all that has gone before. Emerging through what is literally a rocky gate-way, the whole mood of the

Elms on the Genesee Flats.

river seems to have changed with that of its surroundings. In order to make this change as conspicuous as possible, we ascend to one of the two summits of the terminal hills. Standing upon this, and shaded by the grand oaks which crown it, we have but to turn the eye southward to take in at a glance the whole valley below, which is a grand park, reaching far away to the south. The sloping highlands are dotted here and there with rural villages, whose white church-spires glisten in the rich, warm sun-

Flats of the Genesee.

light. Below and around are the meadows and alluvial places known as the Genesee Flats.

The present view embraces broad, level fields, marked out by well-kept fences, enclosing areas often one hundred acres in extent. Should it be the harvest-season, we may distinguish almost at our feet broad fields crossed their entire length by endless rows of richly-tasselled broom-corn. To the right are the justly-celebrated nurseries, with their lines of miniature fruit and shade trees; the distant slopes are dotted with the golden wheat-harvests; while, reaching far away to the south, are the rich meadow-lands of the Genesee. In the midst of all flows the river, its waters giving life and beauty to the numerous groves of oaks and elms which shadow its course. It is, in fact, a broad lawn, unbroken save by an occasional hillock, with here and there groves of rare old oaks, beneath whose shade droves of cattle graze at leisure. These groups of oaks and elms are a marked feature of the flats, and many of our most famous landscape-painters— among others Casilear, Coleman, Durand, and Kensett—have taken up their abode here in order to secure sketches of these "trees," which have afterward figured as among the most attractive features of their finished works.

This valley, like all others watered by rivers taking their rise in neighboring mountain-districts, is subject to frequent and occasionally disastrous inundations. Fortunately, however, the moods of the river are oftenest in accord with those of the varying seasons; for this reason freshets seldom come upon the ungathered harvests. The possibility of this event, however, leads the landholders to reserve their meadows

ROCHESTER, FROM MOUNT HOPE CEMETERY.

East Side, Upper Falls of the Genesee.

upon the flats for grazing purposes, and hence the damage of a flood is mainly confined to the destruction of fences and an occasional hay-barrack. The regular recurrence of these inundations affects, also, the laying out of the highways. Were it not

West Side, Upper Falls of the Genesee.

for the floods, the main avenues north and south would naturally be surveyed along the level land of the flats. As it is, however, these highways lead along the adjacent hill-sides, with an occasional road leading across the valley. Among the important and most frequented of these avenues is that leading from the village of Mount Morris southward, and known as the Mount - Morris Turnpike. It is along this that our southward journey now tends, the objective point being the lovely village of Geneseo.

This village is the shire town of Livingston County, within the boundaries of which the richest of the valley-lands are situated. It stands upon the eastern slopes of the valley, the river, at its nearest point, running half a mile distant. The history of Geneseo is that of the valley itself, since it was here that many of the first white settlements were made. We enter its limits from the south, and the first suggestion of its presence is the old Wadsworth homestead, whose broad porticos, facing westward, command a glorious view of all the rich domain below. The grounds that belong to this old mansion mark the southern limit of the village proper, the entrance to which is bounded by the homestead-grounds upon the right, and an old, prim-looking village park upon the left. Leaving the artist to obtain his desired sketch of the valley from this point, we will turn our back upon him for the present, while we ascend the avenue marking the southern boundary of the town, and reverently enter the " Village on the Hill." Here lies, in the peace and rest that come after noble service, all that remains of one of New York's most illustrious citizens, General James S. Wadsworth, who, after distinguished service in the field, fell " with his face to the foe " in the battle of the Wilderness.

Along the western slope of the hill, upon the summit of which is this village of the dead, rests the village of the living ; and one might go far to find a more perfect rural hamlet. The streets, which run at right angles, are lined with graceful shade-trees ; and the view from those running east and west embraces that of the rich valley in the foreground, and, in the distance, the undulating harvest-fields. That dark opening into the hill-side toward the south is the gate-way through which the river enters the valley ; while, far away northward, that cone-shaped eminence marks the suburbs of the city of Rochester, our next objective point, and the limit of our valley tour.

Transferring ourselves and baggage, including the artist's easel and the tourist's portfolio, from the lumbering stage to the less rural but more expeditious rail-car, we are soon under way, northward bound. The railway that serves as a means of exit from the region of the upper valley is a branch of the Erie, known as the Genesee Valley road. It connects the city of Rochester with the valley villages of Avon, Geneseo, Mount Morris, and now Dansville, the last a flourishing town seated upon one of the tributaries of the Genesee, and thus being entitled to a place among this beautiful sisterhood. At Avon this road crosses the northern branch of the Erie. At this point are the justly-famous sulphur springs ; and, if the health-giving properties of these waters are in any degree commensurate with their mineral strength, Avon deserves a front rank among the health - resorts of the State. Continuing our journey twenty miles

Lower Falls.

farther, following the line of the river along its eastern shores, we enter Monroe County, and approach the city of Rochester.

This city stands in the same relation to the valley as does a storage and distributing reservoir to the streams from which the supply is received. In its early days, the life of the city was dependent upon the harvest of the valley; when these were abundant, then all went well. Having already referred to the wheat-product of the valley, we can readily understand the need and consequent prosperity of the city, which has long been known as the "Flour City of the West." Although now ranking as the fifth city in the State, there are yet living many persons whose childhood dates back of that of the city in which they dwell. From a brief historical sketch on the subject, we learn that, in expressing astonishment at the career of Rochester, De Witt Clinton remarked, shortly before his death, that, when he passed the Genesee on a tour with other commissioners for exploring the route of the Erie Canal, in 1810, there was not a house where Rochester now stands. It was not till the year 1812 that the " Hundred-acre Tract," as it was then called, was planned out as the nucleus of a settlement under the name of Rochester, after the senior proprietor, Nathaniel Rochester. " In the year 1814," writes one of these pioneers, " I cleared three or four acres of ground on which the Court-House, St. Luke's Church, First Presbyterian Church, and School-house No. 1, now stand, and sowed it to wheat, and had a fine crop. The harvesting cost me nothing, *as it was most effectually done by the squirrels, coons, and other wild beasts of the forest.* Scarcely three years, however, had elapsed before the ground was mostly occupied with buildings." From this and abundant kindred testimony, it is evident that the early pioneers of this western region were men of energy and foresight, who saw in the valley of the Genesee the " garden-plot of the West," and in the then village of Rochester the future " Granary of America."

Having already referred to the second series of falls and high banks, we will again return to the guidance of the river as it enters the city limits at its southern boundaries. Its course lies directly across or through the centre of the city, the main avenues, running east and west, being connected by several iron bridges, with the exception of that known as the Main-Street Bridge, which is of stone, and the two wooden railway-bridges.

It is at the city of Rochester that the Erie Canal encounters the Genesee River, which it crosses upon the massive stone aqueduct, that has long been regarded as one of the most important works of American engineers. In its present course the river has rather the appearance of a broad canal, save that the current is rapid, and, at times, boisterous. The shores are lined by huge stone mills and factories, the foundation-walls of which act the part of dikes in confining the waters to their legitimate channels. At a point near the Erie Railway depot the river is crossed by a broad dam, from either side of which the waters are led in two mill-races, which pass under the streets and conduct the waters to the mills along the route. At a point somewhat below the centre of the city, and yet directly within its limits, are the First or Upper Falls. These are ninety-six feet in height, and it is thus evident that; with such a cataract in the centre of the city, the facilities for obtaining water-power could hardly be excelled. The mill-races conduct the main supply along the two opposite shores, and, as the mills are mainly situated below the level of the falls, the full force of the water can be utilized. The illustrations of the Upper Fall have been so designed that the two combined present a full view of the whole front as viewed from the chasm below, the darkened channels through which the water from the races are returned to the river being shown to the right and left.

The brink of this fall marks the upper limit of a second series of high banks similar in general character to those that lie between Portage and Mount Morris. The height of these walls at certain points exceeds three hundred feet. At the distance of about a mile from the Upper Fall, a second descent of about twenty-five feet is followed, at the distance of a few rods only, by the Third or Lower Falls, which are nearly one hundred feet in height. It thus appears that, within the limits of the city, the waters of the Genesee make a descent, including the falls and the rapids above them, of two hundred and sixty feet, and the water-power, as estimated for the Upper Fall alone, equals forty thousand horse-power. Among the interesting features of Rochester are its nurseries and seed-gardens, the largest in the world.

As the river has now reached the level of Lake Ontario, it assumes the character of a deep-set harbor, and the vessels engaged in lake-traffic can ascend it five miles to the foot of the Lower Falls. The port of entry, however, is at the mouth of the river, where stands the village of Charlotte. Here are wharves, a light-house, and a railroad-depot, which road leads direct to Rochester.

Light-house, Charlotte.

THE ST. LAWRENCE AND THE SAGUENAY.

WITH ILLUSTRATIONS BY JAMES D. SMILLIE.

Entrance to Thousand Islands.

IT is three o'clock of a June morning on the St. Lawrence; the little city of Kingston
is as fast asleep as its founder, the old Frenchman De Courcelles; the moon is

ebbing before the breaking day; a phantom-like sloop is creeping slowly across the smooth stream. At the steamboat-wharf there is a little blaze of light and a rush of noisy life, which breaks, but does not penetrate, the surrounding silence. The Lake-Ontario steamer has brought a pack of eager tourists into the town—not to stay, for another vessel is in waiting, ready to bear them down the river, through the rapids and

Light-Houses among the Thousand Islands.

the channels of the Thousand Islands, to Montreal. The pent-up steam screams through the pipes; lamps gleam fitfully among barricades of freight and baggage on the wharf; men's voices mingle hoarsely. "All aboard!" The bell rings out its farewell notes; the whistle pipes its shrill warning into the night, and the Spartan slips her moorings, to the pleasure of the sleepy travellers who crowd her decks and cabins. By this time the east

Among the Thousand Islands.

is tinted purple, amber, and roseate. Night is fast retreating. Ardent young couples, on their wedding-journey, are a notable element among our fellow-travellers; but there are all sorts of other people from the States, with here and there a chubby, florid, drawling Englishman. Most of us are journeying on round-trip tickets from New York, and are as intimate with one another's aims and ends as if we were crossing the ocean together.

We all came up the Hudson in the Vibbard; all occupied the same Pullman car between Albany and Niagara, and will all rush to the same hotels in Montreal and Quebec, as fashion bids us. Soon after leaving Kingston, we bestir ourselves, and choose eligible seats in the forward part of the boat. We chat without restraint, and expectation is rife as we near the famed Thousand Islands. The descriptions we have read and the stories we have heard of the panorama before us flock vividly into our memories. We are all accoutred with guide-books, maps, and books of Indian legend. One sweet little neighbor of ours, in regulation lavender, brings out a neatly-written copy of Tom Moore's " Row,

Between Wellesley Island and the Canadian Shore.

Brothers, row," which she holds in her pretty hand, ready to recite to her husband the very moment St. Anne's comes into view. Meanwhile she is fearful that St. Anne's may slip by unnoticed, notwithstanding the assurances made to her that the much-desired St. Anne's is twelve hours' sail ahead of us. How lightly she laughs as the boat's white stem cleaves the cool, gray surface! and how enthusiastically she repeats Ruskin as the colors in the morning sky grow warmer and deeper, and as the sun rises directly ahead of us, opening a golden pathway on the water! and how prettily surprised she is when her beloved tells her that the Thousand Islands number one thousand six hundred and ninety-two, as may be ascertained in the Treaty of Ghent! Still listening to her childish prattle, we are further occupied with the banks of the river, and the numerous dots of land that lie in our course—the Thousand Islands.

Are we disappointed? That is the question which most of us propound before we proceed many miles. There is little variety in their form and covering. So much alike

Entering the Rapids.

are they in these respects that our steamer might be almost at a stand-still for all the change we notice as she threads her way through the thirty-nine miles which they thickly intersperse. In size they differ much, however, some being only a few yards in extent, and others several miles. The verdure on most of them is limited to a sturdy growth of fir and pine, with occasionally some scrubby undergrowth, which sprouts with northern vigor from crevices in the rocky bed. The light-houses which mark out our channel are a picturesque feature, and are nearly as frequent as the islands themselves; but all are drearily alike—fragile wooden structures, about twenty feet high, uniformly whitewashed. As the Spartan speeds on, breaking the rippling surface into tumultuous waves, we meet a small boat, pulled by a lonely man, who attends to the lamps from the shore, lighting them at sunset, and putting them out at sunrise. Some anglers are also afloat, and anon a large fish sparkles at the end of their line, and is safely drawn aboard. The islands are famous for sport, by-the-way. Fish of the choicest varieties and the greatest size abound in their waters, and wild-fowl of every sort lurk on their shores. They also have their legends and romances, and the guide-books tell us, in eloquent language, of the adventures of the "patriots" who sought refuge among their labyrinths during the Canadian insurrection. As the sun mounts yet higher, and the mist and haze disperse, we run between Wellesley Island and the Canadian shore, and obtain one of the most charming views of the passage. The verdure is more plentiful and the forms are more

Montreal Island.

graceful than we have previously seen. Tall reeds and water-grasses crop out of the shoals. An abrupt rock throws a reddish-brown reflection on the current, which is skimmed by a flock of birds in dreamy flight. The banks of the island and the mainland slope with easy gradations, inclining into several bays; and afar a barrier seems to arise where the river turns and is lost in the distance. Thence we steam on in an enthusiastic mood toward Prescott, satisfied with the beauties we have seen, and arrive there at breakfast-time, five hours and a half after leaving Kingston. Our preconceptions—have they been realized? Scarcely. But an artist in our company tells us, consolingly, that preconceptions are a hinderance to enjoyment, and ought to be avoided, and that when he first visited the Yosemite, last summer, he spent several days in getting rid of idle dreams before he could appreciate the majesty and glory of the real scene.

Below Prescott we pass an old windmill on a low cape, where the insurrectionists established themselves in 1837; and, two miles farther, we catch a glimpse of a gray old French fortification on Chimney Island. Here, too, we descend the first rapids of the river—the Gallope and the Deplau Rapids—with full steam on. No excitement, no breathlessness, attends us so far in our journey. Engravings we have seen represent the water as seething white, with a preposterous steamer reeling through it at a fearful rate. The passengers gather in a mass on the forward deck, and brace their nerves for the anticipated sensation. They wait in vain. The Gallopes and Deplaus are passed almost without their knowledge. But we are nearing the famous Long-Sault Rapids, the passage of which, we know, must be thrilling. An Indian pilot comes on board to guide us through—at least, the guide-book assures us that he is an Indian, and supplements its text with a corroborative portrait of a brave, in war-paint and feathers, standing single-handed at the helm—and, as he enters the wheel-house on the upper deck, he is an absorbing object of interest. A stout, sailorly fellow he appears, without an aboriginal trait about him, or a single feather, or a dab of paint. There are some bustling preparations among the crew for what is coming. Four men stand by the double wheel in the house overhead, and two others man the tiller astern, as a precaution against the breaking of a rudder-rope. Passengers move nervously on their seats, and glance first ahead, and then at the captain standing on the upper deck, with one hand calmly folded in his breast, and the other grasping the signal-bell. Timid ladies are pale and affrighted; young faces are glowing with excitement. The paddles are yet churning the water into snowy foam. We sweep past the scene of the battle of Chrysler's Farm without noticing it. In a few seconds more we shall be in the rapids. The uneasy motions of the passengers cease altogether, and their attention is engrossed by the movements of the captain's hand. As he is seen to raise it, and the bell is heard in the engine-room, the vibrations of the huge vessel die away; the water leaps tempestuously around her, and she pauses an instant like a thing of life, bracing herself for a crisis, before she plunges into the boiling current and rides defiantly down it. It is a grand, thrilling moment; but it is only a moment. The next instant she is speeding on as quietly as ever, without other perceptible motion than a slight roll. The rapids are nine miles long, and are divided in the centre by a picturesque island, the southern course usually being chosen by the steamers. The Spartan ran the distance in half an hour, without steam, and then emerged into the waters of Lake St. Francis, which is twenty-five miles long and five and a half miles wide.

This expanse exhibits few interesting features, and we have ample opportunity to cool from the excitement caused by the descent of the rapids. The banks of the lake are deserted, and the only human habitations seen are in the little village of Lancaster. We are impressed, indeed, from our start, with the few evidences of life in the river country and on the river itself. There are not many farm-houses or fine residences—only a few small villages, of a humble character for the most part, and an occasional town. The drear monotony of our passage through Lake St. Francis is followed by renewed excitement in the descent of the Cedar Rapids, at the foot of which we enter

Lake St. Louis. Uninteresting as is Lake St. Francis, still more so is the sheet of water now before us, bordered as it is by flat lands reminding us of the Southern bayous. But it is here we get our first glimpse of the bold outlines of Montreal Island, rising softly in the background; and here, too, the river Ottawa, ending in the rapids of St. Anne's, pours its volume into the greater St. Lawrence. Contemplating the expanse in the subdued evening light, it impresses us with a depressing sense of primitive desolation—a vague, untrodden emptiness—and infuses melancholy into our feelings without exciting

River-Front, Montreal.

our sympathies. But soon we are aroused to a more agreeable and becoming frame of mind by our little bride in the lavender dress, who is briskly reciting "Row, Brothers, row," to her submissive Corydon:

> " ' Blow, breezes, blow! The stream runs fast,
> The rapids are near, and the daylight's past.' "

A queer-looking barge, with a square sail set, lumbering across our course, and throwing a black shadow on the water that is now richly tinted with purple and deep red; a light-house at the extremity of a shoal, yet unlighted; a mass of drift-wood, sluggishly moving with the current; a puff of smoke, hovering about the isolated village of St.

CUSTOM HOUSE.

MONTREAL FROM HELEN'S ISLAND.

HELEN'S ISLAND FROM MONTREAL.

MONTREAL.

Clair—these things are all we meet in our voyage across the broad St. Louis. Farther up the river there has been little more life—once in a while a monstrous raft coming down from the wilderness, manned by four or five sturdy fellows who live a precarious life in a rude hut perched on the groaning timbers. Nothing more than this—no Indians skimming the rapids in birch canoes, no vestiges of the old life of this region, and no stirring evidences of the newer civilization. Occasionally we have met a steamer, as large as the Spartan, making the upward passage, and apparently moving through the fields on the banks of the river. An incorrigibly practical friend of ours explains: "A vessel of such burden cannot ascend the rapids; and canals, with a system of locks, have been cut in the land wherever the rapids occur. Between Kingston and Montreal there are eight canals, forty-one miles long, and supplied with twenty-seven locks, capable of admitting the largest paddle-steamers." The same friend, incited by our inquiries, has much pleasure in adding several other facts about the river for our information: "The St. Lawrence was originally called the Great River of Canada, and was also known under the names of the Cataraqui and the Iroquois. Its present name was given to it by the explorer Cartier, who entered it with some French ships on the festival-day of St. Lawrence, in 1535. He had been preceded by one Aubert, a mariner of Dieppe, in 1508; but Cartier went to a higher point than Aubert, anchoring nearly opposite the site of Quebec. In 1591, another exploration having been made in the mean time, a fleet was sent out from France to hunt for walruses in the river; and the veteran scribe Hakluyt announces that fifteen thousand of these animals were killed in a single season by the crew of one small bark."

Here the practical man is interrupted. The steamer stops at the Indian village of Caughnawaga, and, after a short delay, proceeds toward the Lachine Rapids. In the descent of these we are wrought to a feverish degree of excitement, exceeding that produced in the descent of the Long Sault. It is an intense sensation, terrible to the faint-hearted, and exhilarating to the brave. Once—twice—we seem to be hurrying on to a rock, and are within an ace of total destruction, when the Spartan yields to her helm, and sweeps into another channel. As we reach calm water again, we can faintly distinguish in the growing night the prim form of the Victoria Bridge, and the spires, domes, and towers of Montreal, the commercial metropolis of British North America. The gentle hills in the rear, well wooded and studded with dwellings, are enveloped in a blue haze, darkening on the southern skirts, where the heart of the city beats in vigorous life. Lights are glimmering in the twilight on the river; black sailing-craft are gliding mysteriously about with limp canvas; the startling shriek of a locomotive echoes athwart, and a swiftly-moving wreath of luminous-looking smoke, followed by a streak of lighted windows, marks the progress of a flying night-train wheeling beyond the din and toil of this dim spot. We feel the sentiment of a return home in reaching a thriving, populous city again, after our day's wandering through the seclusive garden-islands of the St. Lawrence;

and we yawn complacently on our restoration to the electric bells, the attentive waiters, and unromantic comforts of the modern hotel.

A night's rest among these, in a bed of faultless whiteness, prepares us for the following day's tramp through this ancient metropolis of the Indians (which long bore the name of Hochelaga) and modern metropolis of the Canadians. Montreal does not resemble an English city — the streets are too regular — and it does not resemble our own American cities, than which it is more substantially built. Its substantiality is particularly impressive — the limestone wharves extending for miles, the finely-paved streets lined with massive edifices of the most enduring materials, imprinted with their constructors' determination that they shall not be swept away in many generations. There is an honest austerity in the character of the work—no superfluous ornamentation, no clap-traps of architecture. The site is naturally picturesque. It is on the southern slope of a mountain in the chain which divides the verdant, fertile island of Montreal. There are a high town and a low town, as at Quebec; and on the up-

Breakneck Stairs, Quebec.

reaching ground, leafy roads winding through, are the villa residences of the fashionable. The prospect from these bosky heights repays, with liberal interest, the toil of the pedestrian who seeks them from the city. Perched on some balcony, as a king on a throne, he may survey, on the fair level beneath him, the humming streets; the long line of wharves, with their clustering argosies; the vast iron tube which binds the opposite sparsely-settled shore to the arterial city; Nun's Island, with its flowery grounds, neatly laid out; beautiful Helen's Island, thick with wood; the village of Laprairie, its tinned spire glistening like a spike of silver; the golden thread of the St. Lawrence, stretching beyond the Lachine Rapids into mazes of heavy, green foliage; the pretty villages of St. Lambert, Longueuil, and Vercheres; and afar off, bathed in haze and mystery, the purple hills of Vermont. Perchance, while his eye roams over the varied picture with keen delight, there booms over the roofs of the town the great bell of Notre-Dame, and he saunters down the height in answer to its summons—through hilly lanes of pretty cottages on the outskirts into the resonant St.-James Street; past the old post-office, which is soon to be superseded by a finer structure; underneath the granite columns of Molson's Bank—Molson's Bank, as celebrated as Childs's Bank at Temple Bar; through Victoria Square, and on until he reaches the Place d'Armes. Here is the cathedral of Notre-Dame, a massive structure capable of holding ten thousand people, with a front on the square of one hundred and forty feet, and two towers soaring two hundred and twenty feet above. Climbing one of these towers, the view of the river and city obtained from the mountain-side is repeated, with the surrounding streets included. Opposite the cathedral, in the Place d'Armes, is a row of Grecian buildings, occupied by city banks; on each side are similar buildings—marble, granite, and limestone, appearing largely in their composition. In the centre we may pause a while in the refreshing shade of the park, and hear the musical plashing of the handsome fountain as it glints in the bright sunlight. Thence we wander to the magnificent water-front, which offers greater facilities for commerce than that of any other American city. The quays are of solid limestone, and are several feet below a spacious esplanade, which runs parallel with them. The cars of the Grand Trunk Railway bring produce from the West to the very hatchways of the shipping, and cargoes are transferred in the shortest possible time and at the least possible expense. Our practical friend carries us off to the Victoria Bridge, and utters some of his pent-up knowledge on that subject, which we listen to with praiseworthy fortitude: " Its length is nearly two miles. It is supported by twenty-four piers and two abutments of solid masonry. The tube through which the railway-track is laid is twenty-two feet high, and sixteen feet wide. The total cost of the structure was six million three hundred thousand dollars." Then we go to see the Bonsecours Market, the nunneries, Mount-Royal Cemetery, the imposing Custom-House, the Nelson Monument, and the water-works; and in the evening we continue our journey down the river to Quebec.

MARKET-HALL AND BOAT-LANDING, QUEBEC.

We might be travelling through some broad river of France, so thoroughly French are the names of the villages. On one bank are L'Assomption, St. Sulpice, La Vittre, Berthier, Fond du Lac, and Batiscon; on the other, Becancour, Gentilly, St. Pierre, De-chellons, and Lothinier. But the people of these villages are neither European nor American in language, manners, or appearance. Descended from the old French settlers, crossed with the Indian and American, they retain some of the traits of each. Their high cheek-bones, aquiline nose, and thin, compressed lips, refer us to the aboriginal; but they are below the average height, while stouter and stronger, and less graceful, than the French. They are singularly hardy, and therein resemble the primitive

Durham Terrace, Quebec.

Americans, enduring the worst extremes of heat and cold without show of discomfort. In their dress and houses they follow the fashions of the peasants of Normandy. The poorer of them build of logs, and the wealthier of stone. Their houses are alike one-storied, low-roofed, and whitewashed. In their habits they are notably clean and thrifty, simple, virtuous, and deeply religious. A traveller once declared them to be "the most contented, most innocent, and most happy yeomanry and peasantry of the whole civilized world;" and in that opinion all concur who have had an opportunity to observe them. A day might be pleasantly spent with them, but the steamer hastens us on to Quebec, and leaves the spires of their little churches golden in the sunset sky.

From the Top of Montmorency Falls, looking toward Quebec.

Quebec! The historic city of Canada; the city of conquests, of military glory, of bewildering contrasts! It is yet early morning when we arrive there; a veil of mist obscures the more distant objects. As we approach from Montreal, the view obtained is not the most impressive. It would be better, we are assured, were we coming from down the river. But who that loves the ancient, the gray, the quaint, is not touched with emotion on finding himself at the portals of the noble old fortress looking down upon the ample water-path to the heart of the continent? Who is proof at the sight against a little sentiment and a little dreaming? Our minds are fraught with memories of the early explorers, of battles and their heroes, of strange social conditions that have existed and exist in the shadow of yon looming rock, whither our steamer's bow is directed. We can look into no epoch of its history that is not full of color and interest. Illustrious names are woven in its pages—Richelieu, Condé, Beauharnais, Montmorency, Laval, and Montcalm. Two nations' struggled for its possession. We see old Jacques Cartier ascending the river in 1534, and holding a conference with the Indians then in occupation of the site, which they called Stadacona. Half a century later, Champlain, the geographer, enters the scene at the head of a vigorous colony, and builds barracks for the soldiers, and magazines for the stores and provisions. He is not fairly settled before an English fleet speeds up the St. Lawrence, captures Quebec, and carries him off a prisoner to England. Then a treaty of peace is signed, and the city is restored to France, Champlain resuming his place as governor of the colony. Thereafter, for a hundred and fifty years, France rules unmolested, and the lily-flag waves from the heights of the citadel; but a storm impends, and soon England shall add New France to her colonial empire. Two armies contend for the prize: Wolfe, on the land below, at the head of the English; Montcalm, on the heights above, at the head of the French. With the armies thus arrayed, Wolfe is at a disadvantage, which he determines to overcome by strategy. A narrow path twisting up the precipice is discovered, and, on a starlight night, the valiant young general leads his men through the defile. The enemy's guard at the summit is surprised and driven back; the English occupy the table-land which they desired, and where they can meet their antagonists on equal terms. On the following day the battle is fought: Montcalm advances, and covers the English with an incessant fire; Wolfe is wounded in the wrist, and hastens from rank to rank exhorting his men to be steady and to reserve their shots. At last the French are within forty yards of them, and a deadly volley belches forth. The enemy staggers, endeavors to press on, and falls under the furious attack that opposes. Wolfe is wounded twice more, the last time mortally, but his army is victorious; and, as he sinks from his horse, the French are retreating, and Montcalm, too, is mortally wounded.

Who, approaching Quebec for the first time in his life, is not for a moment thus lost in reverie over its past, and, on entering the city, is not charmed with the sharp contrasts the people and their buildings afford? Some one has described Quebec as resembling an ancient Norman fortress of two centuries ago, that had been encased in amber and transported by magic to Canada, and placed on the summit of Cape Diamond. But, while there are streets which might have been brought, ready built, from quaint old towns in provincial France, the outskirts of the city are such as Americans alone can create. At one point we may easily fancy ourselves in Boulogne; a few steps farther, and a crooked lane in London is recalled to us; farther still, and we are in a narrow Roman street; and, across the way, in a handsome thoroughfare, we find some of the characteristics of New York. So, too, it is with the inhabitants, though the variety is not as extensive. Half the people have manners and customs of the French,

FALLS OF MONTMORENCY.

the other half are equally English. You hear French spoken as frequently as English, but it is French of such a fashion as Parisians sometimes confess themselves at a loss to understand.

The Montreal steamer, after passing Wolfe's Cove and Cape Diamond, keeping the city well out of view, lands us at an old wharf a few yards above the Champlain Market, where we get our first glimpse at Quebec. At our back is the placid river, with a crowd of row-boats and sloops and schooners drifting easily in the stilly morning air; to the right is the Market-Hall, a pleasing building of important size, with several rows of broad stairs running from its portals to the water's edge; behind it are the dormer-windowed, slated and tinned roofs of the lower town; behind these, again, on the heights, the gray ramparts, Durham Terrace, resting on the buttress arches of the old castle of St. Louis, the foliage of the Government Garden, and the obelisk erected to Wolfe and Montcalm. Looking to the left is the citadel, fair enough, and smiling, not frowning, on this summer's morning, with the Union Jack folded calmly around the prominent flag-staff. Which of all these "objects of interest" shall we "do" first? We debate the question, and start out undecided. Once upon a time, when Quebec was a garrisoned town, the English red-coats gave the streets a military aspect; and, as we roam about, forgetting that they have been recalled, we are surprised to find so few soldiers. The military works are neglected, and have not kept pace with time. We ramble among the fortifications; here and there is a rusty, displaced cannon; a crumbling, moss-covered wall. The citadel itself, so proudly stationed, is lonely, quiet, drowsy, with no martial splendor about it. One can fancy that the citizens themselves might forget it, but for the noon and curfew gun that thunders out the time twice a day. The garrison is composed of volunteers; no more do we see the magnificently-trained Highlanders, in their fancy uniform. We are also surprised, but not displeased, at the sleepy atmosphere that pervades all; for we have been told that the French Canadians are especially fond of *fêtes* and holidays, shows and processions. They might be anchorites, for all we see of their gayety; possibly they have not yet arisen after the carouse of last night. There is a general air of quiet that belongs to a remote spot apart from the interests and cares of the outside world—a dreamy languor that a traveller is apt to declare absent in the smallest of the United States cities. He himself is as much a stranger here as in London, and those around him perceive his strangeness. We had not walked far, before even a pert little shoeblack's inexperienced eyes detected us as aliens. "He' yar, sir; reg'lar Noo-'ork s-s-shine!" Down in the lower town a great fleet of vessels are at moorings, and the wharves are crowded with men and vehicles; but the traffic makes astonishingly little noise—perhaps because it is done with old-country method, and without the impetuosity that New-York people throw into all their work.

In Breakneck Stairs, which every tourist religiously visits, we have one of those alleys that are often seen in the old towns of England and France—a passage, scarcely

Under Trinity Rock, Saguenay.

fifteen feet wide, between two rows of leaning houses, the road-bed consisting of several successive flights of stairs. Boot and shoe makers abound here, and their old-fashioned signs—sometimes a golden boot—adorn their still more old-fashioned stores. The occupants are idly gossiping at their doors; plainly enough they are not overworked. Yonder are two priests; here some tourists. These are all the sights we see at Breakneck

Stairs. In the evening, Durham Terrace offers a telling contrast to the more sombre quarters of the city. It is one of the finest promenades in the world; adjoining are the Government Gardens; from the railing that surrounds it, the view down the river is enchanting. Seen from the elevation of the terrace, the lower town, with its tinned roofs, seems to be under a veil of gold. It is here, on this lofty esplanade, that Quebec airs itself; and, at twilight, throngs of people lounge on benches near the mouths of beetling cannon, and roam among the fountains and shrubbery of the Place d'Armes. Such dressiness, fashion, and liveliness appear, that we are almost induced to withdraw our previous statement about the quiet character of the city, and to believe that it really is very gay and very wicked. But, as the darkness falls, the crowd begins to disperse; and, when the nine-o'clock gun sends a good-night to the opposite shore, nearly all the promenaders have gone home to bed, with Puritan punctuality.

On the next day we go to Montmorency. We hire a calash, and pay the driver three dollars for taking us there and back, a round distance of sixteen miles. The calash is used in summer only. It is something like a spoon on wheels, the passenger sitting in the bowl and the driver at the point. We jolt across the St. Charles River by the Dorchester Bridge, and then enter a macadamized road leading through a very pretty country, filled with well-to-do residences. Farther away, we pass the Canadian village of Beauport, and get an insight of old colonial life. The houses are such as we referred to in coming from Montreal to Quebec—all alike in size, form, and feature. Thence we follow an English lane through sweet-scented meadows until we arrive at the falls, and, after paying a small fee, we are admitted to some grounds where, from a perch at the very edge of the rock, we can look upon the fleecy cataract as it pours its volume into the river. It is the grandest sight we have yet seen in the Canadian tour. Hereabout the banks are precipitous—two hundred and fifty feet high—and covered with luxuriant verdure; the falls are deep-set in a small bay or chasm, and descend in a sheet, twenty-five yards wide, broken midway by an immense rock hidden beneath the seething foam. The surrounding forms are picturesque in the extreme. In winter, the guide-book tells us, the foam rising from the falls freezes into two cones of solid ice, which sometimes attain a height of one hundred feet, and the people come from Quebec in large numbers with their "toboggins"—a sort of sleigh or sled, as those familiar with Canadian sports will not need to be informed—with which they toil to the summit of the cone, and thence descend with astonishing velocity. Men, women, and children, share in the exciting exercise. Half a mile above the falls we visit the Natural Steps, where the limestone-rock bordering on the river has been hewn by Nature into several successive flights of steps, all remarkably regular in form; and, in the evening, we are returning to Quebec, which, as it is seen from the Beauport road, strikes one as the most beautiful city on the continent.

In the morning we are on board the Saguenay boat, among as varied a crowd as

POINT NOIR, TRINITY ROCK, AND CAPE ETERNITY, SAGUENAY RIVER.

might be formed by the commingling of the cabin and steerage passengers of an America-bound ocean-steamer. Yonder are the people who have come from New York with us, and have shared all our joys and sorrows; here are some recent colonists bound on a "'oliday 'outin';" there is a group of half-breeds, in richly-colored dresses; and everywhere, in the cabins and on deck, are people from Montreal and Quebec, who are going to "Salt-water." At first we imagine that "Salt-water" is the name of a landing, and we look for it in vain in the time-tables; but presently a light is thrown upon our ignorance. Salt-water means Murray Bay and Cacouna, where the Canadians go for their sea-bathing, which they cannot have at Quebec, as the water there is fresh. We are delayed for half an hour waiting for the Montreal boat; but, as soon as she arrives, and transfers a few extra passengers to us, we start out into the stream. For nearly an hour we retrace by water the trip we made yesterday by land, and are soon abreast of the Montmorency Falls, which are seen to still better advantage than on the day before. Afar off, the stately range of the Laurentian Hills roll upward in a delicate haze; and, through the trees on the summit of the bank, the river Montmorency shimmers in perfect calm, with something like the placid resignation of a brave soul conscious of an approaching death. The stream is divided here by the island of Orleans, a low-lying reach of farm-land, with groves of pine and oak embowering romantic little farm-houses and cottages, such as lovers dream of. But, as we journey on, this exquisite picture passes out of view, and the river widens, and the banks are nothing more than indistinct blue lines, marking the boundary of the lonely waters. Few vessels of any kind meet us—occasionally a flat-bottomed scow, with a single sail, so brown and ragged that the wind will not touch it; or a sister-boat to ours; and once we meet one of the Allen-line steamers coming in from the ocean, passengers swarming on her decks from bowsprit to wheel-house. We yawn, and read novels, and gossip, until the afternoon is far advanced, and Murray Bay is reached. About the little landing-place some of the evidences of fashionable civilization are noticeable, and, in the background, is a verandaed hotel of the period. But the land around is wild; and, not far away, are the birch-bark huts of an Indian tribe. The sentiment of the scene is depressing, and, as our steamer paddles off, we cannot help thinking with Mr. Howells that the sojourners who lounge idly about the landing-place are ready to cry because the boat is going away to leave them in their loneliness. At Cacouna, more fashionable people are waiting for the steamer, the arrival of which is the event of the day; but their gayety and chatter also seem unnatural, and they excite our sympathies much in the same manner as do the young man and woman standing alone on the Plymouth beach in Broughton's "Return of the Mayflower." The sun has set before our steamer crosses the St. Lawrence toward the mouth of the Saguenay, and black clouds are lowering in the sky as we glide to the landing at Tadoussac. This also is selected as a watering-place by some Canadians; but the hotel is overcast by older log-cabins, and Tadoussac is still the "remote, unfriended, melancholy, slow station" of the Hudson Bay Company that it was a hundred years ago. The captain grants his passengers two or three hours ashore, and the opportunity is taken by most of us to visit the oldest church in America north of Florida, which Tadoussac contains among its other curiosities. It is a frame building, on a high, alluvial bank, and the interior, as we see it lighted by one small taper, appears scarcely more than thirty feet square. A handsome altar is placed in an octagon alcove in the rear, with altar-pieces symbolizing the crucifixion; and the walls are adorned with two pictures, one a scriptural scene, the other a portrait of the first priest who visited Canada. We are interrupted in our stroll by the steamer's bell summoning us back.

St. Louis Island, from West Bank of Saguenay.

The storm-clouds are drifting thickly across the night-sky; the moon battles with them for an opening. Gusts of wind sweep through the firs. The sea has grown tumultuous in our absence, and, in the increasing darkness, we can discern the billows breaking into a curling fringe of white. The steamer starts out from the jetty, and has not proceeded many yards before the tempest beats down upon her with all its force. The moon is lost behind the banks of cloud; heavy drops patter on the deck. In a storm of wind and rain, the elements in fiercest strife, we enter the dark, lone river, as into a mysterious land.

It is not surprising that the Saguenay, with its massive, desolate scenery, should

Point Crèpe, near the Mouth of the Saguenay.

have inspired early mariners with terror. To them it was a river with marvellous surroundings, with an unnavigable current, immeasurable depths, terrible hurricanes, inaccessible and dangerous rocks, destructive eddies and whirlpools; but, in later days, treasures were discovered in its bounds, and it was frequented by vessels in search of the walrus and the whale. The old superstitions are no longer entertained; but the river is undisturbed — the walrus and the whale have been driven away, and lumber-rafts, coming down from the wilderness, are all that usually stir it. The Indians called it Pitchitanichetz, the meaning of which, you will not be surprised to learn, we could not discover. It is formed by the junction of two outlets of St. John's Lake, which lies in the wilderness, one hundred and thirty miles northwest of Tadoussac, and covers five hundred square miles of surface. From some distance below the lake the river passes over cliffs in several magnificent cascades, rushing between rocky banks from two hundred to one thousand feet high; and, for a distance of sixty miles from the mouth, it is about one mile wide. In some parts, soundings cannot be found with three hundred and thirty fathoms; and, at all points, the water is exceedingly deep, presenting an inky-black appearance. Fish may be caught in great abundance, including salmon, trout, sturgeon, and pickerel.

During the night of storm, the steamer has threaded her way through the hills, and, on a glorious morning, we arrive at a little village in Ha-ha Bay, the nominal head of navigation. The scenery is less massive and sullen here than at any other point, and the character of the crowd at the landing is diversified in the extreme. There are lumbermen, Scotch Highlanders, *habitants*, American tourists, Canadian tourists, English tourists, and aboriginals. Some of the *habitants* have brought with them little canoes, filled with wild-strawberries, which they offer for sale; and, during our detention here, there is considerable bustle. We then resume our journey down the dark river. Ha-ha Bay, with its shrubbery and beaches, is soon out of sight; we are sailing between two towering walls of rock, so dreary, so desolate, that those of us who are impressionable become dejected and nervous. The river has no windings; few projecting bluffs; no farms or villages on its banks. Nature has formed it in her sternest mood, lavishing scarcely one grace on her monstrous offspring. Wherever a promontory juts out one side of the river, a corresponding indentation is found upon the opposite shore; and this has been made the basis of a theory that the chasm through which the black waters flow was formed by an earthquake's separation of a solid mountain. We are willing to believe almost any thing about its origin; it fills us with grief, and our little bride is actually crying over it. The forms are rude, awkward, gigantic; but, like giants, unable to carry themselves. There are no grassy meadows; little greenery of any kind, in fact; only some dwarfed red-pines living a poor life among the rocks. It is a river of gloom, marked with primitive desolation. Occasionally an island lies in our path, but it is as rugged and barren as the shore, formed out of primitive granite, offering no relief to the terrible monotony that impresses us. And, once in a while, a ravine breaks the precipitous walls, and exposes in its darkling hollow the white foam of a mountain-torrent. Near such a place we find a saw-mill, and some attempt at a settlement that has failed dismally. We think of passages in Dante; of—

> " The dismal shore that all the woes
> Hems in of all the universe."

The water is skimmed by no birds, nor is there a sound of busy animal life. Only now and then a black seal tosses its head above the surface, or dives below at our approach, from some projection where he has been quietly sunning himself. Masses of perpendicular rock rise above the surface to an unbroken height of over one thousand feet, and extend still farther below. What wonder that the sensitive little woman is in tears over the awful gloom Nature exhibits? Of course, there are some of our fellow-tourists who are not impressed with any thing except the immensity of the spaces, but it is reserved for her finer senses to hear Nature's voice in the savage tones of the rocks, and to weep at its sternness.

Presently we near Trinity Rock and Cape Eternity, and one of the crew brings a bucket of pebbles on to the forward deck. As these two capes are accounted among the grandest sights of the voyage, there is a flutter of anticipation among the passengers, and the decks are crowded again. A slight curve brings us into Trinity Bay, a semi-circular estuary, flanked at the entrance by two precipices, each rising, almost perpendicularly, eighteen hundred feet above the river. The steepest is Trinity, so called because of the three distinct peaks on its northern summit, and that on the other side is Cape Eternity. Trinity presents a face of fractured granite, which appears almost white in contrast to the sombre pine-clad front of Eternity. And now, as the boat seems to be within a few yards of them, the passengers are invited to see if they can strike them with the pebbles before introduced. Several efforts are made, but the stones fall short of their mark, in the water. For the rest of the day we are toiling through like wildernesses of bowlders, precipices, and mountains. We bid adieu to Trinity and Eternity at Point Noir, thread the desolate mazes of St. Louis Island, and soon are passing Point Crèpe, where the rocks, the everlasting rocks, look in the distance like the channel of a dried-up cataract. Toward night we are in the St. Lawrence again, and as we speed across the brighter waters the moon is rising over Murray Bay, and the wreck of a canoe reposing on the low beach reminds us of the desert through which we have passed.

Mount Murray Bay, St. Lawrence.

THE EASTERN SHORE, FROM BOSTON TO PORTLAND.

WITH ILLUSTRATIONS BY J. DOUGLAS WOODWARD.

Pulpit Rock, Nahant.

T HE coast of New England between Boston and Portland is for the most part
irregular and rocky, and in many spots picturesque. Nature seems to have supplied it with
every variety of sea-coast aspect and beauty, from
the jagged mass of frowning and rough-worn
rock overhanging the waters to the long, smooth
reach of broad, curving beaches, and the duller landscape of green morass extending unbroken to the water's edge. There is no coast on the Atlantic seaboard which presents a
wider choice for the lover of marine pleasures; for the rich city-man and his family who
seek in proximity to the ocean their summer recreation from the cares and excitements of
the year; for the artist searching to reproduce on canvas the visible romance of Nature;

for the gay camping-out parties of students, of youths, and maidens; and for those whose health is supposed to derive benefit from the fresh ocean-breezes, the bathings, and the pastimes offered by the salt-water expanse. Thus, Bostonians and Portlanders have no need to go far from home to find delightful spots for the summer holidays. Within convenient distance of either place are spots where *paterfamilias* may deposit his family

Swallows' Cave, Nahant.

for the summer in a long-porched hotel, or build for them a cosey, picturesque cottage, quite within daily access from his business haunts, whither he may go and repose overnight, and each morning return invigorated to the labors of office or counting-room.

The picturesqueness of the Eastern shore betrays itself as soon as you have steamed away from the Boston docks. Eccentric and irregular peninsulas of land, abruptly widening and narrowing, now a mere thread between water and water, now a wide, hilly space, are encountered at once. East Boston stands upon one of these, and presents a crowded, rather smoky aspect, with its many chimneys, its well-filled docks, and its elevation at the extremity, crowned with the quarter of private residences. The steamboat is forced to make many a curve and winding, and, shortly after leaving East Boston, passes through a straitened channel between the sharp, narrow Point Shirley, a mere needle of a peninsula, and the irregularly-shaped Deer Island, with its spacious Almshouse, shaped like a Latin cross, and its ample accommodation for the paupers of the neighboring city. As you proceed through the harbor, the eye catches sight of many islands of various dimension and contour—some green with lawns, others bleak and arid with herbless sand and rock; here surmounted by a fort, there a hospital or house of correction, sometimes an hotel whither excursions are made in the summer at popular prices. The

The Old Fort, Marblehead.

southern coast looms irregular and sometimes imposing behind, while a glimpse is had of similar eccentricities and rough beauties of Nature in the direction whither you are proceeding.

After passing around Point Shirley, the broad stretch of Chelsea Beach comes into view, extending from the lower part of the peninsula to Lynn Bar. This is the favorite resort of the less well-to-do classes of Boston, while here and there are sea-side residences which betray the taste of a wealthier social class for this neighborhood. There are convenient and cosey hostelries, furnishing refreshment to the merry-makers, and ample provision for the sea-bathing, which is so refreshing to the denizen of the busy and dusty city.

Beyond Pine's Point, which is the strip of land at the northern end of Chelsea Beach, the sea makes one of its abrupt invasions into the line of coast, and has scooped

Salem, from the Lookout on Witches' Hill.

out there a miniature harbor, with uneven coast borderings, called Lynn Bar. This is the inlet to the thrifty "leather-city," which stands just by, intent on supplying mankind with shoes. Lynn Bar is bounded on its eastern side by the long and slightly curved western side of the peninsula of Nahant. From this point of view, you form no conception of the noble picturesque beauties and architectural decorations which this bold and strangely-shaped promontory affords. It is only when you have landed, and advanced to an elevated position, that one of the most, if not the most striking landscape on the Eastern shore presents itself to the sight.

Nahant is about eight miles northeast from Boston, and is easily reached, in less than an hour, from the city by boat. Of all the sea-side resorts of the vicinity, it is justly the most sought; for neither Cohasset, Nantasket, nor Scituate, on the southern shore, can compare with it, as combining each several variety of marine scenery and pleasure advantages. The peninsula, as it stretches out from the main-land, is at first a narrow neck, crossed by a few steps, for some distance almost straight. On one side is the pretty harbor of Lynn; on the other a noble, wide beach, sweeping in a direct line for some distance, then curving, in a short semicircle, round the rocky cliffs beyond which lies the scarcely less lovely and famous Swampscott. This narrow neck begins anon to thicken irregularly, with here and there a sudden eruption of rugged rock, and finally broadens into a rocky, uneven eminence. This promontory is shaped like a horseshoe. On the two sides the shore is rocky, with its Black Rocks, West Cliff, Castle Rock, Saunders's Ledge, Natural Bridge, and so on; while in the convex side of the horseshoe are several exquisite diminutive beaches, lying below the jagged eminences.

Norman's Woe, Gloucester.

A writer, describing the rocky beauty of Nahant, says: "The rocks are torn into such varieties of form, and the beaches are so hard and smooth, that all the beauty of wave-motion and the whole gamut of ocean-eloquence are here offered to eye and ear. All the loveliness and majesty of the ocean are displayed around the jagged and savage-browed cliffs of Nahant."

Few marine localities, moreover, have been so elegantly adorned by the wealth which calls forth the best efforts of the architectural art. Here are noble sea-side residences—of granite, brick, and wood—Swiss cottages and French villas, some shrouded in ivies and parasites, nearly all having, in spacious bay-windows and broad, sheltered piazzas, delightful outlooks upon the ocean. Nor has the naturally bleak and craggy peninsula

ROCKPORT

BASS ROCKS

ROCKPORT

THATCHERS ISLAND LIGHT HOUSES

GLOUCESTER FROM STAGE FORT.

HARLEY

GLOUCESTER AND ROCKPORT.

refused to nourish beautiful lawns and gardens, amply sprinkled with flower-parterres, betraying the artistic care which riches are able to procure.

The artist has reproduced two of the most striking of the many natural wonders which the eternal lashing of the waves has wrought out of the obstinate rock-masses about Nahant. Pulpit Rock lies just by the lower eastern shore of the horseshoe, between the Natural Bridge and Sappho's Rock. It is a huge, jagged mass, rising some thirty feet above the water, with roughly-square sides, broad and heavy below, but projecting abruptly into an angle of forty-five degrees at the top. At a little distance, the upper part appears like a pulpit, upon which some Titan preacher's Bible and prayer-book have been laid ready for service—hence the name; and here, if one is bold enough to venture up the slippery, moss-grown sides, is a famous eyry, whence to contemplate the sea, sitting in the midst of its wash and roar. The Swallows' Cave is farther on, at the lower end of the eastern curve of the horseshoe, between the steamboat-wharf and Pea Island. It is a long, gloomy cavern, overhung by a dome of irregular strata, heaved together in strange, shelving layers. The cave is eight feet high and seventy long, and derives its name from its having long been occupied by colonies of swallows, which built their nests in its sombre crevices, and flew in and out in fluttering multitudes. But the invasion of their retreat by curiosity-seekers has expelled them thence. The cave may be entered for some distance by a row-boat; and here is a favorite cool haunt in the hot summer days, when the beaches are insufferable. Nahant presents other wonders, but none more striking. There are John's Peril, a great, yawning fissure in one of the cliffs; the huge, oval-shaped mass called Egg Rock; a beautiful natural structure, which might almost be taken for a savage fortress, Castle Rock, with battlements, embrasures, buttresses, and turrets, the only kind of counterpart to the castle-ruins which so richly deck European scenes that our new America affords; a boiling and seething Caldron Cliff; a deep-bass Roaring Cavern; and a most grotesque yet noble natural arch, with a cone-like top, and leading to a natural room in the rock, which is known as Irene's Grotto.

Beyond the broad Long Beach, which sweeps from the promontory of Nahant in almost a straight line to Red Rock, is the not less beautiful and fashionable sea-side resort of Swampscott, with its Dread Ledge, and pretty beach, and clusters of charming and lavishly-adorned marine villas; while just northeastward of Swampscott juts out far into the sea the rude and uneven and historic peninsula of Marblehead. This spot was one of the first settled in New England, the town of Marblehead having been incorporated by the Puritan colony just fifteen years after the landing of the Pilgrims at Plymouth. So bleak and bare are the Marblehead rocks that Whitefield asked, in wonder, "Where do they bury their dead?" It is a quaint old settlement, with many queer houses still standing which were built and occupied before the Revolution. The sea penetrates the peninsula with a narrow and deep little harbor; and it is around this that

Bass Rocks, Gloucester.

the town has clustered. Once on a time Marblehead was famous for its fishermen ; and it is the scene of Whittier's poem, " Skipper Ireson's Ride." A hundred years ago it was, next to Boston, the most populous town in Massachusetts. Now its character has almost wholly changed from the olden time, for it has become a brisk centre of the shoe - manufacture. The Old Fort is a plain, hoary - looking edifice, standing on the rugged slope of the promontory looking toward the sea.

Just around the extremity of Marblehead are the harbor and the still more ancient Puritan settlement of Salem. Seven years after the landing at Plymouth, the district between the " great river called Merrimac " and the Charles was set off as a separate colony ; and the year afterward Endicott selected Salem as the capital of this colony. It was called Salem, " from the peace which they had and hoped in it." Of all New - England towns, it bears most plainly the stamp of a venerable antiquity. It is a grave and staid place, and there are still streets largely composed of the stately mansions of the colonial and marine aristocracy ; for Salem was once not only a metropolis, but a port teeming with lordly East-Indiamen, and warehouses packed with the choicest fabrics and spices of the Orient. It is, commercially, a stranded city, reposing upon its memories, and brimful of quaint and striking traditions. It has its antiquarian museums and its historic buildings, and here is sacredly

Point of Cape Ann, from Cedar Avenue, Pigeon Cove.

preserved the original charter granted by Charles I. to Massachusetts Bay. Here, too, is the oldest church still standing in New England, erected in 1634, and whose first pastor was Roger Williams. Salem was the town of witches; and it was on the hill represented by the artist, from which a fine view of the picturesque and drowsy town is

The Merrimac.

had, that the old women who were suspected of dealing in charms and spells were incontinently hanged by the grim old settlers.

In skirting the coast, after issuing from Salem Harbor, you almost immediately reach the broad and far-projecting peninsula at the end of which is Cape Ann, and which forms the northern boundary of Massachusetts Bay. Included between this and Scituate, on the south, is the great, semicircular basin which narrows into the spacious harbor of Boston. The coast between Salem and Gloucester is studded with spots at once naturally attractive and historically interesting. The rocky Lowell's Island, a famous destination for summer excursions, appears in full view from Salem. Opposite to it, on the mainland, is Beverley Beach, with the old town of Beverley, but a few years younger than Salem, in the near background. From one of the promenades here a fine view is had of the sea, with its sprinkling of forts and islands. A little to the north, inland, is Wenham, noted for a charming lake, and the spot of which an old English traveller of two centuries ago said, "Wenham is a delicious paradise;" while beyond is Ipswich, with its "healthy hills," and its ancient female seminary, where the Andover students, says a venerable writer, "are wont to take to themselves wives of the daughters of the Puritans." The quaint village of Manchester lies on the rugged shore; and, soon after passing it, the harbor of Gloucester is entered.

Gloucester is a characteristic New-England sea-coast town. It is the metropolis of the Northern fisheries. Its harbor is one of the most picturesque and attractive on the coast; and the town rises gradually from the wharves, presenting at once the aspect of venerable age and of present activity. All around it are fine points of view seaward, beaches, and rocky cliffs, with a more generous share of the relief of verdure than along the more southerly coast. Interspersed with the residences of the retired captains and well-to-do fishermen, who form a large portion of the population, are fine mansions used as summer residences; for Gloucester, as well as its vicinity, is a favorite resort. Many and various are the scenes in the neighborhood, which curiosity, wonder, and love of the beautiful, have sought out among the rocks and inlets. Of one of these Longfellow has written in "The Wreck of the Hesperus:"

> "And fast through the midnight dark and drear,
> Through the whistling sleet and snow,
> Like a sheeted ghost the vessel swept
> Toward the reef of Norman's Woe."

Norman's Woe is, indeed, a drear and sombre mass of rocks, lying just beyond the shrub-fringed shore, where many a vessel has struck against the ragged reefs in the northeast storms, though on a calm summer's day it adds one of the elements of a beautiful marine landscape. Near by are other curiosities, attractive to the sight-seers who make their headquarters in the vicinity. Among them, perhaps the most notable is Rafe's Chasm, an enormous fissure in the irregular and high-piled ledge, which yawns into the rock a hundred feet, and pierces it to a depth of fifty feet. Here the impris-oned waves at times struggle with fierce and sonorous fury, the noise of their roar, heard long before the spot is reached, endowing them, in the fancy, with the reality of living though insensate savagery. Not far off is another marvellous fissure in the trap-rock; and beyond is the bright and cheerful colony of summer villas which have clustered around Goldsmith's Point.

Cape Ann is really an island, being separated from the main-land by Squam River and a canal called the Cut. Its general appearance is rugged and rocky, with granite hills and ledges, in some places craggy and bald, in others grown over with wild and

APPLEDORE ISLAND.

WHALE BACK LIGHT

CHURCH STAR ISLAND

STAR ISLAND.

PORTSMOUTH. NH

PORTSMOUTH AND ISLES OF SHOALS.

picturesque forests.   From Tompson's Mountain the excursionist obtains a superb view, not only of the sea and immediate coast, but of Massachusetts Bay and Boston, with the yellow dome of the State-House looming in the distance, on the south, and Mount Monadnock, in New Hampshire, in the northwest.   Below may be seen broad marshes, beautified by an abundance of magnolias and water-lilies, with wild, entangled dells and winding brooks, orchards and meadows, and waving fields of grain.   Cape Ann is noted for its trees and flora.   Here grow picturesque tracts of woodland, contrasting pleasantly with the great gray rocks and the azure sea ; there are the oak, the birch, the maple, and the yellow-pine, red-cedars, and the beautiful red-gum tree ; while the wealth of wild-flowers—masses of roses perfuming the air, the trailing arbutus, dog's-tooth violets, tender wind-flowers, innocents and sassafras, columbines and wake-robins—makes the marshy fields and ledge-crevices glow with a kaleidoscope of color and exquisite botanic textures.

Only less romantic than Nahant are the outermost shores of Cape Ann, while the ample foliage adds a feature which even the gardening-art cannot impart to the more southerly resort.   Pigeon Cove, especially, has in these later days become a noted water-ing-place ; for here is not only a noble view of the waters, but the opportunity to enjoy many a delightful excursion amid the lovely scenes and marvellous sculpture which Na-ture has provided.   The little place has been provided with wide avenues and promenades, with groves of oak and pine, which lead to striking landscape-views—among them the Breakwater, which forms the outer wall of the snug little cove, and Singer's Bluff, which overhangs the sea.

Passing from the varied beauties of Pigeon Cove, with its alternate ruggedness, glistening beach, and luxuriant foliage, the northern side of Cape Ann is crossed by an ancient road, which at times enters beneath an arching of willows, and again emerges in sight of the waves and sails.   In a short while Annisquam is reached, and then the ven-erable sea-side village of Essex, just where the peninsula rejoins the main-land.   The coast for a while becomes little notable for any peculiar characteristics of picturesque-ness, until the broad, bay-like mouth of the " great " river Merrimac is approached. From its entrance, the old, historic town of Newburyport, surmounting an abrupt decliv-ity, some three miles up the broad and rapid river, is espied.   Like Salem and Marble-head, it is one of those antique coast-towns which have, to a large degree, lost their maritime importance, while preserving the relics and mementos of a former commercial prosperity.   Few places more abound with old traditions and family histories, and few inspire more pride in their annals and past glories in the breasts of the natives.

The shore between Newburyport and Portsmouth is almost continuously straight and even.   The abrupt eccentricities of bowlder and storm-hewed rock-masses have nearly dis-appeared.   Long and sunny beaches have taken the place of craggy peninsulas and yawning fissures, sinuous inlets and shapeless projections.   Salisbury, Hampton, and Rye,

Caswell's Peak, Star Island.

occupying the larger portion of the brief coast which New Hampshire possesses, are long stretches of sand, interspersed here and there with rocks, but presenting rather the softer and more cheerful than the rugged and awful aspects of marine Nature. Colonies of cosey sea-side cottages, and large summer hotels, line the shores; and, in July and August, Hampton and Rye Beaches are alive with carriages, bathers, and saunterers on the long, surf-washed reaches.

Portsmouth, like Newburyport, is situated on a river-bank, some three miles from the open sea, there being a spacious bay between it and the Maine shore, with an island directly in its mouth. "There are more quaint houses and interesting traditions in Portsmouth," says one writer, "than in any other town of New England"—a proposition, however, which the townsmen of Newburyport and Salem would eagerly dispute. It is, indeed, a singularly venerable and tranquil-looking old place, with many irregular, shaded streets, which look as if they had been quietly slumbering for many generations. Its history is full of incident, and connected with many of the stirring events of colonial and Revolutionary days. Indeed, Portsmouth was settled as long ago as 1623, and was first called "Strawberry Bank," from the exceeding quantity of strawberries which were found growing in its vicinity. It was at first fortified with palisades, to secure it from Indian depredations; and many were the perils through which it passed in the early days. After the Revolution, a French traveller found it with "a thin population, many houses in ruins, women and children in rags, and every thing announcing decline." But, speedily, Portsmouth revived, and became a busy and thrifty port; and so it continues to this day.

The chief natural attraction in the vicinity of Portsmouth is the Isles of Shoals, a

Portland, from Peak's Island.

group of eight bare and rugged islands, lying about nine miles off the coast, communicated with by a comfortable little steamboat, and provided with hotels and cottages for summer visitors. The isles are small in extent, the largest—Appledore—only containing about three hundred and fifty acres. From the main-land they appear shadowy, almost fairy-like, in their dim outline. As the steamboat approaches, they separate into distinct elevations of rock, all having a bleak and barren aspect, with little vegetation, and having jagged reefs running far out in all directions among the waves. Appledore, the principal island of the group, rises in the shape of a hog's back, and is the least irregular in appearance. Its ledges rise some seventy-five feet above the sea, and it is divided by a narrow, picturesque little valley, wherein are here and there timid scraps of shrubbery, and where are situated the hotel and its *chalets*, the only buildings on the island. The solitude and grandeur of the sea are to be enjoyed to the fullest on these gaunt rocks, in whose interstices many a lonely nook may be discovered where, fanned by cool breezes of pure sea-air, the marine landscape may be contemplated amid a surrounding stillness broken only by the lash, murmur, and trickling in and out of the waves. Just by Appledore is Smutty-Nose Island, low, flat, and insidious, on whose black reefs many a stalwart vessel has been torn to destruction. A quarter of a mile off is the most picturesque of the island-cluster, Star Island, with its odd little village of Gosport, the quaint towered and steepled church of which crowns the crest of its highest point; and just by is Scavey's Island. On the west, toward the main-land, is Londoner's, jagged and shapeless, with a diminutive beach; while two miles away is the most forbidding and dangerous of all these islands, Duck Island, many of whose ledges are hidden insidiously beneath the water at high tide, and at low tide are often seen covered with the big, white sea-gulls, which shun the inhabited isles. Mrs. Thaxter, a native of Appledore, and well known as a poetess, thus charmingly describes this fantastic and fascinating group of ledge and trap dike: " Swept by every wind that blows, and beaten by the bitter brine, for unknown ages, well may the Isles of Shoals be barren, bleak, and bare. At first sight, nothing can be more rough and inhospitable than they appear. The incessant influences of wind and sun, rain, snow, frost, and spray, have so bleached the tops of the rocks that they look hoary as if with age, though in the summer-time a gracious greenness of vegetation breaks, here and there, the stern outlines, and softens somewhat their rugged aspect. Yet, so forbidding are their shores, it seems scarcely worth while to land upon them—mere heaps of tumbling granite in the wide and lonely sea—when all the smiling, ' sapphire-spangled marriage-ring of the land' lies ready to woo the voyager back again, and welcome his returning prow with pleasant sounds, and sights, and scents, that the wild waters never know. But to the human creature who has eyes that will see, and ears that will hear, Nature appeals with such a novel charm that the luxurious beauty of the land is half forgotten before he is aware. The very wildness and desolation reveal a strange beauty to him. In the early morning the sea is rosy, and the sky; the line

EVERGREEN LANDING.

WHITE HEAD.

PORTLAND HEAD LIGHT.

PORTLAND HARBOR, AND ISLANDS.

Cushing's Island.

of land is radiant; the scattered sails glow with the delicious color that touches so tenderly the bare, bleak rocks." The Isles of Shoals have latterly become a place of popular resort, and on Appledore and Star Islands are comfortable hotels and cottages, which in summer are filled to overflowing with lovers of the subtile charms of the sea.

Beyond Portsmouth the coast runs tolerably even for some distance northward; then, from Wells Harbor, bends gradually to the northeast, until the isle-crowded entrance of Saco River is reached. It is dotted all along with marine hamlets and fishing-villages, here and there a bit of broken beach, and now and then a slight promontory overlooking the sea. York Beach is the principal sand-expanse between Portsmouth and Portland, and slopes gently to the water from the eminences behind. The coast increases in variegated beauty north of York, and affords ample opportunities for fishermen, bathers, and loungers by the ocean.

Nothing could be more strikingly picturesque, however, than the marine scenery about Portland, or than that most rural of New-England cities itself, as it perches on its high cliffs above bay, valley, island, and sea. It was settled very early in the colonial history, but the great fire of 1866 caused its renovation, and it now bears a fresh and modern as well as otherwise bright and thrifty aspect. Well may the citizens of Portland be proud of its superb site; its exquisite surroundings; its fine, deep, and well-sheltered harbor; its cheerful, shaded streets; its handsome public buildings, and its tasteful environs. The peculiarity of the Portland landscape is that it presents Nature rather in her softer and more cheerful than in her grand and rugged aspects. The many islands which dot Casco Bay are bright, in summer, with the softest and richest verdure and foliage, and are so numerous that, like Lake Winnepiseogee, they are said to equal the number of days in the year. The bay itself is one of the most beautiful on the Atlantic coast, and has been compared to the bay of Naples, so broad and circular its expanse, and so imposingly is it enframed in ranges of green and undulating hills. Cape Elizabeth, which forms the outermost southern point of the bay, is the nearest approach in this vicinity to the rude and jagged eminences already described as lying farther to the south. It is a series of lofty, jutting cliffs, rising abruptly from the ocean, and crowned with wood and shrubbery, which relieve its gauntness. The Twin-Sisters Light-houses stand on the end of the cape; and from these an inspiring view of the bay and harbor, of the distant city rising above its ledges, of the many islands lying close and irregularly between shore and shore, and, in the distance, of the torn and stormy promontories which stretch out north of Portland, is obtained. Nearer Portland is Peak's Island, luxuriant in foliage, and varied with natural bowers and lovely retreats. Here, too, is a favorable stand-point whence to look upon the genial and varied landscape; while Diamond Island, the pet spot for "down-East" picnics, is famous the country round for its groves of noble trees, its occasionally rocky shore interspersed with narrow bits of beach, and its natural lawns of deep-green turf.

One of the largest and most attractive spots in Portland Harbor is Cushing's Island, the edges of which are bordered by high bluffs crowned with shrubs and turf, with here and there a low, rocky shore or a graceful inlet. The island is one of the largest, comprising two hundred and fifty acres, and is provided with a single building, an hotel for summer sojourners. The view from here is perhaps more various and extensive than from any other point, for it includes the harbor, ship-channel, and city, on the one hand, and the towering ledges of Cape Elizabeth on the other. Forts Preble, Scammel, Gorges, and Portland Light, loom in the near distance; the busy wharves of Portland are seen crowded with their craft of many climes; the neighboring islands present each a novel and contrasted aspect of shape and color; the heavy sea-breakers may be seen settling themselves into the smooth, blue ripple of the bay; and sometimes a glimpse is had of the snowy summit of Mount Washington, and its sister eminences, dimly outlined on the far northwestern horizon.

THE ADIRONDACK REGION.

WITH ILLUSTRATIONS BY HARRY FENN.

Ascent of Whiteface.

IT is a common notion among Europeans — even those who have travelled extensively in this country—that there is very little grand scenery in the United States east of the Mississippi River. The cause of this delusion is obvious enough. The great routes of travel run through the fertile plains, where the mass of the population is naturally found, and where the great cities have consequently arisen. The grand and picturesque scenery of the country lies far aloof from the great lines of railroad; and the traveller whirls on for hundreds of miles through the level region, and decides that the aspect of America is very tame and monotonous, and that it has no scenery to show except the Highlands of the Hudson, Lake George, and the Falls of Niagara.

In the State of New York alone, however—to say nothing of the mountains and the sea-coast of New England, or the mountains of Pennsylvania, Virginia, North Carolina, and Tennessee—there are vast regions of the most beautiful and picturesque scenery, to which the foreign traveller seldom penetrates, and of which scarcely a glimpse can be obtained from the great lines of railroad, which have been established for purposes of trade, and not for sight-seeing. West of the Hudson lies a mountainous region, half as large as Wales, abounding in grand scenery, known only to the wandering artist or the adventurous hunter; and beyond that, in the centre of the State, a lower and still larger region, studded with the loveliest lakes in the world, and adorned with beautiful villages, romantically situated amid rocky glens, like that of Watkins, exhibiting some of the strangest freaks of Nature anywhere to be seen, and water-falls of prodigious height and of the wildest beauty.

But the grandeur of the Cats-

The Ausable Chasm.

Birmingham Falls, Ausable Chasm.

kills, and the loveliness of the lake-region of Central New York, are both surpassed in the great Wilderness of Northern New York, the Adirondack, where the mountains tower far above the loftiest of the Catskills, and where the lakes are to be counted by the hundreds, and are not surpassed in beauty even by Lakes George, Otsego, or Seneca. This remarkable tract, which thirty years ago was known, even by name, only to a few hunters, trappers, and lumbermen, lies between Lakes George and Champlain on the east, and the St. Lawrence on the northwest. It extends, on the north, to Canada, and, on the south, nearly to the Mohawk. In area it is considerably larger than Connecticut, and, in fact, nearly approaches Wales in size, and resembles that country also in its mountainous character, though many of the mountains are a thousand or two thousand feet higher than the highest of the Welsh.

Five ranges of mountains, running nearly parallel, traverse the Adirondack from southwest to northeast, where they terminate on the shores of Lake Champlain. The fifth and most westerly range begins at Little Falls, and terminates at Trembleau Point, on Lake Champlain. It bears the name Clinton Range, though it is also sometimes called the Adirondack Range. It contains the highest peaks of the whole region, the loftiest being Mount Marcy, or Tahawus, five thousand three hundred and thirty-three feet high. Though none of these peaks attain to the height of the loftiest summits of the White Mountains of New Hampshire, or the Black Mountains of North Carolina, their general elevation surpasses that of any range east of the Rocky Mountains. The entire number of mountains in this region is supposed to exceed five hundred, of which only a few have received separate names. The highest peaks, besides Tahawus, are Whiteface, Dix Peak,

The Stairway, Ausable Chasm.

CLEARING A JAM, GREAT FALLS OF THE AUSABLE.

Climbing Tahawus.

Seward, Colden, McIntyre, Santanoni, Snowy Mountain, and Pharaoh, all of which are not far from five thousand feet in height above the sea. They are all wild and savage, and covered with the "forest primeval," except the stony summits of the highest, which rise above all vegetation but that of mosses, grasses, and dwarf Alpine plants. These high summits are thought, by geologists, to be the oldest land on the globe, or the first which showed itself above the waters.

In the valleys between the mountains lie many beautiful lakes and ponds, to the number, perhaps, of more than a thousand. The general level of these lakes is about fifteen hundred feet above the sea; but Avalanche Lake, the highest of them, is at nearly twice that elevation above tide-water. Some of them are twenty miles in length, while others cover only a few acres. The largest of these lakes are Long Lake the Saranacs, Tupper, the Fulton Lakes, and Lakes Colden, Henderson, Sanford, Eckford, Racket, Forked, Newcomb, and Pleasant. Steep, densely-wooded mountains rise from their margins; beautiful bays indent their borders, and leafy points jut out; spring brooks tinkle in;

while the shallows are fringed with water-grasses and flowering plants, and covered sometimes with acres of white and yellow water-lilies. The lakes are all lovely and romantic in every thing except their names, and the scenery they offer, in combination with the towering mountains and the old and savage forest, is not surpassed on earth. In natural features it greatly resembles Switzerland and the Scottish Highlands, as they

Whiteface, from Lake Placid.

must have been before those regions were settled and cultivated. The Rev. Mr. Murray says that an American artist, travelling in Switzerland, wrote home, a year or two ago, that, "having travelled over all Switzerland and the Rhine and Rhone regions, he had not met with scenery which, judged from a purely artistic point of view, combined so many beauties in connection with such grandeur as the lakes, mountains, and forests of the Adirondack region presented to the gazer's eye."

This labyrinth of lakes is intertwined and connected by a very intricate system of rivers, brooks, and rills. The Saranac, the Ausable, the Boquet, and the Racket, rise in and flow through this wilderness; and in its loftiest and most dismal recesses are found the springs of the Hudson and its earliest branches.

The chief river of Adirondack, however—its great highway and artery—is the Racket, which rises in Racket Lake, in the western part of Hamilton County, and, after a devious course of about one hundred and twenty miles, flows into the St. Lawrence. It is the most beautiful river of the Wilderness. Its shores are generally low, and extend back some distance in fertile meadows, upon which grow the soft maple, the aspen, alder, linden, and other deciduous trees, interspersed with the hemlock and pine. These fringe its borders, and, standing in clumps upon the meadows in the midst of rank grass, give them the appearance of beautiful deer-parks; and it is there, indeed, that the deer chiefly pasture.

Except these meadows of the Racket, and the broad expanses of lakes and ponds, the whole surface of the Wilderness is covered with a tangled forest, through which man can scarcely penetrate. The trees are the pine, hemlock, spruce, white-cedar, and fir, on the lowest

Lower Saranac Lake.

grounds and higher slopes and summits of the hills; and the maple, beech, white and black ash, birch, and elm, on the intermediate surface. Everywhere lie great prone trunks mantled in moss, while overhead, in summer, the waving plumes of foliage shut out the light, and scarcely admit the air. Under the lofty trees are others, white-birch and aspen, with the saplings of the former trees, and bushes of hopple and sumach, that scarcely see the light or feel the wind. But occasionally the tornado tears through, and leaves tracks which time turns into green alleys and dingles, where the bird builds and the rabbit gambols. Loosened trees lean on their fellows, and others grow on rocks, grasping them with immense claws which plunge into the mould below. All looks monotonous, and seems dreary. "But select a spot," says Mr. Street, the poet of these

Round Lake, from Bartlett's.

woods; "let the eye become a little accustomed to the scene, and how the picturesque beauties, the delicate, minute charms, the small, overlooked things, steal out, like lurking tints in an old picture! See that wreath of fern, graceful as the garland of a Greek victor at the games; how it hides the dark, crooked root writhing, snake-like, from yon beech! Look at the beech's instep steeped in moss, green as emerald, with other moss twining round the silver-spotted trunk in garlands, or in broad, thick, velvety spots! Behold yonder stump, charred with the hunter's camp-fire, and glistening, black, and satin-like, in its cracked ebony! Mark yon mass of creeping pine, mantling the black mould with furzy softness! View those polished cohosh-berries, white as drops of pearl! See the purple barberries and crimson clusters of the hopple contrasting their vivid hues!

Indian Carry, Upper Saranac.

and the massive logs, peeled by decay—what gray, downy smoothness! and the grasses in which they are weltering — how full of beautiful motions and outlines!"

In these woods and in these mountain solitudes are found the panther, the great black bear, the wolf, the wild-cat, the lynx, and the wolverine. Even the moose is sometimes met with. Deer are abundant; and so, also, are the fisher, sable, otter, mink, muskrat, fox, badger, woodchuck, rabbit, and several varieties of the squirrel. There are scarcely any snakes, and none large or venomous.

Among the birds are the grand black war-eagle, several kinds of hawk, owl, loon, and duck; the crane, heron, raven, crow, stake-driver, mud-hen, brown thrush, partridge, blue-jay, blackbird, king-fisher, and mountain-finch. The salmon-trout and the speckled trout swarm in the lakes, and the latter also in the brooks and rivers. The lake-trout are caught sometimes of twenty pounds and more in weight; the speckled trout, however, are not large, except in rare cases, or in seldom-visited ponds or brooks.

Natural curiosities abound in Adirondack. That others are buried in the terrific forests still darkening two-thirds of the surface, cannot be doubted.

Among the curiosities known are Lake Paradox, whose outlet in high water flows back on the lake; the pond on the summit of Mount Joseph, whose rim is close upon the edge; the mingling of the fountains of the Hudson and Ausable, in freshets, in the Indian Pass; the torrent-dashes or lace-work from the greater or lesser rain down the grooved side of Mount Colden toward Lake Avalanche; the three lakes on the top of Wallface, sending streams into the St. Lawrence by Cold River and the Racket, into Lake Champlain by the Ausable, and the Atlantic by the Hudson; the enormous rocks of the Indian Pass standing upon sharp edges on steep slopes, and looking as if the deer, breaking off against them his yearly antlers, would topple them headlong, yet defying unmoved the mighty agencies of frost, and plumed with towering trees; with all the cavern intricacy between and underneath the fallen masses, where the ice gleams

St. Regis Lake.

unmelted throughout the year; and the same rock intricacy in the Panther Gorge of Mount Marcy, or Tahawus.

The Wilmington Notch and the Indian Pass are great curiosities. The former is thus described by Mr. Street, in his "Woods and Waters:"

"At North Elba, we crossed a bridge where the Ausable came winding down, and then followed its bank toward the northeast, over a good hard wheel-track, generally descending, with the thick woods almost continually around us, and the little river shooting darts of light at us through the leaves.

"At length a broad summit, rising to a taller one, broke above the foliage at our right, and at the same time a gigantic mass of rock and forest saluted us upon our left—the giant portals of the notch. We entered. The pass suddenly shrank, pressing the rocky river and rough road close together. It was a chasm cloven boldly through the flank of Whiteface. On each side towered the mountains, but at our left the range rose in still sublimer altitude, with grand precipices like a majestic wall, or a line of palisades climbing sheer from the half-way forests upward. The crowded row of pines along the broken and wavy crest was diminished to a fringe. The whole prospect, except the rocks, was dark with thickest, wildest woods. As we rode slowly through the still-narrowing gorge, the mountains soared higher and higher, as if to scale the clouds, presenting truly a terrific majesty. I shrank within myself; I seemed to dwindle beneath it. Something alike to dread pervaded the scene. The mountains appeared knitting their stern brows into one threatening frown at our daring intrusion into their stately solitudes. Nothing seemed native to the awful landscape but the plunge of the torrent and the scream of the eagle. Even the shy, wild deer, drinking at the stream, would have been out of keeping. Below, at our left, the dark Ausable dashed onward with hoarse, foreboding murmurs, in harmony with the loneliness and wildness of the spot.

"We passed two miles through this sublime avenue, which at mid-day was only partially lighted from the narrow roof of sky.

"At length the peak of Whiteface itself appeared above the acclivity at our left, and, once emerging, kept in view in misty azure. There it stood, its crest—whence I had gazed a few days before—rising like some pedestal built up by Jove or Pan to overlook his realm. The pinnacles piled about it seemed but vast steps reared for its ascent. One dark, wooded summit, a mere bulwark of the mighty mass above, showed athwart its heart a broad, pale streak, either the channel of a vanished torrent, or another but far less formidable slide. The notch now broadened, and, in a rapid descent of the road, the Ausable

Tupper Lake by Moonlight.

came again in view, plunging and twisting down a gorge of rocks, with the foam flung at intervals through the skirting trees. At last the pass opened into cultivated fields; the acclivities at our right wheeled away sharply east, but Whiteface yet waved along the western horizon."

Tahawus has often been ascended, though the task is by no means an easy one.

On Tupper Lake.

Its summit commands a magnificent prospect, which is thus described by Mr. Street in his "Indian Pass:"

"What a multitude of peaks! The whole horizon is full to repletion. As a guide said, 'Where there wasn't a big peak, a little one was stuck up.' Really true, and how savage! how wild! Close on my right rises Haystack, a truncated cone, the top shaved apparently to a smooth level. To the west soars the sublime slope of Mount Colden, with McIntyre looking over its shoulder; a little above, point the purple peaks of Mount Seward—a grand mountain-cathedral—with the tops of Mount Henderson and Santanoni in misty sapphire. At the southwest shimmers a dreamy summit—Blue

Bog-River Falls, Tupper Lake.

Mountain; while to the south stands the near and lesser top of Skylight. Beyond, at the southeast, wave the stern crests of the Boreas Mountain. Thence ascends the Dial, with its leaning cone, like the Tower of Pisa; and close to it swells the majesty of Dix's Peak, shaped like a slumbering lion. Thence stagger the wild, savage, splintered tops of the Gothic Mountains at the Lower Ausable Pond—a ragged thunder-cloud—

linking themselves, on the east, with the Noon-Mark and Rogers's Mountain, that watch over the valley of Keene. To the northeast, rise the Edmunds's Pond summits—the mountain-picture closed by the sharp crest of old Whiteface on the north — stately outpost of the Adirondacks. Scattered through this picture are manifold expanses of water—those almost indispensable eyes of a landscape. That glitter at the nor h by old Whiteface is Lake Placid; and the spangle, Bennett's Pond. Yon streak running south from Mount Seward, as if a silver vein had been opened in the stern mountain, is Long Lake; and, between it and our vision, shine Lakes Henderson and Sanford, with the sparkles of Lake Harkness, and the twin-lakes Jamie and Sallie. At the southwest, glances beautiful Blue - Mountain Lake — name most suggestive and poetic. South, lies Boreas Pond, with its green beaver-meadow and a mass of rock at the edge. To the southeast, glisten the Upper and Lower Ausable Ponds; and, farther off, in the same direction, Mud and Clear Ponds, by the Dial and Dix's Peak. But what is that long, long gleam at the east? Lake Champlain! And that glittering line north? The St. Lawrence, above the dark sea of the Canadian woods!"

The Indian Pass is a stupendous gorge in the wildest part of the Adirondack Mountains, in that lonely and savage region which the aborigines rightly named Conyacraga, or the Dismal Wilderness, the larger portion of which has never yet been visited by white men,

Sand Point, Little Tupper Lake.

A Carry near Little Tupper Lake.

and which still remains the secure haunt of the wolf, the panther, the great black bear, and the rarer lynx, wolverine, and moose. The springs which form the source are found at an elevation of more than four thousand feet above the sea, in rocky recesses, in whose cold depths the ice of winter never melts entirely away, but remains in some measure even in the hottest months of the year. Here, in the centre of the pass, rise also the springs of the Ausable, which flows into Lake Champlain, and whose waters reach the Atlantic through the mouth of the St. Lawrence several hundred miles from the mouth of the Hudson; and yet, so close are the springs of the two rivers, that the wild-cat, lapping the water of the one, may bathe his hind-feet in the other, and a rock rolling from the precipices above could scatter spray from both in the same concussion. In freshets, the waters of the two streams actually mingle. The main stream of the Ausable, however, flows from the northeast portal of the pass; and the main stream of the Hudson from the southwest. It is locally known as the Adirondack River, and, after leaving the pass, flows into Lakes Henderson and Sanford. On issuing from them it receives the name of Hudson, and passes into Warren County, receiving the Boreas and the Schroon, which, with their branches, bring to it the waters of a score or more of mountain lakes and of tarns innumerable.

Thirty years ago, Adirondack was almost as unknown as the interior of Africa. There were few huts or houses there, and very few visitors. But of late the number of sportsmen and tourists has greatly increased, and taverns have been established in some of the wildest spots. In summer, the lakes swarm with the boats of travellers in search of game, or health, or mere contemplation of beautiful scenery, and the strange sights and sounds of primitive Nature. All travelling there is done by means of boats of small size and slight build, rowed by a single guide, and made so light that the craft can be lifted from the water, and carried on the guide's shoulders from pond to pond,

Long Lake, from the Lower Island.

or from stream to stream. Competent guides, steady, intelligent, and experienced men, can be hired at all the taverns for two or three dollars a day, who will provide boats, tents, and every thing requisite for a trip. Each traveller should have a guide and a boat to himself, and the cost of their maintenance in the woods is not more than a dollar a week for each man of the party. The fare is chiefly trout and venison, of which there is generally an abundance to be procured by gun and rod. A good-sized valise or carpet-bag will hold all the clothes that one person needs for a two months' trip in the woods, besides those he wears in. Nothing is wanted but woollen and flannel.

The following list comprises the essentials of an outfit: a complete undersuit of woollen or flannel, with a " change ; " stout pantaloons, vest, and coat ; a felt hat ; two pairs of stockings ; a pair of common winter-boots and camp-shoes ; a rubber blanket or coat ; a hunting-knife, belt, and pint tin cup ; a pair of warm blankets, towel, soap, etc.

There are several routes by which Adirondack can be reached; but the best and easiest from New York is that by Lake Champlain. The steamer from Whitehall will land the traveller at Port Kent, on the west side of the lake, nearly opposite Burlington, Vermont, where coaches are always waiting to take passengers, six miles, to Keeseville. Here conveyances for the Wilderness can always be had, which will carry the travel-ler to Martin's Tavern, on the Lower Saranac, a distance of about fifty miles, which is a long day's drive, but a very pleasant and interesting one. From Martin's, the tourist

Mount Seward, from Long Lake.

moves about altogether in boats, and can, as he pleases, camp out in his tent, or so time his day's voyage as to pass each night in some one of the rude but comfortable taverns, which are now to be found in almost all of the easily-accessible parts of the Wilderness.

It was from this quarter that our artist entered Adirondack. At Keeseville he paused for a day or two to sketch the falls and walled rocks of the Ausable chasm, which afford some of the wildest and most impressive scenes to be found on this side of the Rocky Mountains. At the distance of a mile or so from Keeseville is Birming-

Round Island, Long Lake.

ham Falls, where the Ausable descends about thirty feet into a semicircular basin of great beauty; a mile farther down are the Great Falls, one hundred and fifty feet high, surrounded by the wildest scenery. Below this the stream grows narrower and deeper, and rushes rapidly through the chasm, where, at the narrowest point, a wedged bowlder cramps the channel to the width of five or six feet. From the main stream branches run at right angles through fissures, down one of which, between almost perpendicular rocks a hundred feet high, hangs an equally steep stairway of over two hundred steps, at the bottom of which is a narrow platform of rock forming the floor of the fissure.

From Keeseville the traveller rides westward on a road leading to Martin's, on the Lower Saranac. He will pass for a great part of the way in sight of Whiteface Mountain, the great outpost of the Adirondacks. At the village of Ausable Forks, about twelve miles from Keeseville, he can turn off into a road which leads through the famous White-face or Wilmington Notch, and can regain the main road about a dozen miles before it reaches Saranac Lake. The distance by this route is not much longer than by the main road, and the scenery is incomparably finer. The view of Whiteface from Wilmington was pronounced by Professor Agassiz to be one of the finest mountain-views he had ever seen, and few men were better acquainted with mountain-scenery than Agassiz. Through the notch flows the Ausa-ble River, with a succession of rapids and cataracts, down which is floated much of the timber cut in the Adirondack forests by the hardy and adventurous lumberers, some idea of whose toils and dangers may be formed from the sketch of " Clearing a Jam," the scene of which is at the head of one of the falls of the Ausable, in the Wilmington Notch. From the village of Wilmington our artist ascended Whiteface, which is second only to Tahawus among the mountains, its height being nearly five thousand feet. At its foot, on the southwest side, lies Lake Placid, one of the loveliest lakes of the Wilder-ness. From this lake, which is a favorite summer resort, one of the best views of Whiteface can be obtained.

From Lake Placid to Mar-tin's is a few hours' drive over a rough but picturesque road. Martin's is a large and com-

Watching for Deer, on Long Lake.

The Indian Pass.

fortable hotel on the very edge of the Lower Saranac, a beautiful lake, six or seven miles long and two miles wide, studded with romantic islands, fifty-two in number. The Saranac River connects it with Round Lake, three miles to the westward. Round Lake is about two miles in diameter, and is famous for its storms. It is in its turn connected with the Upper Saranac Lake by another stretch of the Saranac River, on which stands Bartlett's Hotel, one of the best and most frequented of the Adirondack taverns. From a point at no great distance from the house, a fine view can be obtained of Round Lake and the surrounding mountains. A short "carry," of a mile or so in length, conducts from Bartlett's to the Upper Saranac, whence it is easy to pass in boats to St. Regis Lake, our view of which gives a singularly good and accurate idea of the general characteristics of Adirondack scenery. A short voyage in the opposite direction across the Upper Saranac will take the traveller's boat to the Indian carry, or Carey's carry, as it is sometimes called, to distinguish it from another carry, Sweeny's, established a few years ago.

Both lead to the Racket River, the great artery of the Wilderness.

A few hours' row down the Racket brings you to the outlet of Lake Tupper, so named, not from the author of "Proverbial Philosophy," but from the hunter or guide who discovered it. It is several miles in length, and contains many picturesque, rocky islands, covered with evergreens. At its head the wild and little-explored Bog River flows into the lake over a romantic cascade, which forms one of the great attractions of the Adirondacks, being a famous place for trout, and having near by one of the most popular taverns of the Wilderness,

Source of the Hudson.

established a few years ago, and kept by Mr. Graves, who, in 1872, while hunting, was accidentally killed by his son, being shot by him while aiming at a deer, with which his father was struggling in the water.

From Tupper Lake the route of the traveller is up Bog River, through a series of ponds and an occasional "carry"—where the guides take the boats on their backs, as represented in our engraving—to Little Tupper Lake. Thence a series of ponds and carries leads to Long Lake, which, for more than twenty miles, resembles a great river. It is the longest of the Adirondack lakes, though there are many broader ones. From this lake a fine view can be had of Mount Seward, four thousand three hundred and forty-eight feet high. We give also an illustration of the way in which the guides of this region station themselves in trees to watch for deer. The deer are hunted by powerful hounds, which are put on their trail in the woods, and pursue them with

Opalescent Falls.

such tenacity that the frightened animal at last takes to the water. The hunters, with their boats stationed at intervals along the shore, watch patiently till the deer breaks from the woods and plunges into the water. The nearest hunter immediately enters his boat, gives chase, and generally succeeds in overtaking and killing the game.

From Long Lake to the Indian Pass is a very rough journey through the wildest part of the Wilderness. We give an illustration which conveys some idea of the kind of road the explorer who ventures thither may expect to encounter. He will find in it the source of the Hudson at an elevation of four thousand three hundred feet above the sea. From this lofty pool the water flows through Feldspar Brook into the Opalescent River, on which there is one of the most picturesque cascades of the Adirondacks.

Of the scenery of the source of the Hudson, Mr. Lossing, in his "The Hudson from the Wilderness to the Sea," writes as follows: "We entered the rocky gorge between the steep slopes of Mount McIntyre and the cliffs of Wallface Mountain. There we encountered enormous masses of rocks, some worn by the abrasion of the elements, some angular, some bare, and some covered with moss, and many of them bearing large trees,

The Hudson, Twenty Miles from its Source.

whose roots, clasping them on all sides, strike into the earth for sustenance. One of the masses presented a singular appearance; it is of cubic form, its summit full thirty feet from its base, and upon it was quite a grove of hemlock and cedar trees. Around and partly under this and others lying loosely, apparently kept from rolling by roots and vines, we were compelled to clamber a long distance, when we reached a point more than one hundred feet above the bottom of the gorge, where we could see the famous Indian Pass in all its wild grandeur. Before us arose a perpendicular cliff, nearly twelve hundred feet from base to summit, as raw in appearance as if cleft only yesterday. Above us sloped McIntyre, still more lofty than the cliff of Wallface, and in the gorge lay huge piles of rock, chaotic in position, grand in dimensions, and awful in general aspect. They appear to have been cast in there by some terrible convulsion not very remote. Through these the waters of this branch of the Hudson, bubbling from a spring not far distant (close by a fountain of the Ausable), find their way. Here the head-waters of these rivers commingle in the spring season, and, when they separate, they find their way to the Atlantic Ocean at points a thousand miles apart."

THE CONNECTICUT SHORE OF THE SOUND.

WITH ILLUSTRATIONS BY WILLIAM H. GIBSON.

THE vagueness which in many minds attaches itself to the region known as "Yan-kee-land"—which abroad expands itself into a generic term for the whole territory of the United States—has, nevertheless, its sharp lines of definition; and the phrase "from the Hudson to the Penobscot" is hardly a successful rival, in this respect, to the more common expression, "from Quoddy Head to Byram River." The former of these distinctive localities lies on the remote margin of Maine; and the latter is the dividing line of Connecticut and New York, on the border of Long-Island Sound. It is at Byram River that this sketch of the Connecticut shore of that extensive and beautiful water begins. Its scope is the stretch of that varied shore along the Sound, for a century of miles, with a final slight digression to Norwich, at the head of one of its tributary rivers.

The traveller by the Shore-Line route, from New York to Boston, follows the entire line of the Connecticut shore; but, in the swift rush and whirl of his fiery journey, he can get only the briefest and most unsatisfactory suggestions of the beauty which lies all about, if not exactly along, his way. Its most attractive and fascinating aspects are not, indeed, in most cases, to be seen without digression and search, involving delay, and, here and there, delightful excursions. The temptations to this delay are everywhere enhanced by the general comfort of the hotels at and near the important railway-stations.

About twenty miles from our great commercial metropolis lies the first station on the Connecticut shore, that of Greenwich, a very attractive village, occupying finely-wooded slopes just north of the station. Its antiquity is unquestionable; for, two centuries and a quarter ago, it was designated by the Dutch-English Commission, in convention at Hartford, as the western limit of the province of Connecticut. The principal lion of the region is the famous declivity down which the gallant Putnam, of Revolutionary fame, rode on horseback to avoid the close fire of a pursuing troop of British dragoons, who, not daring to follow him in his "break-neck flight," were fain to content themselves with sending volleys of bullets after him. This spot, now called Old Put's Hill, is a long flight of rude cuttings, or steps, made in a steep hill-side for the convenience of the people in reaching a place of worship on the summit of the hill.

The village and vicinity of Stamford will well repay the tourist of ample leisure for delay there. Stamford, like the vignette village of this portfolio of sketches, claims a notable antiquity of origin; but, for a little less than two centuries, it had scarcely more to be proud of than a name. Within the last forty years alone, it has exhibited vitality,

GLIMPSES OF GREENWICH, STAMFORD, AND NORWALK.

and, from being a simple and unattractive hamlet, it has grown into beauty and importance; its hundreds of 1834 almost augmented to thousands in 1874. It is a favorite resort of New-York merchants, many of whom have embellished its heights and knolls with elegant mansions and villas. Much taste, as well as wealth, is displayed in its architecture, making its streets and avenues attractive. Shippen Point, on the Sound, less than a mile from the station, is a place of summer resort to many hundreds, who crowd the spacious Ocean House and numerous smaller places of entertainment.

Close by is one of many ledges of rock which diversify the level aspect and tameness of the Long-Island shore. Pound Rock stretches its dark ramparts into the water, and commands a very fine view of the Sound and its scenery. There are beautiful drives in the adjacent country, with, here and there, pretty glimpses on Mill River, "the ancient Rippowam."

Epicures who are particular in regard to the quality of their oysters will have special associations with the name of the next important place in our eastward progress along the Connecticut shore of the Sound. It is Norwalk, whose fine, picturesque bay affords the bivalves in great abundance, and of proverbial excellence. The oyster-trade is one of the most flourishing of the industries of the now populous and rapidly-growing town—city, perhaps, we should say—of South Norwalk; and the white sails of the numerous oyster-smacks lend one of their chief charms to the prominent points of the harbor in its vicinity. Of these, Roton Point, so happily pictured by our artist, is the resort, by eminence, of the festive parties from the town. It is admirably adapted for picnics, uniting extensive areas with fine groups of noble pines, and these flanked by a broad and beautiful beach.

The scarcely less attractive picture of Wilson's Point is on the opposite side of the harbor, and a little farther up the Sound. It includes a glimpse of the Norwalk Islands. The "Ancient Landmark," with which the artist has flanked, on the right, the pretty, nameless bit of moonlight, is not far from Wilson's Point, and stands, indeed, upon the grounds of the proprietor of that beautiful spot. It is believed to be the chimney of an old Revolutionary building of historic interest, and the subject of many legendary anecdotes. It presents some internal evidence of having been used as a place of concealment, perhaps by Tories hiding from pursuing colonists. Its preservation for so long a time in its ruined condition is said to be the result of government care, utilizing it as a literal landmark to guide vessels over the harbor-shoals.

Norwalk—without prefix—is a twin-town, on the north side of the railway. The hundredth anniversary of the burning of this place by the Hessians will occur in 1879, and afford the enterprising citizens a fine occasion for distinguishing themselves in the popular centennial line!

A few miles east of Norwalk, and in the broad fields of Southport, there was, a hundred years ago and more, an extensive marsh, known as the Sasco Swamp, which

GLIMPSES OF SOUTH NORWALK AND SOUTHPORT.

possesses historic interest as the scene of the subdual of the Pequot Indians by English troops from Massachusetts. There are, indeed, few points along the shore of Connecticut about which some antiquarian interest does not centre in memorials or legends of aboriginal adventures, battles, and defeats.

Southport bears to-day no trace of the fiery ravage to which the Hessian troops, under the notorious Tryon, subjected it in 1779, when it shared the fate of Norwalk, but was more fortunate in having poetic commemoration of its

> ". . . smoking ruins, marks of hostile ire,
> And ashes warm, which drink the tears that flow."

Black Rock is a noticeable village of the township of Fairfield, and quite famous, both for its very excellent harbor and for many beautiful prospects which characterize its vicinity.

Bridgeport, which is reached on the railway, fifty-nine miles from New York, deserves more extended mention than the limits assigned to this paper will allow. It is finely situated on an arm of the Sound, where the Pequannock River empties itself into it. The ground it covers was once owned by the Paugusset Indians, whose name is, somewhat apocryphally, and very remotely, connected with the noble stream bearing the musical name of the Housatonic. In the discomfiture and flight of the guilty Pequots before Mason, the harmless Paugussets were involved in misfortunes from which they never recovered.

Bridgeport has been a city about forty years, and has a present estimated population of more than twenty thousand souls. It is a place of great enterprise and thrift in manufactures, foremost of which are the extensive Sewing-Machine Works; manufactories of arms, cartridges, brass and steel wares, carriages, and water-proof fabrics, giving profitable employment to thousands, and adding rapidly to the wealth of the place.

Seaside Park is justly one of Bridgeport's lions. It is finely situated, looking over the harbor and the expansive Sound beyond. A broad esplanade affords attractive walks and drives on the beach.

Few, if any, New-England cities have a more beautiful street than Bridgeport can show in its Golden Hill, a long line of elegance, taste, and wealth in private dwellings.

Three miles eastward of the city lies old and picturesque Stratford, where the new has not yet displaced the old, where the racket of mills and machinery does not vex the quiet-loving ear, or harrow the nerves of the sensitive; and where one may dream away a sweet summer twilight in the shadows of grand old trees, more ancient even than the quaint but stately houses of the village. These fine, ancient elms make up, together with broad reaches of the stately Housatonic River, the noblest aspects of Stratford. Its light-house is of a quaint style of architecture, matching well the primitiveness of the place, which, however, is not utterly antiquated. The old church, of which Adam

NORWALK from RIVER.

OYSTER BOATS. ROTON POINT.

VIEW FROM WILSONS POINT.

W. H. Gibson

CONNECTICUT SHORE SCENES.

Blackman was pastor in the dim colonial days, has now a handsome though rural Gothic house of worship, in striking contrast to the old, quaint sanctuary of its early devotions.

Five miles from Stratford, eastward, on the railway, and across the broad bosom of the Housatonic, we come to Milford, picturesque with stately, shadowing elms, and a most seductive length of green neatly inclosed. Here flows the silvery Wap-o-waug, giving the railway-passenger free transit over its clear waters by a pretty bridge and bosky banks. Here, too, is a tall monument, built over the remains of many soldiers, cast ashore here from British cartel-ships, in 1777.

A railway stretch of seven miles brings the tourist to West Haven, where he may well miss a train, if only to indulge himself in a pleasant stroll to Savin Rock. It is a walk of twenty minutes, and rewarded, at its close, with beautiful prospects over the Sound and shore alike.

The City of Elms is now close at hand, and there is much in New Haven to interest the intelligent visitor—very much, indeed, of which this sketch can take no cognizance. Its grand avenues of elm-trees are certainly unsurpassed in New England; and the one, especially, which separates the beautiful and attractive Green from the grounds of Yale College, is a great Gothic aisle of such interlacing boughs, and such interwoven masses of rich, green, and sun-gilded foliage, as would surely have either inspired or paralyzed the facile pencil of Birket Foster.

New Haven has a population of over fifty thousand, and the city is not more attractive for its picturesqueness than it is for its intellectual culture and social refinement. These characteristics are doubtless due, in great part, to the influence of Yale College, which, in its real comprehensiveness of scope, in the number of its departments, and in the richness of its educational accessories, more nearly approaches the order of a true university than any other institution in the United States, that at Cambridge alone excepted. It was founded in 1700, and, for now almost two eventful centuries, has exerted a widely-diffused and beneficent influence upon American character and development.

Only two years ago, New Haven divided with Hartford the legislative "honors" of Connecticut, but now her chief and sufficient distinction is her noble and expansive college.

Numerous converging and intersecting railways, extensive manufactures, and a considerable West-India commerce, contribute to the life and wealth of this beautiful city. Its suburbs are adorned with tasteful villas, and afford inviting drives and charming prospects. Of principal interest among its suburban attractions are the crags known as East and West Rocks—two bold and striking bluffs of trap-rock, lifting themselves, in magnificent array of opposition, about four hundred feet out of the plain which skirts the city. Their geological origin was probably some anomalous volcanic convulsion; and their grim heights may have sentinelled, in remote ages of our planet, the flow of the Connecticut River between their august feet to the Sound. Their summits afford very

SCENES IN BRIDGEPORT, STRATFORD, AND MILFORD.

fine but quite dissimilar prospects. East Rock overlooks the ample interval and river-reaches of the Quinnipiac Valley, which are almost hidden from West Rock. The view of the beautiful city from East Rock has afforded to the pencil of our artist rare scope for boldness, amid the average level of the landscape. The cliffs are rough, and difficult to climb, but they well repay the toil of surmounting them, while, from the top of either, the spectator may stretch his vision, and feel, with the poet—

> "What heed I of the dusty land,
>   And noisy town?
> I see the mighty deep expand,
> From its white line of glimmering sand,
> To where the blue of heaven over bluer waves shuts down."

On East Rock there is a little inn, where the weary pilgrim may obtain refreshment in summer. While this rocky crest is more easily accessible than the other, and certainly bears the palm in breadth of view, the West Rock has the counterbalance to these advantages of a positive historic charm in the shape of the Regicides' or Judges' Cave. In a deep cleft, among a wild group of large, loose bowlders, the famous regicides Goffe and Whalley were concealed for several days, in 1661. This cave is reached by a difficult path over the rocky table of the cliff. The legend is, that the regicides were frightened out of this inhospitable place by the glittering eyes of some wild animal glaring in upon them.

The water-supply of the city is pent up on West Rock, in a lake having a superficies of seventy-five acres, and formed by an extensive dam of rock and earthwork. The water-works are planted near the foot of the rock, and close at hand is Maltby Park, a tract of eight hundred acres, most tastefully laid out, and in the course of elegant embellishment.

The view of the city from Fort Hill, which is included in the accompanying series of illustrations, is a picture which well rewards the visitor for an excursion to the point in question, which was once the site of an old fortification, of which, however, few traces remain. The corner vignettes of this beautiful picture have all found some mention in the text, as objects and points of great interest. The meadows, or plains, which lie northward of the city, and out of which the great ranges of trap-rock vault, as it were, into the sky, are well pictured at the bottom of the artistic page.

The railway reach of fifty miles, from New Haven to New London, is less attractive in picturesque elements than the same distance, which this sketch has already overpassed, from Greenwich to New Haven. There are not wanting, however, points of historic interest; and the whole region has attractions to those who love boating and fishing. Fairhaven oysters have a fame of their own.

Branford and Guilford, eight and sixteen miles respectively from New Haven, have their beaches; and numerous hotels invite summer guests to the enjoyment of delicious

THE JUDGES' CAVE

NEAR SAVINS' ROCK

NEW-HAVEN LIGHT

WEST-ROCK

NEW-HAVEN from FORT-HILL

W.H. GIBSON. DEL.

EAST-ROCK AND MEADOWS.

NEW HAVEN AND VICINITY.

breezes, with bathing and boating at pleasure. Guilford is both the birth and burial place of the poet Halleck, although he spent much of his life in New York.

The aboriginal history and traditions of this region, and, indeed, of all the Connecticut shore of Long-Island Sound, are full of interest to the antiquarian and student.

The New-Haven Elms.

Guilford shares with New Haven the fame of having given shelter for a season to the regicides.

Between Branford and Guilford lies Stony Creek, a railway-station, from which a pleasant excursion may be made to the Thimble Islands, a picturesque group of rocky and wooded islets. The names of Money and Pot, belonging to two of this cluster,

NEW HAVEN, VIEW FROM EAST ROCK.

may well suggest to the reader the legends of Captain Kidd and his hidden treasures; and these localities have again and again tempted the cupidity of deluded diggers.

The old and quaintly rural village of Saybrook lies thirty miles east from New Haven, and, just beyond it, the Connecticut River flows into the Sound. Beyond the Connecticut, eastward, lie the villages of Lyme, three of the name, and also of Waterford, covering a reach of seventeen miles to the banks of the Thames River at New London. All this tract was once the home and hunting-grounds of the Niantic Indians, a Narraganset clan, whose somewhat renowned sachem, Ninigret, defeated the Long-Island tribes.

New London, less attractive, perhaps, than either Bridgeport or New Haven, is nevertheless a pleasant town. It has great facilities for traffic and communication both by land and water, railways and steamboats connecting it with New York, and various iron ways leading out of it to the north and east.

The Pequot House, which is picturesquely situated on the Harbor road, about two miles from the city, and at the mouth of the Thames, is one of the most fashionable summer resorts along the shore. It is surrounded by quite an extensive settlement of pretty cottages, rented for the fashionable season to families from the cities; and upon the opposite shore of the Thames are also abundant accommodations for summer guests, though of a little lower rate of expense, if not, perhaps, of real comfort.

The harbor of New London is defended by two forts, which, in these times of peace, frown only at each other from opposite sides of the river. Fort Trumbull is a massive granite structure on the west shore, and in perfect condition; while Fort Griswold, on the eastern side, is little more than the remnant of old earthworks, of historic interest, although there is very near it a well-constructed twenty-gun battery, in good condition.

Around, or rather beneath, the latter, spreads the village of Groton, once a suburb of New London, and now closely connected with it by steam ferries, at one of which the trains of the Shore-Line route are transported bodily across the river. Groton is a centre of historic and revolutionary memories. The tourist should make an excursion to the ruins of Fort Griswold, the scene of the infamous murder of Colonel Ledyard, with his own sword, by the Tory officer to whom he had honorably surrendered it.

Near by is the monument erected in memory of the soldiers who were massacred in that surrender. It is a granite obelisk, nearly one hundred and thirty feet high, and, besides its commemorative tablets, it possesses the charm of such a broad and various view from its summit as one can hardly afford to miss in a level region, and one, indeed, which is not surpassed along the shores of the sound. It realizes fairly the poet's picture of the height—

> " Where was wide wandering for the greediest eye,
>   To peer about upon variety;
>   Far round the horizon's crystal air to skim,
>   And trace the dwindling edges of its brim."

NEW LONDON AND NORWICH.

This point affords the finest view of the city, as well as of the beautiful harbor of New London. The city, jointly with the State of Connecticut, recently gave to the United States a tract of land on the east bank of the Thames, where a navy-yard is established. It borders the widening reaches of the river about the village of Groton.

At New London, the tourist who follows the course of this rapid sketch will have to make a slight departure from the strict shore-line of the sound, taking, if he pleases, the railway, or, better still, a charming drive to Norwich, thirteen miles along the west bank of the picturesque Thames.

He may linger, if he will, a little while at Mohegan, five miles south of Norwich, where, upon the highest land in the village, stands the ancient fortress of Uncas. Here, also, he may see some remnants of the once famous tribe which that brave but treacherous chief led so often on the war-path. It may, indeed, be better that he should not encounter these degenerate sons of the forest—half-breeds at the best—unless he is prepared to resign all his romantic and poetical impressions of the lofty heroism and splendid qualities of the aboriginal red-men of the New-England forests and hills. There is nothing in the present aspect of the Pequot or Mohegan remnants to aid him in the maintenance of his old and it may be obstinately cherished fancies.

Norwich is a larger and finer city than its neighbor, New London, and of a very romantic aspect, much of the town being built on terraces, lying between the Yantic and Shetucket Rivers, which, by their confluence there, make the Thames. It has really noble avenues, with fine trees, antique and modern mansions, and very handsome public buildings.

The monument of Uncas is a prime object of antiquarian interest in the city. It is a granite obelisk, standing in the midst of other memorial stones built to commemorate the ferocious exploits of immemorial chieftains and warriors of the Mohegans. Uncas was once a great sachem of the Pequots, but he became afterward, by revolt and secession, the most renowned leader of the Mohegans for fifty years, during which period he elevated them in point of influence, and held them, in spite of many wars with other tribes, to peaceful relations with the colonists. The monument to Uncas was built in 1841. A cluster of gloomy pine-trees infolds this Indian cemetery, not far from the site of the once highly picturesque falls of the Yantic, which, however, have dwindled greatly from their old renown under the encroachments of both natural and artificial changes, so that the tourist is puzzled to account for the enthusiasm which inspired the early poets and topographers in their praises of the wild, tumultuous lapse of the Yantic.

The glimpse which the artist has given of Norwich, in the fine general view and in the dainty side-scenes which accompany it, are fit suggestions of the picturesqueness of its ways and of its romantic environs, much relieved from the oppressive monotony of the more level shore along which this sketch has been compelled, by the requirements of art, to run.

LAKE MEMPHREMAGOG

WITH ILLUSTRATIONS BY J. DOUGLAS WOODWARD.

Owl's Head Landing.

THE journey northward may be made in thirty-six hours, or it may be extended
through several weeks. The route from the metropolis divides the Connecticut
Valley, that fair reach of glistening stream and forest dell leading beyond into mountain
mysteries. Nature wears her bridal robes, softly colored, fragrant, and bright—

"First a lake,
Tinted with sunset; next, the wavy lines
Of the far-reaching hills; and yet more far,
Monadnock lifting from his night of pines
His rosy forehead to the evening star."

You may start out from your city home for Memphremagog direct; but, in such a path-way as leads through the valley, you will linger, inhaling the breath of the daisy-scented fields, resting the wearied mind with the tranquil sentiment of the Arcadian life that dreams in the brook-side villages on your way. Grander scenes there may be, but they oppress and tire us, and we come back to the Connecticut Valley year after year, loving it the more, and deriving from it the solace that empowers us for renewed toil at the treadmill of city life. Loitering in these pastures a while, we arrive at the foot of Lake Memphremagog in a fit state of mind to appreciate its beauties, not so drowsy and fagged-out as we should be had our journey been unbroken. We disembark at the little Vermont town of Newport; submit ourselves to the regimen of a fashionable hotel; sleep well, and dream of peace. The morning breaks on a bracing day in the season of Nature's most gorgeous transformation; the autumn foliage is crowned with the richest hues; our fellow-tourists have less of the jaded expression that is almost habitual on their features, and so all circumstances are propitious for our voyage over the lake.

Some people tell us that it rivals Lake George, but this admits of difference of opinion; yet it is almost impossible that there should be any thing more picturesque, in the exact sense of that word, than this beautiful expanse with the awkward name. It is overshadowed by mountains and bordered by dense forests and grassy reaches. At one point it is in Lower Canada, and at another in Northern Vermont. It is thirty miles long and two miles wide; the basin that holds it is deep and narrow; numerous islands spring from its depths, where speckled trout, of enormous size, dart and glimmer. These things are imparted to us by an old resident, a freckled, long-faced, discoursive down-easter, as our white steamer leaves her wharf near the hotel and speeds toward the other end of the lake. There is one object already in sight that we have been instructed not to miss —the Owl's Head, a mountain surpassing others around the lake in form and size. But it is yet twelve miles distant, and in the mean time our eyes and binocular glasses are attracted by many other enchantments that the shore sets forth.

Here is a narrow cape jutting out, the shimmering ripples tossing in play around; and yonder the land inclines into two bays, one of them sheltering the boats of some lazy boys, who are stretched on the thwarts, with their vagabond faces raised to the un-clouded sun. The shore varies in character: for a mile it is high and craggy, and then the banks are low and rolling, girt by a belt of yellow sand. The deep water readily imprints the colors on its smooth surface, and duplicates the forms of earth and sky. Past Indian Point there is a small village, and farther on are the Twin Sisters, two fair

LAKE MEMPHREMAGOG, SOUTH FROM OWL'S HEAD.

islands, thickly wooded with a growth of evergreens. Beyond we see another village, and soon we are abreast of Province Island, a cultivated garden of one hundred acres. Nearer the eastern shore is Tea-Table Island, a charming little spot with many cedar-groves, whence cometh the pleasant laughter of a picnic-party, whose fancifully-painted rowboats are moored to a little jetty.

Now we bid farewell to our native heath, and enter British waters, with British soil to the right and to the left of us. There are many farm-houses on the banks, white-painted, and dazzling in the sunlight. It is a national duty for those of us who are free-born Americans to observe that the houses in the Canadian territory are slovenly and uncared for, without the evidences of prosperity and thrift that appear in those situated on our own soil. But let us confess that the scenery of the lake does not diminish in beauty. There are no marsh-lands near its shore, and no stagnant pools. The banks are invariably picturesque, almost invariably fertile and under cultivation. Here is Whetstone Island, so named by some enterprising Yankees, who used the stone found in the neigh-borhood for axe-grinding, until her majesty's government decided that they were trespass-ers, and drove them away. A little farther in our course lies Magoon's Point, a grassy slope coming to the water's edge; and yonder is a cavern with a legend. Perhaps you who have seen so many caverns with legends begin to regard all of them with suspicion; but this one and its legend are veritable. Some marauders have secreted somewhere in the innermost recesses of one of the rocks a treasure-chest of immense value, stolen from a Roman Catholic cathedral. There is no doubt about it. The freckled, long-faced down-easter has seen, with his own sharp eyes, two massive gold candlesticks that were found within a yard or two of the entrance!

We are fast nearing Owl's Head. The boat winds in and out between the cedar-robed islands, and the golden haze vanishes into the clear and breezy day. We do not land during the journey down the lake, but pass Owl's Head, with only a glimpse at its magnificent height. We also speed by Round Island, cap-like in shape; Minnow Island, the most famous fishing-place, where some anglers are now stationed underneath the leafy boughs; and Skinner's Island, once the haunt of an intrepid smuggler, who snapped his fingers in the face of custom-house officers, and whose audacity has been chronicled in many a rhymed story. North of Skinner's Cave is Long Island, covering an area of about a square mile, with a rugged shore. At one place the shore is almost perpen-dicular, and on the southern side there is an extraordinary granite bowlder, balanced on a natural pedestal, named Balance Rock. Hereabout, too, are the villas of some wealthy Montreal merchants, enclosed in magnificent parks on the banks.

Owl's Head is the most prominent mountain, and is cone-shaped. But, in our pas-sage to the head of the lake, we see other heights that do not fall far below it. Here is Mount Elephantus, now faintly resembling an elephant's back, afterward chang-ing, as we proceed farther north, into a horseshoe form. The water deepens; soundings

LAKE MEMPHREMAGOG, NORTH FROM OWL'S HEAD.

show three hundred feet near Gibraltar Point, where the rocks are sheer to the water's edge. The sun wanes toward the west, and the wind grows keener. Yonder is Mount Oxford, not unlike Owl's Head; and here is a landing, toward which our steamer's prow inclines. We are at the foot of the lake. This drowsy little town is Magog, and attracts few of us ashore. A crowd of gaping inhabitants are on the wharf to welcome us, and, as we turn down the lake again, they break into a feeble but well-meaning cheer. The night comes on, and we haul up and go to sleep in a comfortable hotel at the base of the mountains.

In the morning we ascend Owl's Head. The path-way from the hotel is in good condition, overarched by pines and cedars, bordered by pleasant fields. A chorus of birds swells through the thickets; a few brown squirrels flee before us as we advance. The air is filled with the fragrance of wild-flowers, mosses, and ferns. Occasionally, through the green curtain that shelters us from the mounting sun, we catch a glimpse of the untroubled, azure sky. On the way there is a shelving rock, under which we are sheltered during a passing shower; and, proceeding farther, we reach a mass of stone, plumed with ferns, and covered on the sides with a velvety moss. The summit reached, we have such a view as rewards our toil. Looking south, we see the lake from end to end, its islands and villages, the near rivers flashing in the sunlight. Looking north, the picture expands into other beauties; and, to the east and west, there are more lakes, plains, islands, and mountains. The summit itself is riven into four peaks, silent ravines intervening between them. Once a year a lodge of freemasons meets here, and, on the face of the " Mountain Mystery," are written some cabalistic signs of the order.

Mount Elephantus, from the Lake Steamer.

THE MOHAWK, ALBANY, AND TROY.

WITH ILLUSTRATIONS BY MESSRS. FENN AND WOODWARD.

THERE is a part of New-York State around which the spell of the pastoral ages
has surely been thrown, and which gives to it a sentiment of extreme antiquity
for which history refuses to account. A round two hundred and fifty years are all
for which the Muse of History considers herself responsible; and yet, throughout
this region, there is an atmosphere of peace and quiet, as if æons of happy years had
glided away since first man led cows to graze and sheep to nibble at the fat pastures.
This pastoral country is the valley of the Mohawk, a river whose true Indian designa-

The Mohawk at Utica.

tion is unknown, but which has preserved the name of the aborigines who dwelt upon its banks.

The Mohawk rises in Oneida County, about twenty miles north of Rome; flows southeast and east, falling into the Hudson, after a stretch of one hundred and thirty-five miles, ten miles above Albany. It is but a petty stream near its origin, nor is it fed by important tributaries until it has passed the city of Utica. It is clear that the impetus of the city was not derived from the river, but from the Erie Canal; for the streets are all built in the proximity of the latter, and the former is outside of the town altogether. It meanders placidly past, travelling very slowly, and with more turns and bends than that famous river in Asia Minor which Xenophon has immortalized, and from which

we get the word *meander*.
But, though the town neg-
lects it, the farms do not;
and on every side are long,
tranquil meadows, studded
with trees that mount up
from the water's edge with
a most gradual ascent. The
Erie Canal, going still more
slowly than the placid Mohawk, is on one side of it;
and the puffing, panting locomotives of the New-York
Central Railroad go shrieking
past on the other. Beyond
the meadows rise gentle hills,
whose sides are thick with
trees that glance and gleam
in the sunlight as the frolic-
some winds display the upper and the lower sides of
the leaves. The cattle graze
close to the river, near the
bulrushes; and the sheep feed
higher up, where the grass is
shorter and less rank. All
kinds of birds that love the
fat worms of the rich pastoral
soil flit from bush to bush,
or perch upon the tame backs
of the cows, or even upon
the horns of some dignified
old ram. And the river goes
murmuring on through this
scene of quiet happiness until
it comes to a place where
the Adirondack Mountains
have thrown out a line of
skirmishing rocks, and here

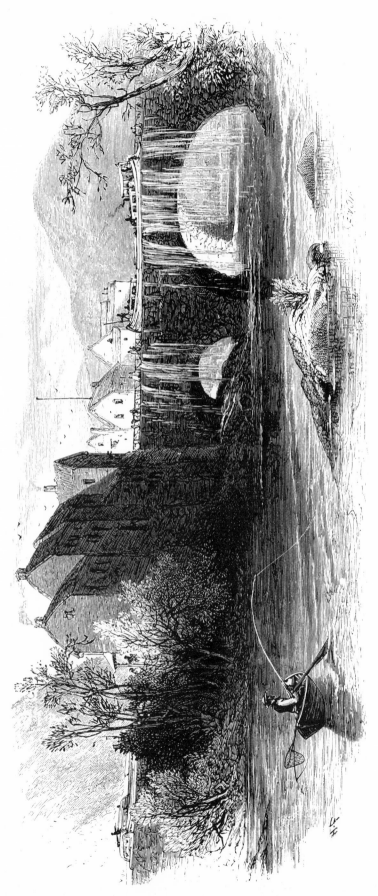

At Little Falls.

the tranquillity of the Mohawk is brought to an abrupt conclusion. This is at Little Falls. It must be confessed that the skirmishers of the mountains, in pursuance of the eternal war waged between the rocks and the rivers, have here made a most tremendous and determined onslaught, for the place is literally heaped with rocks. They are everywhere—cropping up between the houses, over the roofs, in the gardens; bursting out of the sides of the green hills, that here become really mountains; and starting up in the bed of the river in the most perplexing manner. The river here makes a descent of over forty feet, accomplishing the effort in three small falls, which have been turned to great profit by the people of the town, for they furnish water-power to a great many factories. These, for the most part, are upon the island which springs up in the river below the first fall; and this island is perhaps the rockiest part of the whole settlement. The Erie Canal runs through a channel blasted out of the solid rock at the foot of a steep hill, which rises on the east side of the river, and is called the Rollaway.

On the other side rises another hill, not so precipitous, but higher, and terraced upward with grand, curving lines, that show clearly the erosive power of the Mohawk in past times. It had its turbulent youth, also; and the day was when it swept these hills with a fierce current that laughed at such puny obstacles. Now it glides peacefully onward, and sings with a pleased murmur to the fat cattle, and the impudent birds that sip of its waters and toss their heads half disdainfully.

But there are witnesses still extant of what the waters did in the remote past; for here is Profile Rock, where the hard stone has been so mauled, and had its stratification so handled, that the very fair likeness to a human profile has been washed out. That tow-path, where the canal-horses tug and strain so, is the favorite drive of the towns-people, and, indeed, the good folks have nowhere else to drive, being circumvented and hemmed in by their rocky girdle. Accordingly, the Profile Rock is one of the institutions of the place; and the stranger within the gates who should, out of pure "cussedness," refuse to see any resemblance to the human visage, would be considered very— impolite, to say the least of it. The view along the canal tow-path is exceedingly interesting. The side of the Rollaway runs along the canal for several miles, and is clothed with a fine growth of trees—stately, dark pines; white beeches, with gleaming, silvery trunks; and bending aspens, here and there. On the other side is the Mohawk, once more united, for the rocky island terminates at the end of the town. The rocks, however, continue; and, though of no height, are strangely varied in shape, and beautifully mingled with bosky shrubs and thick bushes, waving grasses and delicate harebells. But gradually the Rollaway dwindles to a bank, and the rocks to pebbles; and, after the Suspension Bridge is passed, the Mohawk is itself again, and the pastoral era is renewed.

From this point to Schenectady may be termed the heart of the Mohawk Valley. It is difficult to say which offers the most picturesque and pleasing view—the valley of

LITTLE FALLS.

Profile Rock.

the Mohawk from the Rollaway, looking westward, or from the Suspension Bridge, be-low Little Falls, looking eastward. Both have the same pastoral beauty; both have the same low hills, the same embowering trees. There is a regularity about the lines of the former which will commend itself to the lovers of symmetry, and there is a picturesque looseness about the latter which many will deem more artistic. To Americans—eager, pushing, bustling, ever on the lookout for spheres of action, for possibilities of enterprise—there is a something here of peaceful enjoyment which sinks deep into the heart. It is a restful place, emphatically. Hence we cannot be surprised when we find Schenectady, the capital of this region, partaking of this quiet, unenergetic character; and this city has this, also, in common with the surroundings, that it appears much older than it really is. Its lovers —and it has many—claim for it the title of the oldest city in the State. This claim rests entirely upon the date of the first settlement of Albany, which some declare to have taken place in 1614, and others in 1623; but there is some confusion about the matter, because there was undeniably a time when the Indians called both *Skaunoghtada*, which means "town across the plains." However that may be, in those remote times it is certain that Schenectady proper was more flourishing than Albany. It was at the head of the rich Mohawk Valley, and did an immense business in dairy produce

The Mohawk Valley.

Schenectady, from the West.

and Indian peltries. The Indians seem to have lived in harmony with the Dutch settlers for many years, and it was not until 1690 that they suddenly became enemies. On this occasion, the whole population, save sixty souls, was annihilated; and the town was destroyed by fire. It was burned again in 1748, which gives it quite a history; and the most astonishing thing about it is, that it looks as if it had been existing for untold generations. The Mohawk, at this point, is broad and deep, and the old wooden bridge that spans it is a pretty long one; for the stream has been recruited by several large tributaries since it swept by the city of Utica, the chief contribution coming from the West Kanahta Creek, which, after dashing down the wildly-beautiful Trenton Falls, glides peaceably enough into the placid bosom of the Mohawk, and remembers its past furious excitement only in dreams.

Beyond Schenectady the river sweeps on with a majesty obtained from its increased volume, but the country is not so pastoral as it was. The soil is shaly, and the hills are

Cohoes Falls.

low. At Cohoes there is a great fall; about a mile above the falls, the river, broad and deep as it is, has been hemmed in by a dam, and a great portion of its waters drawn off by a water-power company. The little town of Cohoes is entirely manufacturing. It is the Lowell of New York. Here are the great Harmony Cotton-Mills; and here, also, are some twenty-five woollen-mills, besides paper-factories and other industries. The falls of Cohoes are quite close to the Harmony Mills; and a capital view can be obtained of them, either from the bank in rear of one of the mills, or from an island in the river, at some distance below. Very much depends upon the season of the year as regards the impression which the falls make upon the mind of a traveller. In the dry season there is but little water, and hence the upper part of the falls appears like a series of grand rapids. In the early summer there is one tremendous descent of water, falling over seventy feet. The banks on either side are high and shaly, crowned generally with dark pines at the summit, and showing, below, a diagonal stratification, as if they had been upheaved.

Below the falls the river is divided by a green island, the favorite resort of picnickers from the neighboring city of Troy. This is a great manufacturing centre, especially of metals, and therefore abounding in tall chimneys vomiting forth black smoke. For this reason the inhabitants, who love to call themselves Trojans, prefer to dwell upon the other side of the river, which is only a mile or so from Cohoes. It is here that the junction of the Mohawk and the Hudson takes place, between East and West Troy. There is here, also, a large island, on which the Troy Bridge finds a support for its central part. The view here of the bustling place is inspiriting, and makes one as eager to be up and doing as the pastoral scenes of the Mohawk Valley made us wish to live and die shepherds. Troy is a city of some fifty thousand inhabitants, situated at the mouth of Poestenkill Creek, six miles above Albany, and a hundred and fifty-one miles above New York—an active, enterprising, and bustling city.

Albany, which now numbers over seventy thousand souls within its borders, is a great railroad centre, and the main point of departure for Western travellers. It is the terminus of nearly all the great steamboat lines of the Hudson; but its chief importance is that of being the capital of the great Empire State. Albany is the oldest settlement in the original thirteen colonies, except Jamestown, Virginia. Henry Hudson, in the yacht Half-Moon, moored in September, 1609, at a point which is now in Broadway, Albany. Several Dutch navigators ascended the river to the same place during the next three or four years; and in 1614 the Dutch built the first fort on an island below the present city, which is hence called Castle Island. In 1617 a fort was built at the mouth of the Normanskill; and in 1628 another was erected near the present steamboat-landing in the south part of the city, and named Fort Orange. A quadrangular fort, called Fort Frederick, was afterward built on the high ground, now State Street, between St. Peter's Church and the Geological Hall, with lines of palisades extending down Steuben and Hudson Streets to the river. These fortifications were demolished soon after the Revolution. The place was called, by the Dutch, New Orange, and retained that name until the whole province passed into possession of the English, in 1664, when New Orange was changed to Albany, in honor of the Duke of York and Albany, afterward James II. In 1686 Albany City was incorporated by patent. Peter Schuyler was the first mayor. The Schuyler family possessed the good-will of the Indians to such a degree that, while other settlements were desolated by Indian forays, Albany was never attacked

CITY FROM NEAR OAKWOOD.

TROY AND VICINITY.

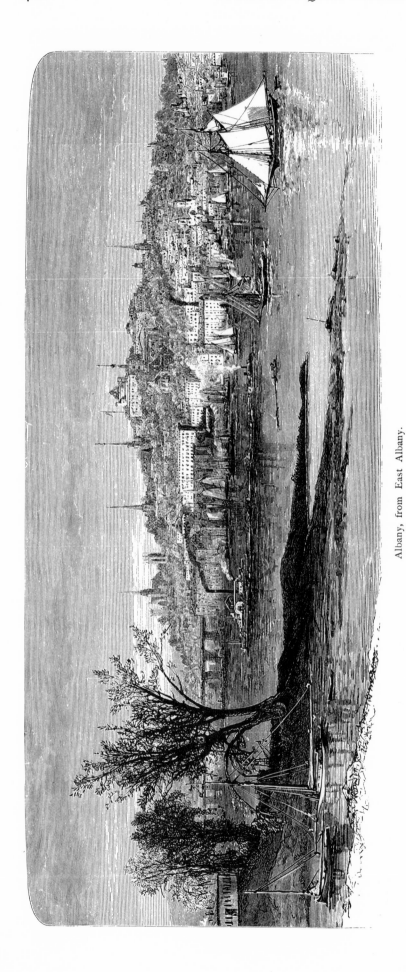

Albany, from East Albany.

by them. Besides its ancient importance as a centre of the Indian trade, Albany afterward became the point where the great military expeditions against Canada were fitted out. It was fortified at an early period; and, although often threatened with invasion, no hostile army ever reached the city. Here assembled the first convention for the union of the colonies. It was held in 1754, Benjamin Franklin being presiding officer.

There are two views of Albany which are specially good; one is from the other side of the river, where the city rises up from the western bank in irregular terraces, the culminating point being crowned with the capitol, embowered amid the foliage of old trees. Soon a more palatial and dazzling building will take the place of the present structure, and will give to the heights of Albany a magnificent apex. Up and down the river, the city stretches far and wide, with coaling-stations and founderies to the south, and, to the north, long ranges of cattle-wards. Above, the hills of the town rise, covered with fine old houses, and towering churches, and massive legislative halls, and huge

SCENES IN AND AROUND ALBANY.

Albany, from Kenwood.

caravansaries of hotels. The other view shuts out the river almost—at least, all the activity along the western bank—and gives to the eye a wider stretch of vision. Looking from Kenwood, one sees the city foreshortened, and gathered into a huge mass; while the two bridges across the Hudson, and the labyrinthine railway-lines of East Albany, become very prominent. The elevators, and the tall chimneys, with their black smoke above, and jet of red fire below, rising from the iron-works, and all the industrial part upon the extremity of the city, come plainly into view. One can see the masses of foliage of the trees in Washington Park, and the brown sedges of the flats above the town. Far in the distance lie quiet hills, on whose sides the reapers are at work on the browned wheat; while at the base are serried lines of trees that may have stood there in the old days, when the Mohawks ruled the land. From the summits of those hills, looking northward, one can see, with the utmost distinctness, the junction of the broad Hudson with the quiet Mohawk.

THE UPPER DELAWARE.

WITH ILLUSTRATIONS BY J. DOUGLAS WOODWARD.

High Falls, Dingman's Creek.

THE artist has been wandering from the beaten path again, on this journey following the Upper Delaware one hundred miles in its course northward. His starting-point is twenty-four miles above the Delaware Water-Gap, at a place called Dingman's Ferry. In the neighborhood hereabout the streams are broken into several picturesque falls, the most important

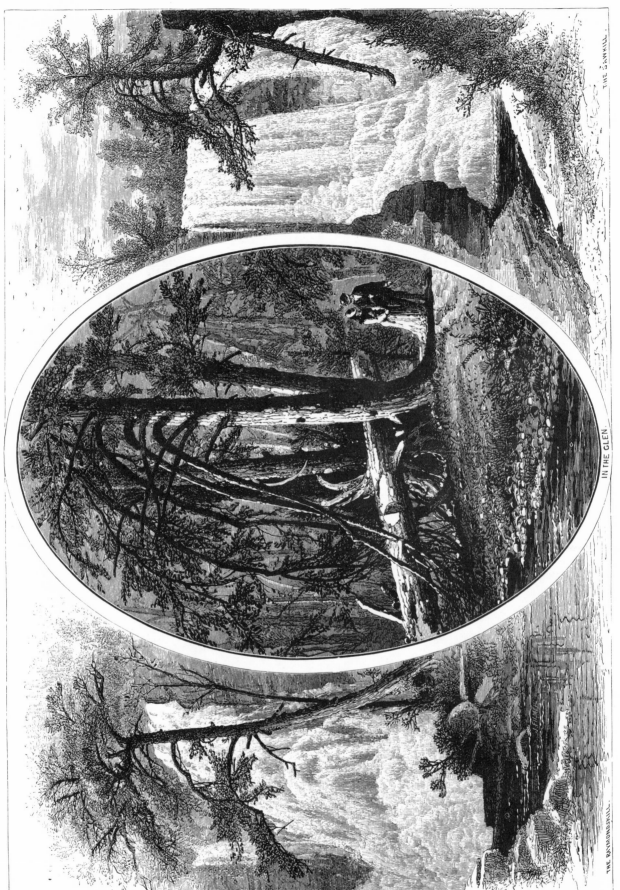

THE RAYMONDSKILL.

IN THE GLEN.

THE SAWKILL.

SCENES IN AND ABOUT MILFORD.

of which are the High Falls, shown in our first sketch. It was in the morning when we first rambled through the bosky approaches to this cascade ; and, after leaping down slippery, moss-covered rocks, we reached the foot, only to find a thin stream of water trickling down, with very little music, and less spray. The weather had been dry—but that fact scarcely consoled us—and we could only admire the tints of the rocks, and the foliage that seemed to grow out of the basin into which the waters made their first leap before rushing through a narrow bit of hill and descending to a lower level. The artist was content, thankful for the smallest share of Nature's bounty ; but the literary soul was disappointed and growling.

We were retracing our steps to the hostelry leisurely, when the premonitions of a storm urged us into a quicker pace. Gusts of wind soughed among the trees, and heavy drops of rain pattered fast on the trembling leaves and parched earth. The sunshine was hidden beneath the gray clouds that came rolling from the east. We considered ourselves in for a wet day, and we dozed near the veranda, puffing at our brier pipes in a mood of bachelor meditation.

But in the afternoon there was clearer and warmer weather, and we again tramped to the foot of the High Falls. If the spirit of the artist was content before, it was aglow now. The scene had changed, and, instead of a mere thread of water, there was a bubbling, foaming, boisterous torrent, echoing its voice in the walls of the hills through the veins of which it found a sparkling way. The moss in the crevices held glittering drops on its velvety surface ; and the branches of overarching trees looked as though they, too, were crystallized. The changing position of the clouds threw shadows across the water, varying its tints, and first giving it the appearance of a pure white, then of a faint green, afterward of a soft blue. The artist drew our attention this way and that— one moment toward yonder darkling hollow in the rocks, as the spray dashed itself into the brown seams ; next toward the water, as the light played ever-new tricks with it ; and then to a little pool formed in the cup of a bowlder. That keen eye of his discovered effects in the smallest nooks, underneath the fronds of the tiniest fern, among the grains of sand that lodged in the crevices, and in the swaying shadows of the forms around. He occupied us constantly for more than two full hours, and was even then inclined to linger, although our journey was long and the time short.

From the ferry we proceeded toward Milford. The stage-road runs along the base of a mountain, so precipitous as to resemble the Palisades of the Hudson. Atoms of rock, rolling down, have made the bed as hard as concrete ; and they have been spread so evenly that travelling is smooth and comfortable. The outlook is magnificent. The sheer wall of the mountain is on one side of us, protecting us from the scorching rays of the sun ; and undulating meadows reach afar in the opposite direction, dotted with many a snug farm-house, painted red or white, that shows its thatched roof over the tops of the orchard. The river glistens through this green expanse, and is spanned, here and

PORT JERVIS AND VICINITY.

POND EDDY.

THE UPPER DELAWARE.

there, by a picturesque bridge. Still farther away are the purple lines of more hills, mysterious in the haze of a warm autumn morning.

Some distance below the village of Milford, we reach the falls of the Raymondskill, in which the artist finds more beauties and wonders. The torrent tumbles from among a mass of foliage down a rock, and is broken several times by projections, which cause it to surge and foam in a grand tumult. Three miles farther in our course, we enter the village, which is prettily situated in a valley, and divided through the centre by a romantic glen. Glens always are romantic, for lovers invariably choose to make love in their shade and quiet. Who that reads novels ever read of a troth pledged in the sunlight? From some inscrutable instinct, it is always done in shadowy places; and here in Milford Glen, on a summer's afternoon and evening, young men and maidens flock, and wander, arm-in-arm, through the narrow paths and murky hollows. The Sawkill, scarcely more than a brook, trembles over the pebbles, and glints vividly as a stray shaft of sunlight breaks through the boughs overhead. Ferns, mosses, and wild-flowers, are sprinkled on the path, and strive to hide the decay of a felled hemlock that rests between two sturdier brothers. It is a lovely spot, picturesque in the extreme, a fit retreat for the shepherds and shepherdesses of the Pennsylvania Arcadia.

Not more than two miles farther north are the principal falls of the Sawkill, which in general characteristics much resemble the High Falls and the Raymondskill. As in the latter, the water dashes against some projecting rocks in its downward course, and is broken into clouds of spray, which the sunshine colors with rainbow hues. The volume of water is, in reality, divided into two separate falls by an elbow of the rock; but, before the two reach the level below, they commingle in one snowy mass.

Following the windings of the river, our next stopping-place was Port Jervis, which borders on New York, New Jersey, and Pennsylvania. Near here the Neversink River enters the Delaware from a valley of great beauty. We followed the artist to a place called Mount William, from which there is a superb view—a wide, extended plain, through which the winding river can be traced for many miles. The afternoon was far advanced, and the sun was declining westward. The whiteness of the light was subdued, changing into a pale yellow, that soon again would deepen into crimson. You see how he has expressed this mellowness in the gray tone of his sketch. He has included, too, a considerable range of ground, bringing in the opposite hills, the town, and the river. As far as the eye can reach, the land is under cultivation. In yonder wide plain there is not one wild acre; and, out beyond the limits of the little town, the farm-houses are numerous, and close together.

After leaving Port Jervis, we touched at Lackawaxen, to get a sketch of the Delaware and Hudson Canal Aqueduct, and thence continued our journey to Deposit, in which vicinity the scenery becomes grander and wilder. The artist's work tells its own story more eloquently than we could, and we have no further notes to add to it.

WATER-FALLS AT CAYUGA LAKE.

WITH ILLUSTRATIONS BY J. DOUGLAS WOODWARD.

Taghanic Falls.

CAYUGA LAKE, in the western central part of New-York State, is noted for a great number of highly picturesque and beautiful water-falls, found mainly at the head, or southern extremity, of the lake, in the vicinity of the town of Ithaca, famous, not only for its surrounding scenery, but for its distinguished Cornell University. The head of Cayuga lies nearly four hundred feet below the level of the surrounding country, while a remarkable feature of this elevation is a number of ravines and gorges, with an almost endless succession of water-falls, formed by the primary streams which drain the middle portion of the northern slope of the water-shed between Chesapeake Bay and the gulf of the St. Lawrence, their first point of rendezvous being Cayuga Lake. In summer, the ravines are frequented by the residents of near towns, and by visitors whose numbers increase year by year, as the fame of the wild, cool retreats spreads abroad. An after-tea walk takes the visitor to Ithaca from crowded streets into the most beautiful of Nature's sanctuaries. In winter, also, the ravines are visited, for the rare spectacle in ice-work which forms about the cataracts.

The most northerly of those ravines which pass through the city is Fall Creek, in which, within a mile, there are eight falls, all of them exceedingly fine. The walls of the chasm are abrupt and high, fringed with a dusky growth of forest-trees. A pathway was worked through it some time ago, and its sombre depths and reverberating waters are now accessible to all who have the courage and endurance necessary to follow the rugged way. Four of the falls range from sixty to thirty feet in height, while a fifth, Ithaca Fall, attains one hundred and fifty feet. In the latter the foaming torrent leaps grandly between the fractured rock. Several times its headway is broken by projections, and narrow courses lead threads of the silvery water from the main channel into the foliage that closes around. Not far from here we also find the Triple Fall, which is, to our mind, the most beautiful of all. It should be named Bridal-Veil Fall. The water pours over the rock in threads, as in a veil of gauze, and is not woven into a mass, as in the Ithaca Fall. But the people who had in charge the nomenclature of this region have avoided romance, and named the places in a matter-of-fact fashion. They have called Triple Fall thus because the stream leaps thrice before it ripples forward again on the level—first over one rock, bubbling on a ledge a while before it descends to the next, and then taking the grandest leap of all.

Before going farther, it is worth our while to examine some curious formations in the vicinity, which somewhat remind us of the eroded sandstones of Monument Park, Colorado. Here is Tower Rock, a perfect columnar formation, about thirty-six feet high, with a sort of groove across the top. The water of the lake stretches out smoothly from its foot, and the banks around are rocky and jagged, hidden in part by the abundant foliage. A still more extraordinary monument of Nature's inexhaustible whims is found in Castle Rock, which has a certain regularity of form, despite its un-usual character. It consists of a massive wall, with a magnificent, arched door-way. One of its peculiarities is that the surface is torn and fractured, and in the deep seams formed some trees and shrubs are living a precarious existence. In the arch of the door-way, for instance, there is a deep slit, whence spring two sturdy trees, their slender trunks appearing bleak and lonely in their exposed situation.

About a mile and a half south of Fall Creek is Cascadilla Creek, smaller than the former, but more delicate and harmonious in its scenery. Between the two ravines, its chimes mingling with their babble, the university is situated, on a fair expanse, nearly

CAYUGA LAKE SCENERY.

four hundred feet above the level of the lake. The principal buildings are ranged on the summit of a hill, which slopes gently, and rises again in richly-scented fields of clover and wild-flowers. The outlook is beautiful beyond description. Nearest is the pretty town, with its regular streets and white houses; then, the luxuriant valley; and, beyond that, twenty miles of the glistening lake are seen, bounded by verdure-clad banks and lofty cliffs. One of the buildings, Cascadilla Hall, is close to two of the most beautiful falls on that stream; an excellent road, built by the toil of self-educating students, crosses the gorge by a picturesque bridge, seventy feet above the stream, afterward winding through a romantic grove, and affording many fine views of the lake and the valley.

Six miles from the city, in a southwesterly direction, is Enfield Falls, a spot of great interest on account of the great depth which a stream, of moderate dimensions, has furrowed into the earth. The water reaches the main fall through a narrow cañon, a hundred feet deep, and then tumbles down, almost perpendicularly, a hundred and eighty feet, into a chasm, whose walls rise three hundred feet on each side. Thence the stream reaches the valley of the main inlet to the lake through a wild, broken, wooded course, to explore which is a task suited only to those who have strong nerves and limbs. The main fall has the same thread-like appearance as Triple Fall, and, like that, it is broken several times in its downward course. The torrent leaps six times over the protruding rock before it reaches the foot, and proceeds on its way in comparative calm. As we stand on a rock in the eddying pool below, and glance upward through the murky chasm, with its sheer walls and sentinel evergreens, the scene is impressive in the extreme, and much more sombre than other parts of the neighborhood. The stream in the main fall of Buttermilk Ravine also issues from a deep channel, with jutting and somewhat steep walls. In this ravine there is another of those fanciful stone monuments which we have referred to.

But the most noted and perhaps the most impressive of all the water-falls about the head of Cayuga Lake is the Taghanic, situated about ten miles northwest from the town, and about one mile up from the west shore. It is more than fifty feet higher than Niagara, and is considered as grand as the Staubbach of Switzerland. The most interesting features are the very deep ravine, the extraordinary height of the cataract, its sharply-defined outlines, and the magnificent view of the lake and the surrounding country that may be obtained in its vicinity. The water breaks over a clean-cut table-rock, and falls perpendicularly two hundred and fifteen feet. Except in flood-time, the veil of water breaks, and reaches the bottom in mist and sheets of spray. The rugged cliffs through which the stream rolls before it makes its plunge are about two hundred feet in depth, and form a triangle at the brink of the fall. From the foot a strong wind rushes down the ravine, the walls of which are here nearly four hundred feet high, and as cleanly cut as though laid by the hands of a mason. This ravine is reached by a series of stairways, hewn in the rock, and by rugged pathways.

ENFIELD FALLS. BUTTERMILK FALLS.

BUTTERMILK RAVINE.

CORNELL UNIVERSITY.

VICINITY OF ITHACA.

THE ROCKY MOUNTAINS.

WITH ILLUSTRATIONS BY THOMAS MORAN.

Tower Rock, Garden of the Gods.

IN a general and some-
what indistinct way,
we may all claim to know
something about the Rocky
Mountains, and we all re-
member the reverence and
awe their name inspired in
our school-days; but our
mature knowledge of them
is neither exact nor ex-
tensive. Perhaps we have
heard of Pike's Peak,
Gray's Peak, and Long's
Peak; but we are hazy as
to their altitudes and characteristics, and could much
more easily answer ques-
tions about the Alps, the
Andes, or the Himalayas,

LONG'S PEAK, FROM ESTE'S PARK.

than about the magnificent chain that embraces an area of sixty thousand square miles in Colorado alone, and nurtures the streams that pour their volume into the greatest and most widely separate oceans. We may have crossed the continent in the iron pathway of the Union Pacific over and over again, and not seen to advantage one of the peaks that cluster and soar to almost incomparable elevations—minor hills hiding them from the travellers in the cars; and we may be inclined to think less of the main range than of the Sierra Nevadas, because the railway has shown us the greatest beauties of the latter. But there is not a false pretence about them; no writer has exaggerated in extolling their grandeur, nor even adequately described it.

The chain is a continuation northward of the Cordilleras of Central America and Mexico. From Mexico it continues through the States and Territories lying between the Pacific and the head-waters of the streams that flow into the Mississippi, spreading over an area of one thousand miles from east to west. Still inclining northward, and still broken into several ranges, it passes into the British possessions to the north, the eastern range reaching the Arctic Ocean in about latitude 70° north, and the western passing near the coast, and ending near Prince William's Sound, where Mount St. Elias, in latitude 60°, stands upon the borders of the Pacific, at the height of seventeen thousand eight hundred feet above the sea-level.

We do not like the word "Backbone" applied to the mountains. Let us rather call them the Snow-Divide of the continent, or, as the main range is sometimes named, the Mother-Sierras. Occasionally, too, they are called the Alps of America by one of those absurd whims of literary nomenclature that insist upon calling New Orleans the Paris of America, Saratoga the Wiesbaden of America, and Lake George the Windermere of America, just as though we had nothing distinctly our own, and Nature had simply duplicated her handiwork across the seas in creating the present United States. The Rocky Mountains are not like the Alps, and in some things they surpass them. From the summit of Mount Lincoln, near Fairplay, Colorado, on a clear day, such a view is obtained as you cannot find on the highest crests of the Swiss mountains. In the rear, and in the front, the peaks ascend so thickly that Nature seems to have here striven to build a dividing wall across the universe. There are one hundred and thirty of them not less than thirteen thousand feet high, or within less than three thousand feet of Mont Blanc; and at least fifty over fourteen thousand feet high. Almost below the dome on which we stand, we can see a low ridge across a valley, separating the river Platte, leading to the Gulf of Mexico, and the Blue River, leading to the Gulf of California. On one side are the famous Gray's and Evans's Peaks, scarcely noticeable among a host of equals; Long's Peak is almost hidden by the narrow ridge; Pike's is very distinct and striking. Professor Whitney has very truly said, and we have repeated, that no such view as this is to be obtained in Switzerland, either for reach or the magnificence of the included heights. Only in the Andes or Himalayas might

BOWLDER CAÑON.

we see its equal. But it is also true that one misses the beauty of the pure Alpine mountains, with the glaciers streaming down their sides. The snow lies abundantly in lines, and banks, and masses; yet it covers nothing.

Even among eminent scientific men there has been a dense ignorance about the Rocky Mountains, and especially about the heights of the several peaks. Until 1873,

Frozen Lake, Foot of James's Peak.

only small areas of our vast Territories had been surveyed and accurately mapped. The greater space had been unnoticed, and uncared for. But in that year a geological and geographical survey of Colorado was made, under the able direction of Dr. F. V. Hayden; and the results have exceeded all expectations. The position of every leading peak in thirty thousand square miles was fixed last summer, including the whole region between parallels 38° and 40° 20′ north, and between the meridians 104° 30′ and 107° west. The ground was divided into three districts, the northern district including the Middle Park, the middle district including the South Park, and the southern district the San-Luis Park. In these three districts the range reveals itself as one of the grandest in the world, reaching its greatest elevations, and comprising one of the most interesting areas

Gray's Peak.

on the continent. As unscientific persons, we owe Professor Hayden a debt of gratitude for reassuring us that the Rocky Mountains are all our forefathers thought them, and not mythical in their splendors. How much more the *savants* owe him, we will not venture to say. We ought to add, however, that he was singularly fortunate in unearthing, so to speak, the most representative scenery, as the photographs made attest; and present or prospective travellers cannot do better than follow in the footsteps of his expedition, as we mean to do in this article.

Early in May we are far north, with a detachment of the Hayden expedition, encamped in the Estes Park, or Valley. Park, by-the-way, is used in these regions as a sort of variation on the sweeter-sounding word. The night is deepening as we pitch our tents. We are at the base of Long's Peak — about half-way between Denver City and the boundary-line of Wyoming — and can only dimly see its clear-cut outline and graceful crests, as the last hues of sunset fade and depart. Supper consoles us after our long day's march; we retire to our tents, but are not so exhausted that we cannot make merry. In this lonely little valley, with awful chasms and hills around, in a wilderness of glacier creation, scantily robed with dusky pine and hemlock, the hearty voice of our expedition breaks many slumbering echoes in the chilly spring night. A void is filled. A man on the heights, looking into the valley, would be conscious of a change in the sentiment of the scene. The presence of humanity infuses itself into the inanimate. It is so all through the region. Alone, we survey the magnificent reaches of mountain, hill-side, and plain, with a subdued spirit, as on the brink of a grave. Our sympathies find vent, but not in hysterical adulation. Our admiration and wonder are mingled with a degree of awe that restrains expression. It would be much more easy to go into ecstasies over the home-like view from the summit of Mount Washington than over peaks that are more than twice as high, and incomparably grander. There are brightness and life, smooth pastures and pretty houses, on the New-England mountain. Out here there are waste, ruggedness, and sombre colors. The heart of man is not felt; we gaze at the varied forms, all of them massive, most of them beautiful, feeling ourselves in a strange world. The shabby hut of the squatter, and straggling mining-camp, deep set in a ravine, are an inexpressible relief; and so our white tents, erected on the fertile acres of the Estes Park, throw a gleam of warmth among the snowy slopes, and impart to the scene that something without which the noblest country appears dreary, and awakens whatever latent grief there is in our nature.

Betimes in the morning we are astir, and the full glory of the view bursts upon us. The peak is the most prominent in the front range, soaring higher than its brothers around; and we have seen it as we approached from the plains. It is yet too early in the season for us to attempt the ascent; the snow lies more than half-way down; but from this little valley, where our tents are pitched, we have one of the finest views possible. The slopes are gentle and almost unbroken for a considerable distance; but, reaching higher, they terminate in sharp, serrated lines, edged with a ribbon of silver light. The snow is not distributed evenly. In some places it lies thick, and others are only partly covered by streaky, map-like patches, revealing the heavy color of the ground and rock beneath. A range of foot-hills of clumsy contour leads the way to the peaks which mount behind them. The park is a lovely spot, sheltered, fertile, and wooded. It

SUMMIT OF GRAY'S PEAK.

is an excellent pasture for large herds of cattle, and is used for that purpose. A few families are also settled here; and, as the valley is the only practicable route for ascending the peak, it is destined, no doubt, to become a stopping-place for future tourists. It is seven thousand seven hundred and eighty-eight feet above the level of the sea, and six thousand three hundred feet below Long's Peak, which is said to be about fourteen thousand and eighty-eight feet high. The peak is composed of primitive rock, twisted and torn into some of the grandest cañons in this famed country of cañons. While we remain here, we are constantly afoot. The naturalists of the expedition are overjoyed at their good fortune, and the photographers are alert to catch all they can while the light lasts. The air is crisp, joyous, balsamic. Ah! that we might never be left alone to hear the secret voice and the dread revelations of these magnificent spaces! But it follows us, and oppresses us; and we are never safe from its importunities without a mirthful, unimpressionable companion. It is a terrible skeleton in the closet of the mountain, and it comes forth to fill us with dismay and grief.

Soon we are on the march again, tramping southward through stilly valleys, climbing monstrous bowlders, fording snow-fed streams, mounting perilous heights, descending awful chasms. Everlasting grandeur! everlasting hills! Then, from cañons almost as great, we enter the Bowlder Cañon, cut deep in the metamorphic rocks of foot-hills for seventeen miles, with walls of solid rock that rise precipitously to a height of three thousand feet in many places. A bubbling stream rushes down the centre, broken in its course by clumsy-looking rocks, and the fallen limbs of trees that have been wrenched from the sparse soil and moss in the crevices. The water is discolored and thick. At the head of the cañon is a mining-settlement, and we meet several horsemen traversing a narrow road that clings to the walls—now on one side, and then, leaping the stream, to the other. The pines, that find no haunt too drear, and no soil too sterile, have striven to hide the nakedness of the rocks; but many a branch is withered and decayed, and those still living are dwarfed and sombre. Bowlder City, at the mouth of the cañon, has a population of about fifteen hundred, and is the centre of the most abundant and extensively developed gold, silver, and coal mining districts in the Territory. Within a short distance from it are Central City, Black Hawk, and Georgetown.

James's Peak comes next in our route, and at its foot we see one of the pretty frozen lakes that are scattered all over the range. It is a picturesque and weird yet tenderly sentimental scene. Mr. Moran has caught its spirit admirably, and his picture gives a fair idea of its beauty. The surface is as smooth as a mirror, and reflects the funereal foliage and snowy robes of the slopes as clearly. It is as chaste as morning, and we can think of ice-goblins chasing underneath the folds of virgin snow that the pale moonlight faintly touches and bespangles. The white dress of the mountain hereabout is unchanged the year round, and only yields tribute to the summer heat in thousands of little brooks, that gather together in the greater streams. The lakes themselves are small basins,

CHICAGO LAKE.

not more than two or three acres in extent, and are ice-locked and snow-bound until the summer is far advanced.

You shall not be wearied by a detailed story of our route, or of the routine of our camp. We are on the wing pretty constantly, the photographers and naturalists working with exemplary zeal in adding to their collections. We are never away from the mountains, and never at a spot devoid of beauty. In the morning we climb a hill, and in the evening march down it. Anon we are under the looming shadows of a steep pass or ravine, and then our eyes are refreshed in a green valley—not such a valley as rests at the foot of Alpine hills, but one that has not been transformed by the cultivator—a waste to Eastern eyes, but a paradise, compared with the more rugged forms around, We are not sure that "beauty unadorned is adorned the most" in this instance. A few hedge-rows here and there, a white farm-house on yonder knoll, a level patch of moist, brown earth freshly ploughed, and a leafy, loaded orchard, might change the sentiment of the thing, but would not make it less beautiful.

We encounter civilization, modified by the conditions of frontier life, in the happily-situated little city of Georgetown, which is in a direct line running westward from Denver City, the starting-point of tourist mountaineers. A great many of you have been there, using its hotel as a base of operations in mountaineering. It is locked in a valley surrounded by far-reaching granite hills, with the silver ribbon of Clear Creek flashing its way through, and forests of evergreens soaring to the ridges. A previous traveller has well said that Europe has no place to compare with it. It is five thousand feet higher than the glacier-walled vale of the Chamouni, and even higher than the snow-girt hospice of Saint-Bernard. Roundabout are wonderful "bits" of Nature, and, from the valley itself, we make the ascent of Gray's Peak, the mountain that, of all others in the land, we have heard the most. We toil up a winding road, meeting plenty of company, of a rough sort, on the way. There are many silver-mines in the neighborhood, and we also meet heavily-laden wagons, full of ore, driven by labor-stained men. The air grows clearer and thinner; we leave behind the forests of aspen, and are now among the pines, silver-firs, and spruces. At last we enter a valley, and see afar a majestic peak, which we imagine is our destination. We are wrong. Ours is yet higher, so we ride on, the horses panting and the men restless. The forest still grows thinner; the trees smaller. Below us are the successive valleys through which we have come, and above us the snowy Sierras, tinted with the colors of the sky. Twelve thousand feet above the level of the sea we reach the Stevens silver-mine, the highest point in Colorado where mining is carried on, and then we pass the limit of tree-life, where only dwarfed forms of Alpine or arctic vegetation exist. A flock of white partridges flutter away at our coming, and two or three conies snarl at us from their nests underneath the rocks. Higher yet! Breathless and fatigued, we urge our poor beasts on in the narrow, almost hidden trail, and are rewarded in due time by a safe arrival at our goal.

ERODED SANDSTONES, MONUMENT PARK.

Foremost in the view are the twin peaks, Gray's and Torrey's; but, in a vast area that seems limitless, there are successive rows of pinnacles, some of them entirely wrapped in everlasting snow, others patched with it, some abrupt and pointed, others reaching their climax by soft curves and gradations that are almost imperceptible. We are on the crest of a continent—on the brink of that New World which Agassiz has told us is the Old. The man who could resist the emotion called forth by the scene, is not among our readers, we sincerely hope. There is a sort of enclosure some feet beneath the very summit of Gray's Peak, or, to speak more exactly, a valley surrounded by walls of snow, dotted by occasional bowlders, and sparsely covered with dwarfed vegetation. Here we encamp and light our fires, and smoke our pipes, while our minds are in a trance over the superb reach before us.

Not very many years ago it was a common thing to find a deserted wagon on the plains, with some skeleton men and two skeleton horses not far off. A story is told that, in one case, the tarpaulin was inscribed with the words "Pike's Peak or Bust." Pike's Peak was then an El Dorado to the immigrants, who, in adventurously seeking it, often fell victims on the gore-stained ground of the Sioux Indians. Foremost in the range, it was the most visible from the plains, and was as a star or beacon to the travellers approaching the mountains from the east. Thither we are now bound, destined to call, on the way, at the Chicago Lakes, Monument Park, and the Garden of the Gods. Chicago Lakes lie at the foot of Mount Rosalie, still farther south, and are the source of Chicago Creek. They are high upon the mountain, at the verge of the timber-line, and that shown in Mr. Moran's picture has an elevation of nearly twelve thousand feet above the level of the sea. Mount Rosalie, ridged with snow, and very rugged in appearance, terminates two thousand two hundred feet higher. Another lake, as smooth and lovely as this, and of about the same size, is found near by, and twelve more are scattered, like so many patches of silver, in the vicinity. The water comes from the snow, and is cool and refreshing on the hottest summer days. Trout are abundant in the streams, and allure many travellers over a terribly bad road from Georgetown. Monument Park is probably more familiar to you than other points in our route. It is filled with fantastic groups of eroded sandstone, perhaps the most unique in the Western country, where there are so many evidences of Nature's curious whims. If one should imagine a great number of gigantic sugar-loaves, quite irregular in shape, but all showing the tapering form, varying in height from six feet to nearly fifty, with each loaf capped by a dark, flat stone, not unlike in shape to a college-student's hat, he would have a very clear idea of the columns in Monument Park. They are for the most part ranged along the low hills on each side of the park, which is probably a mile wide, but here and there one stands out in the open plain. On one or two little knolls, apart from the hills, numbers of these columns are grouped, producing the exact effect of cemeteries with their white-marble columns. The stone is very light in color.

PIKE'S PEAK, FROM GARDEN OF THE GODS.

Upper Twin Lake.

Once more we are on our way, and still in the mountains. We linger a while in the Garden of the Gods, which is five miles northwest of Colorado Springs, as you will see by referring to a map, among the magnificent forms that in some places resemble those we have already seen in Monument Park. There are some prominent cliffs, too; but they are not so interesting as others that we have seen, and are simply horizontal strata, thrown by some convulsion into a perpendicular position. At the "gateway" we are between two precipitous walls of sandstone, two hundred feet apart, and three hundred and fifty feet high. Stretching afar is a gently-sloping foot-hill, and, beyond that, in the distance, we have a glimpse of the faint snow-line of Pike's Peak. The scene is strangely impressive. The walls form almost an amphi-theatre, enclosing a patch of level earth. In the foreground there is an embankment consisting of ap-parently detached rocks, some of them distorted into mushroom-shape, and others secreting shallow pools of water in their darkling hollows. The foliage is scarce and deciduous; gloomily pathetic. A rock rises midway between the walls at the gateway, and else-where in the garden there are monumental forms that remind us of the valley of the Yellowstone.

Teocalli Mountain.

Pike's Peak, seen from the walls, is about ten miles off. It forms, with its spurs, the southeastern boundary of the South Park. It offers no great difficulties in the ascent, and a good trail for horses has been made to the summit, where an "Old Probabilities" has stationed an officer to forecast the coming storms.

Now we bear away to Fairplay, where we join the principal division of the expedition, and thence we visit together Mount Lincoln, Western Pass, the Twin Lakes, and other points in the valley of the Arkansas; cross the National or Mother range into the Elk Mountains; proceed up the Arkansas and beyond its head-waters to the Mount of the Holy Cross. We are exhausting our space, not our subject, and we can only describe at length a few spots in the magnificent country included in our itinerary. At the beginning we spoke about Mount Lincoln, and the glorious view obtained from its summit. When named, during the war, this peak was thought to be eighteen thousand feet high, but more recent measurements have brought it down to about fourteen thousand feet—lower, in fact, than Pike's, Gray's, Long's, Yale, or Harvard, the highest of which has yet to be determined. But its summit commands points in a region of country nearly twenty-five thousand square miles in extent, embracing the grandest natural beauties, a bewildering reach of peaks, valleys, cañons, rivers, and lakes. We find, too, on Mount Lincoln, some lovely Alpine flowers, which grow in profusion even on the very summit, and are of nearly every color and great fragrance. Professor J. D. Whitney, who accompanied the expedition, picked several sweetly-smelling bunches of delicate blue-bells within five feet of the dome of Mount Lincoln. These tender little plants are chilled every night to freezing, and draw all their nourishment from the freshly-melted snow.

Heretofore we have spoken complainingly, it may seem, of the sombre quality of all we have seen, and its deficient power of evoking human sympathy. But at the Twin Lakes we have no more occasion for morbid brooding, but a chance to go into healthy raptures, and to admire some tender, almost pastural scenery. The course of the Arkansas River is southward hereabout, touching the base of the central chain of the mountains. So it continues for one hundred miles, then branching eastward toward the Mississippi. In the lower part of the southward course the valley expands, and is bordered on the east by an irregular mass of low, broken hill-ranges, and on the west by the central range. Twenty miles above this point the banks are closely confined, and form a very picturesque gorge; still further above they again expand, and here are nestled the beautiful Twin Lakes. The larger is about two and a half miles long and a mile and a half wide; the smaller about half that size. At the upper end they are girt by steep and rugged heights; below they are bounded by undulating hills of gravel and bowlders. A broad stream connects the two, and then hurries down the plain to join and swell the Arkansas. Our illustration does not exaggerate the chaste beauty of the upper lake, the smaller of the two. The contour of the surrounding hills is marvellously varied: here softly curving, and yonder soaring to an abrupt peak. In some things it transports us to the western Highlands of Scotland, and, as with their waters, its depths are swarming with the most delicately flavored, the most spirited and largest trout. Sportsmen come here in considerable numbers; and not the least charming object to be met on the banks is an absorbed, contemplative man, seated on some glacier-thrown bowlder, with his slender rod poised and bending gracefully, and a pretty wicker basket, half hidden in the moist grass at his side, ready for the gleaming fish that flaunts his gorgeous colors in the steadily-lapping waters.

We advance from the Twin Lakes into the very heart of the Rocky Mountains, and sojourn in a quiet little valley while the working-force of the expedition explores the

SNOW-MASS MOUNTAIN.

neighboring country. Two summits are ascended from our station, one of them a round peak of granite, full fourteen thousand feet above the level of the sea, and only to

Elk-Lake Cascade.

be reached by assiduous and tiresome scrambling over fractured rocks. This we name La Plata. We are on the grandest uplift on the continent, Professor Whitney believes. The range is of unswerving direction, running north and south for nearly a hundred miles, and is broken into countless peaks over twelve thousand feet high. It is penetrated by deep ravines, which formerly sent great glaciers into the valley; it is composed of granite and eruptive rocks. The northernmost point is the Mount of the Holy Cross, and that we shall visit soon. Advancing again through magnificent upland meadows and amphitheatres, we come at last to Red-Mountain Pass, so named from a curious line of light near the summit, marked for half a mile with a brilliant crimson stain, verging into yellow from the oxidation of iron in the volcanic material. The effect of this, as may be imagined, is wonderfully beautiful. Thence we traverse several ravines in the shadow of the imposing granite mountains, enter fresh valleys, and contemplate fresh wonders. The ardent geologists of the expedition, ever alert, discover one day a ledge of limestone containing corals, and soon we are in a region filled with enormous and surprising developments of that material. We pitch our tents near the base of an immense pyramid, capped with layers of red sandstone, which we name Teocalli, from the Aztec word, meaning "pyramid of sacrifice." The view from our camp is — we

MOUNTAIN OF THE HOLY CROSS.

should say surpassing, could we remember or decide which of all the beauties we have is the grandest. Two hills incline toward the valley where we are stationed, ultimately falling into each other's arms. Between their shoulders there is a broad gap, and, in the rear, the majestic form of the Teocalli reaches to heaven.

In the distance we have seen two mountains which are temporarily called Snow-Mass and Black Pyramid. The first of these we are now ascending. It is a terribly hard road to travel. The slopes consist of masses of immense granitic fragments, the rock-bed from which they came appearing only occasionally. When we reach the crest, we find it also broken and cleft in masses and pillars. Professor Whitney ingeniously reckons that an industrious man, with a crow-bar, could, by a week's industrious exertion, reduce the height of the mountain one or two hundred feet. Some of the members of the expedition amuse themselves by the experiment, toppling over great fragments, which thunder down the slopes, and furrow the wide snow-fields below. It is this snow-field which forms the characteristic feature of the mountain as seen in the distance. There is about a square mile of unbroken white, and, lower down still, a lake of blue water. A little to the northward of Snow-Mass, the range rises into another yet greater mountain. The two are known to miners as " The Twins," although they are not at all alike, as the provisional names we bestowed upon them indicate. After mature delibera-tion the expedition rechristen them the White House and the Capitol, under which names we suppose they will be familiar to future generations. Not a great distance from here, leading down the mountain from Elk Lake, is a picturesque cascade, that finds its way through deep gorges and cañons to the Rio Grande.

The Mountain of the Holy Cross is next reached. This is the most celebrated mountain in the region, but its height, which has been over-estimated, is not more than fourteen thousand feet. The ascent is exceedingly toilsome even for inured mountaineers, and I might give you an interesting chapter describing the difficulties that beset us. There is a very beautiful peculiarity in the mountain, as its name shows. The principal peak is composed of gneiss, and the cross fractures of the rock on the eastern slope have made two great fissures, which cut into one another at right angles, and hold their snow in the form of a cross the summer long.

THE CAÑONS OF THE COLORADO.

WITH ILLUSTRATIONS BY THOMAS MORAN.

Bonita Bend.

NONE of the works of Nature on the American Continent, where many things are done by her upon a scale of grandeur elsewhere unknown, approach in magnificence and wonder the cañons of the Colorado. The river-system of the Colorado is, in extent of area drained, the second or third in the United States. The drainage of the Mississippi is, of course, far more extensive, and the drainage of the Columbia is nearly equal, or perhaps a little greater. It is characteristic of the Colorado that nearly all the streams which unite to form it, or which flow into it, are confined in deep and narrow gorges, with walls often perpendicular. Sometimes the walls rise directly from the water's edge, so that there is only room between for the passage of the stream. In other places, the bottoms of the gorges widen out into valleys, through which roads may pass; and sometimes they contain small tracts of arable land. For the most part, the walls of the cañons of the Colorado-River system are not above a few hundred feet in height; and yet, there are more than a thousand miles of cañons where they rise ten or twelve hundred feet in perpendicular cliffs. The Grand Cañon, which Major Powell calls "the most profound chasm known on the globe," is, for a distance of over two hundred miles, at no point less than four thousand feet deep.

The Green River, which is familiar to every person who has passed over the Union Pacific Railroad, is one of the principal sources of the Colorado. The first successful attempt to explore the Grand Cañon was made by Major J. W. Powell, in 1869. He reached it then by descending the Green River with boats, built in Chicago, and carried by rail to Green-River Station. He accomplished the voyage of nearly a thousand miles in three months, one month being occupied in the passage of the Grand Cañon. Father Escalante had seen the Colorado in 1776, and the map which he constructed shows clearly the point at which he crossed. Fremont and Whipple had seen the cañon; and

Ives, in his expedition of 1857 and 1858, saw the Kanab, one of its largest branches, which he mistook for the Grand Cañon itself. But, previous to Major Powell's voyage of exploration, the course of a great part of the river was as little known as the sources of the Nile; and the accounts of the wonders of the Grand Cañon were held by many to be rather mythical, and greatly exaggerated.

The Colorado is formed by the junction of the Grand and Green Rivers in the eastern part of Utah. The distance from Green-River Station, by the course of the river, to the junction of the two streams, is four hundred fifty-eight and a half miles. The cañons begin very soon after leaving the railroad, and in the series named are Flaming Gorge, Kingfisher, and Red Cañons, Cañon of Lodore, Whirlpool and Yampa Cañons, Cañon of Desolation, Gray, Labyrinth, Stillwater, Cataract, Narrow, Glen, and Marble Cañons. Each has some peculiar characteristic, which, in most instances, is indicated by the name. There is generally no break in the walls between the different cañons, the divisions being marked by remarkable changes in their geological structure. The cañons whose names above precede Cataract, are on Green River before it joins the waters of the Grand.

Labyrinth is one of the lower cañons of the Green River. It is a wide and beautiful cañon, with comparatively low walls, but perpendicular and impassable. Indeed, from Gunnison's Crossing, one hundred and sixteen miles above the junction of the Grand and Green, to the running out of the Grand Cañon, a distance of five hundred eighty-seven and a half miles, there are only two places, and they are not more than a mile apart, where the river and its chasm can be crossed. At one point in Labyrinth Cañon, the river makes a long bend, in the bow of which it sweeps around a huge circular *butte*, whose regular and perpendicular walls look as though they might have been laid by a race of giant craftsmen. At a distance the pile resembles a vast, turret-shaped fortress, deserted and partly broken down. This point in the river is called Bonita Bend, and a view of it has been drawn by Mr. Moran from photographs taken by Major Powell's party. The waters in this cañon are smooth and shoal, and afforded the explorers, for many miles, a grateful rest from the toil and danger of shooting rapids, or making wearisome portages of the boats.

The junction of the Grand and Green Rivers brings together a flood of waters about equal in volume to the flow of Niagara. The Grand and Green meet in a narrow gorge more than two thousand feet deep; and at this point the cañons of the Colorado begin.

The first is called Cataract Cañon. It is about forty miles long. The descent of the river through this cañon is very great, and the velocity acquired by the current is sometimes equal to the speed of the fastest railroad-train. Great buttresses of the walls stand out into the rushing flood at frequent intervals, turning the rapid current into boiling whirlpools, which were encountered by the adventurous boatmen with great peril and

GLEN CAÑON.

labor. At the foot of Cataract Cañon, the walls of the chasm approach each other, and, for a distance of seven miles, the water rushes through Narrow Cañon at the rate of forty miles an hour.

At the end of Narrow Cañon, the character of the gorge changes, and, from that point to the place where the Paria River enters the Colorado, a distance of a hundred and forty and a half miles, it is called Glen Cañon. At the mouth of the Paria, a trail leads down the cliffs to the bottom of the cañon on both sides, and animals and wagons can be taken down and crossed over in boats. The Indians swim across on logs.

A mile above the Paria is the Crossing of the Fathers, where Father Escalante and his hundred priests passed across the cañon. An alcove in this cañon, which the artist has drawn, illustrates the general character of the walls, and the scenery from which the cañon takes its name. The smooth and precipitous character of the walls of Glen Cañon is well shown in the illustration. The chasm is carved in homogeneous red sandstone, and in some places, for a thousand feet on the face of the rock, there is scarce a check or seam.

Buttresses of Marble Cañon.

The most beautiful of all the cañons begins at the mouth of the Paria, and extends to the junction of the Little Colorado, or Chiquito, as it is called by the Indians. This part of the gorge is named Marble Cañon and is sixty-five and a half miles long. The walls are of limestone or marble, beautifully carved and polished, and the forms assumed have the most remarkable resemblances to ruined architecture. The colors of the marble are various—pink, brown, gray, white, slate-color, and vermilion. The beautiful forms, with a suggestion of the grand scale on which they are constructed, are given by the two views in this cañon, which the artist has drawn. But it is only on large canvas, and by the use of the many-tinted brush, that any reproduction can be made, approaching truthfulness, of the combination of the grand and beautiful exhibited in the sculpturing, the colors, and the awful depth, of Marble Cañon.

MARBLE CAÑON.

The Marble Cañon runs out at the junction of the Chiquito and Colorado, at which point the Grand Cañon begins. The head of the Grand Cañon is in the northeastern part of Arizona, and it runs out in the northwestern part, lying wholly within that Territory. Its general course is westerly, but it makes two great bends to the south. It is two hundred and seventeen and a half miles long, and the walls vary in height from four thousand to six thousand two hundred and thirty-three feet. It is cut through a series of levels of varying altitudes, the chasm being deepest, of course, where it passes through the highest. There are in the cañon no perpendicular cliffs more than three thousand feet in height. At that elevation from the river, the sides slope back, and rise by a series of perpendicular cliffs and benches to the level of the surrounding country. In many places it is possible to find gorges or side-cañons, cutting down through the upper cliffs, by which it is possible, and in some instances easy, to approach to the edge of the wall which rises perpendicularly from the river. At three thousand feet above the river, the chasm is often but a few hundred feet wide. At the highest elevation mentioned, the distance across is generally from five to ten miles.

At various places the chasm is cleft through the primal granite rock to the depth of twenty-eight hundred feet. In those parts of the cañon, which are many miles of its whole extent, the chasm is narrow, the walls rugged, broken, and precipitous, and the navigation of the river dangerous. The daring voyagers gave profound thanks, as though they had escaped from death, whenever they passed out from between the walls of granite into waters confined by lime or sandstone. Mr. Moran has drawn a section of these granite walls, showing some of the pinnacles and buttresses which are met at every turn of the river. The waters rush through the granite cañons at terrific speed. Great waves, formed by the irregular sides and bottom, threatened every moment to engulf the boats. Spray dashes upon the rocks fifty feet above the edge of the river, and the gorge is filled with a roar as of thunder, which is heard many miles away.

Fortunately, the wonders of the Grand Cañon can now be seen without incurring any of the peril, and but little of the hardship, endured by Major Powell and his companions. The writer of this, and Mr. Moran, the artist, visited two of the most interesting points in the cañon in July and August, 1873. We travelled by stage in hired vehicles—they could not be called carriages—and on horseback from Salt-Lake City to Toquerville, in Southwestern Utah, and thence about sixty miles to Kanab, just north of the Arizona line. Quite passable roads have been constructed by the Mormons this whole distance of about four hundred miles. At Kanab we met Professor A. H. Thompson, in charge of the topographical work of Major Powell's survey, and, with guides and companions from his camp, we visited the cañon.

Our first journey was to the Toroweap Valley, about seventy miles. By following down this valley we passed through the upper line of cliffs to the edge of a chasm cut

WALLS OF THE GRAND CAÑON.

in red sandstone and vermilion-colored limestone, or marble, twenty-eight hundred feet deep, and about one thousand feet wide. Creeping out carefully on the edge of the precipice, we could look down directly upon the river, fifteen times as far away as the waters of the Niagara are below the bridge. Mr. Hillers, who has passed through the cañon with Major Powell, was with us, and he informed us that the river below was a raging torrent; and yet it looked, from the top of the cliff, like a small, smooth, and sluggish river. The view looking up the cañon is magnificent and beautiful beyond the most extravagant conception of the imagination. In the foreground lies the profound gorge, with a mile or two of the river seen in its deep bed. The eye looks twenty miles or more through what appears like a narrow valley, formed by the upper line of cliffs. The many-colored rocks in which this valley is carved, project into it in vast headlands, two thousand feet high, wrought into beautiful but gigantic architectural forms. Within an hour of the time of sunset the effect is strangely awful, weird, and dazzling. Every moment until light is gone the scene shifts, as one monumental pile passes into shade, and another, before unobserved, into light. But no power of description can aid the imagination to picture it, and only the most gifted artist, with all the materials that artists can command, is able to suggest any thing like it.

Our next visit was to the Kai-bal Plateau, the highest plateau through which the cañon cuts. It was only after much hard labor, and possibly a little danger, that we reached a point where we could see the river, which we did from the edge of Powell Plateau, a small plain severed from the main-land by a precipitous gorge, two thousand feet deep, across which we succeeded in making a passage. Here we beheld one of the most awful scenes upon our globe. While upon the highest point of the plateau, a terrific thunder-storm burst over the cañon. The lighting flashed from crag to crag. A thousand streams gathered on the surrounding plains, and dashed down into the depths of the cañon in water-falls many times the height of Niagara. The vast chasm which we saw before us, stretching away forty miles in one direction and twenty miles in another, was nearly seven thousand feet deep. Into it all the domes of the Yosemite, if plucked up from the level of that valley, might be cast, together with all the mass of the White Mountains in New Hampshire, and still the chasm would not be filled.

Kanab Cañon is about sixty miles long, and, by following its bed, one can descend to the bottom of the Grand Cañon. It is a very difficult task, requiring several days' severe labor. We were forced, by lack of time, which other engagements absorbed, to abandon the undertaking The picture drawn by the artist of a pinnacle in one of the angles of the Kanab is from a photograph taken by Mr. Hillers. The pinnacle itself is about eight hundred, and the wall in the background of the illustration more than four thousand feet in altitude. A railroad is projected from Salt-Lake City to the southern settlements, and, when it is constructed, some of the most remarkable portions of the Grand Cañon of the Colorado will be as accessible as the valley of the Yosemite.

KANAB CAÑON.

CHICAGO AND MILWAUKEE.

WITH ILLUSTRATIONS BY ALFRED R. WAUD.

Glimpse of Lake Michigan.

CHICAGO is as incomparable, in its own way, as Rome. Its history is as brilliant as it is brief, and, of all young American cities, it is the most famous. Less than half a century ago it was an Indian trading-station, with a mixed population of one hundred whites, blacks, and red-men. Long before the site was visited by a white man, it was, as we learn from "THE AMERICAN CYCLOPÆDIA," a favorite rendezvous for several Indian tribes in succession. The earliest recorded were the Tamaroas, the most powerful of many tribes of the Illini (whence the name of Illinois). The word Chicago is Indian, probably corrupted from *Cheecaqua*, the name of a long line of chiefs, meaning "strong," a word also applied to a wild-onion that grew plentifully on the banks of the river that now winds through its busy streets. Let us accept only the first interpretation

THE CITY FROM THE WATER WORKS.

CHICAGO.

of the word, and see in the present glories of the city a transmitted worth from the dusky heroes that once assembled on the spot for words of wisdom or deeds of valor. It was first visited by Marquette in 1673, and shortly afterward by other French explorers. The first geographical notice occurs in a map dated Quebec, Canada, 1683, as Fort Checagou. A fort was built by the French, and abandoned when Canada was ceded to Great Britain. Fort Dearborn was built in 1804, by the United States Government, on the south bank of the Chicago River, near its mouth. In 1812, when the war with Great Britain broke out, the government ordered the fort to be abandoned, fearing it could not be held. The garrison and others marched out, and, when a mile and a half from the fort, were attacked by the Pottawattamie Indians, who massacred sixty of them, including two women and twelve children, and then destroyed the fort. In 1816 the fort was rebuilt, and demolished in 1856. Chicago scarcely advanced a single step in the hundred and fifty years that followed the landing of Marquette. For a long time a few rude timber huts and a mission-house, on the low banks of the creeping stream, comprised the settlement. It had no natural beauties to invite immigrants with a taste for the picturesque. Few trees sheltered it from the hot shafts of the sun. North, south, and west, the prairie reached to the horizon; and, from eastward, Lake Michigan rolled in on a flat beach, with mournful reverberations. But, if it was deficient in beauties, it was rich in natural facilities for commercial intercourse. With the filling up of the West, the town began to show the natural advantages of its situation. In 1831 it contained about twelve families besides the garrison in Fort Dearborn, but in 1833 it contained five hundred and fifty inhabitants. In 1837 it was incorporated as a city, when the inhabitants numbered four thousand one hundred and seventy. In 1850 the population reached twenty-eight thousand two hundred and ninety-six, in 1860 one hundred and nine thousand two hundred and sixty-three, and in 1870 nearly three hundred thousand souls, exclusive of the suburban. It is now the fifth city of the Union.

Chicago is situated on the west shore of Lake Michigan, eighteen miles north of the extreme southern point of the lake, at the mouth of a bayou, or river. The site of the business portion is fourteen feet above the level of the lake. It was originally much lower, but has been filled up from three to nine feet since 1856. It is divided into three parts by a bayou, called the Chicago River, which extends from the lake-shore about five-eighths of a mile, then divides into two branches, running north and south, nearly parallel with the lake, about two miles in each direction. The river and its branches, with numerous slips, give a water-frontage, not including the lake-front, of thirty-eight miles.

The destruction of the larger part of Chicago by fire, in 1871, is still fresh in the memory of every reader—a conflagration the most destructive of modern times, which was followed by a rebuilding of the city with an expedition and in a style of splendor that have made it the marvel of the age. Almost the entire business and much of the

Chicago river from Madison St. bridge.

Portico of the Board of Trade.

Entrance to Chicago River.

Michigan Avenue.

On Wabash Avenue.

SCENES IN CHICAGO.

residence portion of the city were destroyed, the burned area covering nearly three and a half square miles, the number of buildings destroyed being over seventeen thousand, including the Court-House, Custom-House, Post-Office, forty-one churches, thirty-two hotels, ten theatres and halls, the total loss being estimated at one hundred and ninety million dollars.

Upon these ruins has arisen a city of singular beauty. It cannot be claimed, in the rapidly-constructed architecture of the city, that the best taste has always been followed. An excess of trivial ornament is everywhere apparent. But the business portion of the city has fewer evidences of bad taste than elsewhere, while the general effect of the façades is striking and even admirable. In all other American cities there is an unpleasant incongruity in the architecture—splendid warehouses cheek-by-jowl with mean ones, tall structures jutting up by short ones. This unhandsome irregularity is prevented in Paris by municipal regulation, and has for the most part been avoided in Chicago, inasmuch as all the structures are new, erected according to the latest taste and most developed ideas in architecture, and because the builders have seemed to act with some sort of coöperation. The view on the next page, entitled "Madison Street," gives a good idea of the beauty of the façades in the new business portion. This fact gives Chicago the palm among American cities in an important particular.

Our American cities are not usually picturesque. Their sites were selected for commercial convenience; hence they are generally flat. Time has not yet mellowed their tints, nor age given quaintness to their structures. Long rows of handsome business façades, and avenues of embowered cottages, however gratifying to their citizens, do not supply the stuff which the soul of the artist hungers for. But Chicago has one very striking picturesque feature. This is its river, winding through its heart, lined with warehouses, filled with vessels, and crossed by bridges. Here is a grateful change to the monotony of stone and mortar; here are animation, rich contrasts of color and form, picturesque confusion—all that sort of stir and variety that an artist delights in. This river one encounters in almost any direction that he may proceed; and one who loves to watch moving ships, hurrying boats, bustling shores, thronged bridges, can amuse himself for hours in studying the ever-varying picture. There are thirty-three of these bridges; but, ample as this communication might seem, the impatient citizens found that the draws of the bridges were so constantly open for passing vessels that, in order to facilitate connection with different parts of the city, tunnels have been constructed under the river. These add a novel and interesting feature to the city, as well as greatly facilitate intercourse between the parts separated by the river.

A very beautiful portion of the city was not destroyed in the great conflagration. This included several fine avenues of residences extending toward the south. Wabash Avenue and Michigan Avenue are as famous as Fifth Avenue of New York, although not resembling that famous thoroughfare. They are of a semi-suburban character, lined

Chicago river.

Jefferson Park.

Madison Street.

Chicago river from Clark St Bridge.

West Side from Lake Street Bridge.

SCENES IN CHICAGO.

Clay Cliffs, Shore of Lake Michigan.

with tree-shadowed villas and mansions, and fine churches; and here, at all fashionable hours, may be seen gay throngs of carriages, equestrians, and pedestrians.

Chicago has a noble system of public parks, covering an area of nineteen hundred acres, and numbering six distinct enclosures. All are not yet completed. One park lies on the lake-shore, and affords a delightful drive by the green-tinted waters of the great inland sea. Lincoln Park is very charming, with its little lake, its winding stream crossed by many pretty little bridges, its sylvan glades, and its wooded knolls; and Jefferson Park has similar charming features.

Among objects of interest are the great tunnel for supplying the city with water from the lake; artesian wells; towering grain-elevators, from the tops of which expansive views may be had; immense stock-yards; and the usual educational, literary, and art institutions that in every American city spring up side by side with the material interests.

Milwaukee lies about ninety miles directly northward from Chicago, with

SUNSET, LAKE MICHIGAN.

which there is communication both by rail and by steamers. The sail is very pleasant, and occupies only a few hours. If you leave Chicago in the evening, you may see one of the lake-sunsets of which so much is heard—a sunset in which the sun descends behind rolling banks of clouds, shedding the most gorgeous hues on the sky and on the sea. On the way northward the shore of the lake assumes extraordinary forms, especially at a suburb of Chicago called Lake Forest, which is about twenty-eight miles from the city. Here the ground is soft and clayey, and the constantly encroaching surf has worn it into curious columns and peaks, some of them twisted and seamed in the most astonishing fashion. The forms are constantly changing under the action of the

Shore of Lake Michigan.

water, and we are told that, after a gale, during which the surf has been very high, the appearance of the shore is almost completely changed in many places. At one point, a bank reaches to the water in sharply-serrated ridges, which have the exact appearance of miniature mountain-ranges. The narrow line of sandy beach is often strewed with wrecked trees that have been torn from their beds and still hold their leaves. A more melancholy sight than these wanton ravages of Nature present can scarcely be imagined. A short distance from the shore, however, the country is very picturesque, and many Chicago merchants have chosen it as the seat of their summer villas.

Occasionally the shore rises into a noble bluff, sinking again into a beach, with a

THE SHORE AT LAKE FOREST.

gloomy wood in the rear. There are several towns and villages on the route, with here and there a white fishing-station, consisting of a rude hut on a low beach, and half a dozen row-boats. The most important of the towns are Kenosha and Racine. Kenosha lies some fifty miles north of Chicago; it is situated on a high bluff, has a good harbor, and the surrounding country is a beautiful, fertile prairie. Racine, which lies seven miles farther to the north, is in size the second city of the State of Wisconsin in population and commerce, and is noted for a good harbor. It is situated at the

Lake Michigan, near Lake Forest.

foot of Rock River, on a plain forty feet above the level of the lake, and is handsomely laid out in wide and well-built streets. Immense piers, stretching far out into the lake, are a characteristic feature. Racine has a college named after the place.

Milwaukee, like Chicago, is prepossessing. It is the commercial capital of Wisconsin, and has a population of nearly eighty thousand souls. Like Chicago, too, it is divided into three districts East, West, and South, by a junction of the Menomonee and the Milwaukee Rivers. The area embraced is seventeen miles square, and contains

Fishing-station.

Kenosha Harbor.

Kenosha.

one hundred and sixty streets, with fourteen thousand dwellings in nine wards. The river has been dammed, and its banks are the site of several important industries. The ground is more hilly than in Chicago; and Milwaukee, in some particulars, may claim to be the prettier. A large proportion of the population consists of Germans, who give the city a distinctive character and appearance. The Americans say that they are like the inhabitants of a village, and are all familiar with one another's names and business. But, while the visitor is constantly confronted by German signs, and his ears are constantly filled with German sounds, Milwaukee people have the noticeable briskness of manner peculiar to the Northwest.

The city has so many domes, turrets, cupolas, spires, and towers, that you might imagine yourself in some Mediterranean port, especially if it happened that you had never been in a Mediterranean port. The architecture is diverse in the extreme, combining the most widely-different styles; but it is invariably ornate, and lavishes plaster statuary, plaster and iron castings, scroll-work, and filigree, without distinction, on the smallest and largest buildings. As we all know, Milwaukee is called the "Cream City of the Lakes," not because it is famously lactescent, but because the color of the brick used is a delicate yellow. This material produces some very pretty effects, and is used very largely. The outlying residence-streets are well sheltered by trees and shrubbery, and most of the houses have large gardens in the front and rear, with ample porticos reaching out. Grottos and arbors are also found in many gardens, the arbors sometimes being of the most curious form, enlivened by the brightest paints.

The river is navigable for the largest class of lake-vessels two miles inland from the lake, and is spanned by several bridges. The wharves are substantially built out of wood, and are lined with handsome and extensive structures, vastly superior to those found on the water-front of Chicago and New York. Propellers of a thousand tons' burden are moored at the very door-ways of the newest and finest warehouses, and their gangways lead con-

Racine.

CITY OF MILWAUKEE.

MILWAUKEE RIVER, AT MILWAUKEE.

veniently into the best markets. The river, indeed, is an attractive resort, and a pair of four-oared shells are often to be seen pulling briskly among the fleet of steamers and sailing-vessels ever moving in the stream. Milwaukee manufactures nearly three million gallons of lager-beer annually. Immense brick breweries, capacious beer gardens and saloons, abound ; but the beer-drinkers are church-goers, and support sixty religious edifices, of various denominations, besides many excellent literary institutions and schools. Among the curiosities of the place are the elevators, which have a storage capacity for five million bushels of grain, one of them alone having a capacity for one million five hundred bushels. There is also a flouring-mill, which grinds one thousand barrels of flour daily. But we cannot even mention all the things that are to be seen in Milwaukee, and can only add that, as it is one of the most charming, it is also one of the most active and prosperous of the cities in the Western country.

The name "Milwaukee" carries in its sound the evidence of its Indian origin. It is a modified spelling of "Milwacky," the designation given by the Indians to a small village near the site of the present city, and is said to signify "rich or beautiful land." Like so many of the Western cities that we carelessly call new and young, Milwaukee has a history reaching far beyond the time of written records. Not only are there relics here of very ancient Indian habitations, but the mounds found and opened near the town show unmistakable proofs of the residence of an even earlier race, whose very traditions are now extinct.

The authentic and recorded story of the site of the city is, it is true, very brief. We have no mention of any earlier visitor of European race to this region than Father Marquette, the indefatigable French explorer, who came here in 1674. After him, very few, except Jesuit missionaries and occasional traders, visited the place, until the beginning of the present century In 1818 a trader of French descent settled in the Indian village of Milwacky—one Salomon Juneau, whose family were the only white inhabitants until 1835. After the Black-Hawk War, when the Indians were pressed farther to the west, others came and settled near Juneau's block-house. George Walker and Byron Kilbourn appear to share with the Frenchman the honor of founding the actual town. From their village to the Milwaukee of to-day is a change too often repeated in our Western cities to continue a matter of wonder.

A GLANCE AT THE NORTHWEST.

WITH ILLUSTRATIONS BY ALFRED R. WAUD.

WISCONSIN people are generally quiet about the beauties of their State, and submissively listen to a great deal of random talk about lone backwoods and prairie-wastes, that people who have not been there ignorantly diffuse. But if, perchance, when you are planning a summer's vacation, you should feel weary of the more frequented routes of travel, you cannot do better than devote a week or longer to a journey that includes many more picturesque features than these backwoods and prairie-wastes. Go round the great lakes, for instance; break the voyage at one of the lake-ports—say Manitowoc, or Sheboygan—and find your way to the Wisconsin River by the Central Wisconsin Railway.

The guide-books and gazetteers have very little to say on the subject. The most that you will learn from them is, that the natural feature peculiar to the State is the uniformity of its elevation and the shape of its surface, which is neither mountainous, nor flat, nor hilly, but gently undulating; that the river Wisconsin has its entire course within the State, and

In Rood's Glen.

that it flows centrally, and enters the Mississippi, on its eastern border; that the only notable hills in the State are a range to the west of the river, which still do not deserve the name of mountains; that woodland is abundant, and especially increases in thickness near Green Bay, although it is diversified with rolling prairie, marsh, and swamp.

But there is much besides to be seen in this neglected State, and you will do well to pick out your own route, or select the rambling one that we followed last autumn. Near Kilbourn City, a sluggish little town, about half-way between the source and the mouth of the Wisconsin River, touched by the Lacrosse branch of the Milwaukee and St. Paul Railroad, you will find Rood's Glen, a bit of scenery that will vividly recall to your memory Havana and Watkins Glens, the structure of which it resembles very closely, as will be seen in our artist's sketch. It is deep-set between walls of soft-looking limestone and moist earth, fissured and wrinkled into many ledges and terraces, which are so near together in some parts as to almost form a cavern. The bottom is smooth and sandy, covered with a shallow pool, which reflects the bright greenery of the trees and grass that are twisted and interlocked into a natural arch overhead. Some leafy boughs start out from the moss, their stalks interlaced in closest union; and, as they sway and rustle in the breeze, the cool blue of the sky and rifts of fleecy cloud are also mirrored in the silver pool, with the sombre green of the mossy recesses, the brown shadow of the walls, and the lighter, fresher shades of the grass and foliage. It is a beautiful spot, where you may rest in sweet idleness for hours, listening to the cadenced trickling of the spring as it blends with the fluttering of the leaves and the chorus of birds in the fields around.

And not many miles from this unheard-of city of Kilbourn are other scenes, not less picturesque. In Barraboo County, in a basin for the most part walled in with abrupt hills, reposes the Devil's Lake, a sheet of water as pretty as its name is repellent. It is of no great extent, not more than one and a half mile in length; and it does not figure in the maps. But it is a gem of Nature; and, in the autumn, the contrast of its still, emerald-green waters with the rich colors of the foliage, and the weird forms of its gray rocks, is inexpressibly lovely. Its origin was, without doubt, volcanic, the surrounding cliffs bearing evidences of the action of great heat as well as of frost. Round about, too, are many extraordinary forms, a description of which would fill a long and interesting chapter. The Devil's Door-way, of which we give an illustration, is characteristic; and from its portals we obtain an excellent view of a portion of the lake, and the serene vale of Kirkwood, with its orchards, and the vineyards that are already celebrated for their wine. Beyond these are wide reaches of hill and forest, thick with a dusky growth of spruce, pine, birch, oak, and aspen, extending to the water's edge, and abounding with deer and other game. Cleopatra's Needle is another of the curious monuments of Nature's freaks to which we have alluded. It is an isolated column of rock, nearly sixty

DEVIL'S DOOR-WAY, DEVIL'S LAKE, WISCONSIN

Cleopatra's Needle, Devil's Lake, Wisconsin.

feet high, piercing a surrounding bosket at a point where the cliffs are sheer to the bosom of the lake.

Regaining the river, we travel southward, in the track of the railroad part of the way, passing Lone Rock, a dot of an island in the mid-stream. It is nearly circular in form, with an area of not many square yards; and its sides have a streaky, corrugated appearance. A score or so of thin, repressed pine-trees do their best to shield its barrenness and be friendly ; but it will not be comforted, and stands out bleakly, the current lapping and eddying sadly at its feet. At another point of the river the boundary rocks counterfeit the sterns of four or five steamboats moored together, with their several tiers of galleries, one above another; and, as we approach the Dalles near the mouth, there are two isolated rocks on the river-bank—one of them closely resembling a cobbler's awl, and the other slightly suggesting the same unromantic article. Hereabout the stream

Lone Rock, Wisconsin River.

straggles through a desolate, wild, melancholy reach of flat land, with low-lying forests of timber around ; and the general inclination of the scenery to look like something artificial is again manifest in an opposite rock, the outlines of which hint at the paddle-box of a steamer. In the Dalles we pass through six miles of enchanting beauty. The word (pronounced *dälz*), which has become very common in the West, is of French origin, and means "a trough." Hence it is bestowed on this part of the river, which passes between hills of solid limestone, from thirty to one hundred feet high. The forms are among the most picturesque that we have yet seen. Some of the rocks rise sharply from the water, and extend outward near their summits, so as to form a sort of shelter for the luxuriant grass that crops out in slender, wavy blades from the shoals. Others are perpendicular from their base to the table-land above, which is richly verdant with grass, and evergreen shrubs and trees. Here there is a narrow slope, bringing leafy boughs to the water's edge; and yonder a shadowy inlet, its entrance hidden by a curtain of delicately colored, seemingly luminous leaves. The shadows on the water are of exquisitely varied hues and forms. The sky, the clouds, the leaves, are mingled on the unruffled

Steamboat Rock, Wisconsin River.

surface, save where the massive rock intervenes. At the Jaws we move from one spot which we think the most lovely to another that excels, and on through inexhaustible beauties, in a state of unalloyed rapture. There is as much "life" in the Dalles as the most sociable of tourists could desire. On fine days in the summer the water is skimmed by pleasure-barges and row-boats, filled with gayly-dressed people from neighboring towns; and at all times lumber-rafts are descending slowly to the Mississippi, manned by half-savage, outlandish fellows, thoroughly picturesque in aspect, if nothing else. The rocks

STAND ROCK, ON THE WISCONSIN RIVER.

echo the laughter and songs of the pleasure-seekers, who pause to cheer us as we paddle farther down the stream toward the great river of the Southwest.

Scattered over the plains of Wisconsin are found curious earthworks of fantastic and extraordinary forms, relics of a race that inhabited Wisconsin centuries ago. At Aztalan, in Jefferson County, there is an ancient fortification, five hundred and fifty yards

Dalles of the Wisconsin, "The Jaws."

long, two hundred and seventy-five yards wide, with walls four or five feet high. There are also numerous water-falls to be seen—the Chippewa, Big Bull, Grandfather Bull, and the St. Croix—all of them interesting and accessible ; besides, Pentwell Peak, an oval mass of rock, three hundred feet wide, two hundred feet high, and nine hundred feet long ; and Fortification Rock, a picturesque stroke of Nature, which towers one hundred

THE DALLES OF THE ST. LOUIS.

feet high, and on one side is a sheer precipice, while on the other an easy descent is made to the plain by a series of natural terraces.

From Wisconsin we run northward to the thriving town of Duluth and the St.-Louis River, and visit the Dalles of the St. Louis, which are better known, but not more beautiful, than other places we have already seen in our tour. The sentiment of the scene is not inspiriting; Nature is harsh, rugged, and sombre, tearing her way in a water-course four miles long, with a descent of four hundred feet. The banks are formed

Red River, Dakota.

of cold, gray slate-rocks, clad with an ample growth of bleak pine, and twisted, split, and torn into the wildest of shapes. Through the dismal channel thus bordered the current surges with terrific force, leaping and eddying, and uttering a savage roar that the neighboring hills sullenly reverberate. Here and there an immense bowlder opposes and is nearly hidden by the seething, hissing, foamy waves, which dance and struggle around and over it, sometimes submerging it, and then, exhausted, falling into a quieter pace. Occasionally the spray leaps over the banks, and forms a silver thread of a rivulet, which trickles over the stones until its little stream tumbles into the unsparing current again, and is lost. This continuous rapid of four miles is a grand, deeply impressive sight; but on a stormy day, when great white clouds are rolling downward, and the wind adds its voice to that of the turbulent waters, we shiver and sigh involuntarily as we contemplate it.

From Minnesota we cross to the Red River of the North, in Dakota—a stream with an evil reputation for its sadness and loneliness. The names of its surroundings are far from encouraging—such as Thief River, Snake River, and Devil's Lake—but some of the scenery has a quiet, pastoral character, as will be seen in the accompanying sketches. The water is muddy and sluggish, and within Minnesota alone is navigable four hundred miles, for vessels of three feet draught, four months in the year. The banks are comparatively low, and are luxuriantly grassy and woody. There are "bits" of secluded landscape that transport us to New England, but we are soon recalled by a glimpse of an Indian trail through the grass, a canoe toiling against the stream, and a clump of decaying trees in withered, uncared-for desolation.

Indian Trail, Bank of Red River.

THE MAMMOTH CAVE.

WITH ILLUSTRATIONS BY ALFRED R. WAUD.

THE Mammoth Cave of Kentucky is the largest known cave in the world. It is situated near Green River, on the road from Louisville to Nashville. Some explorers claim to have penetrated it to a distance of ten miles; but they probably exaggerate, as the paths through it are so tortuous, and the progress of the traveller is so much obstructed, that they might easily be deceived. Stalactites of gigantic size and fantastic form are seen here, though they are not as brilliant as those that adorn other and smaller caves elsewhere. But, if the Mammoth Cave is deficient in pretty effects, it is crowded with wild, fantastic, and deeply impressive forms, that almost forbid the intrusion of the curiosity-seeking tourist from the surface of the earth.

The railway deposits you at Cave City, and thence a stage-ride of ten miles brings you to an old-fashioned Kentucky hotel, where guides are procured for the exploration. Each person is provided with a lamp; and then you are led, in military order, by a pompous negro, who shouts "Halt!" and "March!" with comical gravity, down a path

SCENES IN MAMMOTH CAVE.

that enters a wooded ravine, and, slanting aside, terminates suddenly at the portals of the cave. The entrance is abundantly supplied with vegetation. Trailing plants descend from the arch above; grass and moss grow thickly around; and the cool beauty of the scene is enhanced by a slender thread of water, which falls continually into a small pool below. But you have little time to linger here. The conductor lights the lamps, and, in a severe voice, calls "Forward!" A few lichens wander a little way in from the entrance, with the daylight, and then all vegetation abruptly ceases. You are ushered into a primitive chaos of wild limestone forms, moist with the water oozing from above. A strong current of air is behind you, as you think; but it is in reality the "breath" of the cave. In explanation, you are told that the temperature of the cave is fifty-nine degrees Fahrenheit the year round, and the cave exhales or inhales, as the temperature outside is above or below this uniform standard. As you proceed farther, the chill felt near the entrance passes away, and the air is still, dry, and warm.

For nearly half a mile on your way you see, in the dim light, the ruins of the salt-petre works that were built in 1808, by persons in the employ of the United States Government. The huge vats and tools still remain undecayed. The print of an ox's hoof is embedded in the hard floor, and the ruts of cart-wheels are also traceable.

Advancing farther, you enter the Rotunda, which is illuminated for a moment by a sheet of oiled paper lighted by the guide. It is over seventy-five feet high, one hundred and sixty feet across, directly under the dining-room of the hotel, and the beginning of the main cave. These things are imparted to you, in a loud voice, by the guide. The lamps throw a feeble light on the dark, irregular walls, broken in places by the mysterious entrances to several avenues which lead from the main cave, and are said to extend altogether a distance of one hundred miles! What if the lights should go out? The thoughtful guide is provided with matches, and he will proudly tell you that there is scarcely a spot into which a traveller could stray that he is not familiar with. As you tramp onward, your companions ahead are rimmed with light; and, if your imagination is active, you might transform them into gnomes or other inhabitants of the subterranean world, albeit their movements are sedate as those of gnomes doing penance. Anon, too, the supernatural aspect of the scene is heightened by the fluttering of a bat that spins out of a dark crevice for an instant, and disappears again in the all-enveloping darkness. If you have courage to look, you will find nests of his brethren in the walls, and a sly rat will dart away at your approach. One chamber, entered from the Rotunda, bears the unattractive name of the Great Bat-Room; and here thousands of the little creatures are found snarling and curling their delicate lips at all intruders. These and the rats, a few lizards, a strange kind of cricket, and some eyeless fish, constitute the entire animal life of this kingdom of everlasting gloom.

From the Rotunda you pass beneath the beetling Kentucky Cliffs, and enter the Gothic Chapel, a low-roofed chamber of considerable extent. Several twisted pillars

THE LOVERS LEAP

THE ALTAR

THE STAR CHAMBER

THE DEAD SEA

THE VESTIBULE . KENTUCKY CLIFFS

ON THE LAKE

THE GIANTS COFFIN

SCENES IN MAMMOTH CAVE.

ascend from the ground into arches formed of jagged rock, and, in the distance, there are two which form an altar of glittering splendor as the light falls on their brilliant stalactites. Near here, too, is the Bridal Chamber, and the guide will tell you how a certain maiden, having promised at the death-bed of her mother that she would not marry any man on the face of the earth, came down to this dark place and was married. He will also tell you that these great stalactites that are so massive take fifty years to grow to the thickness of a sheet of paper. Then, with a sharp word of command, he will lead you on into fresh wonders.

There are rivers and lakes among the mysteries of the Mammoth Cave, and you are floated in a small boat on the dark, stilly, lone waters, among columns and walls, arches and spires, leaden-hued rock and jewelled stalactites, lighted up by a flaring torch in the guide's hand. Memory cannot retain a distinct idea of the thousand weird forms that are constantly flitting before the eye. As you pass one point, a mass of rock assumes a human form, lowering upon you, and the next instant it vanishes from the sight into the darkness.

The next halt is in another wide room, in the middle of which rests an immense rock, in the exact shape of a sarcophagus. This is called the Giant's Coffin, and the guide, leaving you alone for a minute or two, reappears on its lid, his form, shadowed on the wall, imitating all his movements. Above the shadow you will notice the figure of an ant-eater, one of the many shapes with which the ceilings of the caverns are adorned by the oxide of iron. You will then rest a while under the Mammoth Dome, which appears much over a hundred feet high, with its magnificent walls of sheer rock, and at Napoleon's Dome, which is smaller than the former, but hardly less interesting. Afterward the guide will conduct you to the edge of a projecting rock overlooking a hollow, the surface of which is composed of bowlder-like masses of rock, ridiculously called the Lover's Leap. In the Star-Chamber the stalactites assume new forms, even more curious and beautiful than the others; and, in Shelby's Dome, you are ushered into a scene of indescribable grandeur. The height seems limitless, and the eye traces on the walls innumerable scrolls, panels, and fanciful projections of the most varied design and beauty. Under the dome is the celebrated Bottomless Pit, which has a depth of one hundred and seventy-five feet, and a wooden Bridge of Sighs, which leads from this chasm to another, called the Side-Saddle Pit. A railing surrounds the principal pit, and, as you stand holding to it, and peering into the depths, the guide illuminates the dome above, affording one the grandest sights in the cave.

At a point called the Acute Angle there is a rude pile of unhewn stone, called McPherson's Monument, which was built by the surviving staff-officers of that general. A stone is occasionally added to the pile by those of McPherson's soldiers or friends who visit the cave.

NEW YORK AND BROOKLYN.

WITH ILLUSTRATIONS BY HARRY FENN.

New-York Bay.

THERE are few cities in the world so admirably situated as New York. The grand Hudson rolls its waters on one side; the swift and deep tides of the East River wash it on the other; both unite at its southern extremity, where they expand into a broad bay; and this bay is practically a land-locked harbor, that, by a narrow gate-way, opens into the expanses of the Atlantic. The Hudson comes down from the north, a wide, deep stream for a hundred and fifty miles, opening intercourse with the far interior; the East River, which is an arm of the sea rather than a river, opens twenty

The Lower Bay, from Staten Island.

miles from its mouth into Long-Island Sound, establishing by this water-course and tributary streams connection with the New-England States. Bays and rivers completely encompass the place. It is an island, very narrow at its southern or bay end, broadening in its centre to a width of two miles, and narrowing again at its northern extremity. On its eastern side, eight miles from the Battery, is the mouth of the Harlem, a mere bayou of East River, which, running west and then northerly, connects by Spuyten-Duyvil Creek with the Hudson, forming the northern boundary of the island, which, on its eastern side, is eleven miles long. The island is frequently known by the name of Manhattan, so called after the Indian tribe that once made it their home.

Our artist approaches the city by the way of the sea. We sail up the broad expanse of water known as the Lower Bay, nearing the famous Narrows, a comparatively contracted channel, formed by the projection of Long Island on one side and Staten Island on the other. The shore of each island, at the narrowest part, is crowned with forts, fortified by embankments, and both bristle with cannon. The Long-Island shore is comparatively flat, but is handsomely wooded, and some pretty villages and villas peep out from their screens of foliage. Staten Island rises into fine hills, which are crowned with noble mansions and graced with park-like grounds, while at their feet, on the shore, cluster busy and bustling villages.

Through the Narrows opens the Inner Bay; and, as we swiftly cut through the crisp and ever-fretted waters, New York rises before us from the sea, in the centre of the picture; the city of Brooklyn, on Long Island, to the right, spreads a far and measureless sea of roofs, with endless, sky-aspiring spires; the shores of New Jersey extend along the far western border of the picture, on the left, with faint markings of Jersey City a little beyond, on the shores of the Hudson. The picture cannot easily be excelled for beauty; but one or two bays in the world are finer, and none are more animated with stirring and picturesque life. Here are the tall, white-sailed ships; the swift, black-funnelled steamers; the stately steamboats from the Hudson or the Sound; the graceful, winged pleasure-yachts; the snorting, bull-dog tugs; the quaint, tall-masted, and broad-sailed schooners; the flotilla of barges and canal-boats; the crab-shaped but swift-motioned ferry-boats, all coming, going, swiftly or slowly, amid fleets of anchored ships, from whose gaffs fly the flags of far-off nations. New-York Bay, when the air is crisp and bright, the sky brilliant with summer blue, the swelling shores clear and distinct in their wooded hills and clustering villages, the waters dancing in white-crested waves in the glaring sun, affords a picture that can scarcely be equalled. A similar animation marks the two rivers. Our artist has sketched the moving panorama of the East River, also showing the unfinished tower of the contemplated bridge—a picture full of life, color, and light.

Glimpse of New York, from the Narrows.

SCENE ON THE EAST RIVER.

As we approach the city we note the fringe of trees and the circular, fort - like structure that mark the lower border. These are the Battery and the Castle Garden—the Battery a pleasure-promenade, with a fine sea-wall, and the Garden, so called, the great *entrepôt* through which the vast bodies of immigrants from the Old World pass into the life of the New World. Castle Garden was once a fort, afterward a summer tea-garden, then a music-hall and public assembly - room, and is now the headquarters of the Commissioners of Emigration. The Battery was once the only pleasure-ground of the New-Yorkers, and, if its history were accurately and fully written, it would tell a strange story of love and flirtation, of famous persons and fair dames, of ancient Knicker-bockers, of life social and po-litical, interwoven in a varied woof. It has fallen into fashionable disrepute, although it has been enlarged and laid out anew. But the fine old trees that mark the ancient place look scornfully down upon the unhistoric exten-sion, with its feeble new trees and its walks barren of asso-

The Battery and Castle Garden.

A NEW-YORK RIVER-FRONT.

ciation and unfamiliar with romance.

Before entering the heart of the city, let us glance with the artist at a quaint and picturesque scene, lying but a short distance from the Battery on the East-River side. This is a portion of the town which modern improvement has left untouched; the wharves where the old-fashioned ships from far-off ports discharge their precious cargoes; where merchants of the old Knickerbocker quality conduct their business in dark and unsavory chambers; where the old tars, the Cuttles and Bunsbys, are wont to assemble; where the very idea of a steamship is profanation — a venerable, quaint, and decaying place, dear to the hearts of the ancient mariners.

Within the city, our artist takes us at once to the spire of Trinity Church. This famous edifice is comparatively a new church upon the site of one dating far back into the annals of the city. It is a new church, but the grounds around it are marked by ancient and crumbling grave-stones, an antique, tree-embowered spot in the heart of the busiest portion of the town. Trinity Church is less than half a mile from the Battery, standing on Broadway and facing down Wall Street

Trinity-Church Tower.

View from Trinity-Church Steeple.

which all the world knows as the monetary centre of the continent. From the outlook of the spire the picture is a varied one. Looking southward, the spectator sees Bowling Green, a small enclosure at the terminus of Broadway, and, just beyond, the Battery, with the circular mass of Castle Garden. Beyond these are the bay, with Governor's Island and its fort, and the distant hills of Staten Island. The views from our elevated position are all good. The artist has given a glance up Broadway, which gives one an idea of the spirit of this part of the street, shows some of the tall, marble structures, and indicates the bustling throngs upon the pavements below.

The artist has made no attempt to illustrate the varied features of the metropolis, but simply to give a glimpse or two at its interior, by which the imagination may build up a tolerably correct idea of the characteristics of the place.

In one picture he has combined views of three of the most noted of the small parks of the city. Washington Park lies off a little west of Broadway, and is the starting-point of the fashionable Fifth Avenue. The castellated-looking building that stands on its eastern border is the University, a Gothic pile of considerable age and quaint aspect, suggestive of the mediæval structures that lie scattered through the European countries. Union Square is at the bend of the main division of Broadway ; Fourteenth Street is its southern and Fourth Avenue its eastern border. Here are statues of Washington and Lincoln. Madison Square is half a mile north of this, lying with great hotels and business places on its western side, and sedate, aristocratic, brownstone houses on its other confines. It is at a point that is considered the social centre of the city.

From this point our artist takes us to the tower of the novel, Oriental - looking synagogue at the corner of Forty-second Street and Fifth Avenue, from which we have a cursory glance at the highway of fashion. Every city has as handsome streets as Fifth Avenue ; to those, indeed, who like

Broadway, from Trinity, New York.

WASHINGTON SQUARE

MADISON SQUARE

UNION SQUARE

WASHINGTON, MADISON, AND UNION SQUARES.

streets of embowered villas, many are handsomer; but no city has an avenue of such length given over exclusively to wealth and elegance. From its southern extremity at Washington Park to the entrance of Central Park at Fifty - ninth Street, the distance is two miles and a half, and, with the exception of the short space at Madison Square, it presents through this long extent one unbroken line of costly and luxurious mansions. The streets that branch from it to the right and the left have mostly this same characteristic for a quarter of a mile either way; so that, in an oblong square of two miles and a half by half a mile, there is concentrated an undisputed and undisturbed social supremacy.

At the corner of Fifty-ninth Street and Fifth Avenue is the main entrance to Central Park. This park extends northward to One Hundred and Tenth Street, or a distance of two and a half miles, but it is not more than half a mile wide. Central Park is the pride of the metropolis. Less than twenty years ago the greater part of its area was a mass of rude rocks, tangled brushwood, and ash-heaps. It had long been the ground for

A Glimpse of Fifth Avenue.

SCENES IN CENTRAL PARK.

depositing city-refuse, and tens of thousands of cart-loads of this refuse had to be removed before the natural surface could be reached or the laying out begun. Art had to do every thing for it. There were no forests, no groves, no lawns, no lakes, no walks; it was simply a desert of rocks and rubbish. The ground was excavated for lakes; trees were planted; roads and paths laid out; bridges built. The result is a pleasure-ground that is already famous, and only needs a little more maturing of the trees to be one of the handsomest parks of the world. It is not so large as some in Europe, but its size is not insignificant, numbering eight hundred and forty-three acres; while, in its union of art with Nature, its many bridges of quaint design, its Italian-like terrace, its towers and rustic houses, its boat-covered lakes, its secluded rambles and picturesque nooks, its wide walks and promenades, it is unapproached in this country and

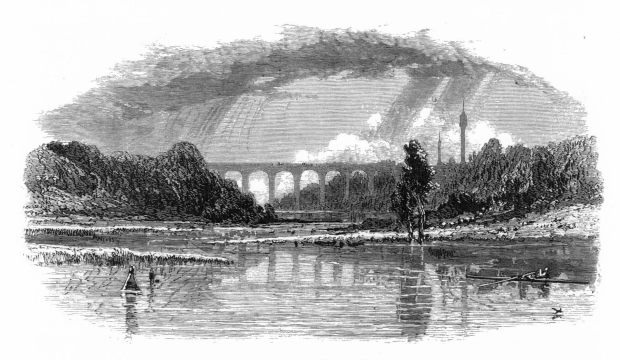

Harlem River, High Bridge.

unexcelled abroad. Our artist gives a few glimpses at places in the park, but it would take a volume to illustrate it fully. One element of satisfaction in the park is that it is not only an art and picturesque triumph—it is a popular success. Its superb drives are thronged with vehicles, while all its paths are occupied on summer afternoons by immense numbers of the people. The enjoyment of the visitors is enhanced by many extraneous means. There are an aviary and a menagerie tolerably well filled, and which are the nuclei of what are destined to be large institutions; and there is also a Museum of Natural History. There are boats on the lakes; a camera; and twice a week there is music. For the children there are nurseries, goat-carriages, camel-riding, swings, "run-rounds," and other devices.

Above Central Park, the whole island has been recently laid out anew in superb drives and broad public ways, where one may always see the fast horses of the bloods. But all here is new, and, with the exception of the roads, unconstructed. There is the animation of crowded thoroughfares, but nothing picturesque. At Harlem River, which forms the northern boundary of the island, there is a change. The banks of this river are high and well wooded. It is crossed by several bridges, and by a viaduct for the waters of the Croton, which are here brought into the town from the rural districts above for the use of the citizens, and which is known by the somewhat incorrect and very prosaic designation of High Bridge. It is a handsome structure, however, of high granite piers and graceful arches, and shows

from different points of view, through vistas of trees, from the open river, from distant hills, from approaching drives, with singular and even lofty beauty. The tall tower shown in the engraving is for the elevation of the Croton to an altitude sufficient to give it force for the supply of resi-

High Bridge and Water-Tower.

dences on the high banks in the upper part of the city. Tower and bridge make a fine effect.

King's Bridge crosses the river near Spuyten-Duyvil Creek, which unites the Harlem

King's Bridge.

with the Hudson. This is an old, historic bridge, identified with many of the early events in the history of the town. The scene here has something of that ripe mellowness and effective grouping of landscape with adjuncts of art that give such a charm

Spuyten-Duyvil Creek.

to old - country scenes. The artist also gives us a glimpse of Spuyten Duyvil near the Hudson, the tall escarpments in the distance being the well-known Palisades of the Hudson.

From Harlem we proceed to the great city of Brooklyn, lying opposite to New York, on Long Island, glancing on our way at two famous points in the East River. One is Hell Gate, situated at a narrow bend of the river, near the point where the Harlem debouches. It is filled with dangerous rocks and shallows; and, as the tide is very swift, the channel narrow, the bend abrupt, there is always danger that a vessel may be driven upon the rocks. Some of the more dangerous obstructions have been removed, and, as we write, extensive subterranean channels are becoming opened under the rocks, which are eventually to be filled with powder, and the shallow reefs blown to atoms. Blackwell's Island begins just below Hell Gate, and extends about two miles southward. It is occupied solely by city institutions, penal and otherwise. Here are the House of Correction, Lunatic Asylum, Workhouse, and City Penitentiary. The beauty of the place is not lost by the uses to which it is put, while its interest is enhanced by its fine buildings and imposing official character.

Brooklyn lies directly opposite to New York; it spreads seaward along Long-Island shore toward the Narrows, and extends along East River for some miles. It is a city without public buildings of interest, and without a commerce of its own, being little

Hell Gate.

more than New York's vast dormitory. It is a very attractive city, however, on account of its handsome streets, its home-like residences, its many churches, and one or two highly picturesque spots. Clinton Avenue is considered the most elegant of the streets. It is not unlike the tree-embowered, villa-lined avenues of many other cities; although unexcelled, it is perhaps quite equalled by some of its rivals. The residences on the Heights are choicely situated, commanding from their rear windows views of New York, the river, and the bay—a wonderfully brilliant and stirring picture.

Brooklyn boasts of a handsome public park, of five hundred and fifty acres in extent, and known as Prospect Park. It is situated on an elevated ridge on the southwest

Blackwell's Island.

border of the city, affording, from many points, extensive views of the ocean, Long-Island Sound, the bays, and New-York Harbor. Fine, broad ways lead out from the park, one reaching to Coney Island, on the Atlantic, three miles distant. There are beautiful groves of old trees in the park, a lake, summer-houses, etc., its natural advantages having been supplemented by many tasteful devices of the landscape-gardener.

SWISS THATCHED COTTAGE

LOOK OUT HILL

ON THE LAKE

PROSPECT PARK, BROOKLYN.

CLINTON STREET

BROOKLYN STREET-SCENES.

Within the precincts of Brooklyn, on what were once called Gowanus Heights, is Greenwood, the handsomest cemetery, probably, in the world. It is over four hundred acres in extent, beautiful, undulating, covered with ancient trees of many kinds, and varied with several lakes—a very rural paradise in its natural attractions, while art and pious devotion have graced it with many noble monuments.

Brooklyn, in size, is the third city of the Union. It has been almost as rapid in its growth as some of the Western cities. In 1800 it contained only four thousand inhabitants; in 1855, after the incorporation of Williamsburgh, two hundred and five thousand; while now (1874) the population is about four hundred thousand.

We should mention that the Brooklyn illustrations are not by Mr. Fenn, as all the New-York drawings are. Prospect Park is by Mr. Woodward; the Brooklyn street-scenes and the view from Greenwood are by Mr. Gibson.

New-York Bay, from Greenwood Cemetery.

WASHINGTON AND ITS VICINITY.

WITH ILLUSTRATIONS BY W. L. SHEPPARD.

The Capitol, from the Botanic Gardens.

THE site chosen by the first Congress for the capital of the United States, and christened by the name of the first President, is a broad plateau, which, on the eastern side, rises to a graceful elevation, and is bounded on two sides by the river Potomac and its tributary called the "Eastern Branch." The main portion of the city, including its business quarter, its public buildings, its main thoroughfares, and its aristocratic residences, stands upon a rather level plain, terminated at the rear by a series of wooded and irregular hills; while the Capitol rears itself upon a sloping elevation, and overlooks a wide extent of country.

Washington has not, until within comparatively recent years, been celebrated for its beauty. Formerly it was an unattractive place, composed in large part of low and mostly wooden buildings, with streets ill-paved and little cared for. Now the national metropolis, thanks to liberal expenditures and a newly-born pride in the government that its seat should be worthy of its distinction, presents an aspect not only of prosperity, but of sights agreeable to the eye and mostly in good taste. Its adornment has betrayed that its natural advantages were greater than had been supposed; and the seeker after the picturesque may find ample opportunity to gratify his quest while observing, at "magnificent distances," the official palaces which have been erected at the service of the republic.

The most striking object at Washington is undoubtedly the magnificent white-marble Capitol, a glimpse of which is caught as the city is approached by rail from Baltimore. It rises majestically far above all surrounding objects, amid a nest of thick and darkly verdant foliage, on the brow of the hill to which it gives its name; its very lofty dome, with its tiers of columns, its rich ornamentation, and its summit surmounted by the colossal statue of Liberty, presents a noble appearance, and may be seen for many miles around; while its broad, white wings, low in proportion to the dome, give an idea of spaciousness which no palace of European potentate surpasses. There are few more beautiful—though there are many larger—parks in the United States than that which surrounds the Capitol. The edifice is approached through an avenue entered by high iron gates; on either side of this are beautiful flower-plots, paths shaded by arching branches, fountains, and copses. A double tier of green terraces is ascended before the base of the

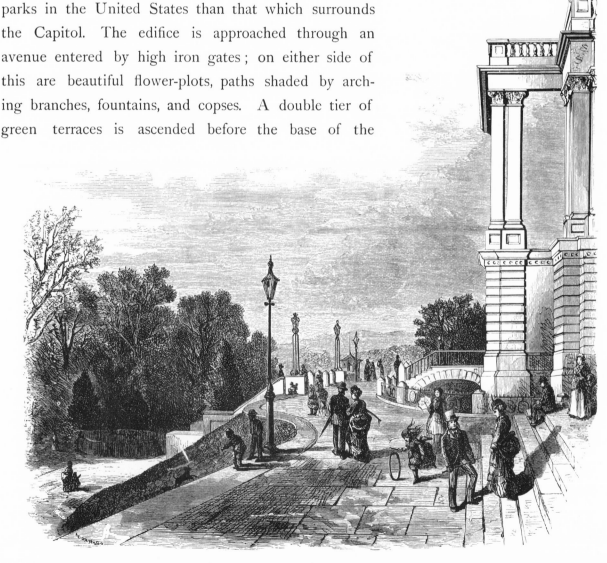

Capitol, Western Terrace.

Capitol is reached; then you find yourself on a broad marble terrace, semicircular in form, with a large fountain beside you, whence you may see the silvery windings of the Potomac miles away, disappearing at last amid the abundant foliage where the Maryland and Virginia coasts seem to blend in the far distance. From this look-out you may discern every part of the metropolis; in the midst of the mass of houses rise the white-marble Post-Office Department and the yet handsomer Patent-Office just beside it. Some distance farther on is to be descried the long colonnade of the Treasury, and the top of the White House, just beyond, peeps from among the crests of flourishing groups of trees; more to the left are seen the picturesque, castle-like, red-sandstone towers and turrets of the Smithsonian Institution, standing solitary on a broad plain al-

In the White-House Grounds.

ready sprouting with young foliage. Between the Smithsonian and the creek the unfinished shaft of the Washington Monument, a square marble torso of desolate appearance, meets the view; while the eye, spanning the Potomac, may catch sight, in the distance, of that lordly old manor-house of Arlington, identified, in very different ways, with the earlier and later history of the country. Georgetown Heights form the far background in the west; more to the north, the picturesque hills, with their wild, straggling growths, which, from the main suburbs and sites of suburban residences of the city, form a striking framework to the scene. A small park also stretches out at the rear of the Capitol, on the east. This presents, however, nothing notable in scenery, its chief adornment being the sitting statue of Washington, in Roman costume, which has been so sharply criticised and so warmly defended. Just outside the limits of this park stands the "Old Capitol," a quaint brick building used by Congress when the Capitol was burned by the British in 1814, in which Calhoun died, and which was used as a prison during the late war.

At the opposite end of the city from the Capitol is the group of departments surrounding the presidential mansion, and enclosing with it pleasant, umbrageous parks and grounds. On one side are the Treasury and new State Departments; on the other, the rather plain, old-fashioned, cosey-looking War and Navy Departments—oddly enough

Smithsonian Institution, near White-House Grounds.

the most placid and modest of the Washington purlieus. The White House is situated midway between these two groups of edifices, and is completely surrounded by open and ornamental spaces. In front of its high, glaringly white portico, with its *porte cochère*, is a lawn, in the centre of which is a corroded copper statue of President Jefferson. This lawn reaches to the thoroughfare, beyond which is Lafayette Square, thickly planted with trees, among which stands Clark Mills's equestrian statue of Washington, and surrounded by elegant residences occupied by senators, diplomats, cabinet ministers, and wealthy bankers. The most picturesque view of the White House, however, is from its rear. The front is not imposing. At the back, a small but beautiful park, profusely

SMITHSONIAN INSTITUTE

VIEW FROM AGRICULTURAL GROUNDS

WHITEHOUSE—FRONT VIEW

WHITEHOUSE—REAR VIEW

TREASURY DEPARTMENT

CITY HALL

PUBLIC BUILDINGS IN WASHINGTON.

View from Red Hill, back of Georgetown.

adorned with plants and flow-ers, varied by artificial hil-locks, and spread with close-ly-trimmed lawns, stretches off to a high-road sepa-rated from it by a high wall. This park is open to the public; and the chief magis-trate and his family may en-joy its cheerful prospect from a handsome, circular portico, supported by high, round pil-lars, with solid arches below, and a broad stone staircase winding up on either side, fairly overgrown with ivy and other clinging parasites. The most prominent object seen from these "President's grounds" is the red Smithso-nian Institution, which from here seems a very feudal cas-tle set down amid scenes cre-ated by modern art. Beyond the presidential mansion and the cluster of department buildings, Pennsylvania Ave-nue stretches over a flat and comparatively sparsely-settled district, until, by a sudden turn, it leads to the ancient, irregular, and now rather unin-teresting town of Georgetown. Its former commercial bustle has departed from it; for Georgetown is older than its larger and more celebrated neighbor, and was once the third or fourth river-port in the United States. It is still, however, a more picturesque place than Washington ; built mostly on hills, which rise above the Potomac, affording really beautiful views of the river and its umbrageous shores. The town has many of those substantial old red-brick mansions where long ago dwelt the political and social aristocracy, and which are to be found in all Virginia and Maryland towns of a century's age, surrounded often with high brick walls, approached by winding and shaded avenues, sometimes with high-pillared porticos, and having, over the doors and windows, some attempt at modest sculptured ornamentation. From Red Hill, which rises by pretty slopes at the rear of Georgetown, a fine view is had of the wide, winding river. The Potomac, just below, takes a broad sweep from west to east ; and, at the place where it is spanned by the famous Long

Glimpse of Georgetown, from Analostan Island.

Bridge, over which the troops passed from Washington to their defeat at Bull Run, it seems to form almost a lake. Washington itself is descried between the trees from the east of Red Hill ; in the dim distance, the shore of Maryland, lofty in places, and retreating southeastward ; and, on the immediate right, the more attractive Virginian shore, with a glimpse of the historic estate of Arlington. A large aqueduct connects Georgetown with this Virginian shore ; and the views from every point of it are full of attractive interest.

Now the Potomac is just below you ; its stream not so turbidly yellow as it becomes farther down. The Capitol, white and majestic, looms high above the metropolis, the rest of which seems a confused mass of houses and spires ; verdant meadows, pastures, and natural lawns, sweeping down by gentle inclinations beneath elms and oaks,

GREAT FALLS OF THE POTOMAC.

LOOKING DOWN THE POTOMAC, FROM THE CHAIN BRIDGE.

are seen on the shore you are approaching; while quite near at hand the portico of Arlington rises on the summit of a higher slope, embedded in the richest Virginian foliage. Just below, not far from the shore, lies a picturesque little island, Analostan, which would almost seem to have floated from some Old-World waters, and been moved quite out of its sphere, in the midst of a young country. For it betrays, half hidden amid creepers and shrubbery, which have for many years been permitted to grow there unforbidden, what seem remains of ancient habitations. One might fancy that it had some time been the site of a baronial stronghold, now fallen in ruins and deserted. Here, in reality, in the early days of the republic, lived a sturdy old Virginian gentleman of aristocratic descent and rank, who played no insignificant part in the formation

Arlington Heights, from Grounds in National Observatory.

of the government, and for some time represented his native State in the old Congress. This was George Mason. He carried the aristocratic idea of lordly seclusion to the extent of seating himself on this lonely, well-shaded island, where he built an old-fashioned Virginia manor-house, and resided in it in solitary state. But, after his death, it seems to have been deserted, and now only serves to adorn the landscape with a somewhat curious and peculiar feature. The walk from the aqueduct to Arlington is by a road whence continual glimpses of the river are to be had through the wild-wood, where the shrubbery grows tangled and rude, and wild-grapes, in particular, abound. Arlington is now no longer what it was before the days of war and consequent change of occupancy came. Those who remember it when Mr. Custis, its venerable owner, was still alive, preserve the impression of an ideal old Virginia manor and estate—one, indeed, which an English noble would not have been ashamed to own. Its site is a most imposing one; the lawn sweeps broadly down from its striking, ample porch for several hundred feet toward the river; its interior, in Mr. Custis's time, was a perfect reproduction of an aristocratic Virginia interior of a century ago. The road was pointed out by which Washington used to ride from Mount Vernon, a distance of ten or twelve miles; and every nook and corner preserved some relic or reminder of the Father of his Country,

Fort Washington.

many of them bequeathed by him to Mr. Custis, who was his adopted son. All about the place had the aspect of wealth, antiquity, and aristocratic ease; and, from the porch, it was, and still is, possible to have a very picturesque view of the capital city, from the Capitol to where the city merges into Georgetown.

The Potomac, for several miles north as well as south of Washington, is bordered by attractive landscapes. One of the pleasantest walks in that vicinity is from Georgetown northward along the banks of the canal, with the artificial water-course on one side, and the broad, winding, and here rather rapid river appearing every moment on the other. A mile from Georgetown by this road, you never would imagine that you were in so close a proximity to one of the "centres of civilization." The scenery is wild, almost rugged. A profusion of brush and shrubbery mingles with the forest-trees along the banks, which rise in continual and irregular elevations; there are few habitations, and such as there are recall the former social status of the border States. After proceeding thus about three miles, you reach Little Falls, which have no other pretensions to distinction than that they are surrounded by very attractive scenery, and form a modest cataract winding in and out among the rocks which here encounter the stream. Over Little Falls is a high bridge, by which one passes in a minute or two from Maryland into Virginia. Piled-up rocks line the shore, and anglers from the metropolis may often be found perched upon them, enjoying the very good fishing which the spot provides. Great Falls, as falls, are more pretentious than Little Falls; they are situated a short distance above. Here the water foams and rushes among jagged rocks, forming numerous cascades and pools as it hastens on. In this region the Potomac has become a comparatively narrow stream, with limpid and rapid waters; and all along its course, as far as Harper's Ferry, its valley presents a varied, unkempt scenery, which makes the jaunt along its shores a thoroughly pleasant one.

But, on the Potomac below Washington, where it is now broader and slower in motion, the aspects are perhaps more worthy of inspection, both because Nature here is more genial and more cultivated, and because at every step there is a reminder of some historical scene, old or modern. Passing down by the steamboat, less than an hour brings you, between verdant, sloping banks dotted by well-to-do-looking and for the most part venerable country-houses, to the landing-place, whence you reach Mount Vernon. It is unnecessary to describe this home of Washington, so familiar to every citizen by description if not by sight.

On either side of the river are Forts Washington, Foote, and other strongholds, familiar to the history of the war of the rebellion. The view northward from Fort Foote is especially fine, comprehending the view at its widest, bay-like expanse, and bringing into clear relief the city of Washington, with the bright dome still dominating all surrounding objects; while the shores in the immediate foreground are composed of gentle cliffs crowned with the rich growths of that Southern clime.

THE END.